JACINDA ARDERN

Other books by Supriya Vani

Battling Injustice: 16 Women Nobel Peace Laureates

Other books by Carl A. Harte

Building Your Own Home:
Tips, Techniques and Thoughts for the Owner Builder

JACINDA ARDERN

LEADING WITH EMPATHY

SUPRIYA VANI and CARL A. HARTE

ONEWORLD

A Oneworld Book

First published by Oneworld Publications in 2021

Copyright © Supriya Vani and Carl A. Harte 2021

ISBN 978-0-86154-030-3
eISBN 978-0-86154-031-0

Typeset by Hewer Text UK Ltd, Edinburgh
Printed and bound in Great Britain by Clays Ltd, Elcograf S.p.A.

Oneworld Publications
10 Bloomsbury Street
London WC1B 3SR
England

Stay up to date with the latest books,
special offers, and exclusive content from
Oneworld with our newsletter

Sign up on our website
oneworld-publications.com

MIX
Paper from
responsible sources
FSC® C018072

To every young girl who dares to dream.

It's about reshaping what it is to be a politician, and demonstrating that you don't have to change your character traits, you don't have to change your personality, that you can be motivated by a different set of goals . . . a different way of doing things.

JACINDA ARDERN

Contents

Introduction

A light drizzle has cleansed the desert air. Under the plaza's lights and the Burj Khalifa, sightseers enjoy a balmy winter evening, if winter can ever truly be said to visit Dubai. Little more than a silhouette against the darkness, the tower above flickers then dazzles with colour and patterns, blue and red reaching 829 metres into the night. Colours turn to blackness. The world's tallest projector screen, the Burj Khalifa, lights with the image of a woman. It is a moving sight: her eyes are lightly closed, her expression gentle as she clasps her hand against the back of another woman in a warm embrace. Above, the words proclaim '*salaam*', 'peace', in Arabic and English.

It is 22 March 2019. The picture was taken the previous Sunday, a hemisphere and cultural world away. Though the woman's head is covered in a scarf and her hair parted in a manner familiar to the Muslim world, hers is a now famous, Western face. It is Jacinda Ardern, prime minister of New Zealand, photographed by Hagen Hopkins at a wreath laying in Wellington, two days after the Christchurch mosque attack on 15 March 2019.

It is a rare tribute in Dubai. The Burj Khalifa usually hosts daily commercial LED light shows, and sometimes national flags of friendly countries, or the odd celebrity or pop band. And, of course, *The Lion King*. In terms of international political figures, Jacinda Ardern joined the likes of Mahatma Gandhi, whose image and inspirational quotes, along with an Indian flag, illuminated the skyscraper on his birthday.

The honour is noteworthy, if not astonishing, given Jacinda's background. Just weeks earlier, she seemed to have no ideological connection to the Muslim world – quite the opposite, in fact. A modern, Western, agnostic feminist living with her partner and bearing a child out of wedlock, Jacinda has campaigned passionately for gay marriage, not to mention equal pay and parliamentary representation for women. To the religious masses in the Middle East, she might well have seemed a picture of Western decadence, rather than an icon of compassion.

This was until 15 March 2019, when Jacinda's response to the Christchurch mosque attack touched millions of Muslims throughout the world. Among them was Dubai's Sheikh Mohammed bin Rashid al-Maktoum. A stern ruler, the sheikh is as far removed from Ardern politically as their countries are from each other geographically. His heartfelt tweet, which thanked Ardern for her 'sincere empathy and support', shows, along with his gesture of projecting her image on the Burj Khalifa, that he was impressed as much by those qualities as by her actions themselves.

This quality, rare in public life, has elevated Jacinda Ardern politically, just as it guides her choices as a woman. From youngest sitting member in Parliament to youngest prime minister of her nation since 1856. From leader of a small, sparsely populated southern country to the ranks of admired international figures. It is a leitmotif that plays throughout Ardern's life, essential to understanding the remarkable woman who is New Zealand's fortieth prime minister.

Ardern's compassion stirred New Zealanders' aspirations for a better, fairer country at the 2017 elections. In the face of a heartless terrorist attack, her compassion raised hopes worldwide for peaceful coexistence between religions. In a world led, at best, by hardened pragmatists, Jacinda Ardern stands out as one of few leaders whose empathy is genuine, not the product of public relations spin or political grooming. Compassion is without doubt her greatest personal and political asset. When a leader has the courage to express compassion, it can reach across political and cultural divides to unite people. Compassion, despite humankind's failings, is cherished by humanity, praised by all the religions and philosophies that underpin our belief systems.

Compassion is described as 'the highest state of spiritual union' in the Bhagavad Gita. The New Testament, Colossians 3:12, exhorts Christians to 'clothe yourselves with compassion'. In the Qur'an, Allah is described as 'Most Compassionate' in the fifty-seventh verse and often throughout. In modern times, the American Humanist Association states that 'humanism is a rational philosophy informed by science, inspired by art, and motivated by compassion'.

It need hardly be said that compassion has been traditionally considered a feminine characteristic. A recent commentary comes from His Holiness the Dalai Lama, who stated in a tweet – that modern medium of wisdom – that 'women have been shown to be more sensitive to others' suffering, whereas warriors celebrated for killing their opponents are almost always men. We need to see more women in leadership roles.'

In the preamble to Supriya's previous book, *Battling Injustice: 16 Women Nobel Peace Laureates*, the Dalai Lama elaborated on his thoughts of women's leadership: 'The lives of the women Nobel Peace laureates detailed in this book by Supriya Vani are clear evidence of my belief that women are naturally more sensitive to others' needs and well-being. They have greater potential for expressing love and affection. Therefore, when, as now, compassionate leadership is required, women should take on a greater role in making this world a better place.' With her government vowing to improve health care for the disadvantaged, to raise New Zealanders' standard of living with new indices, and to tackle child poverty, the New Zealand leader seems to embody the Dalai Lama's observations.

New Zealand is quite familiar with woman leaders, at any rate. Jenny Shipley of the National Party, the nation's thirty-sixth prime minister, held office from 8 December 1997 to 10 December 1999, and Helen Clark, her Labour Party successor, occupied the nation's top position for nearly nine years, until 19 November 2008.

Though Clark is one of her role models, Ardern stands apart from her female predecessors, and not merely for her youth. Shipley, nick-named 'the perfumed steamroller' (along with so many other assertive women), came to power not by popular election but through an orchestrated coup against her party leader and prime minister, Jim Bolger. Notorious while minister of social welfare for her regime of savage cutbacks, her 'ability to inflict pain without flinching' was legendary. Clark, a strong and 'no-nonsense' politician, invited comparisons with Margaret Thatcher, though the English 'Iron Lady' was of a very different political hue. Ardern, on the other hand, distinguishes herself from politicians, male and female, almost every-where, and not only by her idealism and compassion. Idealistic politi-cians turning pragmatic are a cliché; the more soft-skinned in public life quickly develop calluses or quit. Ardern's empathy and commit-ment to her principles, however, are consistent – in her DNA, if you will – and with the pressures of high office, she has not tempered them. In Supriya's interview, she said, 'I never went into politics for the sport of politics, I went into it because it's a place where you can make really positive change.' Her actions are consistent with her words; a rare thing indeed for a politician.

Perhaps all this explains the world's fascination with Jacinda Ardern. It seems the West – or, at least, the progressive West – has caught a second wave of 'Jacindamania', the first of which surged through New Zealand, sweeping her into office in 2017. Her message, innate charisma and humanity are a tonic for those who have lost faith in politics. After the rise of cynical career politicians and a recent trend for strongmen, people see in her a new kind of leader.

Women find her approach particularly appealing; prominent women lavish her with their praise. Former US secretary of state Hillary Clinton described Ardern's victory in the 2017 New Zealand general election as a 'shot of optimism'. The editor in chief of *Vogue* magazine, Dame Anna Wintour, said that she was 'very inspired' by Jacinda. And talk television icon Oprah Winfrey urged women to 'channel our own inner Jacindas'.

For a jaded media, the New Zealand prime minister's openness and genuine charm are refreshing; exciting, even. She is an interview-er's delight (and this we say from experience), speaking frankly about matters affecting her nation and women: her vision for a 'different way of doing things' in politics. Rarely does she seem troubled when she is questioned, and is generous in sharing her experiences and life story.

As a result, there is a clamour in the media about Jacinda Ardern. In international as well as local media, stories abound. Journalists more used to jousting with politicians keenly follow her words, marvelling at her warmth in public interactions and commitment to principles. Others sift through her background, looking for her inspi-ration, garnering clues as to what motivates her. The clues, as we shall see, are there to be found – in this remarkable woman's personal story as also in her country's, in her family heritage and mentors, and from her childhood to her concern for the generations who will inherit the world we will leave behind.

Some of Jacinda Ardern's legacy remains to be decided, however. For all her plaudits for enlightened leadership through some of New Zealand's worst crises, and even with the thumping mandate from the 2020 general election, Prime Minister Jacinda Ardern may yet face greater challenges.

The Christchurch mosque shootings of March 2019 showed Ardern's substance, her courage, compassion and diplomacy. If there were any questions as to her decisiveness, these were erased with her masterful 'go hard, and go early' campaign against COVID-19. Strength, she has demonstrated, can happily combine with kindness, effectiveness with empathy. If any doubt remains, it is whether she can live up to her own aspirations, those she spoke of in her maiden statement to Parliament – 'the words that I wish to haunt me: my values and beliefs, and the things that have brought me here'.

Far more significant for Jacinda Ardern than her adept crisis leadership finding its way into studies and textbooks would be real improvements to living standards, the environment and health for her people, particularly children, that she has spoken of so often. While she steered her nation clear of the coronavirus, she could not help avoid its economic consequences. Ardern successfully marshalled her 'team of five million' Kiwis for the fight against COVID-19. What remains to be seen is whether she can balance a troubled economy while rallying support for the changes she has long espoused; whether she can fulfil her desire for a kinder country, a desire that can be traced far back to her early childhood.

PART ONE

Volcanos and Seismic Shifts

Murupara is a small settlement in the North Island of New Zealand, in a remote part of the Bay of Plenty region. It's a place that feels as if it is drifting, somehow behind in time. Nestled at the edge of the Urewera ranges, near the confluence of the Rangitaiki and Whirinaki rivers, Murupara rests on fault lines: geological, social, cultural, economic. The town divides the pines of the Kaingaroa Forest, planted in the 1920s, and Te Urewera's unspoiled rainforest – straddling the tame country and the wild, peace and upheaval, Māori and pākehā (European), past and future. The place is a scenic backwater with plentiful trout and deer nearby but fewer prospects otherwise, well past its glory days of the mid-twentieth century.

This was a purpose-built logging town which once had hope and prospects. Now, as with much of the region, Murupara has been left behind by New Zealand's 'rock star' economic centres, Auckland and Wellington. Prosperity departed with the decline of the forestry industry and the rise of mechanised timber harvesting. Among the poorest towns in New Zealand, it is famous for gang violence, the occasional vicious dog attack and the sort of dull, hopeless poverty that seems out of place in a developed country.

Some years ago, a judge declared Murupara a 'sad, and on occasions, dangerous town'. The numerous derelict houses, with their smashed windows and overgrown lawns, lend a sadness, a sense of poignancy to the place. The homes are mostly old, erected more than fifty years ago, with low gabled roofs, in that mass-produced style of a town built in a hurry. This, one can see, was once a thriving settlement with around double its current population – home to people with decent incomes and purpose, in another era when meaningful work was one's birthright. In recent decades, this pretty town has endured only with the support of welfare. And not too well, either. According to a University of Otago study conducted a few years ago, Murupara's community suffers the highest level of deprivation in the country.[1]

The residents are typical Kiwis: friendly, polite. They are loyal, close-knit and defensive. Somehow, through tourism or some other means, they believe, this town will have its day again, that the 'gateway to Te Urewera' may yet profit. Tourism brings hope, mostly for popular hunting and fishing expeditions. A recent indigenous, 'authentic' tourism initiative shows some promise. The glory of the town's natural beauty remains, above economics, beyond the rise and fall of governments and fortunes.

The town's beauty is itself beguiling, but the land here has its dark secrets. Beneath this green and pleasant countryside, with its mountain peaks and ridges above and its pastures below, lies a sombre reality. The very forces that created this place threaten to destroy it. Murupara was built in the Taupo Volcanic Zone, one of the most active fields of volcanos in the world.

The Taupo Volcanic Zone extends from south of Lake Taupo, which hides the crater of a supervolcano (some sixty kilometres from Murupara), north-eastwards to White Island in the Bay of Plenty. White Island's volcano is active. It erupted on 9 December 2019, spewing steam and gases, ash and rocks into the atmosphere. Twenty-two people, largely tourists, perished. At a distance of 112 kilometres south-south-west from White Island, Murupara is surrounded by dormant, but by no means extinct, volcanos. The earth's crust here is thin, as little as sixteen kilometres thick; the rage beneath the surface simmers. The countryside rumbles with almost constant earth tremors.

In a land built on shifting tectonic plates, whose immense natural beauty is shaped by the fire beneath, this town is not so unusual, save for its extremes. In time, its claim to fame may well be its link with the fortieth prime minister of New Zealand, who is Murupara's most famous daughter.

Jacinda Kate Laurell Ardern was born into a Mormon family in Dinsdale, a western suburb of Hamilton in New Zealand's North Island, on 26 July 1980. Murupara was her early childhood home, the place where she spent her most formative years.

Aristotle once said, 'Give me a child until he is seven, and I will show you the man.' Just the same, give a child a place, a society for the first seven years of her life, and she will be forever impressed, for better or worse, with what she sees, senses and hears there. Murupara, with its exquisite scenery, small-town bonds and sad turns of fate, has left its indelible mark on Jacinda Ardern.

The te reo Māori word murupara means 'to wipe off mud' – surely an appropriate metaphor for the rougher side of political life she would encounter decades after she lived here. The Ardern family moved to Murupara when Ross Ardern, Jacinda's father, took up the post of town police sergeant, and Jacinda started her primary education at Galatea School nearby. For a time, the family lived in a small, grey-brick house in front of the police station.

Jacinda's mother, Laurell Ardern (née Bottomley), gave up her careers in office administration and teaching – a common decision for so many women of her generation – to support her family. 'I had a choice of looking after the girls or working, I chose looking after the children,' Laurell says. But as she explains, with some regret, decisions as to her future, 'were made by my parents on my behalf . . . [I] would have liked to have attended university as I wanted to be an account-ant, but it was not to be'.[2] After leaving school, she worked in an office at a service station, and in the Te Aroha post office as a telepho-nist; she later taught technology for three years in Murupara. As Jacinda and her elder sister Louise grew into teenagers, the only career their mother would have was in their school canteen.

A mother who has taken a very different path, Jacinda is acutely aware of Laurell's sacrifice. 'Mum is generous to a fault,' she said in an interview not long after she was elected. 'She's very caring and very kind. She made lots of life choices that were all based on me and my sister.' Laurell expresses no regret; far from it: 'I wanted to bring [my daughters] up and put all my time and effort into doing things for them because I knew if I did that, they would be good adults.'[3] The results, it has to be said, are self-evident.

Jacinda is grateful to her mother also, for taking an early lead with that most important parental duty: education. Laurell, she says, intro-duced her and Louise early to words, showing her young girls flash cards of objects around the home, which would help to instil a love of reading as they grew (Jacinda became a great reader of Nancy Drew mysteries and historical non-fiction). Laurell and Ross made sure their girls could read and do simple arithmetic before they went to school. Determined for her daughters to excel, Laurell would place notes of encouragement in their bags, along with their primary school snacks. Before Jacinda entered the world of politics, her efforts had already paid off. Both of her daughters graduated from university, the first in their family to do so.

Naturally, innate character and personality play their part in the Ardern girls' success. One of the earliest pictures of the future New Zealand prime minister is endearing. Baby Jacinda beams a gorgeous, winning smile, as she does in so many of her later childhood snaps and, indeed, her adult photographs. In her childhood photographs she seems to engage with the camera, in just the way she engages with people – brightly and positively. In photographs from her teens, she is still sporting dark-blonde hair, but the direct, thoughtful gaze that is now famous is evident. In the years since, it has changed little – merely matured.

Laurell says she 'could have had a dozen Jacindas', the young girl was so easy to deal with. Her mother recalls that she was 'different to other children. She was mature beyond her years and had incredible common sense. I don't really remember her ever getting into mischief because she was so sensible.'[4]

Sensible and sensitive in equal measure, it seems – qualities that made her acutely aware of the people around her, their feelings and their unhappiness. Though a young girl cannot know the root causes of others' pain – poverty, conflict, sickness and poor mental health – Jacinda sensed that it wasn't right for other young children to go without. She questioned why others at her school didn't have the material comforts she and Louise enjoyed.

Jacinda's empathy would profoundly influence her, setting in place foundations for her political beliefs and destiny as the social-democrat leader of her nation. While the young Jacinda was in her first years of primary school, in the mid-1980s, tumultuous social and economic change engulfed New Zealand. After more than eight-and-a-half years of National Party government under Prime Minister Robert Muldoon, the Labour Party, led by the charismatic David Lange, won an outright majority in the July 1984 general election.

With fifty-six of the ninety-five seats in the unicameral parliament, the country's fourth Labour government embarked on a programme of economic reforms.

The architect of these reforms was Finance Minister Roger Douglas. A third-generation Labour politician and accountant by training, Douglas was a persuasive speaker, a ruthless political operator. In the late 1970s, he became a convert to Milton Friedman's free-market theories, and plotted with his colleagues from the opposition benches. When Labour took office, he and his two associate ministers of finance, David Caygill and Richard Prebble – together known as the 'Treasury Troika' – immediately set to work, radically restructuring the economy. The reform programme Douglas oversaw in the four years before his sacking in 1988 became notorious. It was dubbed, somewhat derisively, Rogernomics.

Rogernomics was imposed on New Zealand in the manner of a revolution. Unlike in most other democracies, there is no upper house of parliament to provide the necessary checks and balances, nor states and their legislatures to contend with, which might well have tempered the government's excesses. Neither does the country have the powerful independent think tanks that exist in Britain and the US that could publicly debate government policy. Academics with the temerity to speak out against Rogernomics' policies found their career paths blocked; journalists were muzzled through their editors. With a party caucus (the Labour members of parliament) ruled by cabinet diktat, Douglas made sweeping changes on many fronts, with little resistance.

In terms of deregulation and implementing free market policies, Rogernomics far surpassed Reaganomics and Thatcherism. From being run, according to Prime Minister David Lange, 'very similarly to a Polish shipyard', the country became one of the most deregulated free-market economies of the industrialised world – and this, para-doxically, from a Labour government. With his steely squint and patrician manner more befitting a corporate CEO than man of the people, Roger Douglas became one of New Zealand's most polarising figures. His programme has been considered alternately a gross betrayal of Labour Party principles and a dose of bitter medicine that the New Zealand economy – reeling under debt, mismanagement and a currency crisis – needed to swallow.

Rogernomics might still divide the pundits, but there's never been much argument about its impact. Sale of government assets, abolition and amalgamation of government departments and massive redundancies, particularly in the forestry sector, hit New Zealand's rural population hard. In one horrific week alone, late in March 1987, some 5,000 New Zealand government workers lost their jobs, a significant number in a country with a small population. Years later, an officer with the Social Impact Unit recalled towns full of men trudging from union meetings to register for unemployment benefits, while their women at home wept. The public's suffering was compounded by the stock market crash of 20 October 1987. Soaring mortgage interest rates touched twenty percent.

Murupara suffered immensely, and just as Jacinda was coming to an age where she could make sense of the world around her. In the turmoil of Rogernomics, the post office, that cherished institution that alongside utility gives rural towns character and a sense of belonging, closed, as did several retail stores. The outlets or offices of the New Zealand Electricity Department, the Bay of Plenty Electric Power Board and New Zealand Railways shut. In just a few years, almost two-thirds of the town's population was reliant on welfare.

Describing the effects of the forestry redundancies, Murupara's townspeople later told, with typical Kiwi understatement, how 'the money dried out' and 'the whole town started to turn over – we were losing people'. 'It was a depressing time,' one said, 'because a lot of friends left the town.'⁵ Like a tree from the immense plantations which sustained it, the town survived, but withered, hollowed out from within.

The young Jacinda was profoundly affected by the human toll of all this. As she told Supriya, 'I have a lot of early memories not about politics . . . but just simply about observing inequality.' She heard whispers of suicides – the girl who babysat her and her sister Louise became jaundiced; her skin yellowed with hepatitis C, and she was no longer able to care for them. In her first year of school, Jacinda noticed that unlike her, some children came to school without shoes – and not for the reason that they liked to go barefoot, as is common for New Zealanders. Their parents simply could not afford to buy them footwear. Or lunch. These unfortunate youngsters walked into school, hungry and barefoot, even on those chilled winter mornings when it rained and the puddles iced over. Years later, she said she 'was troubled by it, even though I was only five. It's stuck with me since then.'

One particular incident stands out for her, and she has mentioned it in numerous interviews. She recalls a time early in her schooling, when she was perhaps seven years old, seeing a boy, alone, barefoot and unwell, crying on the street. Not yet able to make sense of why the boy was crying, what was causing his anguish, the young Jacinda was nevertheless deeply affected. Instinctively, she knew that something wasn't right if this was happening. As she told Supriya, 'When you are a child, you view everything through the simplicity of a child's lens and it just didn't feel fair to me that, you know, that children were having those experiences through no fault of their own.'

That suffering was borne out in statistics. Jacinda's childhood years were a period of increased crime in New Zealand. High unemployment, which rose from four percent of the workforce to peak at eleven percent in 1991, coincided with the worst rates of homicide the nation had seen. It is worth noting that as unemployment fell later in that decade, there was a drop in recorded violent crime, including homicide.

Suffice it to say, the decade from 1985 was a bleak time for New Zealand. Murupara was particularly blighted, and not simply due to the loss of logging jobs and economic crises. New Zealand is reputed to have one of the highest per capita rates of gang membership in the world – more than four times its nearest neighbour, Australia. It was little different three decades ago. Murupara in the 1980s was a hotbed of gang activity, a stronghold for the feared Tribesmen. In the largely indigenous town – around three-quarters of Murupara's population is Māori – the newly formed motorcycle gang found ready recruits in the town's disaffected, bored Māori youth. As did their rivals, the Mongrel Mob.

Power struggles between rival gangs were commonplace in those years, the menace of violence ever present. The local cop was in the firing line, and his family, too. Jacinda remembers her home being pelted by bottles one night, probably by disgruntled gang members.

One particular incident seems to have affected her profoundly, and perhaps for the better. Jacinda recalls walking barefoot to the shops one day, maybe sneaking out to buy a bag of dollar mix lollies from the kind lady, as she described the shopkeeper at the dairy (corner shop). Jacinda knew she was being naughty: Laurell and Ross insisted she and Louise wear Jandals (flip-flops) at least, so their feet wouldn't be cut on the glass shards from broken bottles that littered the streets. As she went, she came upon her father, surrounded by a group of angry-looking men. 'I just froze,' she said. 'I didn't know what to do. Then he spotted me out of the corner of his eye, and he said, "Run along, Jacinda. It's all right."' Her father, she remembers, just stood, calmly talking to the men, and the situation defused.

Her father's manner of handling the dramas around him impressed his daughter greatly. As Jacinda succinctly explains, his approach to the job was 'understanding the situation – and not making a big deal of something that could be worked through'. As a good local cop usually is in a small town, Ross was part policeman, part 'community worker', Jacinda says; perhaps even an occasional psychologist. Ross was the kind of policeman who would use 'his ability to talk to people as his main tool'. In Murupara, this was sometimes a tall order. He had to deal with 'really horrific circumstances and people in significant grief . . . and yet he always maintained a real humanity about him, never became hardened by any of those experiences'.

It is these abilities, to remain cool and humane in adversity, that would distinguish Ross in the force and raise him to higher office, later in life. Three decades after Jacinda left Murupara, the same character traits would bring her to international prominence.

Jacinda is philosophical about how her father's work affected her and her sister. Their proximity to the police station, which saw them witness the darker aspects of the town, must surely have made them wise to the world, and mature earlier than their peers. Jacinda acknowledges, anyhow, the positive side to Ross's work. She remembers, when she was small, a rape victim's mother bringing flowers to the station house at Murupara to thank Ross for resolving her daughter's case.

All the same, it seems Ross's girls couldn't escape the stigma of being the town cop's daughters. Despite being eighteen months Jacinda's senior, Louise was the smaller of the two, a soft target for bullies at their primary school. She recalls, with some humour, that the five-year-old Jacinda took it upon herself to guard her. The one time she remembers being chased and beaten, she says, was when Jacinda was away from school, sick.

The young Jacinda was outgoing, bold and enthusiastic, immersed in her school life, and enjoying the world around her. By all accounts, she possessed that delightful, innocent perspective of a youngster from a small town. When the Arderns lived in Murupara, the family took Saturday shopping visits to Rotorua, a tourist town with hot springs. It is an hour's drive away, over a road traversing rich farmland and meandering through scenic hills. Rotorua, Jacinda says, was 'the big smoke for me . . . [and] always a highlight of my week'.

Jacinda was already beginning to shine in her primary school years, perhaps in her own, childlike way showing the traits that, decades later, would carry her far. One of her teachers, Deborah Taylor, remembers her as 'highly organised, a very engaged and focused learner, polite and respectful . . . [a girl who] set very high goals for herself'.[6]

Not all of Jacinda's experience at Galatea School was pleasant. A dramatic event from those years is imprinted on Jacinda's memory, as terrifying for her as for her classmates.

New Zealand children are used to earth tremors, which are as much a fact of life in 'the Shaky Isles' as rainstorms. The seismic event on 2 March 1987 was another matter altogether. At 1.35 P.M., a mild earthquake rumbled beneath the school. Then at 1.42, just after the children's lunch break, the earth shook with rage, the classrooms heaving from side to side. Jacinda stood beside her teacher. It must have seemed to her and her school friends that the world was about to end. Three decades later, she publicly acknowledged her teacher, who comforted her and her friends.

Thankfully, there was little damage in Murupara from the Edgecumbe Earthquake. In Edgecumbe itself, some sixty kilometres away, near the epicentre of the quake, damage was extensive. Brick chimneys collapsed; railway tracks were buckled into the shape of two serpents slithering together across the plains. An eighty-tonne loco-motive was toppled. At a dairy plant, milk silos collapsed; milk tanker trucks were tossed onto their sides. The earth opened up like a long wound along the faultline, cutting across farmland and a road.

The 1987 Edgecumbe Earthquake was the most severe in forty-five years. It wouldn't be the last Jacinda would experience. In May 2020, she was in the middle of a live television interview from the New Zealand parliament, when an earthquake, 5.9 on the Richter scale, shook the building, known as the Beehive.*She barely flinched, simply saying, 'We're just having a bit of an earthquake here . . . Quite a decent shake here . . . if you see things moving behind me, the Beehive moves more than most.'[7] After the rattling of furniture and fittings stopped, Jacinda simply continued the interview as if nothing had happened.

The year 1987 was the Ardern family's last in Murupara. A class photograph from that year, when Jacinda was in grade two, shows her in the front row next to her teacher (as with so many other notable people, Jacinda bonded strongly with her teachers). She is flashing a charming smile. Her pose seems more eager than that of her school friends, as if she is holding back her exuberance.

It was this very energy, the desire to engage and excel, that would stay with Jacinda, throughout her childhood years and beyond.

---

*The Beehive is the common name for the iconic Executive Wing of the New Zealand Parliament Buildings, so named for its shape, which resembles a skep, a traditional straw or wicker beehive. Formally opened in 1977, the Beehive was conceived in 1964 in a sketch on a restaurant napkin by the Scottish architect Sir Basil Spence, who was dining with Prime Minister Keith Holyoake.

2

A Peaceful Valley

In 1988, when Jacinda was eight, the Ardern family moved to Morrinsville, a neatly kept town in the Waikato region in the upper North Island with a population of some seven thousand. It would be the place where Jacinda said she enjoyed a childhood that was 'as Kiwi as you'[d] get'. Surrounded by fields full of grazing cows to the east and west, the town is bordered by a bend of the Piako River and the Waitakaruru Stream. With hills to the south and the Kaimai Range overlooking from the east, its landscape is more idyllic pastoral countryside than the majestic alpine terrain of the South Island.

It might be a cliché to describe the town and its valley as a land of milk and honey, but this wouldn't be far from the truth of the matter. Waikato's pastures are among the richest in the world. With almost as many milking cows as people in the country, milk and dairy products are a major export for the nation. Morrinsville and its surrounds is one of the most prosperous dairy farming regions in the country; the town hosts a long-established dairy processing industry. Located on the edge of Morrinsville's central business district, if one can call it that, the Fonterra Lockerbie factory produces cream, butter and milk powders, and at peak times processes an astonishing 1.2 million litres of milk daily.

Morrinsville celebrates its dairy heritage with extravagant pride. The sobriquet 'Cream of the Country' is emblazoned on a rustic welcome sign at the town's boundary; the Morrinsville Mega Cow, a 6.5-metre-tall shiny fibreglass sculpture of a Friesian dairy cow, looms over its main street, in front of a car dealership. Smaller, colourful sculptures of cows litter the town centre – cow art, they call it. It's appealing in a cheerful, quirky way. The town's main street, with its Federation shops from the turn of the last century and their modern facades, is witness to a prosperous land.

It is not the kind of town from which one would expect a Labour leader to emerge. At least not one with a decidedly social-democrat inclination. The electorates (constituencies in the UK; in the US, congressional districts) that encompass Morrinsville – Piako and Waikato – have been dyed-in-the-wool conservative for generations; the National Party has held sway since before the Second World War. A young Helen Clark, no less, was dealt an electoral drubbing here in her first tilt at parliament. In 1975, the future prime minister received less than half the votes of her older, National Party opponent, 'Gentleman' Jack Luxton. Jacinda herself made an unsuccessful run at Waikato in the 2008 election, before being made a Labour list member of Parliament. That the country's social-democrat prime minister calls this town home is a peculiarity, almost a source of amusement as much as pride to its residents.

For the Ardern family, the move to Morrinsville brought a welcome change of situation. No longer being the family of the resident police-man in a troubled town was a relief for them all, and Ross wasn't long a local cop. Though at first one of the town's two local officers, he soon took up a post as a Criminal Investigation Branch detective, commuting some thirty kilometres to work in Hamilton. The mood of Morrinsville, more buoyant by far than Murupara's, suited the girls well. The town had proved resilient to Rogernomics' closures and sudden cancelling of farming subsidies. Though it had its share of poverty, with struggling former refugees in among the well-heeled dairy farmers, Morrinsville then, as now, was pretty much an average New Zealand town.

The place fits the trope, too, of New Zealand's arcadian rural life, especially in the picturesque outskirts of the town, where the Arderns lived. Their street was a quiet cul-de-sac, tucked in beside the Morrinsville Golf Club at the town's northern edge. The view takes in two essential aspects of Aotearoa – the Land of the Long White Cloud – fertile pastures and untamed wilderness. To the north-east, across the fairway and rich paddocks, Mount Te Aroha's peak dominates the horizon. Thick with ferns and native forest timber, its upper slopes are occasionally dusted with snow in the winter months.

This was Jacinda's home in a very real sense. Built by her grandfa-ther, the house itself is comfortable, though unremarkable in the streetscape. Girded by a wraparound veranda, it is surrounded by a lush lawn where neighbours say the young Jacinda would collect lost balls from the golf course. The girls lived within walking distance of their school.

Jacinda and Louise's first secondary school in the town, Morrinsville Intermediate School, was where Jacinda's inclination for politics first showed itself. At the age of twelve, she joined the student council. Her fellow council members might have joined for the novelty of it, or more likely to cut class, but the future prime minister was earnest with her duties, it seems. The council's discussions were limited, ranging from the fairness of price hikes for snacks and drinks at the school cafeteria, to questioning rules such as students' dismounting from their bicycles fifty metres from the school gate. Jacinda nonetheless threw herself into her role, even finding a suitable charity for their mufti (casual clothes) day funds.

Perhaps Jacinda's seriousness in this – or more than a hint of bossiness – earned her one of her first nicknames. Her Form 1 teacher, Mrs Bean, called her Aunty Jac, referring to Aunty Jack, a well-known and loved Australian television comedy character of the 1970s. She was an obese, cross-dressing, moustachioed man who wore a single gold boxing glove and a tent-sized blue velvet dress. In her gravelly baritone, Aunty Jack would tell viewers to watch her next show, or she'd 'come over to your house, and I'll rip your bloody arms off'. Mrs Bean must have had quite a sense of humour. The name Jac stuck: to this day, Jacinda's school friends refer to her as Jac, even in writing.

Just a few hundred metres from Morrinsville Intermediate School is the place where Jacinda would begin to blossom, in her teen years. Morrinsville College has always enjoyed a reputation as a decent institution. The New Zealand Ministry of Education currently rates it a socioeconomic decile 6 school, meaning its students aren't from the upper echelons of society – the more moneyed parents would send their children to private schools in Hamilton – but they are not generally from the lower. Like the Arderns and many of its alumni, the school is somewhere in the middle, but punching well above its weight. Morrinsville College is not particularly small, with an enrolment of girls and boys numbering several hundred, but it maintains a personal, community ambience that only small-town schools can.

Perhaps that is the advantage that their rural upbringing offered Jacinda and Louise. New Zealanders are noted for their down-to-earth friendliness, their hospitality, their resourcefulness born of isolation. The Aotearoa countryside is particularly welcoming. Towns here are ideal for families; perfect places, one would think, for raising young children. With its more sizeable population, Morrinsville possessed better opportunities than Murupara for Jacinda and Louise, but was not so large that a talented girl could get lost or overlooked in its places and institutions as she might in a city. And in Morrinsville, the girls would grow up in an area where their family was known.

On both sides of the family, Jacinda's ancestors had lived in the area for generations. Most were farmers from around Te Aroha, though as Jacinda has said, her grandfather 'dug the drains' in Morrinsville. Jacinda's parents and grandparents ran the family farm in Te Aroha, growing apples and pears for export. Later, when Laurell became sick from the agricultural sprays used in the orchard, they raised sheep. The two young girls helped on the farm as they grew.

In these formative years, Jacinda learned the value of hard work. The family home was adjacent to the Morrinsville Golf Club; her grandfather kept a stall stacked with apples near the end of the fairway. Each apple cost twenty cents. Passing golfers would take an apple, dropping a coin through the slot of the honesty box. Stocking the little fruit stall was Jacinda's job; the money from the apples was her pocket money.

The young Jacinda was something of a farm girl, more interested in picking fruit, grading apples and docking lambs with her father, than playing with dolls and dressing up. She even had a pet lamb called Reggie, which she tried to train for the A&P (agricultural and pastoral) show. 'But all I did was teach him how to escape through an electric fence,' she says.

Aside from history, her favourite subject at school was metalwork. The only girl in the class, Jacinda loved turning metal on the lathe, making tools, and developed quite a skill with the pop riveter. She topped the class, much to the consternation of her male classmates.

Given what we know of the adult Jacinda, it's unsurprising that her early career aspirations were more in the social services vein than anything else. She was, she told Supriya, inspired by 'jobs that always had a streak of wanting to help'. Her first ambition was novel, even for a young girl. A clown visited her school and performed at the school assembly. He modelled a balloon animal for her (she still likes balloon animals). 'I remember', she said, 'sitting as a little child, I probably would have been maybe eight years old, watching this clown make the entire school just laugh and be happy. And going home – I kept a little journal – writing in my journal as an eight-year-old, that I wanted to be a clown one day because I wanted to make people happy.'[1]

This would be an astonishing admission from any ordinary political leader. From Jacinda Ardern, it seems completely natural. She is utterly sincere. Indeed, it's hard not to be touched by this sensitive woman who has retained her essential humanity in high office. This is the woman, who at the age of eight, her mother says, formed a 'Happy Club' for her and her classmates, where they would only say good things to each other. This is the leader who genuinely wishes the best for her people – even her opponents wouldn't argue otherwise. One can easily imagine the eight-year-old Jacinda, absolutely earnest as she writes in her journal.

At any rate, it seems she was serious for a while in her ambition. She even learned to play the ukulele, that favoured instrument of a jester, and she still keeps a number of ukuleles. Perhaps she is something of an entertainer at heart. A guest at the Ardern home in the late 1980s recalls being serenaded by the nine-year-old Jacinda and her sister Louise, accompanied by the ukulele. The girls, he remembers fondly, sang him 'You Are My Sunshine' after a family Sunday roast.

Music was an early passion for Jacinda that has never left her. Along with her ukuleles, she keeps a most treasured family heirloom: a violin her great-grandmother Elizabeth McCrae brought to New Zealand when she emigrated from Scotland, which Jacinda has had restored. She learned to play the instrument when she was at school, though with characteristic humility says she 'was never particularly good'. As she grew, she would develop an interest in playing others' music as a DJ, which, it seems, she found more satisfying. Nonetheless, appearing in front of an audience, entertaining people was an early calling for Jacinda.

She nurtured more serious ambitions as she grew. Jacinda told Supriya, 'I went through periods of wanting to be a psychologist [or] a policewoman. For a while, I thought maybe I'd like to write. I went through a whole series of different aspirations. Probably policewoman and psychologist were two of the most significant.' Given her father's occupation, and Jacinda's closeness to Ross, her desire for a career in law enforcement was perhaps inevitable.

It's noteworthy that rather than aspiring to a life in Parliament itself, Jacinda first saw herself in the back offices of politics. She recounts how during a high-school excursion to Parliament, she left her fellow students sipping orange juice in their local member John Luxton's office. She quizzed Luxton's private secretary outside. How could she become a private secretary to an MP? What would she have to study? Jacinda would never have dreamed that she would occupy the ninth floor, the prime minister's office in the Beehive, less than a quarter of a century later.

As she explained to Supriya, 'I never wanted to be a politician. I was really interested in politics, but I didn't think that I would find a path into that place. There are only 120 politicians in New Zealand and I'd only met one . . . I was . . . a teenager before I even met a politician, so it didn't feel attainable.'[2]

Jacinda's teenage interest in politics found its place, though, when she was elected to the Morrinsville College board of trustees. As the sole student representative on the board, she represented her fellow students' concerns passionately, yet showed the kind of common sense that would later distinguish her in office. A case in point is how she handled the perennial issue with school shirts: to tuck, or not to tuck? Naturally, the teachers wanted them tucked in, as they nearly always have, whereas the students wanted to leave them untucked. The crux of the matter for the school was that the students looked scruffy with their shirts hanging outside their trousers and skirts.

A generation earlier, the teachers would have had their way – the young scallywags would be told to knuckle under or face the consequences. With the old century drawing to a close, the students felt empowered to question their elders. Jacinda proposed a novel solution, which, characteristically for her, took care of the concerns of all parties. This was that the uniform shirts be redesigned, so they looked neat untucked.

The board accepted her proposal. In a decision that has not been repeated, Jacinda was allowed to continue as the student representative for a second year.

Encouraged by her success, when she was in her final year of school, Morrinsville College's girls raised another grievance with their uniform: if the boys could wear shorts, why couldn't they? It seemed only logical to Jacinda and her friends, part of the first generation of New Zealanders to grow up under a woman prime minister, Jenny Shipley, who came to power just the year before. Jacinda took the issue to the board, arguing persuasively for what was her first feminist cause.

The board was soon convinced. Girls would be allowed to wear shorts, but with the uniforms already bought, the new rule wouldn't come into effect until the following year, when Jacinda had graduated. It didn't matter much to Jacinda personally, anyway: a practising Mormon, abiding by the church's strictures on dress and conduct, she was happy wearing a skirt. She was simply doing what she was good at – campaigning, advocating; setting a matter right that needed to be set right.

Jacinda's flair for advocacy was matched by her talent for public speaking. It might be surprising, though, to discover that she wasn't comfortable in front of an audience, initially. Indeed, when she spoke at the age of fourteen or fifteen before her school friends, she suffered from dreadful stage fright. Her mouth became dry and she swallowed repeatedly, her mouth only becoming drier, she says, so that her lips stuck to her teeth. 'That might be OK,' she recounted years later, 'if it was just a matter of looking a little funny. But when your teeth provide this much surface area, it literally meant I couldn't talk.'

She persisted, though. Before long she became more comfortable, finding that her inherent capacity for connecting with others could work with an audience as well as it did with individuals. She also participated in drama, playing the role of Elizabeth Proctor in a 1996 school production of Arthur Miller's *The Crucible*, which helped her relax in front of an audience. She won the school speech competition, then in April 1997 took the trophy at the Waikato regional speech contest of the United Nations Association of New Zealand. Fitting for the policeman's daughter was her topic, 'Drug Abuse: The Human Scourge'.

Her old school friend Paula Powelsland recalled, after Jacinda was elevated to the prime minister's office, that she 'just had a natural ability to be a really good public speaker'. She was, Paula said, 'always phenomenal at debating'.

If there is a skill that a teenager should hone and polish for a life in politics, it is debating – that is, the formal, sporting kind. With its time limits and rules that translate handily to Parliament and television, school and university debating is as much a training ground for politicians as school competitions are for sports stars. On the Morrinsville College debating team, Jacinda really shone, displaying the skills that would eventually find their expression in Parliament. To her teachers and fellow students, she was kind, engaging. Against an opposing debating team, she was devastating. At the age of sixteen, Jacinda reached the final of the New Zealand Debating Competition; she remained the Waikato representative from 1996 to 1998. One of her highlights at the rostrum was her leading Morrinsville College's debating team to victory over the team from elite Auckland private school King's College: truly, a victory of the underdog. It seemed, as she later said, she was trying to make debating a spectator sport, like rugby.

That's not to say that Jacinda didn't like sport. She was enthusiastic about it, as she was about almost everything she did, and was competitive. Jacinda especially liked badminton, playing some doubles matches here and there, partnered by her sister Louise. She even won some trophies. It's just that she didn't excel in sport in quite the way she did with her other pursuits.

Perhaps this was a matter of aptitude. Or it may simply be that her skills in sports paled in comparison to her abilities in debating and advocacy. Her appointment as captain of the girls' basketball team was, she explains with typical good humour, more for her dutifulness in organising the team uniforms than for her sporting prowess. Organising, advocating, debating, social work – these were Jacinda's real talents, her preoccupations as a teenager. Jacinda was the student who could be relied on to take responsibility for something – to see it through, to put in effort and time where it was needed.

Along with her work on the student council and contributing to the school newspaper, Jacinda was appointed to the suspension committee as the student representative. There, she helped sit in judgment, so to speak, of her peers who were facing suspension or expulsion from the school. This, Jacinda says, was a difficult responsibility. She might have had no qualms about handing down punishment to bullies and the like. But even at this young age, it was clear to her that many of those before the committee, as she would later say, 'had no emotional or financial support from their families, from their caregivers, or from their community'.[3]

The future prime minister seemed concerned about her fellow students' welfare, whether they were her friends or merely colleagues. Her kind of earnestness, a strong sense for the greater good, may well have been natural. Nonetheless, it was certainly fostered by one of her teachers in particular.

3

The Activist Awakes

There are some teachers whose influence seems to reverberate throughout a student's life. For Jacinda, this teacher was Gregor Fountain.

A young, energetic history graduate, Fountain was in his first post out of Christchurch College of Education, at Morrinsville College. He had an illustrious career ahead of him: he is now principal of his alma mater, Wellington College, a prestigious boys' secondary school in New Zealand's capital. Fountain was Jacinda's social studies and history teacher; he taught her for all the three years he remained at the school.

Fountain's way of thinking and his values made a profound impression on Jacinda during her teenage years. In her first term as prime minister, she paid tribute to her teacher, saying 'he taught me how to question everything, including my own opinions'.[1]

As a teacher in conservative, rural Waikato, Fountain was a curiosity. Unusually liberal, he brought a whole different perspective, a new energy to his subjects and the school's extracurricular life. Fountain's lessons were entertaining to the extent of being a little oddball. He would stage re-enactments of historical events, with the students playing parts. For a lesson on politics, he divided the room into a parliament, giving the students a taste of legislative procedure that might well have inspired Jacinda.

The young, idealistic teacher knew how to engage his students' imaginations. He made his classes entertaining but relevant to his students, relating principles to their lives and their country. On one occasion he taught his class how an enlightened Māori leader inspired the greatest peaceful anti-colonial movement in history.

The story began in the wake of the New Zealand Wars (1845–72), when Māori resistance to colonial rule was crushed. In the late 1870s and 1880s, the spiritual leader Te Whiti o Rongomai mobilised his

people for non-violent civil disobedience, resisting the government's
expropriation of their land. They removed survey pegs, ploughed the
land to slow the building of roads and continually re-erected fences
destroyed by surveyors and road builders. Māori activists packed up
surveyors' camps as they looked on helplessly, leaving them no option
but to withdraw.

When in November 1881 a military assault force descended on
Parihaka, their settlement on the western coast of the North Island,
Te Whiti and more than 2,500 of his people met it with 'passive resistance'. Young girls skipped, boys sang and women awaited with loaves
of bread. During his campaign, Te Whiti and hundreds of others
submitted peacefully to arrest, and when freed, continued their peaceful agitation for the return of their land.

Thousands of kilometres away, a young Indian lawyer read of Te
Whiti's actions. He was deeply affected. Decades later, he would
employ a remarkably similar system of conduct, calling it *satyagraha*,
first in South Africa, then in his native India. The lawyer, of course,
was Mohandas Karamchand Gandhi, better known as Mahatma
Gandhi, whose campaign of peaceful resistance was instrumental to
the British granting India independence.

For this lesson Fountain came dressed as Gandhi. Nobody can
question the effectiveness of his novel teaching techniques. This event
seems to have etched itself on Jacinda's consciousness – she still makes
reference to the curious link between Te Whiti and Gandhi, mentioning it in her interview with Supriya.

Fountain's enthusiasm spilled out of the classroom and into his
extracurricular activities. He encouraged activism, promoting ideals
more in sync with the inner-city intelligentsia than those of the
Waikato. In 1997, he supervised the formation of the Morrinsville
College Human Rights Action Group, whose prime movers were
Jacinda and a couple of her friends. They supported prisoners of
conscience, highlighting human rights violations abroad with their
letters. They even held a Fax-a-Fascist Day – it was the era before the
internet had taken off – where the group fired off faxes to despots
across the globe, denouncing their abuses. A perfect outlet for the
young Jacinda's idealism, the action group seems to have stirred the
spirit of justice within her.

Fountain was proactive and just as he knew the power of theatre for learning, he understood the need to get students involved. It was a valuable lesson for Jacinda's political career, from her Young Labour days onwards. For a 1997 school newspaper photograph, Fountain roped in a few students to swell the Human Rights Action Group's numbers. At the front are the core of the group, which performed most of its work. Fountain himself is at the centre, flanked by Jacinda to his left and her close friend Virginia Dawson to his right.

Fountain's values, and his focus on values as a means of edifying students, resonated with Jacinda. She eagerly probed the history of the New Zealand Wars in all its complexity. In mid-1990s Waikato, history was not simply a subject: the Māori's dispossession of both land and sovereignty by British colonists, the background of the wars, was coming to some kind of resolution, and locally.

In 1995, while Jacinda was attending Fountain's classes, the local Waikato-Tainui Māori reached a settlement with the government, which recognised that the confiscation of their lands during the New Zealand Wars was 'unjust and a breach of the Treaty of Waitangi'. Compensation in the form of land and money was given under the settlement. Jacinda talked with her teacher about the matter. 'She really wanted to get her head around the whole thing,' Fountain recalled.[2]

A little more than two decades later, she would intervene in another Māori land rights issue, similarly a hangover from the controversial 1840 Treaty of Waitangi.

History seemed to show its lessons in the present for Fountain, and Jacinda was keen to apprehend the happenings in the textbooks on a deeper level. For her, as for him, it was not about dates and wars and events, it was about humankind and its motivations. Details that bored many teenagers, Jacinda would find fascinating.

Gregor Fountain left Morrinsville College at the end of Jacinda's penultimate year there. He left a strong impression on his pupil, however, and the pair have kept in touch since.

Her activism continued, as well. Suitably for a Mormon, teetotal girl, Jacinda championed Students Against Drunk Driving (SADDS). The group targeted an issue of particular importance in Morrinsville, as in other rural towns. New Zealand youngsters can apply for their learner driver's licence at the age of sixteen; at sixteen and six months, they might get a restricted licence. Unfortunately, this age is also a time when teenagers begin to enjoy their freedom, parties and alcohol. Boredom, teenage machismo, open country roads and a culture of early unlicensed driving on farms increase the potential for tragedy.

As the daughter of a policeman, Jacinda knew well the dangers of drunken driving. She and some colleagues used the idea of theatre for their activism, something else that Gregor Fountain introduced her to. On the school oval, they staged a graphic enactment of a car-crash scene, to impress upon their fellow students the consequences of drunkenness behind the wheel.

Her commitment to the issue was deeper, and went further, than simply staging demonstrations. John Inger, Jacinda's principal, told Supriya that she took responsibility for organising buses to transport students home after the school ball, so they would not drive home drunk. Even after reaching home herself at 2 A.M., she went back out in the car, driving through the streets of Morrinsville to check that everyone had arrived safely home.

Jacinda showed other community interests as a teenager, beyond her activism and social work. In 1997, the seventeen-year-old Jacinda and her friend Virginia – Jac and Ginny – took on a challenge well beyond the capability of the average young student. A fungus was ravaging local bowling greens, a blight that seemed resistant to the usual commercial solutions. With help from their chemistry teacher, Paul Lowe, and some scientist consultants, the pair worked on the problem in a small room at the back of the science laboratory.

Their teacher was impressed. 'They were happy to approach top scientists at [their] relatively young age.' Jac and Ginny 'drove all around the Waikato to places such as the Ruakura Agricultural Research Centre and the University of Waikato' for their research, he told Supriya.[3]

They were dedicated, too. In personalised lab coats emblazoned with Beavis and Butthead logos, the pair pored over 'hundreds and hundreds of agar plates',[4] as Jacinda later said, until they discovered a bacterium to inhibit the growth of the fungus. Representing the East Waikato region with their project, entitled Bacteria Bowling Fungi, they entered the Realise the Dream national science fair, a competition that was held by the Royal Society of New Zealand (RSNZ). The pair won a prize, which Jacinda would recall later was awarded as much for perseverance as for their results.

Jacinda found herself on television for the first time, talking about the bacteria. 'It must have been a light news day,' Jacinda said, years later.[5] In a TVNZ 1 regional news interview, the young Jacinda, sporting blonde-tipped hair and several earrings, explained the workings of their discovery with maturity beyond her years. Though a little hesitant, she already has a purposeful tone in her voice. Her emphatic delivery would come with the years, with speeches, appearances and debates.

The prize didn't lead anywhere much for Jacinda vocationally. Her appreciation for the subject remained, though, as her championing of science and technology in Parliament years later would show. The prize also provided a highlight of her school years. She was one of twelve teenagers – three of whom came from Morrinsville College (Jacinda, Virginia Dawson and Elene Ly) – in a team representing New Zealand on an RSNZ-sponsored trip to the Asia-Pacific Economic Cooperation (APEC) Youth Science Festival, held in Seoul in August 1998. Some five hundred students from thirty-nine countries participated. Jacinda and her friends were joined by Paul Lowe and Tania Lineham, a highly regarded science teacher from James Hargest College in Invercargill.

Years later, Ardern said with some humour that she looked back fondly on the 'glory days' of the APEC Festival. She wasn't exaggerating, Paul Lowe told Supriya. The South Korean hospitality was a delight to the Kiwi teenagers, who set up a team room at Seoul University to coordinate their activities. Arriving a few days early, the New Zealand contingent quickly found their way around, on buses, on the Seoul Metropolitan Subway and in taxis, then helped orientate students from other countries. There were two types of taxis, Jacinda discovered: local, grey taxis, which were cheap, but for which you needed a sign in Korean to state where you wanted to go, and black ones, which were expensive by comparison, but whose drivers spoke English.

The trip was just the kind of eye-opening jaunt every teenager should have the opportunity to enjoy. Night-time basketball games kept them busy until midnight, during which Jacinda and her female friends surprised the boys with their fierce Kiwi competitive spirit. They were up early at 6 A.M., taking visits by bus to nuclear power plants, research institutes and the like, mixing with their international colleagues. They made a trip to the New Zealand embassy, where Jacinda and her friends put on a cultural performance. Some Kiwi kids did the haka, some spoke in te reo Māori – such a hit with the locals, it made its way onto news channels – while Jacinda and Virginia played traditional stick games. To celebrate Paul Lowe's birthday, Jacinda and her friends hired a train carriage for a karaoke evening. One student – Lowe told Supriya he suspects Jacinda – kindly ordered pizzas for them all.

The girls were so taken with their new friends, they cried when it was time to leave. There were tears again at the airport, when due to horrendous traffic, they missed their flight home. It was left to Tania Lineham to comfort them. They all had to wait three days for the next flight. At any rate, the South Korean experience whetted Jacinda's appetite for travel, which saw her make later overseas trips with even more than the usual Kiwi enthusiasm.

Suffice it to say, Jacinda was an utterly engaged student, a high achiever at school. If she wasn't the best at what she did, she wasn't far behind: she bagged a second prize in the school writing competition and in her final year, was the joint runner-up dux (top pupil) of the school. Unsurprisingly, she was more inclined towards the humanities. Whether out of lack of interest or aptitude, or both, she didn't get on quite so well with mathematics as other subjects. Her maths teacher earned her gratitude, she later said, for telling her she would fail in order to motivate her. Though her teachers didn't perceive her as a genius, Jacinda was seen as a bright student, and earned excellent marks.

What they did see was her potential, which was far greater than her academic results alone might have suggested. Gregor Fountain summed up his thoughts about her at the time, saying, 'I absolutely thought she was someone who would change the world.'[6]

Apart from her academic prowess, her social responsibility, her activism and debating, though, there wasn't anything out of the ordinary about Jacinda. There was no controversy, she wasn't a flamboyant character; there are no skeletons, it seems, that might come rattling out of a Morrinsville cupboard. There was no drinking – not even coffee for the Mormon girl – no wild parties or vamping. Noted for her 'strong morals', Jacinda was a responsible, teetotal young woman who was well liked by her teachers. 'She never put a foot wrong,' according to those who knew her in Morrinsville.[7]

For the average teenager, this might sound prudish – a little goody two-shoes, perhaps. But Jacinda wasn't a saint; she had her own hidden enjoyment of mischief. Once, she taught Louise how to do a burnout on her family home's gravel driveway. 'It was a foolish act given that my father is a policeman and it did not take him long to figure out who the culprit was,' Jacinda says.[8] She seems to have made quite a mess of the driveway, because it took her almost three hours to rake it back into shape. Teenage devilment aside, Jacinda managed to balance her social life quite nicely with her religious, academic and extracurricular duties.

For her peers, she was the 'acceptable nerd',[9] as she has said (perhaps she is being too hard on herself: her school principal John Inger recalls she was 'popular amongst her peers').[10] She wore a nerdy set of braces, but also a fashionable nose stud, and bleached her hair with streaks and layers. She would listen to rock music: Smashing Pumpkins, Metallica, Pantera, Sepultura and Tool, along with the usual drum-and-bass dance music, just as they did. She could socialise and attend parties with them, but as 'both Mormon and the sober driver – that was the benefit they saw from my [church] membership,' she says.[11]

*

Jacinda might have been a model Mormon teenage girl who managed to mix with the cool kids, but for her sister, all was not plain sailing. Of the two, Jacinda was the one whose personality and preferences gelled nicely with her religion: she embraced it, living quite comfortably with the Mormon church, whose expectations seemed to suit her nature. Louise, however, was more rebellious. She would wear short skirts that her mother disapproved of, and they would clash. Laurell became exasperated. It would fall to Jacinda to talk to her sister; explain why it was that she should wear something more 'appropriate'.

Jacinda was a peacemaker early. Louise sometimes argued with her parents, threatening to leave home and locking herself in her room. Jacinda would push notes under the bedroom door which told Louise the reasons why she should stay. Comfortable as a member of the family, church and society in which she found herself, Jacinda was often the binding agent, if you will, that held these units together. It's a personal asset and a rare gift, as helpful in families as in politics.

While it might be tempting to view the Ardern family through the prism of their religion, to feel that the girls had a constrained, austere upbringing, this was far from the case. While Laurell and Ross were a little firmer with their daughters than most parents of their peers, they weren't harsh. They let them watch television, sometimes to excess, as most parents do.

When the girls were young, they had a clever arrangement with them so they could sleep late and undisturbed on weekend mornings. Ross or Laurell would place a bag of crisps next to the television, telling the girls that they could eat the crisps and watch TV – if they let their mum and dad sleep. It was a win-win solution.

This is not to say that Jacinda and Louise were indulged, however. Laurell and Ross, industrious themselves and members of a church that values hard work, were keen to inculcate the value of earning in their daughters. Jacinda was urged by her mother to prepare a CV, which she said as a fourteen-year-old consisted of 'best flan at the cooking competition'. She walked the length of Morrinsville's main street, distributing her CV to businesses as she went.

Her effort paid off with a suitably New Zealand job at the Golden Kiwi, a fast-food restaurant. Most of her friends were off enjoying themselves on a Friday evening, socialising, drinking and attending parties and the like, while Jacinda worked. At the Golden Kiwi, her duties were taking orders at the table and on the telephone, washing dishes, operating the till and serving fish and chips, the most popular takeaway food in the country.

Years later, on the hustings for her successful 2017 campaign, Jacinda paid the Golden Kiwi and her former bosses, Grant and Carol Covich, a visit. They spoke highly of her to reporters, noting she was always on time – a characteristic her party members would run foul of in later years. Jacinda recalled that to prepare her for her job, Laurell gave her half a cabbage and some newspaper and supervised her wrapping it for an hour, until she was proficient – ready to wrap chips at the shop.

After Jacinda took office as prime minister, the Australian ABC ran a segment on her return to Morrinsville College, filming several people who knew her as a teenager. Reporters spoke with Gregor Fountain, who underscored a crucial trait that would guide her in public life. Jacinda, he said, always wanted to 'extrapolate a principle or value' from her lessons.[12]

*

Principle would eventually draw Jacinda Ardern to politics but before then, principle would draw her to her political mentors. The first significant contact Jacinda had with a politician came when, aged fourteen, she interviewed Marilyn Waring for a social-studies project. More recently a professor of public policy at Auckland University of Technology, Waring was a noted feminist and academic and a former National Party member of Parliament. Though their contact was brief, Waring's influence on Jacinda would be strong.

Waring came to prominence as the youngest female member, making her mark as a woman of principle. Something of a maverick and a firebrand, she etched her place in the public's consciousness for her clashes with her party leader and prime minister, Robert Muldoon. For this, at least early in her parliamentary career, Muldoon seems to have afforded her his grudging respect. He appointed her to the chair of the influential Public Expenditure Committee, despite their differences, where he knew she would show neither fear nor favour.

Principle was a hallmark of Waring's political career, and it was principle that brought it to a glorious end. In 1984, while the anti-nuclear debate raged, she took a stand, making it known she would cross the floor of Parliament to support Labour's Nuclear Free New Zealand Bill, which sought to ban nuclear-powered ships from New Zealand's waters and ports. Incensed – and heavily inebriated – Muldoon had Waring summoned to a meeting. He berated her, calling her a 'perverted little liar'.[13]

Waring was unrepentant, to say the least. After returning fire with a threat to sue, she munched on an apple, her feet on a coffee table,

weathering his diatribe as nonchalantly as she could. The National
Party president Sue Wood's attempts to mediate were futile, as Wood
herself later recalled: Muldoon refused to accept Waring's assurance
that she would not vote against the government on supply or other
issues. That very evening, he called a snap election (sometimes jokingly
referred to as the 'schnapps election' for his drunkenness), later declaring that Waring's 'feminist anti-nuclear stance' undermined his ability
to govern.

Muldoon's election announcement on 14 June 1984 foreshadowed
the debacle ahead. His voice slurring from too much brandy and dry,
the prime minister, who had been knighted just a few months earlier,
informed reporters in a wood-panelled Beehive corridor that the election would be held exactly one month later. Responding to a reporter's suggestion that this didn't give his government much time for
campaigning, he declared defiantly that it 'doesn't give my opponents
much time to run up to an election'. Behind in the polls and woefully
unprepared, Muldoon's National Party lost the election in a landslide
defeat.

Waring's career in politics was over. Her status as a feminist icon,
however, was cemented, as was her place in political history. Along
with many young women, Jacinda was impressed with stories of
Waring's courage, and thrilled with the prospect of making her the
subject of her social studies assignment. The fact there was little information to be found on Waring didn't deter her. Jacinda decided she
would speak to her directly. She rushed from her classroom to her
mother at the school canteen, looked up Waring's telephone number
with her and 'left this long, garbled [voice] message, as only a fourteen-year-old could do'.

Waring called her back a few weeks later. After all these years, it's
significant that she can recall such a brief interaction with a high-
school student – the young Jacinda seems to have made quite an
impression on her. Marilyn remembers her having 'specific issues she
wanted me to address . . . "What do you think are the key issues
facing my generation? What do you think about a nuclear-free New
Zealand?"'[14]

Waring seems to have sensed great potential in the young Jacinda.
Indeed, so did her fellow students, her teachers and her own parents.

When Jacinda was in her final year of school, the Morrinsville College yearbook featured the 'Year 13 Poll!', with a number of categories listed. Compiled by the students themselves, the poll was remarkably accurate for several nominees, Jacinda's teacher Paul Lowe remembers. There was 'Best couple', 'Funniest laugh', 'Health nut of the year', 'Most likely to succeed', etc. For the student 'Most likely to become Prime Minister', there was no question: it was Jacinda Ardern. As for her parents, Laurell and Ross Ardern said in an interview after Jacinda took office that they knew their young daughter was 'destined for higher things'.[15]

Ross, usually the quieter of the two in interviews, went further. 'This might come as a shock,' he said. 'But I think both Laurell and I knew from the time she was at high school that one day she would be the prime minister of this country.'[16]

4

Nature and Nurture

What propels a woman to greatness, to the highest office of her country? Is it all natural intelligence and talent, innate characteristics, ambition, or a mix of this with a careful upbringing and parental nurturing? Is there some kind of 'royal jelly' that parents can feed their girls so they might reach their potential, if not to govern a nation, to rule their lives?

Genetics and family characteristics doubtless play their role; there is a recurring theme of strong women in Jacinda Ardern's family tree. Much also can be said for parental example, and Jacinda herself is the first to acknowledge Laurell and Ross as her 'ultimate role model[s]'.[1]

Unsurprisingly, perhaps, the press has emphasised Laurell's influence on her compassion and social responsibility, as does Jacinda herself. Laurell, she told Supriya, is 'very generous . . . the kind of person who would look after people when they were unwell'. Laurell, who taught Jacinda to bake and ice cakes for the elderly at Christmas, praises her for her empathy and generosity. Once, when Laurell was on the remote island of Niue, she called on her daughter to help a friend who was dying. Jacinda, she told a reporter, sat through the night in Waikato Hospital, talking to her friend, brushing her hair, never leaving her side. When Laurell suffered with breast cancer, Jacinda was a 'huge support' to her and her father.

Jacinda has inherited another of Laurell's character traits, it would appear. Laurell, a woman with an independent mind, would sometimes find the teenage Jacinda at odds with her, especially on political matters. The two would often discuss contentious topics, debating their points of view with gusto. Sometimes, neither would relent, continuing their discussions until Ross intervened.

For their famous daughter, at least, Ross has attracted less media coverage than Laurell. It may well be because, as a diplomat and government official – formerly the high commissioner of New Zealand to Niue and later the administrator of Tokelau – he is reticent with the media. Aside from public relations fests, for diplomats no publicity is usually good publicity. This might go some way to explaining why Ross's influence on his famous daughter has been given less media attention than it deserves.

Another factor may be that the importance of a father in a prominent daughter's development has itself been overlooked. In Supriya's book, *Battling Injustice: 16 Women Nobel Peace Laureates*, a curious pattern emerges, one that has not often been emphasised. From Malala Yousafzai back to laureates from the beginning of last century, most appeared to have strongly identified with their fathers: as role models, supporters or inspiration.

This is not to say they all had perfect relationships with their fathers. It is clear, in any event, that a young woman can forge her own path to prominence, as did the first woman Nobel Peace laureate, Bertha von Suttner, in the complete absence of a father (Suttner's seventy-five-year-old father died before her birth). Nonetheless, the strong trend of successful women benefiting from their fathers' support in their early years prevails. For Jacinda Ardern, there is no mistaking Ross's profound influence on her – personally, emotionally, morally and professionally.

Significantly, she genuinely wanted to 'follow in her father's footsteps', as has been the common for young men, but rarely for young women, throughout the ages. Into early adulthood, Jacinda nurtured aspirations of becoming a police officer – even after university, while working for Phil Goff, a prominent Labour politician. It was only the physical rigours of law enforcement work that deterred her: 'The physical side of the exam was too hard,' she said. 'I can remember doing the running and then getting to the big test and the dream just fell by the wayside.'[2] Slightly built and standing little more than 165 centimetres tall, perhaps she didn't feel she would be sturdy enough, anyhow, to withstand the occasional physical assaults that Ross told her were an occupational hazard, something one must endure in the force. Be that as it may, Jacinda says that her father 'always encouraged me [to be a policewoman], but I don't think Mum was so keen'.[3]

Jacinda may have abandoned her ambitions in policing, but a cursory reading of her father's achievements and preoccupations demonstrates that the motifs and themes of his career – amplified, naturally – are echoed in his more famous daughter's.

David Ross Ardern joined New Zealand Police, training at New Zealand Police's training facility at Trentham, in 1974. From police sergeant when Jacinda was in primary school, Ross rose through the force's ranks to superintendent, serving twenty years in the Criminal Investigation Branch and five years as Matamata–Piako area sub-commander. In his four decades with the force, he maintained a repu-tation as a fair, honest, calm officer, noted for his humanity.

Ross was appointed chief of police for the Pacific island nation of Niue, a protectorate of New Zealand, in May 2005. While the island has a tiny, mostly peaceful population of some 1,600, issues arose that required Ross's thoughtfulness and skill in community policing. In Niue, Ross's sense of duty went beyond the usual purview of law enforcement, into the realm of public administration. A New Zealand Police press release years later commended Ross for 'helping the island improve its civil defence readiness, instituting a road safety strategy and advocating on behalf of some of the migrants to the island when they needed support.'[4] In March 2007, after the New Zealand trawler *Jay Belinda* became grounded on the eastern reef of the island, Ross made a public appeal for 'contingency plans to ensure there is not an environmental disaster'.[5]

In 2009, after his tenure as Niue's police chief, Ross was appointed the New Zealand Police liaison officer to the South Pacific and South West Pacific. Stationed in Apia, Samoa, he worked from the New Zealand High Commission. It was through this post that he found himself thrust occasionally into the limelight. Wherever appropriate, he seems to have taken opportunities to make his own measured comment to influence issues for the better. The manner in which he conducted himself, and the concerns he expressed, seem remarkably similar to those of his younger daughter.

Later that year, Ross Ardern was heavily involved in the relief effort following the earthquake and tsunami that struck the Pacific island nation of Samoa on 29 September. He spoke to the New Zealand media days after the disaster: 'I've been in the police thirty-five years, and the damage I've seen here in Samoa is right at the top,' he said. '[Aid] co-ordination is the most important thing . . . The public should think about how they would be placed if their home was totally destroyed – that's how many Samoan families are placed at the moment.'[6]

While chairing the PICP conference in Wellington in January 2009, Ross steered the region's police chiefs to adopting a regional strategy for domestic abuse. In stating that family violence was under-reported to police in the islands, often not perceived as a crime, Ross went to the crux of the issue with words that could easily have been spoken by Jacinda: 'It is easy to say, "Look, that's our culture, to [treat] women in this fashion." I don't think it is in the culture of any coun-try to be able to engage in domestic violence.'[7]

Pertinent statements and humanitarian efforts are one thing; cour-age in crisis, and diplomatic behaviour under the most trying of circumstances, are another. While Jacinda studied conflict and consensus at university, Ross's ability to resolve conflict averted almost certain tragedy. In 2002, he received a Commissioner's Commendation for dedicated conduct during a standoff in 1999 with a man armed with a machete. Ross negotiated for three hours with the man, patiently and calmly. The situation was, as the commendation notes, 'brought to a peaceful conclusion'.

Doubtless, Ross has been an inspiration to Jacinda. There is every indication he is a supportive father whose feelings of pride in her achievements are expressed quietly. He could, however, also be stern at times. Jacinda recalls that if she was late for school, Ross would take her in his patrol car and 'turn on the siren to teach me a lesson'. One can easily imagine the embarrassment the young Jacinda would have felt. At the sound of the siren, every pupil and every teacher would realise that Jacinda had made herself late for school and her father, the town policeman, was admonishing her with some gentle public shaming.

Little wonder she became quite a stickler for punctuality, arriving at her first job, and all those since, on time. Years later, in February 2019, Jacinda publicly chided her Labour Party members of Parliament for being late to a Finance and Expenditure Select Committee meeting, which for want of a quorum was cancelled.

Ross might have been somewhat strict at times, but it is evident that Jacinda shared a strong bond with him. They would spend a good deal of time together, talking about life and all manner of subjects. One of their discussions sparked Jacinda's life-long interest in what is known as the Heroic Age of Antarctic exploration.

It was 1994; Jacinda was fourteen. The family was on a summer holiday, staying in a beach unit, when Ross regaled Jacinda with a story he was reading. It was the tale of the explorer Sir John Franklin's doomed 1845 expedition to navigate the Arctic North-West Passage. Ross told her how in the northern summer a decade earlier, an expedition had exhumed from the permafrost the bodies of three crewmen who had died and been buried on Beechey Island. Frozen in the earth for 140 years, the bodies looked as if they had been buried recently. Autopsies revealed high levels of lead in the frozen corpses, he said, indicating that the crew had been slowly poisoned by their own tinned food. Ross went on to tell Jacinda the tragic story of Franklin, who died afterwards in his ice-bound ship HMS *Erebus*, his crew starving, perishing in the Arctic wasteland.

With her mind already ignited with a passion for history, Jacinda became captivated by the ice-breaking sailing ships and the exploits of their gallant captains. She was fascinated in particular with the iconic Irish explorer Ernest Shackleton, whose travails seven decades later were the polar opposite to Franklin's – geographically, and in their outcome. Jacinda devoured Alfred Lansing's classic of 1959, *Endurance: Shackleton's Incredible Voyage*, which recounts Shackleton and his crew's epic journey of survival after his ship, the *Endurance*, became trapped in pack ice and sank.

Endurance: Shackleton's Incredible Voyage is still Jacinda's all-time favourite book. It's a masculine, old-style non-fiction adventure narrative, the type that a father might share with his son – the title of the *New York Times*' review, 'The Hero Was Man', says much about the book. Utterly spellbound by the account and naturally drawn to heroism, Jacinda idolised Shackleton. For the young and impressionable Jacinda, Shackleton, with his vision and daring, was the antidote to Franklin's haunting, epic tragedy.

The book's significance for Jacinda, and the fact her interest in Shackleton's story was sparked by her father, is noteworthy. Many of Jacinda's interests and characteristics seem to have come from her first male role model – Ross. After Ross, the young Jacinda sought out other male role models and idols – her teacher Gregor Fountain and historical icons such as Shackleton and the legendary Labour leader Norman Kirk – as much as she did female mentors.

Suffice it to say that from her father, Jacinda developed a healthy masculine side, as it were. There were clear indications of her affinity with Ross during her childhood, which was underpinned by quality father–daughter time. A self-confessed 'complete tomboy', the young Jacinda spent many weekends and holidays working on the farm with her father, first with fruit trees, and later with sheep. Ross taught her to drive her first vehicle, a large, red Massey Ferguson tractor.

One vignette she shares from those times evinces the trust she felt for him. One day, she was driving the tractor in the orchard. Disengaging the clutch instead of hitting the brakes, Jacinda held tight on the steering wheel as the tractor ploughed 'straight into a nashi [pear] tree, another nashi tree, and then into my father'. Ross leapt aboard and took over the controls, standing on the brake pedal before the tractor mowed down another tree, or anything else.

For the girl who was to take the highest office of her nation, Ross was more than a father she could admire: he was a role model, a supporter, a provider and believer in her talents – a man on whom she could rely. How successful would any young women be with such a dad?

5

The Mighty Totara

New Zealanders have an oddly intimate relationship with their leaders. Aotearoa's citizens live clumped together in their settlements strung along the coast and the edges of forests, mountain ranges and farmland. The land speaks of its indigenous heritage; Kiwis tend to regard their leaders affectionately as did their forebears. They, the leaders, reflect what society wishes to admire; they must be worthy of its admiration – or not, as the case may be.

Media coverage of politicians here mirrors that of celebrities. Politicians are expected to be approachable, in the manner of television celebrities or sports stars. And like celebrities or sports stars, the average senior politician may be seen out and about in public, as Jacinda Ardern is from time to time, in restaurants and even the odd store (albeit with a handful of burly, suited men in tow). With this closeness, personality politics has taken on an almost familial air in New Zealand. Prime Minister Helen Clark, for one, was often referred to as 'Aunty Helen' by her supporters.

A generation earlier, a very different kind of national leader held sway, in so many ways the diametric opposite of Jacinda. From the mid-1970s to the mid-1980s, the paternalistic Robert Muldoon was in charge. A small, pudgy man with a huge ego, he once campaigned, successfully, under the banner 'Rob Muldoon – Superstar'. He ruled the country, rather than governed it – some would say, like a mob boss (his cheek even sported an Al Capone-style scar, though it was from a childhood accident). His antagonist Roderick Deane, deputy governor of the Reserve Bank, later said, with an economist's understatement, 'He genuinely believed that he knew what was best for the economy and for the rest of us.'[1]

A considered, steady hand may have better suited the times. The

1970s and 1980s was a period of confrontation and dispute, worry and social change for New Zealand. The loss of its major export market when the United Kingdom joined the EEC and the energy crises of the 1970s hit it hard. As the economy reeled, Muldoon, a former cost accountant, borrowed heavily for infrastructure and industrial projects dubbed 'Think Big', while clinging to increasingly futile protectionist policies. When the gains from Think Big projects failed to offset their massive borrowings and with the economy in recession, he imposed a wage and price freeze in September 1982.

It was a vain effort to control the economy, made by a man who fashioned himself as the godfather of the nation – a heavy-fisted, hard-headed godfather. As fond of confrontation as he was a drink, 'Piggy' Muldoon was prone to 'counterpunching' his adversaries, as he put it, wherever they showed themselves: in his party, the cabinet, the opposition, the civil service and the media. His attitude toward his critics was chilling. 'You're never going to get their votes,' he told his friend Bob Jones. '[So] kick the hell out of them.'[2] That he did, often on television. Every few days, his chubby face would take up the nation's screens, where he would issue his latest verbal onslaught. 'There was great bitterness in New Zealand life then,' Jones recalls.[3]

Another, very different leader of the same generation was Labour's thoughtful and charismatic Norman Kirk, 'Big Norm', New Zealand's last working-class prime minister. Even their physical differences were marked. Muldoon was short and balding, whereas Big Norm was tall and had coiffed silver hair. Muldoon was, not to put too fine a point on it, a fairly plain-looking man (though with distinctive features that were a cartoonists delight), while Kirk was handsome, in a regal way.

Born on 6 January 1923, Kirk was more than a year younger than his National Party successor Muldoon, but came to power a term earlier, in 1972. Arguably, it was only through Kirk's untimely death in August 1974 that Muldoon became prime minister.

Kirk died after just twenty months in office and at the height of his popularity, with much promise ahead. In those months, though, he laid the foundations for the modern nation of New Zealand.

Engaging in world affairs, he staked the country's place in the world, away from the aegis of Mother England. As he said, 'Ideas have force, not size.' When he was gone, the world knew that this small country in the Pacific had its own mind and could express itself fearlessly.

In 1972 Kirk withdrew the nation's troops from the morass of Vietnam and, in the following year, he opposed French nuclear testing in the Pacific by taking France to the International Court of Justice. Undaunted by France's flouting of the court's ruling, in July 1973 Kirk deployed two New Zealand navy frigates, HMNZS *Canterbury* and HMNZS *Otago*, to France's test zone area at Mururoa Atoll – a powerful act of diplomatic protest. Also in that year, he cancelled the Springboks rugby team's tour due to public opposition to South Africa's apartheid regime.

Perhaps Big Norm's most significant achievement was his nation building. It was his most powerful stated ambition, to 'cultivate in New Zealand a strong, self-reliant sense of nationhood; to try and get away from this dependent mentality that we acquired in the days of colonialism and which we haven't completely shed yet.'[4]

In terms of international diplomacy, his achievements, as much as his government's actions, speak to this ambition. Domestically, he did much to heal the wounds of colonialism, working towards a cohesive, inclusive national identity. The tradition of celebrating New Zealand Day, or Waitangi Day, was begun in 1973. On that day, 6 February 1973, the suited Big Norm walked hand-in-hand with a Māori boy in traditional dress to the ceremony, showing the nation that a new era of racial cooperation, of reconciliation, had arrived.

On the day of Norm Kirk's funeral, New Zealanders lined Wellington's streets in the winter rain to pay their respects as the cortege proceeded; people thronged the steps as the coffin passed into the cathedral. As his body lay in state near the steps of Parliament, a kaumātua (Māori elder) cried out, 'The mighty totara has fallen!' It was a reference to the beloved totara tree of New Zealand's forests, with its massive trunk, that lives for hundreds of years.

Big Norm was loved across the racial divide: Māori mourners conducted a traditional tangi (ritual chant of mourning and farewell) at St Paul's Cathedral. Such was the outpouring of grief at his unexpected death, it was as if the whole nation had lost a family member. Returned servicemen shed tears openly alongside hippies; Ross Ardern, then a young police recruit, just twenty years old, wept when he heard his hero had died. 'Where were you when JFK was assassinated?' is a question Americans ask of themselves often. For New Zealanders, theirs is 'Where were you when you heard the news Big Norm died?'

For generations of Labour supporters since, the loss of Big Norm is still mourned, as much to the country as to the party and of the man himself. A leader with courage and vision, and a moderation lacking in his successors, his passing has been an endless source of regret for what could have been. If Kirk had survived, Labour stalwarts contend, perhaps the Muldoon years would have been avoided. Muldoon was a National Party usurper, after Kirk, they say. Perhaps Rogernomics would not have torn apart the nation; Labour would not have lost its way for a generation or more, with Big Norm at the helm.

For them, Kirk, with his dark suits, silver hair and avuncular demeanour, his self-taught wisdom and compelling personality, was the consummate prime minister. He knew the struggles of ordinary people, because he had lived them – rat-infested work tenements, years of hard physical labour and building his family home in Kaiapoi, near Christchurch, himself. He even fished, with his own carefully tooled lures, and hunted rabbits with a .22 rifle to help feed his five children. Kirk's struggles grounded his judgement, making his pronouncements as relevant today as they were nearly five decades ago: 'Basically, there are four things that matter to people – they have to have somewhere to live, they have to have food to eat, they have to have clothing to wear, and they have to have something to hope for . . . Everything relates to this human aspiration.'

A man of measured speech and the charisma of a statesman, Kirk was a prime minister everyone could respect, regardless of political persuasion. Even his bitterest opponent in Parliament, Robert Muldoon, described him in his valedictory speech as 'a most remarkable man . . . a great parliamentarian!'[5]

Norman Kirk is a family icon, so much venerated in that familiar New Zealand manner that Jacinda Ardern's first cat was named after him. His portrait is prominently displayed in her office. Kirk is Ardern's favourite prime minister; her political progenitor, whom she so often quotes.

He was the father of modern New Zealand politics. A father the nation lost too young.

6

Family and Politics

There is a small reminder of parenthood in New Zealand politics. It is the title given to the longest-serving member in New Zealand's Parliament: the unofficial position of the mother or father of the House. Helen Clark became mother of the House in March 2005, after nearly twenty-four years in Parliament. Former prime minister Bill English, who was elected in 1990, was father of the House until he retired in March 2018. The title, with honour but no benefit beyond this, is determined by a member's continuous service in Parliament.

Until recently, if it were decided by aggregate time in Parliament, the uncontested father of the House would have been Winston Peters. Entering Parliament in 1979 as a National MP under Robert Muldoon, Peters has endured four decades in national politics. Without a seat for two terms – 1981–4 and 2008–11 – Peters bided his time and grasped his chance to return to the House at the following elections. Though ousted from Parliament in the 2020 election, he is in the 'top ten' of the nation's longest-serving MPs – and there have been some 1,500 Kiwi parliamentarians since 1854. Most New Zealanders cannot remember a time without Winston in public life, his gravelly voice and rounded vowels on radio, his handsome features on the television becoming craggy and compelling with age.

Born on 11 April 1945 in the final months of the Second World War, Peters, who was the oldest sitting member of the House, is not so much the father of New Zealand politics as its cantankerous, whimsical old uncle. One of the more flamboyant characters in New Zealand's political history, he has the vigour, head of hair and rage of a much younger man, with the political acumen to match his years in politics.

Peters is a survivor of the old school, and of expulsion from the National Party: twice he has been written off by political pundits; twice he has confounded them. It would be premature even yet to write his political obituary. In November 2008 Peters lost his bid for his old seat, Tauranga, to the National Party prospect and later leader, Simon Bridges. 'End of the road for Winston', the *New Zealand Herald* headline blared. Gracious in defeat, Peters complimented Bridges, a 'bright young guy', and vowed, 'This is not the end.'[1]

It wasn't, though Bridges would have reason to wish it were. A few years later, Bridges would find himself, as so many others have, on the receiving end of brutal Peters tongue lashings in the chamber. Notably, Winston labelled him a 'joke' and called him 'sunshine', ridiculing his broadest of New Zealand accents. 'I'll tell you about China, but not "Choina"', Peters crowed in February in response to Bridges' interjections. 'I don't know anything about that country unless a new rock has jumped up in the Pacific.'[2] Members on the back benches and the front roared with laughter.

The part-Māori Winston and his party, New Zealand First, are a curious mix of right and left wing, a mishmash of nationalist, socially conservative and old-style interventionist policies. Some observers from the UK have described the party as a 'watered-down UKIP'. In any event, political commentators have given up defining New Zealand First's place on the left–right political spectrum, instead labelling the party, and Peters, 'populist'. It is an inadequate description of the man and his party, in so many ways. Certainly, Peters supports many populist causes, but he sometimes finds himself going against them, such as when he and his New Zealand First members voted against the Marriage (Definition of Marriage) Amendment Act 2013, which allowed same-sex couples to marry legally. The issue should have been put to the people to make the decision via a citizens' referendum, Peters explained.

At first glance, this is the pronouncement of a populist party leader. But Peters goes further than mere populism. It seems he wants to join the government at times, but at others to shake up the political system from within. 'You see,' he says, 'the democratic process that we take part in actually leads to a tyranny, and we believe this is happening in New Zealand . . . politicians do as they wish. Instead of placing the interests of the people first, they put their parties first or pander to some self-interest group in return for prejudice, cash or votes or all three.'³

Anti-elitist, anti-establishment and contrarian would be a more apt description of Winston Peters' politics. He rails against the 'intellectually arrogant elite in government and bureaucratic circles' and relishes a confrontational relationship with the media, which he says is tainted by foreign ownership and political influence. His approach has either stunted his achievement or exalted it, depending on one's definition of success. Former prime minister Jenny Shipley says, 'Winston could have been prime minister but for want of himself. His complexity often got ahead of his capability. Watching him on a good day, he was brilliant'.⁴

Peters himself seems to scorn political success in conventional terms, at any rate: while he accepts high office, he doesn't seem to mind walking away from it when the circumstances suit. As he maintains, he 'genuinely [doesn't] care about the baubles of office'.⁵ He seems to relish his role as kingmaker, far more than the prospect of taking the top job himself.

Unsurprisingly, given his penchant for confrontation, Peters has a chequered history in cabinet. In October 1991, after less than a year as minister of Māori affairs, during which he repeatedly criticised his own party and government, he was sacked by Prime Minister Jim Bolger. Early in 1993, he resigned, or was ousted, from the National Party, then won a High Court decision to allow him to recontest his seat of Tauranga, which he regained. Just three years later, as leader of New Zealand First – and after a marathon seven-week negotiation following the 1996 elections – he was back in cabinet. There, he took his place as deputy prime minister and treasurer, in a coalition government headed by Bolger, the man who had sacked him from the cabinet just five years earlier.

When Bolger was deposed by Jenny Shipley in December 1997, the relationship between Peters and the National Party quickly soured. After a bitter row over the privatisation of Wellington international airport, the new prime minister sacked Peters, who, in August 1998, promptly took himself and his party off the government benches and into opposition.

Winston and New Zealand First seized the opportunity of a confidence-and-supply agreement with the new Labour government in 2005 to introduce the SuperGold Card, a concessions and discounts card for senior citizens and veterans. In the same negotiations, which were significantly shorter than those following the 1996 elections, Peters was handed the ministerial portfolios of foreign affairs and racing.

The former appointment caused an uproar, not least for Peters' anti-immigration stance: 'We are being dragged into the status of an Asian colony and it is time that New Zealanders were placed first in their own country.'[6] His outspoken, blunt manner seemed, for many, to be at odds with the demands of the job. A man who values and cultivates relationships, Peters nevertheless managed his duties quite well. He struck up a friendship with US secretary of state Condoleezza Rice, which seemed to be of some benefit to New Zealand, and took an active interest in Pacific affairs. A few years after her retirement from politics, Helen Clark told documentary filmmakers, 'I have to say [Peters] did a perfectly good job' as minister of foreign affairs.[7]

From there, Peters' career ebbed, at least for a while. After a catastrophic showing at the 2008 election, where Winston and his party were cast into the political wilderness without a parliamentary seat, New Zealand First made a comeback in 2011. The party won eight seats, and in the 2014 elections increased its total to eleven.

Crucial to New Zealand First's success has been the Mixed Member Proportional electoral system (MMP), which was introduced in 1996. Under MMP, which was modelled on the German system, New Zealanders are afforded two votes: one, to choose a local candidate for a geographic seat; the other, for their preferred party, which determines the number of list seats the party receives. Of the parliament's 120 seats, sixty-five are general electorate or geographic seats; a further seven are for Māori electorates. The remaining 48 seats in parliament are selected from the party lists (compiled and publicised before the election by each party) according to the proportion each party receives of the party vote. If a party receives at least five percent of the party vote, it is awarded list seats.

List seats allow minor parties that might not win a single geographic seat, to take their place in Parliament and exert influence. From

MMP's inception, none have succeeded in doing so more than New Zealand First. Largely through New Zealand First's list seats, Peters played kingmaker for both major parties, with governments of the National Party under Jim Bolger and the Labour Party, under Helen Clark. As the 2017 election loomed, it seemed inevitable Winston Peters would again play his role of deciding the government.

No leader or potential leader in New Zealand, in any event, has been free to ignore Peters and his influence. Jacinda Ardern was herself questioned about him in an interview in mid-2012, when, the interviewer noted, she seemed 'a little fascinated' by him. Ardern described Peters, accurately, as a 'true politician' who 'knows his constituents and how to push their buttons'. Her response to the question of why the liberal left treated him as 'some likeable, irascible uncle' is insightful, and somewhat ironic, given his later role in her rise to power: 'You can treat someone as an uncle . . . but that doesn't mean that you want them to lead the family dinner, does it?'[8]

In little more than half a decade after she spoke these words, Ardern would be talking with this very same political uncle, deciding exactly what place he should take at the nation's dinner table.

*

It was a family member who introduced Jacinda to national politics: a woman. Although Jacinda has said her parents 'weren't overly political people',[9] her paternal aunt, Ross's sister Marie Ardern, was. A staunch Labour Party supporter and member since her youth, Marie was Jacinda's inspiration in joining the Labour Party at the age of seventeen. Marie remembers Jacinda asking her opinion about whether she should pursue a career in politics. 'Darling,' Marie said, 'if you want to do . . . politics . . . come down to New Plymouth with me, and I'll show you how we do a campaign.'[10]

The campaign she spoke of was for the October 1996 general election in the New Plymouth electorate, which encompasses the town of the same name and its surroundings on the North Island's Taranaki Peninsula. Jacinda was sixteen. Marie and her dedicated young niece knocked on doors, delivering leaflets and canvassing tirelessly for the sitting Labour member, Harry Duynhoven, who retained his seat in a landslide victory. Jacinda, with her natural charm, quickly earned her reputation as a 'good doorknocker'.

A political streak runs through Jacinda's father's family, even though it seems to have remained latent within Ross himself. Jacinda's grandmother Gwladys was an ardent Labour supporter – as Jacinda would say in her maiden speech to Parliament, 'the true political beast in my family' – and a secretary of the Piako Labour Electorate Committee. Gwladys took her duties seriously. When the polls approached, she would take a collection bucket to the shops in Te Aroha, raising money for her beloved party. If a shop owner turned her down, she would refuse to shop there again. One of Jacinda's most cherished mementos is a newspaper clipping from 1968, yellowed with age, picturing Gwladys with Norm Kirk, four years before he won office. The pair stood for a photograph before attending a Hindu wedding at Te Aroha racecourse. Gwladys is in a formal dress, hat and gloves next to Big Norm, who true to his sobriquet, looks imposing in his trademark dark suit and tie. Big Norm's face wears a calm half-smile; Gwladys's expression is of muted happiness, as if she is trying to contain her delight. Jacinda has the clipping of her grandmother and the late prime minister framed, displayed on her wall at home.

Another photograph shows Gwladys in action. Jacinda keeps it on her electorate office desk. Taken a few years later, in 1975, it captures her with a small group of her party colleagues at an outdoor event for the general election that year. Four women surround one man, smiling, wearing pink campaign ribbons on their lapels. With Gwladys's arm tightly around him, their male colleague holds a hexagonal sign, 'HELEN CLARK LABOUR PIAKO'.

Doubtless, Gwladys was equally passionate about politics as her granddaughter four decades later. Repulsed by the demagoguery of Prime Minister Robert Muldoon in the 1970s, she would turn off the TV set any time he appeared, keeping it off for ten minutes lest she see his face again. Perhaps this goes some way to explaining Jacinda's teenage admiration for Marilyn Waring, the woman who humbled the bombastic National Party prime minister.

Not all family members have been Labour supporters, and the Ardern name was not new to politics in New Zealand before Jacinda took her place in Parliament in 2008. A distant cousin, Shane Ardern

– who Jacinda once told Parliament is her third cousin by marriage, 'distantly related' – was a prominent National Party member of Parliament between 1998 and 2014. Shane rose to notoriety in September 2003 for driving a vintage tractor called Myrtle up the steps of Parliament House before a cheering crowd, demonstrating against a proposed agricultural emissions research levy nicknamed the 'fart tax'. Jacinda once made a witty reference to the incident, telling a journalist, 'I learnt how to drive a Massey Ferguson [tractor] before I learnt to drive, but just knew it was impolite to drive it up stairs.' Though on opposite sides of the political fence, and apart from the odd disagreement in the debating chamber, Shane and Jacinda are on good terms.

Another relative, Jacinda's second cousin Hamish McDouall, made a bid as the Labour candidate for the seat of Whanganui in 2008, the year that Jacinda entered Parliament. Like Jacinda, Hamish was unsuccessful in his bid for a geographic seat, but ranked sixty of seventy-seven on the Labour Party list, he was not granted a list seat either. He polled second in Whanganui in the 2011 and 2014 general elections, before running in the mayoral elections of Whanganui District Council in 2016. There, Hamish won comfortably, garnering 2,900 more votes than his nearest rival. In 2019, his former opponents acknowledged his competent leadership, and he was re-elected unopposed.

Interestingly, Jacinda's inclination for public life seems to derive from the women of the family, who were no shrinking violets, to say the least. They were, indeed, a particularly strong lot: Gwladys Ardern was her family's matriarch, and a local personality associated with the race club. Gwladys's mother Elizabeth McCrae, who emigrated from Scotland, brought with her two chief possessions – a violin, which was handed down to succeeding generations, and tellingly, a pistol.

That some of Jacinda's women ancestors set out alone from the United Kingdom, making the longest voyage of migration in human history to New Zealand (some 14,750 miles), says much of their mettle. The fact that these women would willingly submit to the boredom and miserable conditions aboard the ships – along with heavy seas on the southern reaches of three oceans before the treacherous Tasman waters – is testament to their fortitude.

Kate Wiltshire, née Rider, Jacinda's great-great-grandmother, is a case in point. The most prominent of Jacinda's early ancestors in New

Zealand, she is still remembered in the family and history books as New Zealand's first national woman sports star. Kate was a celebrity whose image and exploits graced the pages of papers and magazines of the day, enjoying a professional career as a long-distance pedestrian and theatre performer. This she did in a time when such pursuits were frowned upon in polite society, yet she managed to garner respect. Perhaps it's fitting that Jacinda was given the middle name Kate after her ancestor, who was a true feminist before the word found its way into common parlance.

Kate's story is almost as outstanding as her great-great-granddaughter's, and certainly more colourful. A working-class woman, she emigrated from London at the age of nineteen in 1872, marrying Joseph Wiltshire a few months after her arrival.

In the late 1800s, long-distance pedestrians were the most famous of sportspeople, their feats of endurance attracting crowds, gambling and press attention. Joseph had been a pedestrian in England, and when he decided to resume his career in New Zealand, Kate accompanied him on his record-breaking attempts, walking with him, wearing striking costumes and attracting attention as she did.

Despite the failure of an ambitious attempt at a 1,000-mile (1,600-kilometre) walk with Joseph in Dunedin, Kate took on her greatest challenge on a Friday night in May 1876 at Auckland's City Hall: a 100-mile walk in 24 hours. This was a feat that had only recently been accomplished by men.

Kate's style drew an audience as much as her ability as a pedestrian. Dressed in a costume that was described as similar to a trapeze artist's, her 'beautiful black curls' hung free over her back; her décolletage was adorned with loops of pearls and her wrists with bracelets. A petite woman, she had character to match her looks – like her great-great-granddaughter nearly a century and a half later. And like Jacinda, Kate had, a reporter commented, 'an air of determination about her which showed she was capable of great things'.

This was to be Kate Wiltshire's day of greatness.

The Artillery Band struck up a tune for her to start the first of 2,833 laps of the circuit in the hall, and she began. Serious money had been wagered both ways on her attempt. A local publican bet £25 that she would fail. As the late hours became morning, Kate endured ankle pain, exhaustion and a singing, drunken sailor accompanying her waving a flag, but she strode on. At 7.30 P.M., the hall was full to witness her finish. The audience cheered, waving handkerchiefs and hats, the band played 'See, the Conqu'ring Hero Comes' to deafening applause as Kate finished.

Kate had earned the accolade 'The Greatest Female Pedestrienne in the World'. She could never surpass this, her greatest accomplishment as an athlete, though later in the same year, she supported Joseph's successful bid to walk 1,000 miles at a course in Wellington.

A drama outside the event almost ruined his attempt. Around the 500-mile mark, Joseph was charged in court with threatening a man with a pistol. Kate's appearance for her husband in court created such a stir that it was reported in the press, in dramatic detail. She took to the witness box, waving the loaded pistol around in court with a flourish as she spoke, terrifying onlookers. At one point, the gun was pointed at the magistrate's head, who apparently in on the gag, winked. The gallery cleared from her path in haste as she left the witness box to instruct her counsel, who likewise found himself looking down a barrel.

The charge was eventually dropped. The Wiltshires settled down to a quieter life, having two boys and seven girls, one of whom, Lydia, was Jacinda's great-grandmother. Predictably, perhaps, Kate was an ardent supporter of women's rights, being among the 31,872 women (and some men) who signed the 1893 Women's Suffrage Petition. Her signature in its cursive, nineteenth-century hand can still be seen on the original document – a small but significant contribution to a historic campaign.

Later in 1893, New Zealand's women became the first in the world to vote in parliamentary elections. Another Kate – Kate Sheppard, one of the leading lights of early modern feminism – is honoured for her role in this with her portrait on the New Zealand $10 note.

Sheppard was an eloquent speaker, whose words set the tone for feminist activism in the next hundred years. She spoke of the disempowerment of women with a clarity that resonates, more than a century and a quarter later. There is 'no greater anomaly,' she declared, 'than the exaltation by men of the vocation of wife and mother on the one hand, while, on the other, the position is by law stripped of all its attractiveness and dignity'.

Her words on women's political rights are lucid; perfect common sense: 'Women are entitled to share in the privileges of citizenship. If we have to obey the law, we want a voice in the making of that law. If we pay taxes, we want a voice in saying how that tax money is spent. If we are interested in politics, we want full liberty of thought and action. In short, we want a voice in the form of that most sacred possession – a vote.'

Sheppard's exhortation at the end of her many pronouncements was, 'Women, take the matter up!' And they did – all through the twentieth century, and still.

7

Suffrage and Suffering

Jacinda Ardern owes as much to women such as Kate Sheppard and others who followed – her political antecedents – as to her ancestors. A woman who is aware of history and the sacrifices of her forebears, Ardern keeps a portrait of Sheppard in her office and has made mention of her and Kate Wiltshire in numerous speeches and articles. She visited Sheppard's former house in Christchurch for a Facebook live 'sneaky tour' of the property during the 2020 election campaign, showing the dining room where Sheppard worked on the petition.

It is hard to imagine that before 1893, Kate Sheppard, Kate Wiltshire and all other women were classed with lunatics, minors and criminals, considered unfit to vote in New Zealand – or anywhere in the world, for that matter. It is even harder to imagine now that it was not until 1920 in the US, and 1928 in Britain, that women were granted equal franchise with men.

The path to equal voting rights for women may have been swifter in New Zealand, but it was by no means easy. Sheppard, as a leading figure of New Zealand's Woman's Christian Temperance Union, faced staunch opposition from the liquor industry. If women were given the vote, brewers and distillers reasoned, prohibition might very well result, and they would be out of business. They mobilised, lobbying politicians – most notably the boorish Henry Fish, who deployed petitions opposing women's suffrage. Attracted by Fish's bounty for each signature garnered, touts circulated these in bars and public gatherings. Sometimes, they tricked men into signing them.

Then there was the belief, prevalent in those times, that equality was somehow dangerous; allowing women to vote went against the very order of nature. Fish himself asserted that 'bringing women into contact with politics will destroy that refinement, that delicacy of character, which has been her greatest charm hitherto'; that 'angels of the house' would become part of a 'shrieking sisterhood'.

An anti-women's suffrage cartoon of the period says much about male chauvinists' fears. In it, a woman is pictured, striding in through the door of her home in the manner of a patriarch. She points her umbrella at a downtrodden man, who is standing by a stove, his hair in curlers, pan in hand, cooking. Toddlers fight on the floor nearby; a baby shrieks in a cot. In the background, a wall is festooned with parodies of quotations, such as 'Frailty, thy name is man'. 'What, dinner not ready yet?' the woman asks. 'What have you been doing?' Some men evidently feared that women would reverse the order of things; that they would be the ones forced into servitude.

The majority of New Zealand men were less concerned. While political chicanery from Premier Richard Seddon and others delayed women's suffrage, widespread support saw it granted in New Zealand with none of the angst and brutality the movement endured in the mother country.

It seems odd now that in their quest for equal voting rights (which is now regarded as a basic and inalienable entitlement), women in Britain felt driven to desperation and violence. Hunger strikes were met with force-feeding; peaceful demonstrations encountered gangs of thugs, police beatings and, most horrifyingly, public sexual assault. The British suffragettes' campaign took a darker turn in the years leading up to the First World War. After a peaceful demonstration at Westminster was quashed violently on what came to be known as Black Friday, 18 November 1910, women activists unleashed a slew of attacks. Their arson, bombings, sabotage, assaults and vandalism would doubtless now be regarded as acts of terror. The war brought the increasing violence in Britain to an end, and by 1918 a limited female franchise was introduced with little opposition, though it would take another ten years for full voting rights to be achieved.

New Zealand can be proud of its early record in women's political rights, prouder still that men and women cooperated to bring about change that seems only logical. After the early promise of the late nineteenth century, however, women's participation in politics lagged for much of the twentieth century. Two crippling world wars and their aftermath took their toll: women voted, but stayed largely on the fringes of the political process.

When a woman did make her way into Parliament, and later cabinet, these were anomalies. Women were not eligible to stand for a parliamentary seat until 1919, and it would be a further fourteen years before the first woman was elected. Even then, sentiment – and the proximity of the woman in question to a male in politics – seems to have played a role in this watershed event.

Elizabeth McCombs hailed from a family famous for its socialist women activists. In her youth, she felt overshadowed by her two elder sisters, Christina and Stella, who regarded her as unlikely to excel, because she was 'lazy at school'. In her middle age, however, McCombs came into her own. Elected to Christchurch City Council in 1921 – only the second woman councillor – she joined, and later chaired, the city's Electricity Committee. It was there that her efforts saw her city's households enjoying the cheapest electricity in the country, an important achievement for the domestic feminism she espoused.

McCombs was active in public life as few can be. She was elected to the Christchurch Tramway Board and became a North Canterbury Hospital Board member. In 1926, she became one of the few women justices of the peace in New Zealand. Perhaps her most enduring contribution to public life was the building of women's rest rooms and a crèche in Christchurch's Cathedral Square. Women, McCombs knew, were entering public places in their own right; they deserved proper, decent amenities, corresponding to those already in place for men.

She was committed to social welfare, too. In the early 1930s, while the Great Depression raged, McCombs played her part in alleviating suffering. Taking her place on the hospital board's Benevolent Committee and the committee administering the Mayor's Relief of Distress Fund, she helped distribute aid to those most in need.

Despite her demonstrated effectiveness in local government and public administration, a seat in Parliament seemed to elude McCombs, as it had the nine other women who contested seats in New Zealand before her. The first woman to be endorsed as a candidate by the Labour Party, McCombs unsuccessfully stood for the seat of Kaiapoi in 1928. Though she polled last of the three candidates, it was a close election, mere hundreds of votes separating them. McCombs felt, as many women candidates have until the current generation, that being a woman had hampered her chances of winning (it's worth noting that the political icon Annette King recalls voters telling her in 1984 – more than half a century later – that they would not vote for her, simply because she was a woman). In 1931, when she contested the seat of Christchurch North, she decided to confront the issue, campaigning under the slogan 'Vote the First Woman to the New Zealand Parliament'.

As has so often been the case in New Zealand national politics, the woman candidate was thrust by her party into an all but unwinnable electoral battle. McCombs's main competitor for Christchurch North, Henry Holland, was a former mayor of Christchurch, a respected local personality who had delivered a crushing defeat to her husband James in the 1917 mayoral election. Unsurprisingly, she came a distant second behind Holland.

Still, McCombs would not give up her parliamentary ambitions. Despite reservations from some of her local members that she could not win the marginal seat of Lyttelton, she was endorsed by the Labour Party to contest a by-election held in September 1933. The seat had become vacant upon the death of the sitting member: her husband, who had died of a heart attack the previous month.

The election campaign was one of the more spectacular in New Zealand and, needless to say, controversial. McCombs's rivals were two men, one of whom, Frederick Freeman, had come close to unseating James two years earlier; the other, Edward L. Hills, was a young, disaffected Labour Party member.

Hills made some jarring statements then that today would be outrageous in this generation. At a public meeting he squarely took aim at McCombs, in a blatant sexist attack: 'I believe the same as Hitler believes, that a woman's place is in the home,' he declared, and then went further, saying, 'I believe the difficulties of the country are too great for women to grapple with.'[1]

Members of the meeting – likely McCombs's supporters – were having none of it. 'The men have made a hash of [governing],' a man interjected, as he and others took Hills to task. Hills's ideas were 'old-fashioned', a woman remarked, and another young man suggested that women had managed their homes very well with little money (New Zealand was still reeling then from the Great Depression), and opined 'they could do the same with the country'.

Freeman, a man with political experience comparable to McCombs's, steered clear of the issue of gender, probably aware that it would more than likely do his campaign more harm than good. He might have been painfully aware that sentiment was on the side of his former rival's widow, who the press said was 'regarded as one of the most capable women in the Labour Party'.[2] McCombs herself was happy to again confront the issue, reviving her earlier campaign motto, 'Vote the First Woman to the New Zealand Parliament'. It was, she told her supporters, her 'late husband's greatest desire that I should sit in Parliament'.[3] They had hoped to work together there, she said.

Reporters seemed unperturbed by the fuss over a woman running for a parliamentary seat and for the most part remained impartial. Newspapers could not resist capitalising on the controversy, though, publishing the more tendentious readers' letters, from both sides of the debate.

The issue seemed to polarise society: either people (mostly women) were heartily in favour of having a woman in the House, or they were fervently opposed to it, as if women were quite incapable of carrying out the duties it entailed. The more extreme seemed to believe that women, whose 'hearts invariably run away with their heads', would somehow endanger the entire public administration if elected to Parliament.

Preparations for the result of the by-election on 13 September 1933 were sensational. Loudspeakers were installed in Cathedral Square along with powerful lighting, and billboards to advertise the latest count were erected above the *Press* newspaper's city and Lyttelton offices. Nearly everyone, it seemed, was eager to know the outcome.

At the end of polling, it became clear that McCombs had fared far better than her husband at his last electoral outing. She trounced Frederick Freeman by a margin of 2,669 votes, whereas James had come within thirty-three votes of losing the seat to him. And Edward L. Hills's grandstanding saw him utterly rejected by the voters, with a pitiful 263 votes.

A crowd of some 2,000, mostly women, braved driving rain and the spring chill to greet McCombs in victory at Cathedral Square. Her speech, or what could be heard of it, was stirring. 'I am proud to be the first woman to be elected to our Parliament,' she said. 'It will be my endeavour to live up to the tradition the women of New Zealand have established for taking their full share of the burden of government.'[4] The rest of her oratory was drowned out by cheering.

A woman in Parliament meant the institution was to change – in subtle ways, perhaps, but permanently. The 'Ladies Not Admitted' signs had to be taken down from outside the billiard room and Bellamys, the parliamentary restaurant. Protocol and official addresses would be different.

This led to speculation in the newspapers. 'Will the Governor-General in the speech from the throne address the House as "Honourable Lady and Gentlemen",' the *Press* mused, 'or will he compromise with "Honourable Members"?'[5] Then there was the issue of attire. Men entered the chamber bareheaded. Would McCombs wear a hat?

The governor-general took perhaps the most logical course in his speech to the House on 21 September 1933. From that day, 'Members of the House of Representatives' was to become the standard address for elected members.

Near sixty and suffering from asthma and other ailments, McCombs was in the last years of her life when she stood in the House for her maiden statement on 28 September 1933. The chamber was adorned with three bouquets for the occasion. Bareheaded along with her male colleagues, she was dressed in a tailored suit, over a light silk blouse with a turnover collar. It was dignified attire, fitting for a historic day.

'She appeared somewhat nervous,' a reporter later wrote. But McCombs's words show only the stern spirit of the woman; a feminist flourish:

> I wish to express my sincere thanks to the honourable members of the House for the very kind reception which they have accorded me. It seems to me that a very good working basis has been established, and I trust that nothing will happen during my term of

office that will disturb the harmony of the relations so created. I would like to warn honourable members, however, that women are never satisfied unless they have their own way. It happens in this case that the woman's way is the right way.[6]

From there, McCombs issued forth an impassioned, authoritative oration that was to set the tone of her short career in Parliament. She spoke of crippling unemployment, about which, she declared, 'the Government of this country seems to have withdrawn into a kind of mental euthanasia'.[7] She highlighted the onerous burden of taxation on the working poor, the lack of opportunity and education for youth, and cuts to the education budget for the underprivileged. Gently challenging the government members opposite, she said, 'Many of the honourable gentlemen on the government benches, I think, are accustomed to a rural life and to the delightful freedom of sunny paddocks. I do not think they altogether understand the conditions of life in the cities today . . . I know of several cases where a whole family lives in one room.'[8]

McCombs's speech was compelling, and extended by several minutes over her allotted time. Before concluding, she urged that women be appointed to the police force, noting that they had been employed in the force in Scotland and England for many years, and successfully so.

McCombs's parliamentary career continued as it began, but not for long. Realising that her chances of swaying government policy were negligible as an opposition MP, she used her position to highlight issues close to her heart, speaking on them in the House. Her activism seems to have played its part in New Zealand's 'cradle to grave' welfare system, the first of its kind in the world, introduced in September 1938.

She would not live to see it. As her health began to fail, McCombs did not relinquish her seat. She had waited years for the opportunity to represent the least fortunate in society, and was determined to make the very best of her opportunity. Despite poor health, she continued to undertake the weekly trip by train and ferry, from Christchurch to Wellington, when the House was in session. She died an MP in June 1935, at the age of sixty-one. Her son Terry succeeded her.

Despite sitting less than two years in Parliament, Elizabeth McCombs's influence on public debate endured. Her ideas were either far beyond her time, or simply rooted in profound, timeless common sense. Her championing of equal pay for women, recruitment of women into the police force and more equitable unemployment benefits set the women's empowerment agenda for feminists decades later. It's worth noting that McCombs' humanitarian concerns are mirrored in Jacinda Ardern's, and although their maiden speeches and styles seem as far removed in fashion as in time, the substance is remarkably similar.

*

Once a woman had found her way into Parliament, it was inevitable that one would find her way into the government ministry. She was to come from the same side of politics. Elizabeth McCombs paved the way for another Labour Party member, Mabel Howard, to became the country's first cabinet minister in 1947, as minister of health and minister in charge of child welfare.

Like McCombs, Howard came to Parliament through her familial ties to a prominent man, though in her case it was not her husband, but her father, Ted Howard. Ted, an ardent socialist, was a leading light in the early Labour Party, an MP for Christchurch South from 1919 until his death in 1939, and a long-standing party whip.

Well respected by his electorate, Mabel was every bit her father's daughter. As an early supporter of Ted's career, she would stand below his platform at his speeches, applauding and punctuating his points with the odd 'bloody oath'. When Ted died, she was endorsed by the local branch to contest his seat, Christchurch South, in the coming by-election, but was passed over in favour of the mayor of Christchurch, Robert Macfarlane. In 1943, she won Christchurch East convincingly in a by-election.

A feisty woman who conceded she 'was more manly than most women', Mabel Howard smashed her way through the thick glass ceiling that hung low over women of her day. In her trade union career, she learned judo to ward off thugs. As the only woman secretary of the Canterbury General Labourers' Union, she would confront members whose dues were in arrears at their homes, climbing stairs and even the occasional ladder to do so. Howard preferred to walk or take a bus rather than a taxi or chauffeur-driven car, even during her ministerial career, and when she did take a car, she would offer people lifts. Her short, stout figure was often seen plodding along the streets of New Brighton, wearing ill-fitting old dresses, a beret and men's shoes.

Howard became famous for enlivening parliamentary debate in ways novel, even scandalous for the day. In 1954 during a debate, she held aloft two pairs of sizeable bloomers in the chamber. Both labelled 'OS' (oversize), the undergarments were clearly differently proportioned. Her intention was to demonstrate the need for clothing size standardisation, and her proposal for this attracted bipartisan support. Another time, she threw a rock onto the floor of Parliament to illustrate the poor quality of bagged coal. The rock, she said, had been found in a coal bag. She continually raised the issue of smog and air pollution, decades before the environment became a *cause célèbre*. Most of Howard's attention was, as with McCombs, centred on improving the lot of the underprivileged. She highlighted the plight of the poor and the environment, again issues similar to those taken up by Jacinda Ardern six decades later.

Incidentally, the Labour Party created a rule that members should not seek re-election for their seats after the age of seventy. This was explicitly to force the ailing Howard, who was suffering from dementia and recurring pneumonia, into retirement in 1969.

Women taking their rightful place in politics was decades away from Howard's era, in any event. The unusual cases aside – brave outliers with familial links to political parties – women were simply not seen as fit for a career in politics, and given scant opportunity to prove otherwise, for most of the twentieth century. Parliament was male-dominated – and remained a bastion of paternalist tradition.

It is noteworthy, if not alarming, that only eleven women were elected to Parliament during the fifty years following the legislation that allowed them to contest seats. Until 1960, only one woman – and that was Mabel Howard, who won the new seat of Sydenham with an outstanding 75.2% of the vote – had entered Parliament in a general election, rather than a by-election. Even as late as 1984, women guests to Parliament were not permitted to sit on the floor of the chamber, an honour extended courteously to male guests. This scandalised the women MPs in David Lange's new government, who promptly and successfully lobbied for change.

Women in Parliament – and more, in cabinet – remained the exception until nearly a century after Ardern's great-great-grandmother Kate Wiltshire signed the Women's Suffrage Petition. The list of women's 'firsts' in New Zealand politics has a cluster of names and titles in the 1980s and 1990s, corresponding with the number of women in Parliament rising into double figures (twelve in the 95-seat House in 1984). Helen Clark became New Zealand's first deputy and acting prime minister in 1989, and two years after Jenny Shipley became the nation's first female prime minister in December 1997, Clark succeeded her as the first elected female prime minister.

Ardern's generation was the first to be brought up with women holding key posts in national politics. Hers was the first, she says, where girls felt that women in leadership was 'normal'.

8

Emerging

It's easy to see patterns in things with the benefit of hindsight. Apart from some pipe dreams of following her father into New Zealand Police, Jacinda Ardern was on track for a career in politics after leaving Morrinsville College. Perhaps one could say her career had already begun. Her work volunteering in Harry Duynhoven's office during holidays, and campaigning for the MP and associate minister in two elections before she was out of her teens, was invaluable experience of national politics.

Indeed, it was during her time at Duynhoven's office that Jacinda truly became aware of the power of politics to influence society for good – and to influence people's lives, in real and meaningful ways. She recalls a pivotal experience from those years. 'I remember I'd gone to Harry's office when a constituent came to see Harry and got talking to a staff member,' she says. 'This was a grandfather caring for his grandchild, he had health problems and his grandchild was unwell and he was desperate because he couldn't buy school books or treat his asthma.'[1] Duynhoven made representations on the grandfather's behalf to help him. Sitting outside the office later in her car, Jacinda marvelled at 'how amazing [it is] that you can be in Wellington on the one hand changing everything, and then come back here and just change the world for one person.'[2]

Inspiration and aspiration need to be honed and channelled, and for Jacinda, as for most, this would be through education. Though she recalls 'angsting' over where she should study, the choice that she made shows that she knew – on some level, at least – exactly what she wanted, and how to go about it. She had toyed with the idea of travelling overseas to study, but feeling 'terrified' at the prospect of being so far from home and family, Jacinda settled instead on the University of Waikato in Hamilton.

The University of Waikato was a practical choice. As well as being close to home, it allowed Jacinda to continue her work at the Golden Kiwi. She also worked in a gift shop – and a supermarket, as did 'half the caucus', she told a Labour campaign audience years later. Her wage there was $5 per hour – meagre earnings, perhaps, but enough to pay for her car's running costs, shuttling to and from university. At one time, Jacinda held all three jobs, changing into her 'chippy' uniform at the back of the gift shop before heading to the Golden Kiwi for her Friday night shift.

Though unpleasant, one workplace incident became an 'awakening' experience for the teenage Jacinda. New checkouts installed in the supermarket were poorly designed, causing numerous accidents for the checkout operators. A proud young union member, Jacinda guided them in recording their injuries in the workplace incident log book, according to proper procedure. Her boss immediately confronted her. He took the incident log book, ripping the pages from it in front of her in anger. Jacinda was shocked with the brazenness of his action as much as by his bullying. 'It was a real lesson for me about the need to stand up, even if it was a scary experience,' she says. The incident served to firm Jacinda's resolve to advocate for 'vulnerable workers'.[3]

Otherwise, Jacinda's life in these years seems so very ordinary, though industrious, and her focus intense. Her choice of university likewise. If the alma maters of previous leaders are any guide, the University of Waikato is hardly a place one would expect to find a future prime minister. Her three predecessors as prime minister, Helen Clark, John Key and Bill English, attended the universities of Auckland, Canterbury and Otago respectively – older, more established institutions. The University of Waikato has climbed the international rankings over the last few years, though, garnering respect and students.

Established in 1964, it is a young institution, modern and well appointed, with a sizeable number of international students and the highest Māori enrolment in the country. The University of Waikato doesn't boast the tradition of the universities of Auckland, Canterbury,

Otago or Wellington, which are perhaps the equivalent of the North American Ivy League colleges. Nor does it have a Latin motto. In its rather plain coat of arms, a book is emblazoned between the stars of a Southern Cross, underscored by 'ko te tangata' in te reo Māori, meaning 'for the people'. With its lack of pretence, the University of Waikato is just the kind of institution where one would expect to find a modern, social-democrat politician in the making.

The town in which it is based, Hamilton, is likewise free of the airs and graces of New Zealand's urban centres. It has the reputation of being the country's 'bogan capital'. For those not from New Zealand or Australia, 'bogan' is a slang term for an unrefined, unsophisticated person. Bogan has become a subculture, a label worn almost with pride in Australia and New Zealand. Tattoos, tight black jeans, mullet haircuts and heavy-metal band T-shirts are de rigueur, as are modified Fords and Holdens with loud exhausts and wide wheels. Burnout competitions and illegal drags on public roads exasperate the more staid members of the community here.

Jacinda's study was for a mainstream, though suitably modern course: bachelor of communications studies (BCS), majoring in public relations, with a minor in politics, at Waikato Management School, a faculty of the university. This might have appeared an unusual combination, but in hindsight, and in the age of digital communication, it couldn't have served her better.

Jacinda quickly distinguished herself at university. Her communications professor, Debashish Munshi, speaks of his straight-A former student in glowing terms: 'We teach students, but there are some students we learn from as well, and I would say that [Jacinda] was one of those students,' he says. 'The simple things like humility, social consciousness – you can see what a great communicator she is.'4

Naturally, the faculty is thrilled with its famous alumna's success. Professor Munshi's colleague, communications professor C. Kay Weaver, observes with a satisfied chuckle, 'We don't have to use Obama's speeches anymore in class. We can use Jacinda's.'5

Toward the end of Jacinda's time at Waikato, an opportunity for overseas study presented itself. Now a little older and rather more confident, she was quick to take it up. She departed a few weeks after her twenty-first birthday, to spend the final semester of her degree at

Arizona State University (ASU) in the city of Tempe. It was a coura-geous step. A photograph of Jacinda with Laurell, taken before she set off, reveals an expression of untempered optimism in her smile and eyes.

Her sense of adventure and the novelty quickly faded in the US. It was a rude shock for Jacinda, compared to the joyful, carefree experi-ence in Seoul three years earlier.

The weather in itself was ordeal enough. She had left New Zealand in its cool winter months, quite unprepared for an Arizona summer. The region is the hottest in the US, with average maximum tempera-tures in that season hovering around forty degrees Celsius. ASU was, Jacinda says, 'large, hot and sprawling', such that lecturers drove golf carts from class to class to avoid walking in the heat. She found the sight of this amusing – that is, until she saw a student knocked over by a lecturer in his cart.

The scale of ASU is intimidating enough. Among the largest public universities by enrolment in the US, the Tempe campus alone covers some 270 hectares – larger than Jacinda's home town, Morrinsville. The place could hardly be further removed from the environment Jacinda had grown up in. The lush Waikato region is a stark contrast to the Arizona desert, and while the University of Waikato is by no means small, a campus with some 50,000 enrolled students is in another league altogether. Inevitably, perhaps, this mammoth institu-tion could be impersonal, despite its reputation as a party college – a far cry from the University of Waikato's cheery, laid-back ambience.

Some things in Arizona were simply baffling for a young Kiwi, too. In Parliament a few years later, Jacinda would recall how 'along the highways where the prisons were located . . . there were signs – as often as the signs we have here indicating speed limits – that stated: "Do not stop and pick up passengers. Prisoners likely to be roaming free."' It seemed incomprehensible to her that escaped convicts should be walking freely about the countryside, let alone thumbing a ride.

The whole experience of studying in Arizona was a trauma for Jacinda, who quickly became homesick, 'wish[ing] that I was at home with everything that was familiar, and with everyone that I loved'.[6] A small-town Mormon girl with no taste for sorority antics and drunken parties, Jacinda felt isolated, too. She discovered that with the soaring temperatures, 'people in Arizona do not walk'. Sometimes, she got lost, and with two buses to catch to travel to college, would often miss one and have to walk anyhow in the heat, cars honking at her all the way. Jacinda's 'overwhelming memory' of her semester at ASU 'was that heat stroke was awful, and that I was lonely'.[7]

Her time at ASU became more strained with the 11 September 2001 terrorist attacks, the fallout of which seems to have made a profound impression on her. The attacks rocked American society; the shock waves were felt on campus at ASU, as everywhere. A woman attuned to others' feelings, Jacinda could not ignore the collective grief and recriminations that swept the country after the attacks. Still, she had no thought of quitting. Despite all the challenges and discomfort in Arizona, she 'stuck it out' and finished the semester and her degree.

*

After graduating in 2001 with her BCS, Ardern began her political career in earnest, learning the ropes backstage, as it were. Her first job in Wellington was as a fill-in private secretary and assistant for Harry Duynhoven, who was then the associate minister of energy. She was quickly noticed as she accompanied Duynhoven on his field trips to oil wells, offshore exploration sites and mines.

Such workplaces were, and still are, a man's world almost exclusively – no woman had ever been in this position before. The presence of the associate minister's attractive, personable young assistant caused quite some wonderment. Once, when Ardern went with Duynhoven to inspect a mine, its managers were taken aback that she actually intended to go into the pit's murky depths with him. Hasty arrangements had to be made for a pair of overalls and hard hat.

It was during her time with Duynhoven's office that Ardern found a place in the party organisation. Her friend Tony Milne introduced her to the New Zealand Young Labour Committee. The committee didn't need much convincing. Milne nominated Ardern, and she was elected vice-president of Young Labour in 2003. Having a competent, dedicated woman on the committee – an honorary position – worked for everyone. She didn't even need to campaign.

The committee was right to bring her on board: Jacinda could be relied on to take responsibility for a task and wasn't afraid to dedicate effort and time to the position. In the summer of 2004–5, she was the chief organiser, the force behind the Young Labour Clarion Tour, which was the first of its kind.

The tour was named after the Clarion Cycling Clubs that journeyed the English countryside in the late nineteenth and early twentieth century, handing out socialist pamphlets and discussing political ideas. In late 2004 New Zealand, there was no cycling for the ten Young Labour volunteers. They toured the country in a minibus, the length of the two islands, Northland to Southland (the regions in the far north and far south of the country respectively), some 3,000 kilometres. On the way, the Young Labour members performed community service – cleaning beaches, separating recycling from rubbish, handing out condoms to revellers on New Year's Eve.

More inclined to be revellers themselves, most young men and women – of any political persuasion – wouldn't think of spending their summer holidays this way. Little wonder that after Ardern left Young Labour, it wasn't until the summer of 2010–11 that the next Clarion Tour was convened. That she managed to muster her colleagues, prising them away from their parties and summer indulgence to make the Clarion Tour successful, is quite some testament to her ability as an organiser.

Her dedication was noted. The energetic young Mormon woman might have stayed away from the vices of her colleagues, but she was cool enough without, and accepted them as they were. Her charm, energy and willingness to get things done seemed intrinsic to her nature, as was an uncanny ability to inspire others. In 2005, Ardern was elected international secretary for Young Labour.

By this time, she had made other moves upwards. Armed with a recommendation from Duynhoven, she applied for a job that was to take her about as close to the centres of power as any 25-year-old could go. She would work in the best possible position for a future prime minister: researcher and adviser for a senior national politician.

Her first boss in cabinet was Phil Goff, a Labour Party stalwart with an impressive reputation. More recently the city of Auckland's mayor, Goff was then minister of foreign affairs and a former candidate for party leader. He would go on to lead the party in 2008. As one of Goff's advisers, Ardern would assist and coordinate matters for him, in his office, and outside.

She remains close with her former employer. In support of Goff's announcement in November 2015 that he would run for the office of mayor the following year, she posted a photograph with him from those years on her Facebook page. The post stated that Goff was 'one of the hardest working people I have ever seen in action . . . Phil was the best [of bosses] (even laughing off one of my more memorable mistakes) . . . he's also a wonderful human being'. Goff is equally complimentary of Ardern. As well as praising her as 'vigorous, enthusiastic and charming', Goff makes a point about her that is perhaps the key to her appeal: 'What you see is what you get'.[8]

Goff's office gave Ardern her first close-quarters experience of power. With his determination, his acumen and industriousness, Goff himself was a powerful influence on Ardern. It was in Goff's office, too, that she would be noticed – sought after by the most powerful women in the country.

9

When the Student Is Ready

Phil Goff's office was exalted enough – working for the minister of foreign affairs is no small achievement – but Ardern's next job was in another league. Headhunted from Goff's staff for the prime minister's office – recruited by Heather Simpson, Helen Clark's head of staff – she would spend the year leading up to the 2005 general election working on the ninth floor of the Beehive. She shared her office space with Grant Robertson, her close friend and supporter ten years her senior, who would be significant in her rise to power a little over a decade later.

Working as an adviser for Prime Minister Helen Clark was a coup for Ardern, but she was well aware of the exacting standards that the job required. Almost as soon as she was appointed, she took a trip to Whitcoulls, a well-known bookstore in Wellington, where she bought a book on grammar, 'because,' she said after she was elected to Parliament, 'I always had a bit of a failing when it came to grammar, and I knew it was one of Helen's things'.[1] Buying the book would prove a sound decision.

The job of adviser to a senior politician is broader even than the term implies. Clark describes Ardern's former role thus: 'to work in the back office and put together background materials for Prime Minister Questions, things like that'. Ardern herself says, 'My job was a little bit of everything.'[2] Along with assisting and coordinating matters for Clark as she did for Goff, Ardern 'also had a bit of over-sight [on] certain portfolios on behalf of Helen,' she says. 'It was a diverse job; that's probably why I liked it.'[3]

It challenged her, too, and Ardern relishes a challenge. Working for Clark was an opportunity to experience politics at its pinnacle, under one of her country's most respected leaders of modern times.

It made her learn 'very quickly to be a little more accurate', too. Clark, a former lecturer in political studies at the University of Auckland, had never quite shrugged off her former vocation, it seems. A couple of documents Ardern fired off to her were returned, with grammatical corrections marked in red pen. It was 'a little bit like getting your school assignment back',[4] Ardern says. It couldn't have been better preparation, though, for a life in high office, where one's every mistake is magnified.

Helen Clark was exceptionally busy – 'her diary was incredible,'[5] Ardern recalls – but still she found time to walk about the office, mug of tea in hand, to talk to her staff. Ardern remembers her 'deep passion for politics that always extended beyond New Zealand'.[6] She once discussed with her and the other staff the latest developments in the US election cycle, even as her own political survival looked uncertain.

The New Zealand election itself loomed. Grant Robertson and Ardern were part of a youthful team brought together for what was perhaps the greatest challenge of Clark's career: the 2005 elections. The party desperately needed the injection of energy that Ardern, Robertson and others brought to her campaign. Being young themselves, they could tap into issues that resonated with their contemporaries. Ardern came up with the policy for interest-free student loans, which has been popular among New Zealand's youth since, for obvious reasons. Needless to say, the policy stayed, even through two terms of National Party government. With such youth-oriented offerings, party strategists sought to mobilise young voters on election day.

Helen Clark's Labour Party government needed all the help it could get at the ballot box. It had enjoyed two decent terms in office, even delivering the National Party its worst electoral defeat in 2002, yet two years later, Labour's support had flagged. History itself seemed to be against re-election. New Zealanders are on the whole fairly conservative politically. No Labour government had lasted beyond two terms since the 1940s; a prime minister governing for twelve years, as Keith Holyoake did between 1960 and 1972, was a distant memory. But other forces were in play. Before Ardern joined her office, Clark's popularity had waned, her approval ratings had fallen from their dizzy heights of a couple of years earlier. Worse, the Labour

Party found itself on the back foot to a resurgent National Party, its leadership quite prepared to test the boundaries of public discourse. Led by the former governor of the Reserve Bank of New Zealand, Don Brash, the party campaigned aggressively over issues that were to divide the country along racial and ideological lines.

Brash's campaigning started early, well before the election, and it wasn't the campaign that saw his approval ratings rise. It was a speech that became famous – many would say infamous – which he delivered at the Orewa Rotary Club in January 2004. The fallout from what came to be known as the Orewa Speech continued at least until the election the following September. The speech, its content and impact are still debated.

Brash took the stage at the Rotary Club under the banner of 'Nationhood', but quickly broke old taboos by making bold statements about race; Māori and pākehā relations were the focus of much of his rhetoric. A 'grievance industry' – words Brash hammered home a number of times – had been allowed to 'blossom' under Labour with Māori claims for compensation for expropriated land under the 1840 Treaty of Waitangi, he charged. Brash spoke of 'one rule for all', attacking Labour's inaction on a court ruling handed down six months earlier.

The National Party leader hit a nerve, particularly among older voters. In June 2003, New Zealand's Court of Appeal ruled in *Ngati Apa v Attorney-General*,[7] among other things, that 'the definition of "land" in Te Ture Whenua Māori Act 1993 did not necessarily exclude foreshore and seabed'. This seemed to open the door to Māori ownership claims on beaches and seas. Many New Zealanders were alarmed at the prospect, however remote, of losing access to the country's beloved beaches and waters. The Labour government's announcing its intention of passing legislation on the matter did little to assuage their concerns.

Politically, the effect of the Orewa Speech was dramatic, and the fallout from the court ruling fuelled one of New Zealand's most significant protests of the last half-century. Brash's popularity soared – his party surged past the government in the opinion polls. If the election had been held early in 2004, in the wake of the Orewa Speech, the National Party would surely have trounced the Labour Party.

Bitter recriminations were the backdrop to the election the following year; protests and heated debate raged within the government.
Labour was under attack from the National Party on one side, Māori
groups on the other, and even from within its own ranks. A Māori
junior Labour minister, Tariana Turia, resigned her seat over the
government's stance, then successfully contested it as an independent
candidate in the ensuing by-election. On 5 May 2004, a 15,000-
strong hikoi (protest march) that had begun thirteen days earlier in
Northland assembled outside Parliament in Wellington, Māori flags
aloft.

Clark pressed forward regardless. On 18 November 2004, the
Labour–Progressive government's Foreshore and Seabed Act passed
the House, effectively declaring the foreshore and seabed the property
of the Crown. On the same day, an activist drove an axe through the
window of Clark's Auckland office, leaving it embedded in the glass.
A note left at the scene vented anger at the legislation, apparently
claiming 'the broken glass symbolised broken faith, broken trust and
shattered justice, and the axe represented steadfastness and determination'. Police promptly charged the culprit with sedition, which
only added to the imbroglio.

This was the backdrop to Ardern's first election campaign at close
quarters, albeit one which she was not herself contesting. It was a
baptism of fire. For a hardened political veteran such as Helen Clark,
it was taxing, but for Ardern it was, she would later say, 'extraordinarily stressful'.[8] At least part of the stress was owed to the confrontation
being so utterly against her nature. With her sensitivity to Māori
rights and inclination for consensus rather than political brawling,
Ardern was conflicted.

The foreshore and seabed controversy was not the only unusual
challenge for the prime minister's office. The Exclusive Brethren, a
subset of the Christian evangelical movement, funded a campaign
against the Labour Party, distributing its own leaflets in support of
the National Party. It was 'surreal', Ardern said, years later. 'It
seemed something out of a novel, the idea of a religious sect having
that amount of influence – and pouring that amount of money
into your opponent's campaign just didn't seem very "New
Zealand".'[9]

While the Labour government clawed back its advantage after the Orewa Speech, Brash campaigned heavily on reducing taxes as the polling day loomed. The gap between the parties narrowed. Headlines in the weeks preceding the election said it all: 'Poll puts National in front, tax cuts policy influencing voters'; 'NZ opposition extends poll lead on governing party 13 days from election'; 'Polls point to cliffhanger New Zealand election'.

The mood on election night in the Labour camp was subdued. Staffers often bear the burden of worry during an election more than the politicians themselves and Ardern, always one to shoulder responsibility, felt the pressure as much as anyone. Her nerves almost collapsed when it seemed that the Nationals had edged out Labour.

Ross Ardern, knowing how his sensitive younger daughter would feel, rang Jacinda to reassure her. More than a decade later, Jacinda recalled their conversation: '[Ross said] "Don't worry. You'll be able to find another job" – because he could hear how upset I was. And I remember saying in this broken voice, "It's not about my job. What about all the people who'll have to pay market rents in their state houses?"' [10]

She need not have worried, though she was left on tenterhooks for some time. While the election was held on 17 September, it was not until 1 October, after recounting was complete and it was clear that no coalition deal could be struck, that the Nationals' hopeful leader conceded defeat. From the party's worst ever showing at the 2002 election, the National Party opposition had almost doubled its party vote and the number of members in the chamber. Labour had prevailed in the popular vote with a mere two percent margin, and held only two seats more in Parliament than its major rival. With a coalition with the Progressive Party, and confidence and supply agreements with United Future, the Green Party and New Zealand First, Labour would govern for another term.

Years later, Ardern would say that 'the joy of winning was even more marked because it had felt so tough'. [11] Tough, but educational. The 2005 campaign gave vital lessons to the woman who would later lead the country – in a brutal, boot-camp kind of way. She remembers the prime minister's office as 'an intense environment . . . everyone around you was working equally as hard and no one harder than

Helen.'[12] There, in the crucible of the election campaign, the team members' relationships with colleagues and seniors in Labour were forged. These relationships would be crucial to Ardern's ascent in the party a few years later – even sustaining her in government.

The 2005 election might have been Labour's fight for survival, but there was still time for 'fun moments as well' on the ninth floor of the Beehive. Ardern's reported impersonation of her mentor was a case in point. One of her lesser-known talents is mimicry, and it is said she can be quite convincing. To keep the office mood lively, she apparently gave the occasional impersonation of their boss, giving a near-perfect rendition of Clark's contralto voice, her punctuated delivery. It was all in good fun, and if she heard about it, Clark didn't seem to mind. After all, imitation is the sincerest form of flattery.

The fun even extended to the campaigning itself. At that time, Ardern shared a flat with three of her colleagues on a street in Wellington called The Terrace, which runs directly south from the Beehive. They decided on a novel campaigning device that at that time only twenty-somethings could have dreamed up, its cheekiness reminiscent of Jacinda's teenage Human Rights Action Group's Fax-a-fascist Day. The staffers set up a telephone free-call information line: 0800 BRASH, a number they advertised liberally around the capital. It was connected to a landline at their flat. Callers would listen to a series of satirical National Party policies – 'Press 1 to sell off state assets, press 2 . . .', and so on.

The cleverness of the stunt made it a roaring success. Indeed, it was almost too successful. The number was shouted out on air on national radio programmes; soon, thousands of callers had rung the number to enjoy the joke. Everyone in Labour was laughing – until the telephone bill arrived, anyhow. Thousands of reverse-charge calls at commercial rates gave the four junior Labour Party staffers an astronomical telephone bill, that even with their incomes combined, they simply couldn't afford. It fell to the charming mastermind, Jacinda, to negotiate with the telephone company to reduce the bill.

The experience of a general election from within the prime minister's office had been invaluable. But though the campaign had been exhilarating and Clark's team had averted a seemingly inevitable defeat, Ardern was exhausted. Given her nature, this is hardly

surprising. Ardern is typically all in or nothing; her absolute dedication to her job in the prime minister's office – or any other duty she
undertakes – meant she gave as much as she could, and more.

Unsurprisingly, Ardern was valued highly on the ninth floor of the
Beehive. G. J. Thompson, Clark's press secretary, noted that Ardern
was universally liked; an excellent addition to the office: 'She had the
basics down pat and was good in groups and off the cuff. She was
doing stuff without pissing people off. And she connected with
people.'[13] She managed to impress her boss, too – Heather Simpson,
that is, Clark's long-time chief of staff. The two women, Helen and
Heather, were so often seen together they became known as H1 and
H2 (Grant Robertson, then Ardern's close friend and colleague on the
ninth floor of the Beehive, was apparently referred to as H3). Simpson
is a Southland woman, renowned for her exacting standards and
suffering no fools; she was described by Helen Clark herself as 'the
most powerful women in New Zealand'. Who knows to what extent
she was joking.

Another party heavyweight who noticed Ardern in the Beehive
was Paul Tolich, a unionist in the Labour caucus. Impressed with
Ardern's skill in liaising with the unions – essential for proper mobili-
sation on the hustings – Tolich would become her supporter. He
would be instrumental later, in a key moment in her career.

That Ardern managed to shine in the highest office of the land,
under the jaundiced eyes of political veterans, speaks volumes for her
dedication and ability. At the end of the 2005 election, she was now
well known; her reputation preceded her – in Labour circles, anyway
– as a capable party member whose talent marked her for greater
things. The woman who would become her most significant mentor
recognised her promise, more than anyone.

Mentor and Role Model

No one played a greater part in the making of Prime Minister Jacinda Ardern than Helen Elizabeth Clark, the thirty-seventh prime minister of New Zealand. Indeed, it would be hard to overstate her influence on the young Jacinda, or the importance of their relationship in moulding her into the leader she would become.

Their relationship began, as do many good relationships, before the pair got to know each other – before they met, even. Clark knew Ardern's grandmother Gwladys, who campaigned for her in Piako when she was a 25-year-old Labour hopeful. As Ardern made her presence felt in New Zealand Young Labour, Clark heard reports of her. She told an interviewer years later, 'I didn't know [Ardern] very well – because she's thirty years younger than I am – but she was clearly someone who was on the rise . . . She was definitely recognised as a rising star from at least her early twenties.'[1]

For Ardern, Helen Clark was an icon: it was under her that the stigma of Rogernomics, which Clark deemed a 'ghastly period', was erased, and Labour returned to government. Ardern had cast her first vote in 1999, and predictably, it was for the Labour Party that Clark led.

Ardern is only too ready to acknowledge the older woman's part in fostering her talent and guiding her career. A portrait of Clark takes pride of place on her office wall on the ninth floor of the Beehive, alongside that of Big Norm Kirk, and above Kate Sheppard's. In public speeches, Ardern has often paid tribute to Clark. In her maiden speech to Parliament, she said, 'There are many reasons why I joined the Labour Party, but it was Helen who made me proud to be a member . . . My generation grew up under Helen's leadership and many do not know how good they had it.'[2] In 2012, she told interviewers that 'Helen played a big part' in her entering Parliament to a list seat; Helen had 'carved a path' for women like her to follow.

At first blush, though, Ardern and Clark seem a strange pair to forge a deep friendship, one that clearly transcends politics. Beyond their political affiliations and office, it might appear strange, too, to draw parallels between Jacinda Ardern and Helen Clark. Superficially, at least, the thirty-seventh prime minister and the fortieth prime minister of New Zealand are so different, it seems almost odd to compare them.

Ardern, at thirty-seven, was in the prime of her life when she took office, while Clark was just three months shy of her fiftieth birthday. Ardern became a staple for fashion magazines, whereas Clark, adopting an androgynous style for her years as a senior politician, seems to have sidestepped the issue of fashion and her gender by dissociating herself from it altogether, as much as she was able. She could, though, display a stylish flair during her early years in Parliament. As with Ardern, she had a liking for black couture, complete with black boots – also an Ardern favourite. A shot of her as a young MP in 1983 shows her hair in a chic bob. But serious-looking trouser suits were almost her uniform while in office, and since. As for her hair, a columnist once suggested, 'She probably shuts her eyes while her secretary snips it with hedge clippers.'

All this knitted together well with her sober, somewhat dour prime ministerial persona, her deep contralto voice and masculine intonations that saw her treated as seriously as her male counterparts. Doubtless, it worked: 'formidable' is a word often associated with Prime Minister Clark. One can only guess, though, how much of this was cultivated. Labour Party backroom figures worked on her image relentlessly, one way or the other, it seems.

The clue to this transformation in Clark is seen when one looks at other women in politics who were her contemporaries: Marilyn Waring, Ruth Richardson and Jenny Shipley. There is precedent for this, almost a tradition for women in politics. A case in point is a politician from another generation that Clark has often been compared with – rather uncomfortably for her, it must be said: Margaret Thatcher. Thatcher apparently practised vocal exercises with a National Theatre expert, at the suggestion of theatre great Lawrence

Olivier. A comparison of an interview she gave as a new MP with her later oratories is startling. It is clear that she lowered her speech register considerably, so it sat roughly halfway between the registers of the average woman and the average man. This gave her speech a more masculine sound, hence more gravitas.

With her voice's natural contralto register, Clark didn't need to lower her speech. As with many women politicians before her, though – and of course men, too – her public persona was a little crafted. At least, her tough exterior was exaggerated to defend against the prejudices of her time. Much of this was from her own, conscious efforts to modify her behaviour and image, it seems. Her biographer Denis Welch notes, 'She saw early on that you couldn't afford as a woman to appear too serious or too feminine.' Or too funny. Clark's close friends talk of her uproarious sense of humour, which was barely seen in public. She had to temper, even hide it, along with her femininity.

Twenty years after Jenny Shipley became her nation's first woman prime minister, after eleven years of women in power and then two male leaders in New Zealand, the world was a very different place. Women were beginning to make their mark at the pinnacle of politics: Michelle Bachelet, the president of Chile; Beata Maria Szydło, Poland's prime minister; Kolinda Grabar-Kitarović, president of Croatia; President Tsa Ing-wen of Taiwan, and Katrín Jakobsdóttir, prime minister of Iceland, to name a few. New Zealand was among those countries ready for a different kind of woman leader – a woman who displayed her femininity, who felt secure dressing in the manner of her choosing; a woman who was openly compassionate and campaigned on issues close to other women's hearts: children's welfare, equality, well-being. They were happy to elect a leader with humour, who would see beyond dry economic and political issues to oversee a kinder administration. Jacinda Ardern was to become a prime minister quite unlike any the country had seen.

Nevertheless, the two Labour Party woman who've held the nation's top job are remarkably similar in many other respects. Though they were born more than a generation apart – Clark on 26 February 1950, Ardern thirty years later – the similarity of their life themes, interests and backgrounds is striking.

Both were from all-girl families – Ardern with one sister, Clark three. Curiously, Jenny Shipley, New Zealand's first woman prime minister, also had three sisters, and came from an all-girl family. It may well be that living in an environment with only girls allowed the three future women prime ministers to develop confidence; perhaps they felt more free to express their ambition, in the absence of male siblings.

Clark and Ardern were both born in Hamilton, spending their early years in the Waikato region: Clark's family dairy and sheep farm was situated on the slopes of Mount Pirongia, near Te Pahu, some sixty-five kilometres from Morrinsville and ninety kilometres from the Ardern family's farm, in the shadow of Mount Te Aroha. Helen and Jacinda were each blessed with a 'typically Kiwi' upbringing; as 'farm girls', they relished their healthy rural, outdoors lifestyle. They still have the essence of Waikato farm girls, beneath their sophistication.

Their education and interests are likewise similar. At school, both women showed a keen interest in history and music – Clark was an accomplished pianist, Ardern learned the violin – while each became politically active in their teens. Both studied politics at university. Before their parliamentary careers, they ran in equivalent electorates, Piako and Waikato, unsuccessfully. And both won the seat of Mount Albert comfortably before being elevated to the office of prime minister.

Perhaps more easily overlooked are their shared character traits. Clark and Ardern have iron wills (though this not so obvious with Ardern), and do not back away from a challenge. Both are utterly dedicated to an objective, which is an essential characteristic of a good leader. Each is comfortable with herself, on her own terms, and both have stable domestic partnerships with supportive partners. Clarke Gayford, like Peter Davis before him, is happy; willing to be the great man behind the great woman.

For the men, too, there are parallels and divergences. Gayford and Davis are equally devoted. Davis was happy to take on the burden of domestic duties, cooking and cleaning, though he has hardly spoken about it publicly. The media-friendly Gayford's answer to reporters questioning his role with Ardern is frank and modest: 'There's no title . . . Look, my job is just to make sure that [Jacinda's] OK, and be in the background, going, "Have you eaten your lunch? Have you slept properly? You've got lipstick on your teeth." . . . that's my job.'³ Unlike Davis, Gayford is often seen by his partner's side. Two decades ago, the husband of a prime minister sitting with her baby at the United Nations General Assembly, as Gayford did in September 2018, would have been unthinkable.

The changing times and how they affected Ardern and her mentor differently are summed up in one key event. On the eve of the November 1981 general election, at which Clark would win the seat of Mount Albert, she and Davis came under immense pressure. Senior party figures delivered the soon-to-be-MP an ultimatum: she must marry Davis, for the public and for the party. It was simply not acceptable to have a single woman running for Parliament (let alone for the prime ministership) – especially not one 'living in sin'.

One of Clark's former lecturers, the late Ruth Butterworth, recalled her grief – not at being married to Davis per se, for the pair had been living happily together for some five years already, but simply that marriage itself was 'so deeply against her principles'. Clark 'was resistant . . . crying on the day' of the wedding, Butterworth said.⁴

Thankfully, Helen and Peter Davis have enjoyed four decades of marriage. Perhaps Helen would not have managed her gruelling nine years in office without Peter's steadfast support. The social pressures of the times, however, meant she was not afforded the freedom of personal choice that Jacinda Ardern and Clarke Gayford enjoyed, decades later. Most New Zealanders seemed not the least perturbed by their woman prime minister living unmarried with her partner – even more so than Australians and their prime minister Julia Gillard seven years earlier, who had faced some pressure from conservative media. Save for some sniping over maternity leave, New Zealanders were delighted at their first couple having a baby, too. Helen Clark can no doubt gain some satisfaction from seeing her protégée experience a lifestyle choice she herself was denied.

Before Labour's campaign launch for the 2017 general election, Clark made reference to the two women's similarities: 'We are both out of the Waikato. I'm from the west Waikato, she's from the east Waikato. We both came into Parliament reasonably young, Jacinda younger than I was, but reasonably young. Both got the leadership positions reasonably young. Both MPs for Mount Albert. So people will see a lot of similarities.'[5]

Ardern's and Clark's approaches to the role of prime minister have numerous parallels as well. The two women have an absolute commitment to gender equality, which they carry with aplomb. Neither have shown any inclination to make their gender an electoral issue, which is perhaps best summed up by Clark's statement, 'I've never sought election on the basis of being a woman. I've always sought election as the best person for the job.' Ardern likewise.

Both, too, conduct themselves with dignity, mostly avoiding the type of roughhouse politicking some of their male colleagues – and occasionally a female politician – seem to relish. Each is nevertheless articulate and performs well in public debate. Ardern values honesty; her frankness with the public has won her support, just as it did for Clark.

Along with so many similarities between the mentor and protégée are marked differences. Their models of leadership itself are almost diametrically opposed. Ardern favours a consensus-building approach to her prime ministership, where she consults and is supported by her ministers, an approach essential to her political survival in the coalition with which she formed government. Clark, however, was more a top-down leader: most decisions were made by her, Heather Simpson and Deputy Prime Minister Michael Cullen. While theirs was a good combination, Clark's opponent and successor John Key notes that 'they just cut every minister out – every decision was made on the prime minister's floor . . . [of] the Beehive'.[6]

Their personalities and ways they present themselves are likewise very different. Ardern is noted for her kindness and reaching out to people (which Clark is quick to appreciate) whereas the elder stateswoman's flinty resolve and sheer presence are her trademark. Ardern's public persona, which differs little from the Jacinda known to family and friends, is warm and engaging: members of the public sometimes ask to hug her, and often she obliges. This would have been rare with Clark. Known to her supporters as Aunty Helen, she was a stern aunt.

Her 'direct stare [and] impassive delivery', her bearing earned her respect, but kept her at a distance.

Despite this difference, which is as clear to New Zealanders as to the politicians themselves, some of Clark's characteristics have been a template for Ardern in public life – her defence against the barbs that politicians generally and women politicians in particular suffer. Suffice it to say, Clark had to endure a litany of sexist attacks during her career. Curiously, she has revealed that the jibes against her lessened when she became prime minister. This says much of the kind of scurrilous nonsense she faced earlier, much of which remains thankfully unpublished. At the start of her career, the least she faced was the predictable 'She'll never be any good', simply because she was a woman. When she had proved herself as the most powerful woman in the country, she was referred to as a 'political dominatrix', a 'black widow', enduring endless harping on her physical appearance, and false allegations about her sexuality.

Among the most egregious attacks were the bumper stickers, sponsored by trucking companies opposing increased road user charges, during Clark's final general election campaign. The rear of trucks in New Zealand's South Island were emblazoned with the stickers, reading 'Ditch the Bitch'.

Discussing the 'nasty stuff' (her off-hand description of gender-based abuse) that she endured throughout her career, Clark told a reporter that 'you build a brick wall around that kind of thing'.[7] Ignore it, get on with the job, and become known as one of the nation's most respected public figures. This is just the approach Ardern would need to take, years later. Jacinda's family always worried that she was too thin-skinned for the brutal world of politics; the cut and thrust of public life, whose cruelty is often directed at successful women. Clark was, her biographer Denis Welch says, 'steady, guarded and cautious and unflappable', which allowed her to weather decades in public life. Ardern, however, readily concedes that 'I probably wear my heart on my sleeve a bit too much, I probably overshare.'

Perhaps she knew instinctively that there was much she could learn from the older woman, aside from observing Clark's brilliant political management at close quarters. Despite their contrasting personalities, she might adopt some of Clark's ways for her own survival. If she couldn't build metaphorical brick walls as Clark did, she would have to build fences, porous though they might be, to filter whatever came to her.

One incident during her time in the prime minister's office gave Ardern particular insight into her boss's character, and skill in handling adversity. It came when Clark visited the University of Canterbury, for one of her numerous campaign appearances. Back in the office, Ardern watched the live television coverage of the event in alarm. Images flashed on the screen of a terrifying, fully fledged protest: Clark was 'crowded out by a flood of students', angry and bearing huge placards, many of which bore degrading slogans.

The office phone rang; Ardern took the call. It was Clark. She was completely unfazed, talking with Ardern in an even manner about how they might avert a similar situation in future. Ardern was impressed as much as baffled by the older woman's composure. 'Anyone else,' she says, 'you would expect to be quite shaken.' This utter calm, complete resolution in the face of crisis, was a strategy that Ardern would adopt herself while in office.

As role model and mentor, Prime Minister Helen Clark was the best that 25-year-old Jacinda Ardern could ask for. Her interest in Jacinda and fostering of her talent gave the younger woman an entrée to elite national politics that would serve her well, twelve years later.

In the southern spring of 2005, however, as chilly Wellington warmed and Labour settled into its third term in office, Jacinda felt drained. She recalled 'thinking, I need to get out for a while, I need to see the world because I worried that if I stayed I would be consumed'.[8] Aside from her trial by fire in the Beehive, the upheaval and elation of the election, the year had seen a profound shift within her. This was not a shift that would change her personality, much less shake the foundations of her character. But it would bring about change nonetheless.

11

Resolution

With the general decline in organised religion in the West, more people than ever identify themselves with such terms as 'lapsed Catholic' and 'secular Jew'. For Mormonism – the Church of Jesus Christ of Latter-day Saints, or LDS – those who leave the church are referred to as 'ex-Mormons' or 'post-Mormons'.

Jacinda Ardern may not actually refer to herself as an ex-Mormon or a post-Mormon. In response to a question posed to almost every leading politician, 'Have you smoked marijuana?' she simply said, 'I was raised Mormon and then I was not Mormon.'[1]

While Ardern is one of a growing contingent of younger people who have left the church, the LDS is hardly languishing. Mormonism stands apart from most mainstream Christian denominations, defying the overall trend of dwindling church congregations. Though its growth rate has slowed in recent years, its numbers have swelled from around two million in the 1960s to some sixteen million. Driving its success have been dedicated congregations, a high fertility rate and missionaries' door-to-door proselytising.

It was the latter, starting with an unexpected knock on the door which for so many of us is familiar, that brought the Ardern family into the LDS. Jacinda's grandmother Gwladys 'always had the cake pans full, and the missionaries all seemed to come around',[2] Ross Ardern's twin brother Ian recalls. Though it seems they visited the Ardern home in Te Aroha as much for her baking as for preaching, their visits seem to have made an impression. Gwladys converted, and the rest of her family followed her into the church. She and her husband Harry did not join the church officially, though, until their children were baptised; Ross and Ian were baptised at the age of eight.

The Ardern family are still active in the LDS, part of a devout community of Mormons in New Zealand. In this century, numbers of the Mormon faithful in the country have swelled to more than 40,000 – or 113,000, if church figures are any indication. The focal point of the LDS's activities in the country is the Hamilton Temple – the first of its kind in the southern hemisphere – which opened in 1958.

Surrounded by rolling green fields in the outskirts of Hamilton, the temple stands on a rise with white post-modern neatness, like a latter-day mediaeval cathedral. Graced by manicured gardens and a spire reaching forty-eight metres into the heavens, it's impressive enough for adults. One can imagine the stark grandeur of the place, the sheer scale and wonderment of it for children. This is where the Ardern family came for their Sunday church services, and it is where members of the extended Ardern family continue to worship today.

In recent years, Jacinda's family has become more prominent in the LDS. Ian Ardern, a school principal, was a bishop and in 2011 became a general authority of the church, which is a most prestigious position in Mormonism. As a General Authority Seventy, Elder Ian S. Ardern is among the senior Mormons worldwide having administrative and ecclesiastical authority over the church.

Jacinda's immediate family have not been so active in the church's hierarchy, but they were nonetheless serious about their religion. The more devout of the sisters, Jacinda was a fully practising member of the church. Sunday services took precedence over netball (Laurell and Ross allowed Jacinda to make this her own choice) – she is quick to admit she was not that good at netball, anyway – and drinking alcohol was strictly out of the question. Coffee and tea were eschewed with a little less rigour. Clothing was tidy and demure (Mormons in the US frown upon garments that reveal what are sometimes referred to by the church faithful as 'porn shoulders'). Naturally, too, there was the door-to-door 'tracting', spreading the word, which is obligatory for a good Mormon.

The strength and comfort a Mormon receives from the church's community is as much a source of pride in the LDS as the reputation of Mormons as being good neighbours. Little wonder, then, that Mormons who leave the church are usually quite determined and committed to their decision – far more so, usually, than those who leave other denominations. The average lapsed Catholic might even attend Christmas and Easter services for family's sake. Leaving the LDS, in contrast, often entails complete religious disavowal and a robust social uncoupling. A post-Mormon may struggle to cope with the loss of a place in the community that comes with quitting the church.

For Jacinda, leaving the church was not so traumatic socially – it had been a slow drift for her, rather than a rupture. With her varied circle of friends and strong ties to the Labour Party, which is a society in itself, she didn't feel isolated. For a woman who had lived according to the church's tenets for the first twenty-five years of her life, however, it was a momentous decision.

The reasons for a departure from the Church of Jesus Christ of Latter-day Saints can be varied. For Jacinda, the tipping point that led to her making a life away from the church was its response to legislation: the Civil Union Act 2004, which grants the right for gay couples, along with heterosexual ones, to forge a civil union. When the bill came before Parliament, the Mormon church, along with many other religious groups, firmly opposed it. The church's stance against the act triggered a spiritual crisis for Jacinda, bringing to the fore a 'cognitive dissonance' surrounding her beliefs, she says, that had vexed her for some time.[3]

Shortly before she was elevated to the office of prime minister, Ardern explained her thoughts on leaving the church: 'Even before the Civil Union Bill came up, I lived in a flat with three gay friends and I was still going to church . . . and I just remember thinking, this is really inconsistent – I'm either doing a disservice to the church or my friends. Because how could I subscribe to a religion that just didn't account for them? . . . I could never reconcile what I saw as discrimination in a religion that was otherwise very focused on tolerance and kindness.'[4]

The Civil Union Bill was clearly an issue close to her heart. Ardern felt so strongly about the rights of gay couples to make a legal commitment to their relationships that she made her own statement in support of the bill. As one of a thousand activists, she paid $20 to put her name to a full-page advertisement in support of the bill, which was published on 22 November 2004 in the New Zealand *Sunday Star Times*.

The declaration and centrepiece of the advertisement reads like a credo drafted by Ardern herself: 'We support the Civil Union Bill and the Relationships (Statutory References) Bill. We believe our country's laws should reflect the diversity of relationships within society, treat all people in relationships fairly and equally, and not discriminate against de facto and same-sex couples.' Among the columns of names surrounding the declaration, Ardern's name is printed in the advertisement, a few rows down from that of her close friend and later cabinet colleague and deputy prime minister Grant Robertson, who is openly gay.

This was not simply an ideological matter for Ardern. As with many of the other causes she has championed – poverty, domestic violence and even girls wearing shorts at school – it may not have affected her personally, but it was nonetheless an issue that she felt strongly committed to, on a visceral level.

This revealed itself to her gay friend and colleague Tony Milne, in the months after the Civil Union Bill came into force. In 2005, when the pair worked together on the ninth floor of the Beehive, he recalled accompanying Ardern to the OutTakes Gay and Lesbian Film Festival. There, they watched the 2003 romantic comedy-drama *Latter Days*, which would win the Audience Award for Best Feature of the festival. It also provoked an uproar from the LDS.

The film's plot line centres on Aaron, a closeted gay Mormon man, and his affair with Christian, his openly gay neighbour. There are some lighter moments, centred on Christian's trying to seduce Aaron for a bet. But the film has its serious side, portraying realistically the stigma of homosexuality within the church. When Aaron is outed, he is shunned by his family; he faces an excommunication tribunal and treatment to be 'cured' of his homosexuality. Aaron and Christian's relationship is rent asunder by the turmoil. There is a tearful dénouement, though, when they reunite with a friend, who tells them they will always have 'a place at my table, and a place in my heart'.

Tony found the film pleasant; decent enough. The credits rolled, and as the lights came up, he looked over to Jacinda. She was in tears.

The LDS's uncompromising approach to homosexuality and civil unions may have been 'the big crunch point' for Jacinda. There were,

however, 'other things' that led to her leaving the church. While she
does not elaborate, she is forthright in her opposition to tithing, a
practice where adherents of the faith are obliged to donate ten percent
of their earnings – most often calculated on their gross income – to
the church.

Doubtless, an even more substantive cause for Jacinda's departure
from the church was her feminism. As women were taking their place
at the forefront of society in the 1960s and 1970s, the LDS seemed to
hold doggedly to traditional roles. Edicts from the church seemed
anachronistic in the extreme, dated even by the standards of a generation earlier. A senior church leader, Bruce R. McConkie, wrote in
1966 that a 'woman's primary place is in the home, where she is to
rear children and abide by the righteous counsel of her husband'.[5]

Even recently, aside from watershed issues such as recognition of
LGBTQ church members, the LDS seems to have held firm to the
tenets of a bygone era. It was only in December 2018, more than two
decades after Jacinda's campaign for girls to have the right to wear
shorts at Morrinsville College, that the church announced that (adult)
women LDS missionaries would 'have the option to wear dress slacks'.
Only in the current decade has the church made its first, tentative
overtures to feminists.

It wouldn't be hard to imagine the discomfort a feminist, even one
of such tolerant disposition as Jacinda Ardern, might feel in the LDS.
Her decision to leave the church would thus come as little surprise to
her friends and former teachers. Gregor Fountain says that it was
'pretty obvious to me that [Jacinda's] feminism and Mormonism were
going to clash'.[6]

Her family, nevertheless, were quite taken aback by her decision,
though each member had quite different reactions. Jacinda never
discussed her decision with Ross, but says Laurell was 'very disappointed' at her leaving the church. Ultimately, though, her parents
were 'fantastic', she says. 'Families who cut off people for leaving [the
church] – that's just awful.' Louise, whose 'slight rebellious streak' as
a teenager had already distanced her from the LDS, was shocked,
because the church 'was such a massive part of her life for so long'.
Louise is quick to note that 'even though [Jacinda] doesn't go to
church anymore, she would still hold many of the values'.[7]

Indeed, Jacinda's values have altered little over the years. She now identifies as an agnostic because, she explains, 'atheism seems so vehement to me. I respect people who have sets of values in any faith.'[8] She seems to maintain an open mind to religion, of all persuasions. At the beginning of the 2020 election campaign, in August, Jacinda attended the Sri Radha Krishna Mandir in Eden Terrace, Auckland, for a Hindu puja held specially for her.

Typically, Ardern remains on good terms with the LDS and its members, locally and overseas. In May 2019, she hosted a friendly meeting with President Russell M. Nelson, leader of the LDS, who arrived at the Beehive with a delegation which included her uncle Ian. She accepted a leather-bound Book of Mormon as a gift from Nelson, who was most complimentary of his former church member and her achievements.

So what of her faith? Her religion since leaving the church, Ardern says, has become the Labour Party, though at least one humanist writer has suggested she is one of their own. From a cursory reading, humanism sounds much like a religion without God: values such as compassion, a moral code and ethics along with the betterment of oneself, are at its heart. By this definition, perhaps Jacinda Ardern is a humanist. Her compassion, charity and care for humanity that were her spiritual foundations, in any event, remain unchanged since her departure from the Mormon church.

Many of the post-Mormon changes that Ardern has exhibited – such as a more relaxed approach to clothing, and a taste for red wine and Glendronach 18 Scotch whisky – seem somehow superficial, incidental beside the humanity that she has retained from her former faith. She still has the unflappable sincerity and wholesome goodwill which is a hallmark of the LDS's adherents. And she still embodies the commitment to hard work that is typical of Mormonism.

Indeed, the Mormon way of life seems to have stood her in good stead for her political career – it may have even given her an edge against her opponents on the hustings. An electoral campaign, with door knocking, street meetings and debates (some impromptu), is not for the faint-hearted. But as Ardern declares, 'nothing is as hard as door knocking for God!'[9]

12

Overseas Experience

Freedom and the pleasures of youth had found scant place, if any, in Jacinda Ardern's life. Up until now there had been little time for leisure, no floating between jobs or 'finding herself'. After her stratospheric rise from assistant to a junior minister to favoured adviser of the prime minister in a couple of years, and the stress of the 2005 general election – not to mention her spiritual reckoning – it's little wonder she needed a break. She was twenty-five. Her age and her circumstances made it a perfect time for her OE (Overseas Experience). She needed a change of scene, time to take stock of her life.

The OE is a time-honoured rite of passage for many New Zealanders. Its prevalence is such that New Zealand has reciprocal working holiday schemes with some forty countries to facilitate it. Typically, twenty-something youngsters will head to London and work in casual labouring or waitressing gigs while taking trips to the continent: 'seeing the world', broadening their horizons and savouring a host of new experiences before returning home.

Unlike countless young Kiwis before her, Ardern didn't head directly to the UK, which was considered 'home' by many New Zealanders of earlier generations. Almost on a whim, she says, she made her way to New York, applying for a work permit, so she might find employment as a political researcher.

New York was an intriguing choice for Ardern's OE. As a wide-eyed 21-year-old student in the final semester of her degree, she had had an experience of the US that was somewhat disappointing and uncomfortable. Now, just four years later, the young, idealistic socialist woman with a strong social conscience was heading to the Big Apple, a place Frank Lloyd Wright described as 'a great monument to

the power of money and greed . . . a race for rent'; a noisy, overpopu-
lated city where 'you could be frozen to death in the midst of a busy
street and nobody would notice', according to Bob Dylan. New York
couldn't be further from the tranquil familiarity, the friendliness of
Morrinsville.

Perhaps Ardern was determined to take on the greatest challenge,
to conquer her fears, proving to herself she could find her place in the
world as far away from her family and support structures as possible.
America and especially New York state, as the birthplace of the LDS,
had been influential on the young Jacinda. On some level, she might
have wanted to reconcile herself with the United States.

More logical would have been to head directly to London. The visa
process in the UK was simple and the city hosted an established Kiwi
expatriate community, with friends or contacts who might have
helped her find her feet with a place to live and work. In New York,
she had plenty of time on her hands, simply waiting for her visa.

Others on their OE might have taken this opportunity to travel,
see the country and party, but not Ardern. True to the humanitarian
principles she had been raised with – hospitality and charity is a
strong suit on both sides of her family – she quickly volunteered in a
soup kitchen. And not just any soup kitchen. Ardern worked in the
iconic CHiPS (Community Help in Park Slope) soup kitchen and
women's shelter in Brooklyn.

CHiPS is an institution in New York. With its side wall covered by
murals of women at work and play, rising three storeys over its antique
brickwork, the centre has a decidedly socialist, feminist ambience,
though it was founded by the Catholic Church. Along with other
volunteers, Ardern made meatballs and soup to help feed the couple
of hundred poor and homeless men and women who came to the
centre daily.

She also remained politically active in these months, busying
herself with a workers' rights campaign. As a pro bono campaign
assistant, Ardern organised home-care workers who had suffered
without an employment contract for a decade. She even stood with
them on a picket line. She recalled years later, with some humour,
that the chants she had coined 'sounded fine in a Kiwi accent, but
never sounded quite right when belted out by Americans'.

Her New York sojourn might have been eventful and enjoyable, but it was hardly productive. After six months without a work visa and with her savings dwindling, Ardern realised she had to find steady employment – elsewhere, and quickly. She began applying for jobs in the UK, one of which was for a senior policy adviser in the Cabinet Office, a government department. Bolstered by a CV that for a 25-year-old was beyond impressive (working for a junior minister, a cabinet minister, then a prime minister), she underwent an interview by telephone. She secured the job, which meant she would be working under William Sargent, the CEO of Framestore, the visual effects company behind the Harry Potter film franchise, but ultimately for Prime Minister Tony Blair.

Accepting the role was, Ardern says, a 'totally pragmatic' decision. She had misgivings about working for Blair, whom she viewed as culpable for the disastrous Iraq War, but 'I wanted to live overseas,' she said. 'I wanted to have that time and experience abroad. I was doing amazing voluntary work that I loved, but I needed to live so I took the job.'[1]

In London, Ardern was a little taken aback with the scale of the Cabinet Office. She was one in a unit of eighty, and there were many units in the office. For much of her time in the UK, her job involved working as an assistant director for the Better Regulation Executive, a unit that was later transferred to the Department for Business, Enterprise and Regulatory Reform. There, she engaged with small businesses – in short, 'trying to make their lives easier'.[2]

Many people assumed that Ardern would have forged some kind of relationship with Blair, as she did with Helen Clark during her time in the Beehive. But she didn't even meet the British prime minister during her period of duty in the Cabinet Office. Her stint with the British government coincided with the end of the Blair era, which stretched across a little more than a decade, from 2 May 1997 to 27 June 2007.

Ardern's abiding memory of Blair from these years was of witnessing his final speech to Parliament, and the realisation of the fleeting nature of power that came over her as she did so. Blair finished his speech by saying, 'And that is that, the end.' 'I still remember that moment,' Ardern recalls. 'You can have that enormous career in politics . . . and then suddenly, pouff. That's that. It's done, and you're gone.'³ This was a great lesson for Ardern to learn early, a humble realisation.

Later in her sojourn, Ardern was seconded to the Home Office as senior policy adviser under the chief inspector of constabulary, Sir Ronnie Flanagan. There, she assisted with his Review of Policing in England and Wales. At least in some manner, however remote, she was fulfilling her dream of working for law enforcement.

Jacinda's OE wasn't all work. Now a scientist, Louise Ardern was also in London, and the sisters took some trips together. They travelled to the Netherlands and Scotland, then late in 2007 made a special trip to Argentina, to learn Spanish. There, they stayed in Buenos Aires for a month in the kind of circumstances twenty-somethings seem to be immune to, if not relish. Jacinda and Louise shared a cramped room without a window, sleeping on sofa cushions for mattresses on the floor. At the end of their time in the city, at any rate, they had managed to grasp basic Spanish (this was, as events would transpire, of more help to Louise, who would later marry Colombian-born Ray Dussan).

Their travel was helped in no small part by Jacinda's contacts in the International Union of Socialist Youth (IUSY). IUSY, while not widely known outside political circles, is a huge umbrella group, the largest socialist youth organisation in the world. With 145 member organisations, comprising social democrat, socialist and Labour Party youth organisations from 106 countries, IUSY enjoys UN Economic and Social Council (ECOSOC) consultative status. Formed in 1907, it became a forum for young socialists to meet and share methods and experiences, developing policies and principles with their counterparts abroad.

In New Zealand's Young Labour, Ardern had held the post of international secretary, which was her entrée to IUSY. As international secretary, she had made contact with countless delegates throughout the world, before she left for London. She had also met many in person. As New Zealand's IUSY delegate, Ardern attended the IUSY Congress in 2004 in Hungary with her friend Tony Milne, where she and hundreds of her colleagues gathered to determine through voting the organisation's public policy.

With her easy, personable nature, Ardern had made many friends in IUSY; on her trips from London, she met her IUSY counterparts wherever she could, cementing numerous relationships. Perhaps she was a natural networker, but her connections were deeper and the esteem in which she was held in IUSY was stronger than networking alone could account for. At any rate, her friendships in IUSY would be a deciding factor in elevating her to her first prominent position, which would be within the organisation itself.

It almost didn't happen, though later it might have seemed destined. Ardern's rise in IUSY followed a pattern that would be repeated in the coming years: she would seem utterly out of contention for a post, before sweeping gracefully into it as if some unseen force were behind her.

After Ardern left for London, her position as New Zealand Young Labour international secretary was taken over by her friend Kate Sutton. Prior to the 2006 IUSY Festival, held in Alicante, Spain in July, Ardern was made aware by her colleagues in the organisation that according to IUSY rules, she was ineligible to serve as New Zealand's delegate on the board, as she was no longer active in Young Labour. Disappointed, she nevertheless arranged for Sutton to take her place. Ardern would step down and nominate Sutton as New Zealand's delegate on the board at its meeting in Alicante.

Ardern's supporters at the board meeting, however, would have none of it. In an extraordinary turn of events, they argued that upholding the spirit of the rules was more important than abiding strictly by the letter of the rulebook. How could they let a minor rule disqualify such a valuable delegate as Jacinda Ardern? They had plans for her, anyhow – plans that made such a trifling matter as not being currently active in Young Labour seem inconsequential.

At the end of the meeting's discussions and resolutions, Ardern had not only been reconfirmed as her country's delegate on the IUSY board. Her colleagues had nominated her, unopposed, as the next IUSY president, to take office in 2008 when the current president's term expired.

This was extraordinary, in several ways. Most presidents had been from Europe and South America. A couple had been from the Indian subcontinent and east Asia; all but one had been men. Jacinda would be the first New Zealander to occupy the post – and only the second woman in IUSY's 101-year history.

More extraordinary was the strength of advocacy that elevated her to the position. Among all the ambitious young socialist delegates, Ardern had managed to garner such emphatic support that they would overlook her ineligibility and make her the sole nominee for president. Assuredly, her standing in IUSY had been built over a period of years. But the incident showed that somehow, Ardern possessed something special. Perhaps it was the 'stardust' that her future opponent Prime Minister Bill English would speak of years later.

Another remarkable feature of the whole episode was her reaction. Ardern had assured her friend of a position on the board, yet had ultimately kept the position herself, securing the top job in the organisation in the process. She was truly distressed: she had let her friend down and unlike most politicians, who might view such a turn of fate pragmatically – even with a quiet sense of satisfaction – she agonised over it. For her part, Kate Sutton may have been disappointed, but was gracious in congratulating Ardern; happy, she said, that the first New Zealander would take up the position. Significantly, the pair's friendship didn't seem to suffer in the least from the incident. Ardern may have won in a coup. But it was, like others in which she would later triumph, bloodless.

Becoming IUSY president was a coup for Ardern in other ways. When she took up the post late in January 2008, the New Zealand press proclaimed her election to the post a 'huge achievement'.[4] It was both a stepping stone and a proving ground for her. Though the position holds little real power, as president of IUSY, Ardern could gain invaluable exposure on an international stage, showcasing her oratory and diplomatic skills.

Quite unsurprisingly, the speeches she made in her role as president of IUSY are peppered with instances of the word 'comrade' and references to the failures of capitalism. Her post was, of course, the head of a socialist organisation, and 'comrade' has been a socialist term of address since the late nineteenth century. Her detractors would make much of this later, which is perhaps equally unsurprising. What is more noteworthy about Ardern's speeches from this period is the confidence with which she spoke, and her conviction. There was some tension in Jacinda's voice and mannerisms, which is still present, at times, years later: the tension, perhaps, of a woman determined to excel, a woman who places immense pressure on herself – or a sign of a tussle somewhere within her, between self-doubt and resolute self-belief, the latter obviously prevailing. The tension, at any rate, doesn't detract. On the contrary, it almost enhances the power of her delivery.

Of greater importance than the speeches and publicity were Ardern's visits to refugee camps, which tempered her political spirit, gave her a broader perspective than would be expected for a Kiwi politician. The first was in eastern Nepal, to a camp filled with people from Bhutan, who lived in simple huts with mud floors. The second was in Tindouf, Algeria. There, Sahrawi refugees from Western Sahara had lived for decades, waiting for the resolution of a UN-sponsored peace process for their return from exile.

In a photograph from her visit to Algeria, Ardern is wearing a hijab – publicly perhaps for the first time, but not the last – and smiling while she gives an interview on Algerian radio. Another of her in Tindouf shows her in a more typical pose: crouched down, her hand extended to a toddler's while a pair of young girls, probably his sisters, look on. In the background are the cement and earthen flat-roofed dwellings of the camp, stretching low across to the horizon like rocks among shifting sands.

The experience of seeing the people from these camps, who 'just wanted the chance to go home', lingered for Ardern. It would influence her approach and her government's policy towards refugees less than a decade later. Her visits to the West Bank and Lebanon, war-ravaged regions about as far removed from peaceful Waikato as one can imagine, and the crushing squalor of Mumbai's slums, would likewise prick a compulsion within her to help. She knew, however, that making a 'big dramatic shift' was beyond her. Also, as she later said, 'I missed things and I missed people and I always felt drawn home.'⁵

Jacinda would miss London – her sister Louise, her expat friends, work, her favourite Yorkshire Tea and Branston Pickle. But the time was ripe for her to go back home. While she was in London, party heavyweights in Wellington had been making plans for her. She was about to be called back to New Zealand, to embark on a new phase of her life that would start before she returned.

Baby of the House

The British prime minister Harold Wilson once said, 'A week is a long time in politics.' No one would argue otherwise. The period between general elections can seem short for New Zealanders, however. While the overwhelming majority of democratic countries have parliaments with four- or five-year terms, New Zealand's Parliament, like Australia's, has a maximum term of just three years. No sooner has everybody recovered from one election campaign and its fallout than another begins. Parties seem to be perpetually in campaign mode or, at least, with an eye on the next poll.

Not long after Jacinda Ardern made her way to London in 2006, her name was being mentioned in party inner circles as a prospect for the 2008 election. Naturally, she had made a favourable impression on several Labour Party powerbrokers, including her former bosses Phil Goff and, of course, Helen Clark. Another was the Labour Party stalwart who eventually put Ardern's name forward for the party list. Curiously, he was not a parliamentarian, but a unionist: Paul Tolich, a veteran in the Labour movement who had been active in leftist politics since before Ardern was born.

Tolich, or Tolly as he is known to his friends, met Ardern during her days in Harry Duynhoven's office. He had been impressed with her then as he was later, when she liaised masterfully with the union movement during Clark's 2005 campaign. Tolich, who became one of Ardern's supporters and advisers, was a member of Labour's New Zealand Council. He recommended her to the thirty-seven-member Moderating Selection Committee (MSC), which decided the 2008 party list.

The process for deciding the Labour Party's list, as with the National Party's, is in two tiers. First, regional lists are compiled in a quasi-democratic manner, then the MSC, made up of venerable Labour figures, meets in the months preceding the election to finalise the party list. The Labour Party's MSC has considerable discretion; ultimately it has more oversight and control of the process than the National Party counterpart has of its own.

Beyond that, the Labour selection for list seats seems for outsiders an opaque, bewildering process. A right-wing political blogger has referred to it unkindly, and unfairly, as a 'knife fight', though it would be naive to think back-room jockeying and party machinations don't play their part in it. Little wonder, anyhow, there is so much fascination with the party list: careers and political futures are built on it.

Jacinda Ardern's own career is a case in point. Suffice it to say, though, that she didn't need to lobby for her position on the 2008 party list. Earlier, while she was in London, she had been contacted by her former boss, Phil Goff, and asked to run for a seat in Parliament at the next election. Initially, she declined, but when he called and asked the second time, she agreed; this ambivalence towards holding office, so unusual in politics, would become a feature of Ardern's political career. Once she had indicated her willingness, her supporters – Tolich, Goff, Clark and others on the MSC – would champion her cause.

That they did, and effectively.

For the Labour powers that be, Ardern was the right person at the right time. She had a constellation of factors in her favour: she was young, talented and committed, and she was supported widely within the party. This alone would have guaranteed her a decent position on the list. Conscious that the ageing old guard, Clark, Michael Cullen *et al.*, would soon retire, the MSC set its sights on promoting a fresh, younger generation of Labour politicians. Along with Ardern, Chris Hipkins, Grant Robertson, Stuart Nash (great-grandson of Walter Nash, twenty-seventh prime minister of New Zealand), Phil Twyford, Kelvin Davis and Carmel Sepuloni were recruited to the Labour team for the 2008 election. All were relatively young; all would be eventually become ministers. Hipkins and Robertson found their way through preselection to safe seats, while the others were given a ranking high enough that they could make their way into Parliament on a list seat.

Another factor in Ardern's favour was her gender. Her friend Kate Sutton, a member of the Labour New Zealand Council, had campaigned for a 50/50 gender balance for Labour in Parliament, and she was backed by several prominent women in the party. This meant the committee had a particular focus on women candidates, who, as usual, were in the minority. With her background and skills, there was no perception on the committee that Ardern was being gifted a seat for being a woman. She fulfilled all the criteria for a young, promising MP.

Ardern was, however, almost unknown outside the Labour Party, and to the press, aside from her mention as the new president of IUSY at the start of the year. She was not in the country and indeed, had not shown any intention of contesting a geographic seat.

Perhaps the first public indication of Ardern's imminent political career came in an article in the *Dominion Post,* around seven months before the 2008 election. A reporter had obtained a leaked copy of the Wellington region party list. Below the five sitting MPs, at number six, was a new name – Jacinda Ardern, 'a former staff member in Helen Clark's Beehive office',[1] the reporter noted. More newsworthy then was Labour's recruitment of Dr Rajen Prasad, a former chief families commissioner and former race relations conciliator.

Ultimately, when the MSC finally announced the list on 31 August 2008, it showed Ardern was ranked twenty. She was still in London. Such a ranking, pundits noted, indicated the hopes the committee vested in its young candidate. The only candidate higher on the list who, like Ardern, was not a member of Parliament was Prasad, many years her senior and with a wealth of experience in public life.

Ardern's placement on the list was more than an unequivocal statement of her party's faith in her ability. At number twenty, she knew that save for an electoral calamity, she was sure of taking a list seat. She proposed that she should stay in London until the election, campaigning with a New Zealand London voters group. That was to be her contribution to the campaign.

Ardern's idea was canny. Both Labour and National parties sought to woo expat voters. Many of her often left-leaning, twenty-something fellow expats would happily cast their votes for Labour, given a nudge in the right direction by the charming activist with a winning smile. She had witnessed their admiration for Helen Clark, less than two years earlier, when she opened the New Zealand Memorial at Hyde Park in November 2006, with Tony Blair and the Queen. She saw Clark step from her official vehicle to 'a spontaneous eruption of applause' from her young compatriots.[2]

Despite Ardern's likelihood of success in cornering the London OE vote, Clark had other ideas. Flying back from an OE to a party seat seemed almost dilettantish – not a fitting start to her protégée's career. To the cynical press gallery, as well as those who had no knowledge of Ardern's work for the party over the preceding twelve years, it might very well seem that she had been gifted a list seat. Ardern would have to earn her place in Parliament, and be seen to have earned her place, Clark decided. She would have to contest – but not necessarily win – a geographic seat: Waikato.

In retrospect, it's hard not to feel that fate was playing its part here. Perhaps it was merely coincidence that Waikato needed a candidate, and that Gwladys Ardern, Jacinda's grandmother, had campaigned there for Clark generations earlier. Or perhaps on some level, Clark wanted Ardern to follow in her footsteps. Maybe it was simply fitting under the circumstances that Ardern should campaign on her home turf. Whatever the case, Ardern would contest the seat of her home town.

At first blush, this was a quixotic tilt at a parliamentary seat. Waikato had been a safe National Party seat for generations: no one from a left-leaning party had held the seat, or its predecessor, Piako, for seven decades, and anyone in Labour who had tried – including Helen Clark – had failed miserably.

The media, though, was positive about Ardern's campaign, while realistic about its chances of success. 'If youthful enthusiasm won elections Labour's newest recruit, Jacinda Ardern, 28, would win Waikato hands-down,' a local reporter declared. But 'the *Waikato Times* was told you could stick a cat on a stool and say he was running for National, and it would win.'[3]

The odds were stacked against Ardern, far beyond Waikato being a safe National Party seat. Her chief opponent and incumbent, Lindsay Tisch, was a warhorse who had held the equivalent, abolished seat of Piako since 2002. Prominent in the service organisation the Lions Club and a justice of the peace, he was a one-time National Party president and party campaign manager for the 1996 general election.

Ardern was taking on a political veteran and popular local, and dealing with the incumbency effect in a safe National Party seat. Moreover, she was in London when her campaign began.

There are some familial echoes of duty here, of taking on a thankless task, of soldiering on against the odds. As secretary of the Piako Labour Electorate Committee, Gwladys Ardern had helped choose candidates for the seat and supported their campaigns, knowing their chances were slim to nil. Now her granddaughter was doing her duty for the sake of her party. In political parlance, she was a sacrificial-lamb candidate.

Jacinda was under no illusions as to the nature of her campaign. Still, she was not prepared for the shock of her return, just three weeks before the poll date. In London, she had been surrounded by upbeat, positive expats, many of whom still supported Labour whole-heartedly. While they and she had been abroad, however, the winds of public opinion had shifted away from the party. Polls indicated strongly that New Zealanders wanted a change, and none more than in conservative seats such as Waikato.

Thankfully, Jacinda was surrounded by friends and family. Her other grandmother, Margaret Bottomley, proudly lent her a red mini-van – its Labour Party colour a happy coincidence – which was topped by a matching, four-sided party sign, 'Ardern Labour'. Jacinda used the minivan to ferry her friends and party workers to meetings and around the district for doorknocking. Her aunt Marie Ardern, a seasoned campaigner, joined them.

While Ardern campaigned with gusto as she had since her teens for Harry Duynhoven, it was clear to her 'where people were at . . . where it was going to go'.[4] National Party supporters in Waikato – the majority of voters – are often plain-speaking country folk. Ardern and her party workers were regularly met with coolness. The blue National party hoardings, dominant on the Waikato Expressway, were like standards of Waikato's allegiance.

Perhaps this was the first time Ardern had been on the wrong side, as it were, in her home town. Nonetheless, she fought for her party with courage, earning respect in the process. Jacinda, the 'sacrificial lamb', would shine in defeat, her loyalty and effort duly noted by the party leadership.

Defeat in one's first election is no bar to career advancement. On the contrary, it seems to be a baptism of fire for future leaders. The great New Zealand Labour prime ministers of the last half-century, Norman Kirk, David Lange and Helen Clark, all endured electoral defeats early in their careers yet proceeded, their reputations unblemished, to win parliamentary seats and hold the highest executive office in the land. Perhaps this is simply the nature of party politics. It's interesting to note that all British prime ministers from Thatcher to Johnson lost in their first attempt at a parliamentary seat; the majority of Australian prime ministers from the same period, likewise.

When the chief electoral officer released the official election results on 22 November 2008, it showed an electoral rout: Ardern had received just 7,272 votes to Tisch's 20,122. Elsewhere, there was little cause for celebration. Clark, Ardern's mentor and party leader, had retained her own seat, but her nine-year term as prime minister was over. The National Party under John Key had won ten more parliamentary seats than at its last showing, forming a government with the Māori Party, ACT and United Future.

Despite the gloom for her party, and her not unexpected drubbing in the poll, Jacinda's political career had now begun. She had managed to secure a seat in Parliament as a list MP. She was the youngest sitting member of Parliament – the baby of the House, the ninety-ninth woman to be elected.

*

Maiden speeches in Parliament, unlike so many aspects of politics, are treated with a certain dignity and sentiment. It is long-established protocol for other members to refrain from interjecting and reciprocally, the fresh member avoids overly contentious and partisan topics. The exceptions are rare.

Jacinda Ardern's speech on 16 December 2008, as with so many aspects of her career, didn't breach rules or break convention, yet nevertheless managed to be outstanding and memorable. She spoke passionately yet managed to strike that delicate balance of highlighting issues without sanctimony or courting offence. Her speech was frank yet entertaining, and at times humorous.

Maiden statements, as they are referred to in New Zealand, are allotted fifteen minutes and, according to the New Zealand Parliament website, are 'an opportunity for new MPs to make a strong start and set the tone for their time in Parliament'. Ardern's statement, lasting a few decorous seconds shy of the limit, did this to the fullest.

The baby of the House wore a black dress suit; her mentor, Helen Clark, in remarkably similar attire, looked on. Ardern's streaked blonde hair had gone; now it was the dark brown she is known for today, and tied back neatly. She was striking and charismatic before uttering a word.

She began her speech with the usual pleasantries and a warm tribute to Clark, her party leader, who watched with a half-smile on her lips. 'Maiden statements', she said, 'are a bit like words spoken in a heated argument; like it or not, they will come back to haunt one.'[5] This seemed to echo the maiden speech of the second woman in Parliament, Catherine Stewart, who said in 1939, 'I must be exceedingly careful of my utterances lest in ten years' time some of my statements may be quoted from Hansard against me.' Nearly seven decades later, Ardern turned this on its head: 'Today I will share with members the words that I wish to haunt me: my values and beliefs, and the things that have brought me here.' With that challenge, she made her statement a declaration of intent.

She spoke of the deprivation she saw in her childhood, that gave rise to her commitment to social justice. In stressing the need to 'reduc[e] poverty in this country', particularly for children, she declared that children living in need were 'not part of an underclass, as I have heard them called; they are part of our community'. While outlining her childhood education in Morrinsville, Ardern called for the teaching of te reo Māori in the nation's schools.

With a dig at the opposite benches, Ardern stated that it was 'unspeakable that . . . we now have a parliamentary select committee to question the science of climate change itself'. She declared that the detriment would be to 'the future generations, whom some people in this House do not yet believe they have a responsibility to'.

Her speech made overtures to business, talking of the 'delicate balancing act . . . that protects citizens whilst also allowing business and public services to flourish'. In conclusion, she paid tribute to her family members and campaign helpers, along with her colleagues in the party.

Ardern's maiden speech was well received on all sides. Her delivery was punctuated with smiles and self-deprecating humour that engaged and amused MPs of all political persuasions. 'Some people have asked me whether I am a radical,' she said. 'My answer to that question is very simple: "I am from Morrinsville." Where I come from a radical is someone who chooses to drive a Toyota rather than a Holden or a Ford.'

A murmur of laughter echoed throughout the chamber. The members would hardly have been surprised that Jacinda's first car was a Toyota, her trusty 1979 Corona.

While many MPs seem to read from a script for their maiden speeches, Ardern spoke like a seasoned orator, consulting her notes here and there, but maintaining eye contact with her audience. The effect was palpable. There was a sense in the chamber that here was someone to be watched, a woman of principle and intellect whose presence and likeability would elevate her to the front bench.

She ended her speech with the te reo phrase 'Tēnā koutou, tēnā koutou, tēnā koutou katoa' ('Greetings to all of you'). Her words brought applause from both sides of the chamber, and a standing ovation, as is common, from her own side. She was surrounded, and warmly embraced by her Labour Party colleagues. It could hardly have been a more auspicious start to a parliamentary career.

Earlier in that session, another young parliamentary debutant, Simon Bridges, the National Party MP for Tauranga, made his own maiden statement. It was a stiff, traditional performance, far removed from the easy charm of Ardern's speech a short time later. Bridges would become a jousting partner for Ardern on television. Later, upon taking office as prime minister, she would face him as leader of the opposition.

The 2008 election seemed to usher in a new guard of young politicians, on both sides of the House. A week before Ardern, another young woman gave her maiden speech to Parliament, from the opposite side of the House. Nikki Kaye, the National Party MP who had won the seat of Auckland Central, made her speech in quite a different manner to Ardern. Even her appearance seemed Ardern's diametric opposite. She wore an ivory suit, matching her blonde hair, free over her shoulders. With her hands mostly firm on the bench in front of her as if in fierce parliamentary debate, she spoke formally, and forcefully, consulting her notes below. There was barely a hint of a smile in her delivery, and no attempt at humour.

Less than six months in age separates Nikki Kaye and Jacinda Ardern, Kaye being the elder. Her suburban upbringing, politics, well-heeled family background, schooling and somewhat confrontational style were quite removed from Ardern's, yet there were a number of similarities between the two young politicians. Their careers after their parliamentary debuts in December 2008 would be compared and intertwined for more than a decade. It seems only fitting that the pair would face off in the following poll. Perhaps predictably, their contest was the most publicised of the 2011 election – for all the wrong reasons.

14

Battle of the Babes

The first issue that Jacinda Ardern raised in her maiden speech was the welfare of children, and it is fitting that an early question she tabled in Parliament, to the minister for social development and employment, Paula Bennett, related to children, a boot camp that was being conducted for young offenders. The question is recorded in Hansard, question no. 18659 (2009) of 27 November 2009: 'What are the ages of the young people currently taking part in the military-style activity camp concept test at Te Puna Wai o Tuhinapo youth justice residence?' Naturally enough, 'Socialist Cindy', as she was nicknamed by her opponents, was fobbed off by the minister, who exhibited a particular dislike for her. But it was the first of many references to children by Ardern in her capacity as MP and prime minister.

The media was largely quiet about Ardern for some time. That is, until it had something newsworthy: an electoral contest between two young, attractive women, which came to be known in the press as 'the battle of the babes'.

It was for the seat of Auckland Central in the 2011 general election, and the clichés abounded. The local press – male reporters, naturally – made it a sexist tour de force: 'Nicola Laura Kaye, 31, in the blue corner; Jacinda Kate Laurell Ardern, 31, in the red corner. Poor old Denise Roche from the Greens doesn't fit in the metaphorical wrestling ring. "If this is the Battle of the Babes, I'll be the auntie," laughs Roche, 48. "I don't want to be in the ring." '[1] Next was a sly comment on a suggested jelly-wrestling match for the two women, who had heard the same, tasteless joke dozens of times.

Ardern and Kaye sidestepped the innuendo as best they could. The pair even made light of the situation, agreeing to pose for a photograph together, Ardern in a black skirt and jacket over an orange and beige top, Kaye in a green dress and blue jacket. The plan to capture the pair in party colours of blue and red, National and Labour, was scotched, a reporter claimed, when someone spilled red wine over Kaye's blue chiffon number at the rugby.

Labour leader Phil Goff tried to steer the debate onto serious matters, emphasising Ardern's local support and ability. 'You're not voting for your MP on the basis of their looks,' he said. 'It's not a beauty contest.' His opposite, prime minister John Key, spoke highly of Kaye's work ethic and ability.

The candidates themselves said the hype around their election campaign gave them a platform to raise relevant issues, and seemed careful not to rise to the bait of the gender issue. 'It's not something I get hung up on,' Ardern told a reporter. 'There does still seem to be a bit of novelty around the fact that we're young women in politics. I hope, one day, we get to a place where that isn't a novelty anymore.'[2]

The temperaments and backgrounds of the candidates provided contrast enough to make the contest even more intriguing. Ardern, as always, was a paragon of charm and thoughtfulness, while Kaye was energetic and forceful. Ardern's focus in her youth had been social work; Kaye was a former champion sportswoman. Kaye hailed from the leafy, affluent Auckland suburbs of Epsom and Kohimarama, while Ardern was the small-town farm girl from Morrinsville. Kaye was educated at the elite Corran School, a private girls' school with its Latin motto, whereas Ardern made her mark in a coeducational government school, with its te reo Māori exhortation 'Kia U Ki Te Pai' ('Whatever you do, let it be your best') – a motto that she surely took to heart.

Despite these differences, there were many similarities beyond their youth. Ardern and Kaye had prodigious debating skill; both had worked for their party leaders, then set off for OEs in London before entering Parliament in 2008. Kaye had been vice-chairman of the International Young Democrat Union (IYDU), a centre-right youth political organisation, while Ardern was a former president of IUSY. The pair were exceptionally well-matched opponents. They had even appeared occasionally on television together, as panellists on the Young Guns segment of TVNZ's breakfast show. Both represented their parties' hopes, not simply in the electorate, but for the future.

Both made impressive efforts at campaigning, too, knocking on thousands of constituents' doors. They did so with great expectation. Auckland Central was once a Labour stronghold, but gentrification of the inner-city area in recent years had made the seat marginal. Kaye won it in the 2008 election from the long-time Labour incumbent Judith Tizard, and in the 2011 election, it was one of the most hotly contested seats.

The incumbent began with distinct advantages. She was a local, respected for her efforts for the electorate, and her party's government was still popular, expected to win a second term – New Zealand's National Party has always held office for at least three consecutive parliamentary terms. And indeed, election day on 26 November 2011 saw Labour under Phil Goff defeated soundly by John Key's National Party. But while Labour's vote was greatly reduced, Ardern managed to reverse the trend in Auckland Central.

It meant for a nail-biting election evening for the two young women. With twenty-two percent of votes counted, Kaye took a narrow lead of seventy-seven votes. Soon afterwards, though, she drew further ahead, and at 10.40 P.M., she gave her victory speech. Kaye had held off Ardern's surge to retain the seat by the narrowest of margins: just 717 seats. Ardern had lost, but valiantly, increasing her party's vote by 4.69%. Ranked lucky number thirteen on the Labour Party list, she was anyhow guaranteed to return to Parliament on a list seat, which she did.

Kaye and Ardern's interaction continued in Parliament and outside. Ardern kept her office in Auckland's College Hill, in a villa that was adjacent to Kaye's office. This was a fateful and happy decision for reasons only tangentially related to politics, as she would see.

Ardern and Kaye shared a desire to make a difference in social and environmental issues. Each wanted changes – somewhat similar – to adoption laws, and there was talk of broad cooperation between them, though they made parallel efforts. In May 2012, Kaye along with Green Party MP Kevin Hague drafted a bill dealing with adoption, international adoption and surrogacy. The bill was sponsored by Hague for a ballot in October, but never drawn. Meanwhile, Ardern had introduced her own Care of Children Law Reform Bill to Parliament, which was drawn from the ballot for consideration on 30

August 2012. If the bill was passed, civil union couples, heterosexual and gay, would be eligible to adopt children. The bill was defeated forty-two to seventy-eight.

Ardern had another close, but more genial association – at least in those years – with another National Party politician: Simon Bridges, the young National leading light, whose parliamentary career also began in 2008. The two jousted weekly on air as panellists on TVNZ's *Young Guns*, which was broadcast live on a Thursday morning. They would meet and have friendly chats in the green room, before debating before the cameras, mostly in a good-natured manner, with plenty of banter to keep the viewers entertained.

That the two were put forward by their respective parties for the show indicates the confidence that party decision makers vested in them. It was well founded: within just a few years, both would lead their parties. For the viewers, they were charming, good-looking and well groomed, seeming far more like professional television anchors than politicians.

Their chemistry was such that it was widely, and wrongly, assumed the two were romantically involved. At any rate, their appearances worked as well for them as for their parties. Ardern and Bridges had an easy charm for the cameras, could debate without offence and even had the grace to agree, on the odd occasion. Their on-screen appearances were almost a partnership, working far better than did Ardern with Nikki Kaye in the same segment. Unsurprisingly, there seemed to be a lack of warmth between the two women opponents for Auckland Central.

Television, at any rate, was not the only area of the entertainment industry where Ardern shone. New Zealand's fortieth prime minister has a particular talent as a disc jockey – though, humble as she is, she prefers the term 'tune selector'. She has showcased her ability numerous times: at high school, at various events in university, and later. One of these was for a 45-minute selection of songs at the famed Laneway music festival in Auckland in January 2014. It was, Ardern later said, the pinnacle of her 'career' as a DJ; the most memorable for its profile, as well as the significant personal price the gig exacted.

The festival was held at Silo Park, a public events, carnival and gathering space on the waterfront that was once an industrial site.

Many events were held in the space, between a cluster of six silos on one side and a larger one on its own, thirty-five metres high, on the other: iconic landmarks that once served as storage vessels for cement. For Ardern's Laneway music festival appearance, the larger silo's interior was decked out as the Red Bull Thunderdome – equipped with a powerful PA system and LED lights: ample electronics and wattage to bombard the senses rather than merely excite them.

As a politician, Ardern's set attracted more media attention than that of most artists in the festival. There was even speculation in the press as to whether she would include political anthems, and a witty query if she would play Split Enz's 'Six Months in a Leaky Boat', a journalist's pointed reference to the ongoing leadership woes within the Labour Party. With unflappable sincerity, Ardern said that would be 'unkind', but that 'someone joked that if I don't play "I See Red" [also by Split Enz] it would be political suicide'. 'I'm aiming for things people want to dance to,' she said, and was keen to ensure there was no 'dead air'.[3] According to one of the event's organisers, she 'got the Thunderdome jumping'.

She also showed a dimension of herself beyond that usually revealed by politicians; if taste in music is any indication of character, Ardern's set for the festival speaks of her sensitivity, sense of humour – and love of quirky cover songs.

Looking the part in a blue and green, psychedelic-patterned sleeveless top, she started her eclectic set with Beyoncé and Andre 3000's 'Back to Black' from the *Great Gatsby* soundtrack, a smooth and haunting number with a compelling beat – a perfect choice for an alternative music festival. The next was another song of love that has soured, a hardened, pepped-up version of George Michael's favourite 'Careless Whisper', by Gossip. 'Bang Bang (My Baby Shot Me Down)', by Terry Reid, followed – an emotional version of Cher's classic.

'Black or White', Michael Jackson's hit song from 1991, when Ardern was just beginning high school, made its appearance in vastly different form by the Kiwi indie outfit Street Chant. Perhaps Ardern was finding a cooler, more upbeat place for the soundtrack of her childhood years.

Punk, its rough, self-destructive anarchy vastly removed from

Jacinda Ardern and her life of responsibility and order, seems to hold some fascination for her. Tom Jones and the Pretenders made their place in the set with an Iggy Pop number, 'Lust for Life', along with the perverse Sid Vicious cover of 'My Way', and 'Common People' by William Shatner, its semi-spoken lyrics stark alongside punkish Britpop.

Like a true professional, Ardern ended the set on a light note. 'Yummy Yummy Yummy', that cute song from the 1960s, was given its indie, uber-cool yet hilarious punk makeover by Love Toy.

Ardern didn't emerge unscathed from her experience at the Red Bull Thunderdome. The enclosed space of the silo interior, with its concrete walls, acted like an amplifier, which after nearly one hour, was simply too much for Jacinda to take. She remembers the event for its intensity and enthusiastic reception, as much as for the permanent damage it caused to the hearing in her left ear. Trooper that she is, Ardern didn't complain, though she joked that it was all downhill from there for her DJ career.

Ardern seemed utterly at home at festivals, enjoying herself with a musical audience as she did at her political appearances – though with a DJ crowd, there was no work, only pleasure. At some festivals, she would even join the audience to dance for a number or two. She showcased a surprising repertoire of music, her musical taste veering from power pop, like 'Wannabe' by the Spice Girls (a favourite she played years earlier in a high-school function), and RnB, like TLC's 'No Scrubs'; to heavy, with Judas Priest's hard rock 'Breaking the Law'.

Another of Jacinda's favourite songs, though one that she wouldn't likely play at such an event, is Janis Joplin's version of a Nina Simone classic, 'Little Girl Blue'. It's a melancholy, bluesy number, perhaps at odds with her upbeat, optimistic personality; a song with lyrics of aching loneliness. If Jacinda had suffered her own share of loneliness until now, it would not be for much longer.

15

Catch of a Lifetime

As early as 2012, Jacinda Ardern was regarded, as the political journalist Guyon Espiner noted, 'as a future [Labour Party] leader – often the kiss of death in politics'. She brushed the label off, making it clear she had no desire to lead her party. Instead, she was keen to stress that she had a 'long list of policy goals . . . around [the] well-being of families and kids'.[1]

It was just as well – at that time, anyway. Labour was in the doldrums; the heady days under 'Aunty Helen' in the first years of the century seemed a lifetime away. Infighting, conflicting ambitions in the shadow cabinet and a divided caucus left the party in no shape to counter the National Party government of John Key, whose popularity seemed immune to scandal.

Ardern's career progressed, anyhow. Naturally, she took on as much as she could manage, and more, as is her way. In January 2014, she was elevated to the shadow cabinet. She had previously been assigned numerous minor shadow portfolios, and in 2014 became responsible for police, corrections, arts, justice and small business. It was the election year; she had barely any time for socialising and spending time with her family.

When she was not in Wellington for parliamentary sessions, Ardern lived in Auckland's inner west in Freemans Bay, a formerly industrial, working-class suburb. Her chic apartment was one in a light, modernist block, built as public housing in the mid-twentieth century.

The neighbourhood has a chequered history. Concerned with vice and squalor in the middle of the last century, the government razed the suburb's seediest parts for urban renewal. In the following decades, as in so many Western cities, the city's fringes, formerly homes of vice and workers' disenchantment, became fashionable. A National Party government sold the apartments in the block. The next Labour government bought some back.

It takes a brave woman, one at ease with herself, to open the doors of her apartment to the media. Ardern happily hosted some journalists in her home, even allowing them to tour the place. Their glimpses and their observations of her private world in the years before she took office are revealing.

The fact that she quite willingly brought reporters into her home in itself says much about Jacinda. While she is, by her own admission, 'terrible at creating preventive barriers' for herself, it is more the case that she doesn't seem to need them; she has nothing to hide. One cannot discern a difference in the public and private Jacinda Ardern – not even an elision between one role and another. Nor is there a shift of mood as she steps between private and public spaces, unless a journalist is being particularly obstreperous.

Those media personalities who did visit her at home found Ardern a genial host. One of those was the high-profile columnist Michele Hewitson, who met her for an 8 A.M. interview in April 2014. Michele's interviews are respected, noted for their perspicacity – she is sympathetic, but clear-sighted and fair in her assessments.

She described the apartment as being like Jacinda: 'nicely turned out and fashionable but not in a swanky or precious way'. The second-hand armchairs, she was told, Ardern had bought online on a discount site, then covered in a Florence Broadhurst fabric. This is vintage Jacinda: stylish but frugal, and homely. Hewitson's observation that Ardern 'comes across as terribly sensible and annoyingly earnest but she is also fun' is about as kind as you might expect of a veteran journalist.

As Ardern took Hewitson through the apartment, the journalist noted two features that alone say much about Ardern's approach to work, leadership and life. One was a to-do list, a blackboard in the kitchen, bearing just two words that are normally one: Every Thing. The other was a historic photograph in monochrome, hanging on the wall. In this photograph, the great early twentieth-century explorer Ernest Shackleton and his crew are launching their lifeboat, the *James*

Caird, from the shore of Elephant Island in the Southern Ocean, on 24 April 1916.

The iconic image speaks of hope in the face of disaster. Shackleton's ship, the *Endurance*, trapped in pack ice, had broken up and sunk in the Weddell Sea off Antarctica. His crew's survival depended on Shackleton sailing with some of them to South Georgia, a journey of some 800 nautical miles through horrendous conditions – hurricane-force winds and gargantuan waves, as winter approached – to seek help. Shackleton's voyage in the *James Caird* after the photograph was taken is one of the great ocean journeys in history.

That Ernest Shackleton is one of Ardern's personal heroes is itself significant. Perhaps the most heroic explorer of the Heroic Age of Antarctic exploration, Shackleton was known for his boundless optimism, a rare gift of inspiring his crew members, whom he treated equally; his resilience and ability to lead his men from catastrophe is legendary.

Elements of Shackleton's skippering the *James Caird* and his crew away from the wrecked *Endurance* to safety would be seen in Ardern's leadership. Shackleton's attention to morale, his leading from the front are perhaps as natural for Prime Minister Jacinda Ardern as they were for the explorer. In the meantime, Ardern immersed herself in work. She seemed to be burning the candle at both ends. Another reporter visiting her at her apartment for an interview seemed to have poked around more than even the nosiest guest, noting that the refrigerator contained little other than condiments.

Ardern wanted a partner, someone with whom she could have a family. She revealed in an interview that she had 'spent a good amount of time in not particularly good relationships'.[2] It seems she had felt a gap in her life, one that had remained for some time; she needed, as she said, 'someone you really adore'.[3] This gap would soon be filled.

*

Sometimes, the usual order of things is reversed: the smallest of actions can have great consequences, a rival can be your greatest ally. This is especially so in the topsy-turvy world of politics. Jacinda

Ardern has Nikki Kaye to thank for a small action – or inaction – that was to have the happiest of ramifications.

Predictably, with her glamour and magnetic personality, Ardern was often invited to high-profile events in Auckland, where she mixed with her friends from the political and entertainment worlds. One such friend is Colin Mathura-Jeffree, a well-known New Zealand model, actor, television host and spokesperson. In 2012, the tall, dark and handsome Mathura-Jeffree was named New Zealand's sexiest man by *Metro* magazine. In May that year, he told Supriya, he featured on the cover of *Metro* and was invited as an honoured guest to the magazine's Restaurant of the Year Awards in Auckland, an institution in the city. What better companion to share his moment of triumph than Jacinda Ardern?

The pair had been friends since they met at a Peer Sexuality Support Programme graduation event, where they were guest speakers. There, Mathura-Jeffree remembers her 'engag[ing] the entire room like a master orchestra conductor: her narrative so smooth, informative, warm and all encompassing – it was like I was slowly drowning in Manuka honey'.[4] When he took to the microphone, he said, 'Wow! Who wants to talk after that amazing speech? Do you all get the feeling we've just been spoken to by the future prime minister of New Zealand?'

Ardern shrugged off Mathura-Jeffree's compliment. He says she never liked his addressing her in that manner. Not that it stopped him.

Mathura-Jeffree has been quizzed by reporters about the evening of the *Metro* Restaurant of the Year Awards in May 2012, perhaps more than any other in his career. He remembers how he embarrassed his friend, whom he describes as 'a force of nature', by introducing her as usual as 'the future prime minister of New Zealand'. He cannot recall much, though, about the most momentous happening of that evening – for his friend, and indeed, the country – which was another introduction he made. What he can recall, however, is that there were 'lots of smiles'.

The smiles were between Ardern and another handsome man, his features suggesting his typically Kiwi, mixed European and Māori heritage: broadcast personality Clarke Gayford, who was the host of the evening.

Gayford was himself already famous. An affable, well-regarded celebrity in New Zealand, he had broadcast on radio for the Edge and Channel Z, and hosted the drivetime shifts on More FM and George FM. In television, he boasted an impressive résumé, hosting and appearing as a guest presenter for numerous reality programmes: first in his own *Cow TV*, then *United Travel Getaway* in 2007, the New Zealand version of the *Ultimate Guinness World Records* in 2008 and in 2010, the third season of *Extraordinary Kiwis*. Later, he would go on to host a fishing show.

For Ardern and Gayford, there was little more than smiles and polite conversation at their first meeting. But a year later politics threw them together again.

A man with a keen eye on political developments, Gayford was alarmed when in May 2013, Prime Minister John Key introduced the Government Communications Security Bureau and Related Legislation Amendment Bill. Contentious provisions of the bill would afford the government greater powers to intercept and store data, leading, perhaps, to the 'mass surveillance' of New Zealanders, critics maintained. Gayford could see the obvious undermining of privacy that, if passed to become legislation, the bill would entail for ordinary Kiwis. His fears were well founded, as would be shown by the revelations in investigative journalist Nicky Hager's book *Dirty Politics: How Attack Politics Is Poisoning New Zealand's Political Environment* the following year.

Gayford wrote to his local member, Nikki Kaye, outlining his concerns about the bill. She didn't respond – the bill was sponsored by her party leader. He recalls his fateful next step: 'I thought, well, Jacinda's sitting on the other side [of politics], so I wrote this letter and said "how can I help?" '[5]

The pair met for coffee. Clarke was delighted that Jacinda shared his liking for Concord Dawn, 'a fantastically awesome heavy New Zealand drum and bass outfit'. Their shared love of music was important. So passionate was Clarke about music, he says he quit radio because he became disillusioned, forced to play the same songs, in a different order, each day. He was also pleased to discover their mutual commitment to ecology and interest in addressing social issues facing New Zealand. As he would later say, 'We kind of align on most things.'[6]

Another coffee appointment followed, then another. Eventually, Clarke invited Jacinda out for a fishing trip. This was a crucial test of their compatibility; a sure indication he was serious about the relationship. His younger sister Pene remembers Clarke being 'fanatical' about fishing from his early childhood, and insisting on his loved ones accompanying him. One Christmas Day, he took Pene out in a dinghy fishing, staying so long on the water that her Walkman batteries went flat and they missed their Christmas dinner.

Clarke and Jacinda's first date augured the blissful courtship that followed. Clarke recalls, 'It was a Champagne day [31 December 2013]. It was a day you don't want to have first off . . .'[7] It was idyllic, so satisfying, it might very well mean the relationship would deteriorate from there, he thought.

Interestingly, Clarke had expressed a similar sentiment in a comedy skit years earlier, for the YouTube channel Rattle Ya Dags. In 'Bad Relationships', he suggested starting a new relationship badly, so it could only get better:

Improve the relationship slowly, therefore surprising your partner – 'Oh, you brought me flowers, you never brought me flowers before.' Surprise! You will also never hear those words 'Remember when you used to, you were so much nicer when you used to do that'. Start slowly, improve slowly. Everyone wins. Trust me – I have had literally hundreds and hundreds of really successful relationships.[8]

On his first fishing date with Jacinda, Clarke couldn't have been further from the mark, although their relationship had doubtless begun slowly. Their day on the water sounds like a scene from a romance movie. 'The sea was glass flat and we had a huge pod of dolphins join us. It was literally Jacinda's first cast and she was like, "Oooh! Something's pulling!" She pulled in a 5.4kg snapper. And she said, "Is that good?" And I was like, "That's real good!" And after that, she caught a huge John Dory – and then a whale showed up!' 'The signs', Clarke says, 'couldn't have been clearer.'[9]

As both were public figures, it was necessary that Jacinda and

Clarke kept their relationship away from the public eye. Most new relationships need privacy; those of public figures more so, where they might be magnified in the attention of others a thousand times. Somehow, Jacinda and Clarke managed to maintain tight secrecy around their relationship – for far longer than would be expected, anyway.

It was only in September 2014 that the *New Zealand Herald* gossip column Spy asked in its headline, 'Is romance blossoming for MP?' Jacinda and Clarke, the paper said, were seen 'getting cosy at Ponsonby bar Golden Dawn'. Curiously, Jacinda told the reporter there was 'nothing to report' about Clarke. Clarke said, risibly, they were 'just good mates'.[10] Indeed.

Months before the Spy article, as her romance with Clarke simmered, Jacinda had cheekily told Michele Hewitson she hadn't been in a relationship for years. She laughed at the 'empty [Google] search' the reporter had performed, looking for details of her boyfriend. Before long, anyhow, Clarke and Jacinda felt ready to make their relationship public. They moved in together, buying a villa in the fashionable Auckland suburb of Point Chevalier.

Later, with Clarke's hit television show *Fish of the Day* screening on the National Geographic channel to millions of viewers in thirty-five countries, the pair heard all manner of witty references to fishing and their relationship. Perhaps the most appropriate and enduring of these refers to Jacinda as Clarke's 'catch of a lifetime'. Clarke takes these in jovial spirit, for as he says, Jacinda is 'definitely . . . the best thing that's ever happened to me'.

They are indeed a perfect mix, to the public as to their friends. In some ways, Jacinda and Clarke seem to contrast, but in others, according to one journalist who knows them both, 'they're two peas in a pod: dynamic, smart and witty'.[11] Both are seasoned professionals in public life, used to living in the limelight, which is invaluable for Jacinda's career with its unique challenges.

Peter Davis, Prime Minister Helen Clark's husband, a retiring sociology professor, was rarely seen in public with his wife, and beyond the odd letter to a newspaper, abstained from public comment.

In terms of personality, Jacinda and Clarke are a blessing for one another. In the way that is the hallmark of all successful marriages, as it were, they are a study of likenesses and contradictions. Clarke is more casual, spontaneous and devil-may-care than his life partner. Jacinda appreciates his laid-back, young-man-of-the-sea charm, dubbing him Huckleberry Finn for the way he so often appears in shorts – even for interviews – and how he seems always to have a fishing rod in hand.

Jacinda tends to worry about other people and details; shouldering responsibility – too much, perhaps. This is a trait that has been consistent throughout her life; one that Clarke cherishes, yet moderates. He tells of a time where Jacinda woke at 2 A.M., worried that there was no milk in the house for his morning cup of tea. She rose and soaked some almonds, so she could blend them into almond milk for his tea at dawn. 'It was the best cup of tea I've ever had, and I hate almond milk,' he says.[12]

Conversely, when Jacinda's penchant for caring too much or focusing on issues becomes a burden for her, she has Clarke to gently remind her to ease her self-imposed pressures. 'Clarke really tries to pull me back from the precipice of anxiety a lot,' Jacinda says.[13] He does so in the most gentle, and sometimes subtle, manner.

While in England, Jacinda was gifted a novelty mug by her flatmate, with a tongue-in-cheek message. The mug, decorated with a retro photograph of a woman's face looking cheekily out from surrounding polka dots, features the text 'I will not obsess, I will not obsess, I will not obsess'. Always quick to acknowledge her faults rather than hide them, Jacinda cheerily describes it as 'a legitimate tease'. It is one that Clarke is so keen to emphasise that when the original mug broke, he bought 'mug version 2.0' for her on the internet.

Naturally, Jacinda's intense focus is tempered itself by an innate thoughtfulness. Consummate politician that she is, she is most comfortable taking a considered approach – not reacting to a situation without assessing all points of view and facets of it. Clarke credits Jacinda with broadening and moderating his perspective: 'Through Jacinda, I've actually become less tribal, more understanding of an alternate view.'[14]

In these words, he has perhaps identified some of Jacinda's greatest strengths, attributes that have marked her for leadership in a country that has long been riven with political, economic and tribal divides. Aotearoa, the Land of the Long White Cloud, was calling out for a leader who was capable of spanning those divides – a leader for everyone.

PART TWO

16

Ambition or Ambivalence?

Feminism the world over faces a nagging question, one that seems to gain impetus as the century progresses: why, after decades of activism, equal employment opportunity and anti-discrimination legislation – not to mention ceaseless public debate – are there so few women in the upper echelons of leadership? It grates that while there has been change for women, so much for the better in the last half-century, corporate boardrooms are still, by and large, old boys' clubs, peppered with the odd woman here and there. The vast majority of heads of state, too, are men.

There is a myriad of reasons for this, and an even greater number of explanations, many of them contentious. Most of these have been well discussed.

First, a corporate and political culture steeped in masculine competitiveness, rather than consensus decision making, means many a worthy woman leader is overlooked. Then there is the subtle marginalisation in the workforce of women who choose, as a majority do, to have a family, or prioritise their children's needs over work. Lack of familial support for women in power, which has traditionally been afforded most men, takes more out of contention, as do the often extreme, 24/7 demands of most corporate CEO and senior political posts. Women, unlike many of their male counterparts, tend to favour a balance between their professional and personal lives.

None of these could be considered definitive, and few explanations offer helpful insight. This information is useful for policy makers and activists, but less so for women seeking to fulfil their potential.

For career women, Jacinda Ardern's rise to the summit of political life is a case study, because the challenges she has encountered are so very familiar. Unlike a number of women outliers holding office,

Ardern hasn't compromised her personality to suit her career; she hasn't become 'masculinised'. Assertive and effective in politics, she invokes a style that a broad spectrum of people, of both sexes, may seek in coming generations: the strong woman – as opposed to the strongman – who embodies astuteness, along with the ability to bring opposing forces together for a greater goal.

So much the better. Seeking counsel, weighing options with others to determine the most appropriate course of action beyond the limits of one's experience and personal conviction, doesn't sit well with a patriarch. It may be a woman leader's very essence, a strong suit that allows her flexibility to adapt to new or unforeseen circumstances. Absolute certainty and self-assurance could well be the 'strongman' politician's weakness, rather than strength.

Although Jacinda Ardern is a confident, strong woman, absolute self-assurance is not one of her character traits. This is where so many can relate to her, and learn from her rise to power. Ardern demonstrates that one doesn't need preternatural self-possession and an absence of self-doubt to succeed. Most people struggle with confidence issues, self-doubt or anxiety. Many of us have misgivings about fulfilling our potential, as well.

Few, however, share their struggles so openly, and in public, as Jacinda Ardern has done; fewer still in positions of power.

'I'm constantly anxious about making mistakes. Everything in politics feels so fragile,' she told a magazine interviewer. 'I do live in constant fear of what might be,' she says, acknowledging that her anxiety is 'just who I am'.[1] Her honesty, her frankness about such a personal issue is remarkable, almost unprecedented in politics.

At least as remarkable, in the upper echelons of public life, is Ardern's lack of cut-throat ambition. From the time she was touted as a leadership prospect for the Labour Party and a potential prime minister, she voiced her ambivalence towards assuming office. This is hardly unusual in politics: most politicians deny their ambitions emphatically, until the very hour of their leadership challenge. Ardern's qualms about New Zealand's 'top job', however, are sincere.

In a radio interview in June 2014, she described the prime ministership as an 'awful, awful job', and she meant it. Earlier, she had told a reporter that Helen Clark 'had to give up everything' for her position – and she was not willing to do likewise. She had 'no desire' to be prime minister.[2]

Ardern's experience of Clark's tenure, and the strain of her mentor's last successful election campaign in 2005, had left their mark. She describes that election year as 'extraordinarily stressful'. So stressful was it that her OE was as much a sabbatical as a means of broadening her horizons. She might have nurtured teenage ambitions of running the country, but her encounter with the ninth floor of the Beehive had left her cold.

It seems she was scotching any likelihood of her becoming prime minister by talking of her anxiety – shooting her prospects in the foot, as it were. A ministerial post would be more than enough for her, she had concluded – one where she could pursue policies for the betterment of children and families. In addition, she and Clarke Gayford wished to have a family of their own, and they were trying to conceive.

Perhaps there was one other factor holding Ardern back from taking high office, one so familiar to professional women. It is often referred to as the 'confidence gender gap', though the gap itself might have less to do with confidence and more with masculine bravado. For his testosterone level, daring or sheer foolhardiness, a man might seek a promotion well beyond his level of competence. He might take a swing at the seemingly impossible and in doing so, even find success. Women, however, as Ardern notes, have a 'natural tendency . . . to wait until they have every skill required'[3] before they put themselves forward for a higher position. She cites as an example Helen Clark's own 'questioning whether she had the credentials to . . . go and work at the UN'.[4] That is, after she had been a successful prime minister for three terms in her own country!

The confidence gender gap is discussed in the book *Lean In: Women, Work, and the Will to Lead.* Facebook COO, Sheryl Sandberg and Nell Scovell, cite a Hewlett-Packard internal report that states that while men commonly apply for jobs for which they only fulfil sixty percent of the criteria, women will, for the most part, apply for positions that they are one hundred percent qualified to occupy.

Perhaps this is feminine self-abnegation, or maybe it is a milder version of another factor that is worth discussing – imposter syndrome. In 1978, the academics Pauline Rose Clance and Suzanne Ament

Imes wrote in their paper 'The Imposter Phenomenon in High Achieving Women: Dynamics and Therapeutic Intervention' that 'despite outstanding academic and professional accomplishments, women who experience the imposter phenomenon persist in believing that they are really not bright and have fooled anyone who thinks otherwise'.[5]

While accepting the Gleitzman International Activist Award in a virtual conference from the Beehive in December 2020, Ardern said that although 'there was never a point in my life that I can recall where I thought, "I can't do that because I'm a woman . . . I have on many occasions thought, "I cannot do that because it's me". Imposter syndrome is real.'

And it counts against women's ambition and career progress.

Likewise does natural caution, which is obviously more associated with women than men. A conscientious woman tends to put pressure on herself, well beyond that which is reasonable. She doesn't want to let herself and others down, as she might see it, by not performing a task as she feels she should – that is, to the highest standard possible.

As much as her desire to have a family and her suffering imposter syndrome, it is this, perhaps, that held back Jacinda Ardern's ambition. The clue here lies in her own words. She describes herself as a 'high-guilt' person – guilt in this sense simply being conscientiousness turned inward. The fact is that while she brushes off most criticism, she acknowledges that 'if people attack me for not doing enough on behalf of the causes that I feel strongly about, those are the things I take to heart'.[6]

For all her misgivings, Jacinda had long harboured dreams of becoming New Zealand's prime minister – indeed, since her teenage years. An *Otago Post* article from April 1997 now seems quaintly prophetic: 'Jacinda for PM', declares the title, beside a photograph of a smiling Jacinda. In her school uniform, she is holding a large trophy for the speech competition she had just won. 'Champion speech-maker Jacinda Ardern,' the article says, 'has a huge goal – to be New Zealand's first female Prime Minister'. Jenny Shipley's ouster of Prime Minister Jim Bolger in December that year, meant Jacinda would never achieve one part of her goal. But despite all her qualms – her dread of the onerous demands of the job, her self-doubt, her feelings of inadequacy that she has so openly shared, her lack of feeling ready to assume the mantle of power – her ambition remained. And despite it all, her ambition to be prime minister was achieved.

For this, Jacinda is a role model for anyone who has a goal but lacks overwhelming confidence. Ardern says the best advice she has for young women is, 'When opportunities come up, say, "Yep, I can do that job." '[7] That is, don't wait until you feel ready – you may never feel ready, or be fully qualified in every respect. Don't let self-doubt, imposter syndrome, perfectionism, lack of confidence or misplaced conscientiousness undermine your ambitions.

Ambition, in any case, is not the only factor to determine success. Aside from talent – and, dare it be said, luck – circumstance and timing have their own way. The first in a chain of events that drew Ardern to the prime minister's office came in December 2016, when former Labour leader David Shearer resigned from Parliament.

17

Turmoil and Teflon John

David Shearer is, as his old school friend Phil Goff said, a 'special guy'. Before entering politics by winning the Mount Albert by-election in June 2009, he had spent two decades working for the UN in some of the world's most dangerous places, at the worst times: Somalia, Rwanda, Liberia, Kosovo, Afghanistan and Lebanon. He was the deputy special representative of Secretary-General Ban Ki-Moon in Iraq. Shearer and his wife Anuschka Meyer were named the *New Zealand Herald*'s New Zealanders of the Year in 1992, in recognition for their running one of Somalia's largest aid camps during the country's civil war. In 1994 he was awarded a Save the Children's International Award for Gallantry for his service in areas of conflict. A brave and capable administrator, Shearer had survived the bombing of Belgrade and an armed hold-up in Mogadishu.

It wasn't enough for him to endure the Labour leadership. Seemingly anointed for power – other candidates were passed over so he could take Helen Clark's former safe seat of Mount Albert – Shearer was one of several Labour leaders whose careers foundered after the Clark era. He was, as much as anything, a casualty of a party that turned on itself in opposition.

To say the Labour leadership was an uneasy crown after Helen Clark's retirement is an understatement. Phil Goff's tenure of more than three years between 2008 and 2011 resulted in an electoral defeat worse than that of 2008: the party lost nine seats and 6.86% of its party vote in the 26 November 2011 general election. Three days later, Goff fell on his sword, along with his well-regarded deputy, Annette King.

In the leadership battle that followed, three Davids ran: David Cunliffe, David Parker and David Shearer. Parker quickly withdrew, endorsing Shearer. Jacinda Ardern supported Shearer over Cunliffe and Shearer prevailed. Shearer's tenure, though, was blighted by the ambitions of his shadow ministers, most notably Cunliffe. After a little over a year and nine months, in which he faced accusations of indifferent performances in Parliament and before the media, he resigned the leadership, saying, 'My sense is I no longer have the full confidence of many of my caucus colleagues.'[1]

It was at this point that Ardern began to play her part in the upper echelons of the party. Along with fellow MP Megan Woods, she nominated her friend Grant Robertson for the Labour leadership contest in September 2013. Robertson ran against Cunliffe and Shane Jones. With strong trade union support – along with that of the rank and file – Cunliffe was victorious by a wide margin in the leadership poll. He fared no better, however, than his predecessor, and his tenure was shorter.

The 2014 general election sealed his fate. Hampered by political infighting – a political pundit made reference to 'bitter factionalism . . . turmoil and bloodletting' in the party – Cunliffe led Labour in what he later called 'the craziest and in some ways the most unfortunate campaign in recorded memory'.[2] Since 2008, Labour had appeared hopelessly overmatched, on the back foot to the popular prime minister, John Key, whose friendly image as a 'confident, laid-back, in-charge kind of guy' camouflaged the darker workings of his government – even when they were publicised. Released on the eve of the 2014 election, investigative journalist Nicky Hager's book *Dirty Politics: How Attack Politics is Poisoning New Zealand's Political Environment* created a furore, painting a picture of a government determined to win at almost any cost, hell-bent on destroying its adversaries. Senior figures in the National Party government, including Minister of Justice Judith Collins and John Key's senior media adviser Jason Ede, it emerged, were involved in covert campaigns of leaks and smears against the government's opponents.

Sensationally, information held by the New Zealand Security Intelligence Service was hastily declassified in July 2011 and provided to the notorious right-wing blogger Cameron Slater, who used it to discredit Labour Party leader Phil Goff. Slater, who was instrumental in mudslinging on behalf of the National Party, was shown to have close ties to Collins and Prime Minister John Key.

Despite the scandal for National surrounding Hager's revelations, the 2014 general election in September would be a disaster for Labour.

Jacinda Ardern again stood against Nikki Kaye for the seat of Auckland Central. Before the campaigning began, she had already suffered a setback. Early in the year, an electoral boundary redistribution had moved one of her key strongholds in the electorate, the traditionally left-leaning, arty suburb of Grey Lynn, to the adjacent seat, Mount Albert. Making matters worse for her was the lack of proper leadership and unity in the Labour Party, which meant policy indecision and general ineffectiveness. Weakened by infighting and the clashing ambitions of several party leading lights, Labour couldn't seem to gain traction on the issue of greatest concern to voters: the rising inequality in New Zealand. Undoubtedly, there was greater inequality in New Zealand than there had been thirty years earlier, and it should have fallen to the Labour Party to address it. David Cunliffe's bids to make inequality an election issue, however, came to little.

If anything, he made himself look foolish. Taking aim at John Key's $10 million mansion in the fashionable suburb of Parnell, Cunliffe attempted to paint the wealthy prime minister as out of touch with the average New Zealander. He might have been better served by speaking of Key's Hawaiian holiday home. When it was pointed out that he himself owned a luxurious property on Marine Parade in Herne Bay, one of the more sought-after addresses in Auckland, Cunliffe quickly backpedalled.

His attempt to appease women voters was more damaging. At a Women's Refuge symposium, Cunliffe began a speech by saying that he was 'sorry for being a man' in view of domestic violence. It was a perfect meme moment, before memes' popularity reigned. Howls of protest followed, then jeers and derision. Some New Zealand men saw it as an insult, others as a cheap attempt to curry favour. To women, it seemed inauthentic. Ultimately, this was Cunliffe's weakness: he didn't seem believable; unlike Key, he wasn't genuine to voters.

Ardern made the best of her situation, though with a confused policy direction from Labour, and with electoral boundaries redrawn such that victory was unlikely unless Nikki Kaye faltered. If the party couldn't convey clear-cut policies that would address voters' needs, she would address voters herself. She had #AskJacinda billboards erected, with space on them for voters to write questions for her.

It seemed to resonate – far better than her leadership's campaign. Still, though the result was even closer than in 2011, Ardern could not unseat her opponent. Only 600 votes separated the pair and now, she had lost twice to Nikki Kaye.

The Labour Party fared dismally, suffering an electoral rout – the worst result for Labour in a general election since 1922. The party attracted a mere 25.13% of the popular vote, against 47.04% for the National Party.

No politician likes losing, but Ardern took electoral defeat – twice, no less, in the same electorate – sportingly. She had lost by the narrowest of margins against the incumbent, one of National's best performers, and she would live to fight another day. She even made light of her lack of electoral success, in public. Speaking of her childhood in June 2014, and winning a seat on the board of trustees at Morrinsville College, she said with a laugh, 'And it was probably the last time I won an election.'[3] At any rate, with the enviable rank of five on the Labour Party list, Jacinda was returned to her list seat in Parliament after the 2014 general election.

Inevitably, there were calls for Cunliffe's head for the debacle of the electoral campaign. Within a week of the 20 September election day, Cunliffe announced a leadership spill (election). Astoundingly, given the election result and sentiment against him in the Labour caucus, he intended to recontest the party's top job. His deputy, David Parker, occupied this thankless, seemingly cursed post for a little over a month, while party leadership aspirants positioned themselves for a battle. Annette King, the veteran MP, former cabinet minister and former deputy leader under Phil Goff, took Parker's place as deputy.

One of those contesting the leadership was Grant Robertson, a stout man with friendly, astute features, who had been one of Jacinda Ardern's closest friends and confidants for more than a decade. At his campaign launch in the beer garden of the King's Arms, a popular Auckland pub that is now closed, he announced to no one's surprise, that Jacinda Ardern would be his deputy, his 'running mate'. Robertson's supporters welcomed her with a hearty cheer, the loudest ovation of the day.

Robertson admitted frankly that Ardern's popularity would be beneficial to his campaign. The premise of his leadership bid was, he stressed, a 'long-term project . . . to rebuild' the party – which meant, implicitly, a changing of the guard. To underscore the point, Robertson's supporters wore red T-shirts emblazoned with 'New Generation to Win – Grant 2017'. 'The new generation of leadership is going to have to take on the next generation of challenges,' Ardern said. She spoke graciously, saying she was honoured to be asked to join Robertson's campaign. Robertson was, she said, 'my colleague, but first and foremost my friend'.[4]

A close friend indeed, and a supporter. On an Edge radio afternoon show just a few months earlier, Ardern had jokingly replied to a caller that if she were forced to marry an MP, it would be Robertson – because he's gay. In another interview, she light-heartedly blamed him for introducing her to swearing and drinking, which she claimed she never did before she met him.

Robertson and Ardern shared a political partnership, in any event, that dated back a decade. They entered Parliament together – Robertson even took a stand for Ardern's place on the party list, though the matter was probably already decided. A journalist claimed years later that when Robertson was nominated for a seat in Wellington in 2008, he bluntly told the membership, 'I won't accept a nomination until Jacinda Ardern is on the list as well.'[5] The pair were, and continue to be, ideologically well matched; a formidable team.

Ardern could well have run for leader in her own right, and she had support from the public to do so. In the days following the 20 September election debacle, a poll conducted by 1 News showed her a clear favourite for the job: forty-one percent of respondents named her as their preferred Labour leader, while David Cunliffe trailed at twenty-four percent. Robertson polled a mere twelve percent, and Andrew Little could only manage a dismal five. This indicated an enormous swell of public confidence in Ardern, just as it evinced the public's coolness toward her party's male prime ministerial aspirants.

One year earlier, a TVNZ poll from Colmar Brunton suggested there was a modest fifteen percent support for her to lead her party. Twelve months and an election debacle on, the public mood was now clear: Labour needed a change, a new prospect who could speak directly to people on issues with sense and dignity – someone who could offer a viable alternative to Prime Minister John Key. None of the Labour prospects, other than Ardern, seemed to evoke much enthusiasm from voters.

In the wake of the 1 News poll, the network's Facebook page was flooded with comments in support of her candidature. Jodie Loos wrote, 'Jacinda Ardern for sure, Labour needs some young blood, because she's a woman, young, with fresh eyes.' The support came not only from Labour voters. Tania Oxton commented, 'I didn't vote Labour but I like Jacinda. She is young, vibrant, speaks knowledgeably about subjects and has a sense of humour. Labour could do with someone like her leading them.'

The Robertson–Ardern leadership ticket, which someone in the press dubbed 'Gracinda', had its detractors. Cunliffe, and some in the Labour Party caucus, labelled the pair 'beltway babes', a jibe that suggested they were insular; brought up within and cosseted by the political system. Ultimately, though, Cunliffe withdrew from the leadership battle, after a caucus meeting that Annette King would later describe as 'brutal . . . probably the toughest I've ever seen the caucus.' David Shearer, who was tipped to make a bid for a second stint as leader, made it clear he would not run. Finally, the contenders for the Labour leadership were Grant Robertson, Andrew Little, David Parker and Nanaia Mahuta.

The Labour leadership battle was a serious affair, almost as hotly contested as the general election itself. Fourteen rank-and-file meetings were convened, where thousands of party members heard the candidates speak. Of course, backroom machinations would be as much a factor in the outcome as the party vote. Under new Labour Party rules, forty percent of the votes are for party members, another forty percent are for caucus members, and affiliated unions are given twenty percent of the votes.

After one round of voting, it was clear that Parker and Mahuta were not in the race. Robertson was far ahead in caucus and membership votes, whereas in the affiliated union vote, Little, a former head of the Engineering, Printing and Manufacturing Union (EPMU), prevailed. It was this that saw Little edge out Robertson for the leadership, after the third round of voting, on 18 November 2014, by 50.52% to 49.48%.

Unquestionably, Robertson's impressive showing, much improved from his previous leadership bid, owed much to his star running mate. Jacinda Ardern had missed becoming deputy Labour leader by the slimmest of margins. So close was it, that if just one member had switched allegiance, the result would have been reversed. Losing narrowly was becoming painfully familiar to her.

The Labour Party would soon have reason to regret its decision. Little made the shrewd decision to keep Annette King as his deputy, which with her high standing in the party and acceptance by all its factions, served to consolidate party unity. But while Little revived Labour's esteem for a few months, he couldn't keep his party's approval rating above thirty percent, try as he might. His personal approval ratings – polls as to his status as preferred prime minister – were far worse.

As opinion polls told a sombre tale in 2016, there were whispers of exasperation in the caucus. A principled politician and determined campaigner, Little seemed to lack the charisma vital for a successful party leader. He was 'wooden', his detractors said, and not even oration lessons seemed to help much. He simply lacked the emotion, the sensitivity that would help him convey political messages to people. National Party opponents had long cast him as 'Angry Andy', taunting him in Parliament and media with the nickname. Its imputation had stuck.

Worse for Little was the calibre of his opponent. He was utterly eclipsed by John Key, undoubtedly the most popular New Zealand prime minister since Big Norm Kirk.

*

No one in Labour would want to face John Key at the peak of his career. A polished performer, Key showed none of the hubris or antagonism that dogged some of his National Party predecessors. He was approachable and engaging, a natural with the media. With a likeable persona – he smiled readily and often – Key and his down-to-earth banter appealed to the Kiwi liking for modesty. It showed at the ballot box.

New Zealanders' relationship with their leaders, it must be said, is quite unlike those of their siblings and cousins in Australia and the UK, where politicians are often viewed with contempt. Kiwis are far more inclined to show affection for their leaders; John Key was often mobbed when he appeared in public. Crowds of children and adults vied for a selfie with Key, who behaved with the aplomb of a veteran TV star.

A man used to success and comfortable with it, Key had already enjoyed a stellar career in business before he entered politics. Living in a poorer neighbourhood of Christchurch in a state house (public housing) and brought up by a widowed mother, Key had his sights set on winning early. In his twenties and thirties, he rose to the upper echelons of finance, enjoying the trappings of wealth and a jet-set lifestyle. Almost every week, he would travel to Wall Street as one of the world's eminent currency traders. His career exposed him to rarefied luxury and celebrity contacts. Early in his political career, he told an interviewer that Paul McCartney, whom he once sat beside on a Concorde flight, was 'a really good guy'.

Key's privileged life did not seem to show when he entered politics in 2002. Perhaps because of his humble beginnings, and in spite of his wealth – Key was reportedly the richest member of the House, and lived in his Parnell mansion – Key appeared so very normal. He was a Kiwi everyman, if you will – there wasn't a hint of the born-to-rule, patrician attitude in him. Key made little reference to his former role as head of global foreign exchange at Merrill Lynch.

Whether wholly genuine or somewhat cultivated – he was known as the 'smiling assassin' during his time at Merrill Lynch – Key's very ordinariness seemed to resonate with the public. His liking for rugby and unsophisticated tastes endeared him to a broad cross-section of the electorate and he had no qualms in telling a reporter his favourite film was Rowan Atkinson's spy spoof *Johnny English*, or that his favourite novels were John Grisham thrillers. His preferred music was easy listening, and his favourite artwork was a painting hanging in the Speaker's Lounge in Parliament, he said. His tastes, the reporter wryly noted, were 'immaculately populist, inoffensive and middle-of-the-road'.[6]

His public behaviour was, too – for the most part, anyway. He was happy to pose for a photo opportunity in barbecue chef's attire sipping from a beer bottle; he wore silly hats; a woman's magazine cover displayed Key cuddling a puppy. On election night in 2011, 26 November, Key appeared in front of television cameras, barefoot and wearing a blue polo shirt, to personally pay for Pizza Hut pizzas he had ordered. Business in Pizza Hut boomed that evening. Key won by a landslide.

For the Labour Party, Prime Minister John Key was a nightmare opponent. His uncomplicated appeal meant he could connect with the working class and aspiring middle class that were Labour's demographic stronghold. Key could sweep swinging voters into his net, and even poach traditional Labour voters, while his economic conservatism maintained the National Party's traditional vote bank.

For Jacinda Ardern and other social democrat politicians, Key's dismissive attitude to social and environmental issues was troubling. Under his National government, conditions for the underprivileged deteriorated. Child poverty increased, even as HSBC's Australia and New Zealand chief economist, Paul Bloxham, famously hailed New Zealand's 'rock star economy' for its outstanding growth.

In some respects, the deprivation in certain areas of New Zealand mirrored the Murupara of Jacinda Ardern's childhood. A report by the children's commissioner suggested poverty in New Zealand was more grave in 2015 than it had been in the 1980s: child poverty had doubled, and one in three children faced hardship. But when questioned on a radio programme about the issue in December 2015, Key laid the blame on the poor themselves, citing drug use and inter-generational welfare dependency as causes. Without explicitly saying so, Key implied the poor were junkies and inveterate freeloaders.

As Labour spokesperson for children, Ardern weighed in immediately. The prime minister's comments linking drug abuse to poverty were 'completely irresponsible', she said, adding, 'He offers no evidence in support and is demonising tens of thousands of families who are living in poverty.'[7] It was the classic social-democrat-versus-conservative debate, but the statistics leant firmly towards Ardern. The vast majority of children living in poverty had at least one parent in full-time employment, and by and large, drug and alcohol usage was no greater for their families than for the rest of the community – less, even.

Key's comments, consistent with others he made during his tenure, were, at least in part, a matter of playing to the gallery. In 2011, he said that 'anyone on a benefit actually has a lifestyle choice', claiming 'poor choices' were the cause of poverty.[8] And while such pronouncements were unhelpful in addressing the problem – children, who had little choice in the matter, went hungry just the same – Key knew his views would find favour among taxpaying voters.

With a decent majority, his way with the media and voters, and an almost clairvoyant sense of public opinion, John Keys never looked particularly troubled by Labour, while Labour's factional infighting and cloak-and-dagger leadership intrigues were to the National Party's advantage. Furthermore, on real, substantive issues – scandals, even – Labour could hardly make an impression on the prime minister. Nothing seemed to stick to 'Teflon John', as he had been dubbed by reporters in his first term.

Revelations in 2014 of dirty politics, skulduggery behind the scenes and meetings with unsavoury characters had little real effect on opinion polls. When a café waitress stepped forward in April 2015 to reveal that Key had repeatedly tugged her ponytail, despite her protests – surely a textbook case of harassment – Key dismissed the matter as 'a lot of fun and games'. There were 'lots of practical jokes' at the swanky Parnell café, he claimed. Teflon John's approval rating in the wake of what came to be known as 'Ponytailgate' actually increased.[9]

Key's popularity saw his reputation weather other undignified behaviour, which seemed only to reinforce his 'jokey blokey' persona. He camped it up, mincing down a catwalk dressed in a Rugby World Cup volunteers' uniform early in 2011 (Key later admitted he was being 'a bit stupid'). In October 2015, Key appeared on Radio Hauraki to play the game 'Thank You for Your Honesty', admitting that he didn't trim his pubic hair, had urinated in the shower, thought the Virgin Mary was not a virgin and confirmed he had never sent a 'dick pic'.[10]

There had been a string of other inappropriate actions from Key, ranging from what he described as a 'light-hearted joke' suggesting a Māori tribe might 'have him for dinner' in 2010,[11] to a radio show late in 2015, where he was interviewed in a cage and made off-colour references to prison rape. While another politician's career would have been marred by one of these gaffes, Key's reputation remained unblemished.

He was, indeed, recognised widely in New Zealand for his generally sound economic stewardship. With almost perennial good humour – he rarely showed his anger – he steered the nation through the global financial crisis, and saw it through the wholesale destruction and loss of 185 lives in the 2011 Christchurch earthquake. John Key seemed good for New Zealand's morale.

The only consolation for Labour was the inevitable effect of time. During 2016, the polls began to change. As his third term in office began its final year, the National prime minister was no longer the darling of the electorate he once had been. With his approval rating dipping from nearly fifty percent to below thirty-seven percent on some polls, the man whose finger always rested firmly on the pulse of the public mood knew his time was nigh. On 5 December, he held a press conference. At the conclusion of a gracious speech, he told the assembled reporters, 'I've got nothing left in the tank,' and said that 'at an appropriate time prior to the next election'[12] he would vacate his seat in Parliament. Deputy Prime Minister Bill English would replace him.

Three days later, on 8 December 2016, it was time for another leader to announce his retirement. The erstwhile Labour Party leader, David Shearer, had been called back to the United Nations by Secretary-General Ban Ki-Moon: he was to head the UN Mission in South Sudan (UNMISS), a peacekeeping mission. This meant his parliamentary seat, Mount Albert, would become vacant.

Jacinda Ardern was rumoured to have had her eye on the seat for some time. She and Clarke Gayford lived in the Auckland electorate, named after the peak of a dormant volcano that presides over the landscape, some seven kilometres to the south-west of the city centre. As soon as Shearer's announcement of his impending retirement became public, talk began of Ardern contesting the seat in a by-election. When the by-election was announced, she was first to throw her hat into the ring.

18

Star on the Rise

Mount Albert is a most unusual parliamentary seat. One might even call it a seat of destiny. More than a safe Labour electorate, it had only ever been held by the party – by four Labour members, one of whom died in office – since it was created in 1946. Helen Clark held the seat (and for one term the equivalent seat Owairaka) from 1981 until her retirement from Parliament in 2009. Robert Muldoon waged an unsuccessful, sacrificial-lamb campaign there in the 1954 election. Jacinda Ardern was to become the third prime minister to have contested Mount Albert.

Not much seemed to stand in her way of winning the seat. She and Clarke Gayford had moved into Point Chevalier, within the electorate, earlier that year; she was the sole party nominee – there wasn't even talk in the media of a rival for pre-selection; at least, not beyond Labour leader Andrew Little's hinting to media at a 'long queue' of potential candidates, as had vied for the seat in 2009 (no such queue materialised). More than this, within days of David Shearer's valedictory speech in Parliament on 13 December, Prime Minister Bill English announced that the National Party wouldn't field a candidate.

For a governing party not to field a candidate in a by-election is rare. English justified the decision by stating the obvious: Mount Albert was a safe Labour seat, and the National Party was focused on winning the general election later that year. Labour deputy leader Annette King was quick to seize on this, pronouncing the Nationals' stance 'gutless' and telling media that English, who had taken office just days earlier upon Prime Minister John Key's resignation, was 'running scared from his first test as a leader'. Characteristically, Ardern was more measured in her observations: 'By-elections are an opportunity to put up a set of ideas and vision, so to not use that opportunity certainly does strike me as surprising.'[1]

Privately, she was surely less surprised. The National Party had nothing to gain in the by-election – only funds to waste in a pointless campaign. Also, the party's prestige could suffer by contesting the all-but-unwinnable seat. Fielding a candidate against such a strong Labour personality as Jacinda Ardern could only paint a picture of a vulnerable government. A few weeks earlier, in a by-election for the Mount Roskill electorate immediately to the south-east of Mount Albert, Labour had given the National Party an electoral drubbing – a 'bloody nose', Andrew Little crowed. No leader would wish to undermine his government's morale, just months from the general election, with a second by-electoral loss.

Ardern stated her intention to contest the seat with her usual grace, staking her claim diplomatically. Along with living in the electorate, she pointed out to reporters that parts of Auckland Central, the electorate she had twice contested, had made their way into Mount Albert in a recent electoral boundary redistribution (this included her former stronghold, Grey Lynn). Running for the by-election would thus be 'logical'. It would also be, she declared, an 'exciting opportunity to be a part of a by-election'.[2]

For Ardern, there was far more to the by-election than excitement. First, party gossip had it that Helen Clark, who had held the seat before David Shearer, had wished her protégée to contest it in the by-election following her retirement. Labour leader Phil Goff had put paid to that, supporting his friend Shearer among the eight vying for candidature in Labour's preselection process. With his resignation, the opportunity for Ardern to run for Mount Albert finally presented itself.

More significant by far would be the boost to Ardern's political career, its security and her confidence, that winning Mount Albert engendered. Such was the value of a geographic seat to Ardern, that before Shearer's retirement she had intended to run for a third time in Auckland Central. 'It'll be nice to feel like I have the role of representing an area,' she said. 'I always like to feel anchored, I guess.'[3] Anchored emotionally, as well as politically.

Historically, a politician's mandate, her moral legitimacy, has stemmed from the support of local constituents, and for this popular election to Parliament was the litmus test. In Auckland Central, Ardern had performed creditably in her electoral showings. But while she had pruned Nikki Kaye's winning margin to just 600 votes, the narrowest in New Zealand's 2014 general election, she still had fallen short in her bid for a geographic seat. There are no second prizes in elections – except, perhaps, for list seats.

List seats, for the party vote, came into being upon the introduction of the MMP (mixed-member proportional representation) voting system in 1996, which was modelled on the German system. Unquestionably, MMP and its list seats has helped women make their way into Parliament. On both sides of the House, male incumbents largely dominated safe electorate seats until recent years, which meant women had to compete for more marginal seats – or those that are absolutely unwinnable.

Ardern and Kaye are cases in point. In 2008, the two women, noted for their talent within their parties, had to contest an unwinnable seat and a marginal seat respectively. Their contemporary Simon Bridges, also noted for his talent, was gifted the premier National safe seat of Tauranga for his first parliamentary campaign. It was a virtual shoo-in, and he has remained there, comfortably ensconced, since.

While a list seat has all the legal validity of an electorate or geographic seat, it doesn't quite have its prestige. List MPs – those who have never won a geographic seat, at least – are sometimes spoken of snidely in the House. It is difficult for them to escape the perception that the party has placed the candidate in Parliament, rather than the candidate taking a seat by merit of direct election. This a moot point in New Zealand politics.

Undoubtedly, Ardern's two list seats, and the other of her political appointments, had been decided on merit. All of the latter were, naturally, shadow appointments, the most prominent being spokesperson for youth affairs and associate spokesperson for justice (youth affairs), spokesperson for social development, and spokesperson for justice, children, small business, and arts and culture. The full list of her positions and responsibilities in the party up until the time of the by-election was more impressive:

Youth affairs 2008–11

Youth justice 2008–11

Employment 2011

Associate arts 2011, 2013

Social development 2011–13

Children 2012–

Police 2013–14

Corrections 2013–14

Arts 2013–

Justice 2014–

Small business 2014–

Auckland issues 2015–

Ardern had not, however, prevailed in any kind of election – not in adulthood, at any rate. From her presidency of IUSY to her list seats in two parliaments, her way seemed, to some critics, to have been paved for her. Direct election to a geographic seat would be a more satisfying achievement by far than appointment to Parliament by virtue of her party's decision.

This by-election victory would be less than absolutely satisfying for her, however. The decision of all centre-right and right-wing parties not to field candidates meant there was to be no real 'opposition' in the election; nor would there be any real ideological battle. From the social democrat Ardern and Julie Anne Genter from the Green Party to the Communist League, all the candidates were ostensibly on the left side of politics.

This meant a strange contest for the seat, ostensibly between Labour and the Greens – parties whose policies were markedly similar, and relations so cordial that they were subject to a memorandum of understanding. Endorsed in May 2016, the memorandum stated that the parties 'agreed to work together on matters of mutual interest', 'working cooperatively . . . to change the Government at the 2017 election'.

There was at least talk of an election battle, from one of the whole list of left and centre-left candidates: four independents, and seven fielded by minor parties. Of those, Geoff Simmons of the newly formed Opportunities Party was the only candidate with enough funding and backing to garner a serious number of votes. Simmons, a well-known economist, would 'prove', his party leader Gareth Morgan declared, 'to be a thorn between two roses [Ardern and Genter]'.[4]

A very small thorn, it would seem. A hardened political veteran, former Labour Party President Mike Williams described the 2017 Mount Albert by-election as 'the most low-key by-election I've ever seen'.[5]

The only obvious sign of the by-election was a cluster of the different candidates' hoardings in front of some trees, on a strategic corner where traffic passed on its way to Auckland airport. The simplest and most striking was Ardern's, which took pride of place at the centre. Such was her public profile, there was no need for it to state her full name. With a red backdrop and her photograph, it simply stated, 'Vote Jacinda on 25 Feb.'

Aside from these, 'there's hardly a ripple in Auckland', Williams said. 'I've been involved in by-elections since Onehunga in 1981 . . . but I have never seen anything like this.'[6] There were no polemics or heated debate; no dramatics or grandstanding, no controversy or recriminations, and not even a hint of rancour between the candidates.

Nothing, it seemed, would detract from the geniality of the two major contestants. Ardern and Genter struck up a very likely friendship during the campaign, even driving each other to their respective campaign events – carpooling, as Ardern described it. Of almost the same age, and with politics that were barely distinguishable, the pair had hardly spoken during their time in Parliament. On the hustings, they became close, sometimes handing out leaflets as they stood together. 'This isn't a fight to the death. It's actually a conversation, and we both have things to offer,' Genter told the media.[7]

A relaxed, friendly conversation was the most appropriate way to describe the organised 'debate' the pair had at the Satya Chai Lounge, an Indian street food restaurant and bar in Sandringham, along with Geoff Simmons. The trio sat together with the moderator, journalist Simon Wilson, at a rustic bench held up by tea crates, with a backdrop of jute coffee bags. It was 15 February, ten days from polling.

The event had the ambience and bonhomie more of a cool, left-wing book launch than a debate between candidates for a seat in

Parliament. Rather than contrasting policies and gaining the upper hand in verbal battle, which is the usual purpose of electoral debates, the breadth of common political ground was canvassed. Housing affordability and transport infrastructure were quickly flagged as major issues. The discussion served to illustrate the level of cooperation in a 'Labour government in coalition with the Greens',[8] which Ardern cited as a means to overcome several local transport problems. As if to illustrate the point, Ardern and Genter matched dance moves together.

On social media as well, Ardern and Genter's was the 'least bitter rivalry in New Zealand politics', a journalist observed, and the pair were only too happy to show it. There were selfies with funny faces together, and another of Ardern photobombing Greens leader James Shaw – Ardern's old friend from her London days – as he took a shot of himself with Genter for Twitter.

None of this levity detracted from Ardern's focus in campaigning, though. As usual, she set the highest standards for herself. Even without a credible opposition, so to speak, she told reporters she was 'certainly feeling a lot of pressure' to perform well. One of the campaign mantras, she later said, was 'Take nothing for granted; make every vote count and earn it'.[9] Jacinda had lost narrowly in two elections, and there was no way she would leave the slightest opportunity for defeat. She and her campaign workers doorknocked thousands of homes, made thousands of telephone calls to voters in the electorate, and convened no fewer than fifty-five street corner meetings and nine café meets. In fact, some 100 volunteers had a target of knocking on 5,000 doors each day for the campaign. As Ardern told reporters as the campaign came to its final day, 'We put in a huge effort.'

While the result of the election was a foregone conclusion, the extent to which Ardern would distinguish herself was a matter of great interest for pundits. For them, the ramifications of a big win were clear. A *Stuff* news headline seemed to crystallise the question that was on every political pundit's mind: 'Could Jacinda Ardern's star rise further on a Mt Albert by-election win?'

It was a question that surely weighed on the Labour Party leader. Andrew Little had visited the electorate several times in the week preceding the poll, lending his support to Ardern's campaign. The day before the by-election, he joined Ardern for a final public showing at the local Sandringham Road shopping strip, looking every bit the party politician with his sharp blue suit and copper-coloured tie. With Ardern's celebrity factor, the media paid particular attention to the event. There was the customary press-the-flesh, with Little's star list MP making her usual impression on the public. Her disarming warmth, her sincere charm worked its usual magic, delighting her supporters and thawing National voters' reserve. For this final outing of the campaign, she wore her 'power colours': a red blouse with black coat and skirt, and ankle boots.

Cameras followed. A reporter posed a ticklish proposition to the Labour leader: a strong showing from Ardern, it was said, could lead to calls from within the party for her to be appointed deputy leader. Little quickly rebuffed the suggestion, as did Ardern, who said such talk was 'just people trying to put pressure on me'.[10]

A strong showing was expected. But as the results poured in, in the early evening of a sunny Saturday, 25 February 2017, the magnitude of Ardern's victory soon became apparent. Ardern and her supporters had gathered at the Point Chevalier Bowling Club for the Labour post-election event, high with expectation. When the early counting figures came in, she could barely contain her nerves. Cameras followed her as she approached Little, who stood with a group of Labour Party functionaries in the car park. 'Looking good!' she remarked as she was shown the latest figures.

While her trademark smile was broad, her self-critical side was still evident, even in her moment of triumph. Ardern could not help but 'alternate between looking at margin and turnout' – as if she could be held responsible for voters' apathy, a few months from a general election, where most voters saw the by-election result as a foregone conclusion. But Ardern shouldered responsibility, as if by her work alone she should have achieved more. Her leader, thrilled by the resounding victory, was amused. 'I knew you'd be nervous . . . a knife-edge result,' Little quipped.[11] Ardern had won in an electoral rout of the field, receiving an astounding 76.89% of the vote. Julie Anne Genter received 11.45%, and Geoff Simmons 4.56%. She had exceeded her best expectations.

Her victory speech to party workers and functionaries in the humble club room of Point Chevalier Bowling Club was heartfelt, her expression elated. Standing by her side was Little, whose face had lost its usual solemnity, replaced with a beaming smile. Her voice at times brimming with emotion, Ardern thanked numerous members of her campaign, entertaining her supporters with her usual humour: 'I learnt never to have a street corner meeting not on a corner. If you have a street corner meeting . . . mid-way down the street, people may come up to you and say "Oh, my goodness, what has number 32 done? Why are you protesting there?"' [12]

She finished her speech with a vow that at the time sounded like humdrum political rhetoric, but now seems prophetic: 'We will work even harder in September [for the general election] when we will turn all of this into party vote to change the government.' [13]

Now, Ardern had the grass-roots victory that had so long eluded her, and it was sweet. A photographer captured Clarke Gayford holding her in a tight embrace, a bunch of flowers in hand, delight on his face as if the two were the only people in the room.

For the public, the victory was equally significant. It had long been clear that Ardern possessed the voice, a rare humanity that could cut through the white noise of political discourse that had left New Zealand voters tuning out. Now the voters had spoken, the party machinery – the caucus, the shadow cabinet; the powerbrokers and union delegates – had no excuse to overlook the young woman from Morrinsville. Senior party members could no longer dismiss Ardern as a 'beltway babe'. And with steady rumblings of discontent at Andrew Little's performance, there was a chorus in the media and serious talk in the party backrooms of elevating Ardern to the deputy leadership.

Only, the woman herself seemed hesitant.

19

For the Party

In the aftermath of the by-election, Ardern described speculation of her becoming deputy leader in a Radio New Zealand interview as a 'distraction', saying it was 'not an issue'. Her party leader, Andrew Little, made it clear there was 'no vacancy' in any event, and said, 'Don't expect any change.'

The incumbent deputy leader, Annette King, was even firmer on the matter. A Labour stalwart who had loyally served as deputy for Phil Goff and Little, King bridled at the suggestion she should stand aside for Jacinda Ardern. Such talk, the 69-year-old former minister said, was 'ageist' and 'sexist'. No one had questioned her competence. She was younger than Winston Peters, the New Zealand First leader, it was noted, and nobody had suggested he retire or stand down on account of his age. An article in the *New Zealand Herald* even claimed King 'went a little bit Trump' in claiming the media was against her. Without actually quoting her, the reporter stated she 'questioned what Ardern could offer that she did not, other than relative youth'.[1]

Calls in the media, in various guises, to elevate Ardern to the deputy leadership were nothing new. David Cunliffe had been asked by reporters in 2013 why she hadn't been selected as deputy leader. Then, the question was fobbed off: Cunliffe simply said she had been 'considered' for the post. Now, with a general election in sight, and Labour as far as ever from government, the question had far greater urgency – in the party and the media.

Perhaps the media's pressuring King was a cunning attempt, too, to light the powder keg beneath the Labour leadership that journalists had been complicit in placing there. If they thought their reporting might blast a rift between prominent Labour identities, though, they were to be disappointed. Loyalty and friendship – and shared history

between women of different generations – meant the media provoca-
teurs were to be denied the sensation they craved.

*

The first thing anyone notices about Annette King, apart from her
shock of short blonde hair turned white, is her well-shaped, hazel-
brown eyes – a small legacy, perhaps, of her mixed European and
subcontinental heritage (her Ceylonese great-great-grandfather was
the first of his people to emigrate to New Zealand). Her gaze is pene-
trating, but in a charming way. King is one of those rare individuals
whose larger-than-life persona brings people together, entertaining
and enlivening, rather than dominating.

She can dominate when the need arises, however, as it does sometimes in politics. The veteran of innumerable parliamentary encounters, King more than held her own on the floor, throughout her career.
The woman hailed as an icon by Helen Clark (King returns the
compliment) could, it was claimed, 'control [the Labour] caucus with
one pinky finger'.

King entered Parliament in 1984 when David Lange's Labour
Party stormed the government benches, held for nearly nine years by
Robert Muldoon. By the time she left politics, she was the longest-
serving woman member of Parliament in New Zealand. Apart from
the three years from 1990 to 1993 – she lost her seat in the 1990
general election in the backlash against Labour's Rogernomics debacle – King was in the thick of New Zealand national politics. She held
several key cabinet posts in the Clark government: health, police,
transport and justice. In the party, as well as deputy leader under Phil
Goff and Andrew Little, she was a member of the Moderating
Selection Committee from 1996.

King made her presence felt in Parliament, and early. In the
twilight of his political career, Muldoon, a man who would sniff a
political threat as a hound does a fox, declared that the young former
dental nurse 'put the horror in Horowhenua', her electorate.

She certainly found ways to get under the National Party strongman's skin. One could barely feel sorry for the former prime minister,
with his habit of hurling insults and making drunken, offensive

comments. One of these was directed at King and a colleague. Muldoon noticed King speaking late one evening in Parliament with her fellow Labour MP, Fran Wilde. 'Muldoon looked across and said, "I know who you're going home with tonight," the implication being that Fran Wilde and I were lovers,' King recalls. 'We both laughed at him.'

King had her revenge. One of her early mentions in parliamentary debate, an interjection, shows the wit she would become famous for. Muldoon was on the receiving end of it:

Mr Shirley: I invite the House to picture the scalp of the Leader of the Opposition [Sir Robert Muldoon] being delivered like the head of John the Baptist, with no heir apparent.

Annette King: No hair!

Mr Shirley: There is no heir – the Opposition is bald of all talent . . .[2]

King had a way of tackling discrimination against women in Parliament that was equally humorous and good-humoured. Parliament's billiards lounge, with its five full-size billiards tables, was a male bastion that endured until the late 1980s. Men would sit in musty leather chairs, chatting and taking pot shots of the sporting, social, and political kind, the atmosphere thick with smoke and testosterone. Women, King remembers, were not welcome. Rather than complain, she decided to play a few games of billiards – badly, she would later say – to make a point.

Her act of defiance in 1984 with two fellow woman parliamentarians, likewise new to the House, created more of a stir. Women's toilets in Parliament, the women found, were far too few and out of the way for convenience. The trio decided to take their own affirmative action. Armed with screwdrivers late one evening, they removed the 'Gentlemen' signs from the toilet doors, replacing them with felt-tip, hand-written 'Unisex' signs. The next morning saw quite some humour, but consternation and embarrassment among the men, King recalls, because 'the men's urinals weren't removed at the same time'.

Humour, and her ability to not take politics personally, helped King maintain her reputation and sanity, in the brutal arena that is

New Zealand national politics. Jacinda Ardern reflected on her attributes: 'What I observed is the fact that she would fight the good fight . . . push hard but then move on. She can let stuff go . . . I think that's seen her through a lot.'[3]

Ardern recalls one instance where she gained some insight into this peerless woman politician that would be useful for her own career. 'I remember watching Annette in a really robust exchange in the House once . . . and then . . . maybe 20 seconds later . . . Annette has got her iPad out and she's playing a game . . . [She has an] ability to push hard . . . and just manage whatever stress she had . . . whereas I would stew over something. I really love that about Annette.'[4]

Despite besting many a foe on the opposing benches, King managed somehow to do so without rancour, while maintaining respect. She was the 'glue' that was 'key in holding things together'; 'a party person' who never sought the party leadership. Perhaps most significant about King is her generosity. She was only too happy to act as the mentor to a whole generation of younger Labour parliamentarians, the most prominent of whom is Jacinda Ardern.

By the time Ardern won the Mount Albert by-election, she and King had been close for years. Jacinda wasn't the least shy in praising her party's deputy leader. In a radio interview in 2014, she said that King 'is awesome, she's like the aunty everybody wants in their life'.[5]

The pair first met in early June 2008 in London. King was staying with the then high commissioner to the United Kingdom, Jonathan Hunt, while she was visiting in her capacity as New Zealand's health minister. Hunt invited Ardern over to the high commissioner's plush residence in Kensington for drinks. With both Ardern and King being gregarious, personable women sharing similar political leanings and social concerns, it was inevitable that a friendship would spark. The pair hit it off immediately. Ardern was vivacious and bubbly, King recalls.

Naturally, there was more to the evening than socialising. King finally had the opportunity to get to know the young Labour woman whose dedication and talent had so impressed party movers and shakers. It was important that the younger woman pass muster with King. King was a long-standing member of the Moderating Selection Committee, an influential senior member of the party. However

assured the women's rapport, her blessing would be needed for
Ardern's high ranking on the Labour Party list, which would see her
enter Parliament just months later.

Naturally, Ardern received that blessing, though when she first
entered Parliament, the two women were not especially close. The
challenges of an entirely new life as a member of the House, though,
meant Ardern gravitated toward the older woman.

So too did a whole generation of new Labour members. Along
with Ardern, Grant Robertson, Chris Hipkins and Megan Woods –
each of whom would become cabinet ministers in Ardern's government – confided in and sought the guidance of 'Aunty Annette'. In
this, they felt comfortable, their trust assured. It was well known in
party circles that King was loyal. She stayed aloof from the cloak-and-
dagger machinations that felled many a politician of her era; anything
said to her in confidence would remain with her.

King would also become Ardern's moral and emotional support.
Early in her career, Ardern was hurt by the nasty comments about her
in social media, that 'she was a lightweight, she was all teeth', King
recalls. King was sympathetic, but firm, telling her simply, 'Don't take
any notice of it.'[6] *Illegitimi non carborundum.* She would tell stories of
her early days in Parliament that put Ardern's worries in perspective.
Her message was clear: Rise above it. I survived, and so will you. King
might have been a 'kind aunty', but she was not an overindulgent one.

Politics, and a need for support, drew Ardern to King, but their
relationship would soon deepen, spanning their professional and
personal lives. It was in a mutual friend's crisis that their attachment
was truly forged. That friend was Darren Hughes.

Among the most promising young Labour politicians of his time,
Darren Hughes was something of a wunderkind. In the 2002 election, Hughes won the nation's most marginal seat, Otaki, at only
twenty-four years of age. He held the seat for two terms. Like Ardern,
Hughes was the baby of the House, though he was four years younger
when he gave his maiden speech.

More remarkable was Hughes's interest in politics at an age when
most children were playing with toys – as he said wryly, his involvement in party politics began 'well below the legal age'. When he was
still in primary school, at the age of eight, he met his local member,

whose close friends and campaign managers, Lloyd and Marea Falck, lived next door. The keen little boy asked if he could help post flyers into letterboxes. His local member was Annette King.

The eight-year-old Darren was more than simply passing time with King. Utterly captivated, he 'sat in awe at her feet', her friends recalled. Annette stayed close with Dazza, as she and his close friends called him, throughout the years, mentoring his career in the party through Young Labour. He was elected to Parliament in what was ostensibly her old seat. He boarded in her home in Wellington, when Parliament was in session. She was his political aunty; perhaps as close to him as any real aunt could be. Just as Annette King was his aunt, Darren Hughes was referred to by party insiders as 'the son Helen Clark never had' – without doubt, a rare honour.

Hughes was seen as a future leader; his rise in the Labour Party was as prodigious as his talent. With boyish good looks and ginger hair, repartee and debating skill, Hughes loomed large in the House. At the age of twenty-five, he was made junior whip. He became a minister at twenty-nine in Helen Clark's government (albeit holding a minor portfolio: statistics, and was associate minister for social development and employment). In opposition, he was given the education portfolio, and looked certain to take a senior cabinet position when Labour was returned to power.

That is, until an unfortunate incident in March 2011. The details of the incident are still unclear, though the media spoke of witnesses, early in the morning of 2 March, seeing a distressed, naked young man on the road near King's home in Hataitai, Wellington, where Hughes stayed. The man was quickly intercepted by police, and an investigation ensued.

As soon as an unnamed MP's involvement in the incident became public, speculation in the media abounded. Its prurient interest saw a resort to some outrageous tactics. King said a journalist from the *Herald* threatened that he would report that she herself was seen in her dressing gown and slippers, chasing a naked man down the street, if she would not grant him an interview. Journalists and a photographer tried to trick their way into King's home, telling her cleaner they were allowed into Hughes's bedroom. Refused entry, they traipsed around the exterior of the home, taking photographs. The *Dominion*

Post ran a story under the scurrilous headline, 'Former Police Minister in Sex Scandal'.[7]

Hughes, a private man who never spoke publicly of his sexuality, was mortified. At first, he stayed holed up at King's home. But as the media began to swarm, he fled Wellington for Auckland. There, he sought refuge with his good friend and supporter, Jacinda Ardern.

All the while, the police investigation plodded along. On 8 June the police announced that they would take no further action in relation to the incident. In terms of a substantive issue, the matter petered out entirely – the naked man questioned by police did not wish to comment; his family likewise, requesting that the media respect their privacy. There was not even a hint of civil action and public recriminations, the well-beaten path for those turned away by the police. Hughes, who maintained that he had 'done nothing wrong' from the beginning, was vindicated.

It was too late for his career. After weeks of 'frenzied media attention', Hughes handed his resignation to Labour Party leader Phil Goff. Goff initially rejected it. A day later on 25 March, he announced at a hastily arranged press gathering that Hughes had resigned from Parliament.

A party man through and through, Hughes later explained: 'I could see that our political opponents . . . would use it as a battering ram . . . I thought the best thing for the party – it was election year – was to get out of the way.'

Jacinda was with her friend Dazza throughout the ordeal, harbouring him from the media storm in her Auckland apartment. As she spoke with him at length, she admired his 'superhuman ability' to view his plight philosophically. For 'not one moment did I hear any anger about the situation he was in', she later said.[8]

Through their shared ordeal with Hughes, Ardern and King's friendship became more intimate. On a whim, Ardern would buy clothes for herself and King, such as the occasional jacket that would suit them both, one in each of their sizes. Then, when they were attending sittings of Parliament or a function, they would 'have to make sure we didn't wear [the jackets] on the same day', King said.

Ardern's description of King as a favourite aunty might sound unlikely in a political friendship; it would probably be contrived from another politician, but it is honest and accurate. Annette truly became like family to Jacinda.

The older woman even took an interest in Jacinda's romantic life in a manner that perhaps Jacinda's own mother wouldn't have dared. She knew that Jacinda loved children, that she yearned for a stable relationship; it worried her that Jacinda didn't have a partner. Annette played matchmaker, arranging dates for her with eligible bachelors she deemed worthy. Annette was 'protective of Jacinda', she later admitted. When Jacinda finally met Clarke, Annette fretted that he might be unsuitable for her, that the man with a former reputation as a party boy might not be serious. She recalled saying to her husband Ray, 'I don't know whether he's the right one for Jacinda.' She later said she was 'totally wrong. He's absolutely the right person for her . . .'[9]

The best of relationships are challenged by fate; patterns have a habit of repeating, in different forms and guises, in ways which confound. Six years after Darren Hughes fell on his sword, it was Annette King's turn to make her own sacrifice for the party, though under very different circumstances.

At the end of 2016, with public approval of the party in the doldrums, the caucus was becoming restive. A year earlier, shadow cabinet minister Phil Twyford had given King his hint that it was time she stepped aside, so Ardern could take her place as deputy leader. King spoke with Andrew Little, who it seems was somewhat noncommittal on the matter.

Now, with the election in sight, the press weighed in heavily. Audrey Young from the *New Zealand Herald* suggested in January 2017 that, with the 'slate of strong young women' in the Greens, and anticipating new talent making its way to the front bench in the National Party, among them Nikki Kaye, 'Little and King would be foolish not to rethink the deputy's job'.[10] Ardern had been in the running for deputy party leader, even in the first few months of Little's leadership. She and King spoke openly themselves about which of them should become the deputy leader. Ardern recalled that it made 'absolute sense' for King to be appointed. She knew what Little and the party heavyweights understood: the caucus needed King's experience, her influence and diplomacy to help bind it together, after years of factional splintering.

With the 2017 election in view, however, and with Little's personal approval ratings sinking, a change of tack seemed inevitable. Labour simply could not afford another electoral shipwreck that might well see it overtaken as the major opposition party. Internal researchers looked desperately for a new direction for the party.

Their results were sobering, while encouraging. Unmistakeably, the research concluded that Little's appeal was far greater to the public with Ardern beside him. Little, a politician who, though sincere, had difficulty connecting with voters, seemed to bask in Ardern's warmth, her natural affinity for people. The research simply confirmed what was already known, inside the caucus and in the community at large. With Ardern's resounding victory in Mount Albert, pressure mounted within the party, and in the media, for King to step aside for the younger woman.

There were factors other than youth and charisma in Ardern's favour. She had a strong base in the nation's commercial capital, Auckland (the 'juggernaut of votes', according to one political journalist); she was the face of the Labour Party for younger voters; and Andrew Little was an unabashed fan. Unfortunately, the press's meddling took away the initiative from Little. It would have been far better for King, as for everyone, if the issue had been handled in party backrooms, rather than in the newspapers. A veteran fighter who had survived three decades of triumphs and disappointments, King came out swinging when reporters surrounded her. On 27 February, the Monday after Ardern's by-election victory, King made it clear to all and sundry she had no intention of resigning her post.

She was justified in defending herself. Perhaps only time and perception – and as she suggested, ageism and sexism – counted against her.

Little found himself in quite a bind. In view of King's excellent performance and her dedication to the party – not to mention her standing in the caucus – demoting her would have been sheer political folly. Neither would there be any nudge from Ardern: she simply would not have contemplated challenging her friend and mentor. Political correspondent Patrick Gower said he thought it would be 'easier to move Mount Albert than move Annette King' from her position as deputy leader.

The matter eventually came down to private discussions between King and senior members of the party – and of course, her husband Ray and her friends. Some of the discussions were with Ardern, who remained in close contact with King throughout the ordeal. Ardern was 'uncomfortable', she says, about the media suggesting King should resign, and even more so for 'the pressure it was putting on my friend who was doing a great job . . . I felt like somehow I was being used as leverage against her.'[11] The leverage was effective: within a week King had had a change of heart.

Ardern was aware that King would announce to the media that she would stand aside as deputy leader of the party; she knew, also, that King would publicly give her blessing for Ardern to take up the role, which she had already privately given. She was not prepared, however, for King's more dramatic announcement.

It came in a conference call meeting on the morning of Wednesday 1 March. With the caucus on the line listening, King announced she would resign as deputy leader of the party. Further, to the surprise of nearly everyone apart from Andrew Little, she said that at the forthcoming election, she would retire from politics altogether.

Ardern was shocked. King had not even hinted at her intention to leave Parliament. Ardern had expected, as had so many in the caucus, that King would stay on in a cabinet position – probably as health minister – to bolster the party with her experience. The blow of the news left her 'close to tears . . . because I felt in part I had contributed to [King's decision to retire]'.[12] Ardern only had a short time to compose herself before she fronted the press alongside Little.

Little and Ardern appeared on camera with Radio New Zealand reporter John Campbell after the announcement. Ardern's expression was uncharacteristically subdued. While she spoke of the issues of housing affordability and child welfare, she said she was 'saddened' by the party's loss of King, whom she described as a 'stellar member of Parliament'. Little was at pains to stress that King, a 'strong-willed woman', had not been pushed. He confirmed he had tried to persuade her to stay on in a frontbench position, 'because she's fantastic'.[13]

At any rate, with King's blessing, and the backing of Little and the caucus, Ardern's path to the number two spot in the Labour Party was a *fait accompli*. She would be formally appointed – unanimously, of course – at a caucus meeting on Tuesday 7 March, which made her the youngest deputy leader in Labour Party history.

Ardern's elevation to deputy leader had not been without cost. But by the metric of political power plays and party leadership battles, it was a bloodless, almost genial, coup. Indeed, most remarkable about the whole affair was that Ardern's friendship with King would remain untarnished.

Ardern's hesitancy in taking power until it was virtually thrust upon her, her refusal to engage in backroom intrigue to further her position and her thoughts for the welfare and feelings of others would be intrinsic to her rise to power. All are confoundingly rare in politics. Likewise, her decent behaviour would set her apart from many of her colleagues, some of whom could be quite objectionable, especially under the cover of parliamentary privilege. Often, she was a target for political thugs. Her manner of handling their mudslinging and general nastiness speaks of her humanity, as much as her discipline.

20

Pull Up the Ladder, or the Woman?

'Zip it, sweetie.' Surely this sentence, directed at Jacinda Ardern in Parliament, is a clear example of male chauvinism. Patronising, sexist and belittling, it is the kind of speech that brings Parliament into disrepute. The words were spoken in anger by a minister under pressure from Ardern and several of her colleagues in a question time in November 2012, but this hardly excuses such behaviour. The remark might well have attracted parliamentary censure – if it hadn't been spoken by a woman: Minister of Social Development Paula Bennett.

Instead, 'Zip it, sweetie' became almost a meme, a tagline voted Massey University's winner of the Quote of the Year Competition for 2012. Dr Heather Kavan from the university's School of Communication explained its appeal succinctly: 'There's something almost primal about two women fighting . . .' No doubt. And men, too – which is why we have competitive boxing and mixed martial arts matches.

Ardern laughed off Bennett's snideness, tweeting, 'Kids in the gallery could be forgiven for thinking they were watching a *Hairspray* revival.'[1] A few months earlier, she had endured sniping from a prominent National Party member, Maggie Barry. Barry suggested Ardern was not qualified to raise a question on paid parental leave, asking, 'How many kids do you have?' When the opposite side of the House erupted with indignation, Barry added, 'Don't be so precious, petal.'

More than five years later, Ardern would face off against Bennett – deputy leader of the opposition against deputy prime minister. The media looked forward to the parliamentary fire-fight with glee.

The first salvo from the National Party, on 15 March 2017, didn't come from Bennett, however. It came from Ardern's nemesis in Auckland Central, Nikki Kaye, and it was an extraordinary, *ad hominem* attack. Ardern's elevation to the deputy leadership was a 'superficial, cosmetic facelift', Kaye said. While there would be 'a whole lot of photo ops' with Ardern's image 'across every billboard', she had 'absolutely failed our generation on her first day in the job'; she had 'cut and run', Kaye declared. Barry, by now conservation minister, followed up with her own verbal broadside, saying Kaye had 'nailed it': Ardern had 'achieved almost nothing', referring to the 'punishment' that Annette King had suffered for her loyal service.

If 'Zip it, sweetie' was a *Hairspray* revival, this was *Mean Girls 2*. The *New Zealand Herald*'s headline on 15 March, 'Gloves off: National MPs target Jacinda Ardern in series of attacks', encapsulated the drama in the House. Yet it didn't highlight one crucial fact: the members attacking Ardern were women. An opinion piece the following day suggested this was a calculated attack by a government concerned at Ardern's popularity. There seemed no better way to attack her than to denigrate her popularity itself as 'all show and no substance'.[2]

Ardern refused to be drawn into a slanging match. She made mention, however, of her old agreement with Kaye to only speak of issues, and refrain from personal attacks during campaigning, noting that she had 'stuck to that'. Obviously, and for the first time, Kaye had not. Ardern held firm to the high ground, saying, 'I'm going to stick with the way I like to do politics'[3] – debating the issues, rather than attacking the personalities.

Things were little better with the National's Judith 'Crusher' Collins, another of Ardern's detractors in the House. Collins, a woman with a steely glare who seems to relish confrontation, was known as Crusher from her time as police and corrections minister, when in 2009 she proposed legislation not simply to impound the cars of illegal street racers, but to crush them. She revelled in the sobriquet – indeed, she seemed to cultivate the image it implied. An inveterate political infighter, she was at the centre of smear campaigns with the right-wing blogger Cameron Slater, which came to light in 2014 with Nicky Hager's book *Dirty Politics*. Her notorious hacked emails published in the book revealed she referred to Ardern as 'my little pony'.

Ardern loathed being called a pony but didn't rise to the bait. Perhaps she didn't want to dignify it with a response. Unquestionably, the treatment meted out to her by senior government politicians – fellow women politicians, no less – had the flavour of bitchy high-school bullying. While it might be tempting to suggest the women involved had been used as proxies by their male colleagues, wary of a backlash should they target Ardern, the spontaneity of at least some of the attacks, and the way the National Party women seemed to relish going on the offensive, suggests otherwise. So much for sisterhood.

The worst Ardern would do in return would be to offer questions in Parliament, and in the media, that turned up the heat on the ministers. She focused on flippant remarks Collins had made on poverty and families in need in October 2016. Earlier, when challenged by a reporter for thinking everyone was nice, she had offered her as an example of someone who she didn't think was nice, but admitting that Collins would 'hate to be described as nice',[4] anyhow. Likewise, she posed prickly questions to Paula Bennett about failures in government training programmes and employment, saying Bennett was 'bouncing all over the place with jobs', making 'ludicrous'[5] claims about the job market.[6] Ardern stuck to the rules of propriety, and her vision of a different way of conducting politics. She plays the ball, not the man or woman.

Ardern's experience with her woman colleagues is far from unusual – it is, indeed, far too common. So prevalent is the phenomenon of women campaigning against other women as they rise in seniority, there's even a name for it: queen bee syndrome.

Queen bee syndrome is a strange, almost perverse counterpart of the discrimination and sexual harassment women have suffered since time immemorial, highlighted in recent times by the #MeToo movement. On one hand, women tread their way around male sexual predators from the shop floor to the boardroom. And on the way upwards, they contend not merely with unsympathetic men and systemic discrimination, but sometimes with women above them who seem to resent their rise, and are hell-bent on stopping it.

Marilyn Waring has spoken of this phenomenon. Ardern has referred to her discussion of the issue in interviews. Waring, the teen-age Jacinda's idol, saw it was necessary for a woman to get her 'foot in the door . . . [for] the next feminist coming behind'.[7] Waring, the 'amazing politician [from] the seventies,' Ardern recounts, 'said there [are] two types of women in this world. There are ones who fight so hard to get where they're going, they shove their foot in the door, and they pull through as many women as they can. And there are others who pull their foot out and close it shut.'[8]

What is it that leads the latter kind of women to stop their junior sisters from progressing in the workplace? Using another metaphor, why would a successful woman, whose climb to positions of power has been fraught with challenges far beyond those of her male colleagues, try to pull the ladder up behind her?

The concept of queen been syndrome has been controversial since it was suggested by G. L. Staines, T. E. Jayaratne and C. Tavris in the book *The Female Experience* in 1973. There are numerous studies that support its existence, that corroborate anecdotal evidence of women feeling victimised at work by women managers. One, by the Workplace Bullying Institute in 2017, suggests that while most workplace bullies are men, women bosses largely direct their hostility towards their female staff. The survey shows that in the sample of respondents, two-thirds of victims of female bullies were women.

Explanations for the queen bee phenomenon are fairly logical. The root of it, of course, is competition. As Ardern says, '[Women] feel a sense they had to work really hard and fight really hard to get where they are, and then they feel a sense of competition amongst other women.'[9] Perhaps a woman manager might feel that the personal sacrifices she has made to reach her position distinguish her from her colleagues. Helping them climb the corporate ladder may well seem a stretch too far for her generosity – she may even feel she would let herself down by doing so. Thus, some women who climb the corpo-rate ladder, breaking through the glass ceiling themselves, could pull up the ladder behind them, and reinforce the glass ceiling for others below them.

Some experts say that queen bees exist, but are far less common in most workplaces than people might believe. They suggest that queen bee behaviour is a woman's response to sexism – that is, she distances herself from other women as a defence in an inherently sexist environment, so she won't be targeted.

Whatever the prevalence of queen bees in a normal workplace, Ardern seemed to have run into a small swarm of them on the floor of Parliament – women who were in the upper echelons of their party, well ensconced in the Beehive.

Parliament, at any rate, is no ordinary workplace: if there is a queen bee to be found, politics is a most likely place to find her. Narcissists, obsessive compulsives, Machiavellian types, authoritarians, and those with paranoid tendencies, abound in Parliament. Queen bees might fit nicely in at least half of these categories.

Hence, for every Aunty Annette – and former parliamentarian Fran Wilde (now Dame Fran), whose encouragement and mentoring brought Annette into politics – there are others who, like the former UK Conservative prime minister Margaret Thatcher, revel in being the most prominent woman in Parliament, and are quick to stifle female competition. Thatcher, an archetypal queen bee, made her cabinet a veritable old-boys' club. Of all the cabinet ministers Thatcher appointed between 1979 and 1990, only one, Baroness Young, was a woman – and she had been raised to the peerage on the advice of Thatcher's predecessor as Conservative Party leader, Ted Heath. Other competent women were sidelined.

At any rate, New Zealand's Parliament, as with most legislatures almost anywhere, was founded by men, to suit men's needs, proclivities and expectations. A clear illustration would be that New Zealand's sittings were originally timed between the tupping (breeding) and the lambing seasons so as to leave members, mostly farmers in the early years, free for their farm work. Typically, just before lambing season, legislation that was pending was rushed through the House, a fact lamented by the more conscientious parliamentarians.

To say that most women find New Zealand's Parliament repellent – as women do about other parliaments throughout the world – is an understatement. Members find themselves in verbal battles in the House that sometimes descend into exchanges demeaning the institution as much as the members involved. After watching parliamentary question time, many competent women leaders recoil from the mere thought of spending days in the debating chamber.

Even the hardiest of women describe Parliament as a hostile workplace. Judith 'Crusher' Collins is scathing of the 'toxic work environment' in Parliament which is, she declares, 'the worst environment I have ever worked in' (she was a lawyer before entering politics). It is 'similar to what I imagine a 1920s boys' boarding school to have been', she says, comparing it to *Lord of the Flies*.[10]

Ardern's thoughts on this are subtler, though she speaks of the general unfriendliness of Parliament, and politics in general, for women. Aside from 'systemic issues', Ardern told Supriya, women are less prevalent in politics, in part because it 'is perceived to be an ugly place, where there are personal attacks, where you sacrifice a lot, [from] a woman's perspective . . . for what's perceived to be little reward, because . . . there's very few people who thank a politician, and I understand that'.

In her interview with Supriya, Ardern posed a question that is for the next generation to ponder: 'So how do we attract women, who don't . . . seem as obviously motivated by power, to be motivated into . . . a profession where that seems to be the only selling point?' She offers a wise suggestion: 'For me,' she says, 'it's about reshaping what it is to be a politician, and demonstrating that you don't have to change your character traits, you don't have to change your personality, that you can be motivated by . . . a different set . . . of goals, and that actually you can take a bit of ego out of it as well. And so it's modelling a different way of doing things.'

She went further, giving advice that is important to all women who might aspire to leadership – especially to those who may feel that the old model of leadership runs counter to their very nature. 'My message to girls and women', Ardern told Supriya, 'would be that empathy and compassion and generosity are all important leadership traits, and that they should not be deprioritised against assertiveness and confidence . . . I think too often, because we've had fairly consistent role models in leadership roles that have had fairly consistent traits, we perhaps think that the personalities that we have don't suit environments like politics, when that's absolutely untrue. And I have said often, it takes courage to be an empathetic leader.'

Spoken as it was in autumn 2019, Jacinda's final statement on the topic takes on greater significance, in view of the 2020 COVID-19 pandemic: '[I] think if anything, the world needs empathetic leadership now, perhaps more than ever.'

21

Turning Point

If there was a single defining point in Jacinda Ardern's life, it would be on her thirty-seventh birthday on 26 July 2017. That moment would also see a change in fortunes for the Labour Party, as if the fate of the party and hers were interwoven. As she would say in the weeks afterwards, 'This will go down as the most extraordinary period of my entire life.'[1] Just days after her birthday, she would be propelled to the forefront of public life in dramatic fashion. Not that she expected this, much less engineered it.

The month of her birthday was eventful enough. July began for Ardern with celebration, and much drama in between. The formal 2017 parliamentary election campaign period had begun a week earlier, on 23 June, though the parties had been jockeying for position for many months. As elsewhere, New Zealand's three-month regulated period (for election advertising expenses) prior to election day is the final lap of a long, gruelling race, which usually begins when politicians return from their Christmas and New Year holiday, and shake themselves out of their summer torpor.

As the pace of campaigning gained momentum, Ardern, along with her senior Labour colleagues, was kept busy, though with muted hopes. Party heavyweights and rank and file alike knew the indications for the party were gloomy. Even with Ardern in the deputy leader's position, which at first had given the party a breath of life in the opinion polls, Labour's polling was back to lacklustre. The party appeared almost certainly to be headed for its fourth consecutive electoral defeat – and a sound defeat, at that. The mood in the Labour camp was sombre.

Jacinda's mood was sombre for another, personal reason. Her sister Louise, who, like a few of her fellow New Zealanders, had found the expatriate lifestyle to her liking and made London her home, would soon be married. She and her partner, Ray Dussan, had lived together in London for ten years; they had a three-year-old daughter, Isabella, and were expecting their second child. Their wedding was scheduled for the beginning of July, in a relaxed village an hour from Barcelona, almost as far from New Zealand as could be (Spain is its antipodes). Jacinda had already given her apologies: in an election year, she simply couldn't afford to be out of the country, even for her sister's wedding. Louise was understanding, but sad that Jacinda wouldn't be with her.

Jacinda herself was filled with regret. Two powerful, compelling responsibilities wrenched her in opposite directions – her family and the party: an almost impossible choice for a woman whose loyalties to both were fundamental to her. As Louise's wedding day approached, Jacinda's distress got the better of her. She spoke with her shadow cabinet colleagues and, most importantly, her party leader, Andrew Little. She later wrote a Facebook post on the matter: 'I knew I'd made a massive mistake. I remember telling Andrew, and he totally agreed, "you have to go".'

Her change of plan would be all the sweeter for Louise, she decided, if it was a surprise, so she quietly booked a flight, arriving the day before the nuptials. Without announcement, Jacinda arrived at the sunny villa where Louise, Ray and their guests were staying. In the mobile phone video she took of her reunion with Louise, she is seen walking into the villa, having a few quiet words in Spanish with a staff member to find out where 'Louisa' was, before making her way to the poolside. There, Louise sits on a lounger, talking with her partner and friends. Jacinda calls out to her in a forced whisper, 'Louise!' Louise leaps to her feet in astonishment, the sisters embrace, tears mingling with laughter.

Jacinda, always the woman who is there in times of need and crisis for others – for celebration or mourning – did her duty. For this event, as with so many others, she was everything the situation demanded: maid of honour, sister and representative of the family. The following morning, Louise and Jacinda set off to the village in search of a makeup artist and hair stylist. Jacinda supervised as Louise was readied for her big event. At the 6 p.m. wedding, Louise wore a simple lace gown. Beside her, walking down the aisle in a teal dress, was Jacinda, cracking silly jokes so Louise wouldn't cry and ruin her makeup.

Jacinda shared a heartfelt message on Facebook: 'Today I walked my beautiful sister down the aisle, and I feel so privileged and lucky to have been able to do that.' It accompanied the video of Jacinda surprising Louise at the poolside.

Jacinda would soon have her own surprises, which would change her life utterly, in a matter of weeks.

*

The jockeying for position before the polls is most prominently played out in the media between Labour and the National Party in New Zealand. But the jockeying between the minor parties is no less fierce. It might, indeed, be more so. Every election is a fight for the minor parties' survival, with Labour and the Nationals taking the vast majority of seats in Parliament between them; the number of small parties makes for slim pickings. If a minor party's vote falls below the mandated cut-off of five percent and it doesn't win a geographic seat, it is banished to the electoral wilderness for the following three years, which may well amount to political oblivion. And so, the public duelling between the Green Party and New Zealand First started not long after campaigning began. In a TVNZ interview, the Greens' Metiria Turei took aim at Winston Peters, saying his was a 'very racist approach to immigration'.[2] Peters returned fire later, claiming the Greens had 'racially separatist policies'.[3]

Numbers, as much as ideology, were behind the fracas. The polls in late June and early July showed the two parties faced a tight contest for third place in the election: the 1 News–Colmar Brunton poll, taken in the first week of the month, had the two parties level at eleven percent of the popular vote.

Counting against the Greens was their media profile, their perceived blandness beside the colourful Peters. The Greens had only managed to capture one percent of media coverage in the 2014 election, and it reflected at the polls. Powerful though his contempt for journalists might be, Peters' preternatural talent for attracting media attention gave him a decided edge at the hustings.

Perhaps it was this that led Turei, the co-leader of the Green Party, to take a bold decision to speak out; to engage in a public confessional, if you will. It was anyhow to have consequences not just for her and her party, but for Labour and its leadership as well. Hers is a sobering case of how in politics, a few well-placed – or poorly placed – words can have a profound effect, far beyond what one could imagine at the time.

Labour might have been prepared for Turei's bombshell, but it could do little to stop it, or mitigate its effect. The Greens and Labour were tied by their memorandum of understanding, in which a 'no surprises' clause said they had to 'give each other prior notice and the details of major announcements and speeches'. Neither party had the right to vet the other's speeches, though Labour would surely have wished it did. Labour advised against Turei's disclosures, for what it was worth.

Before the home crowd of the Greens' annual general meeting on 16 July 2017, Turei revealed 'the lie I had to tell to keep my financial life under control',[4] which was that she had deliberately withheld information from the welfare authorities, Work and Income New Zealand, about her domestic purposes benefit. In the early 1990s, she had, she said, concealed from the department rent money she received from flatmates, so her benefit would not be affected. She and her young daughter needed the benefit to survive, she told her party faithful.

In short, Turei openly admitted she had committed welfare fraud. Her motives for doing so were ostensibly to start a dialogue about the punitive nature of welfare in the country, and how it condemned ordinary people to abject poverty. Doubtless, she hoped to snare votes, too, bringing the Greens to centre stage of the media's election coverage.

In this, she was initially successful. Her revelations won her sympathy: many people recognised the plight of single mothers on welfare, the difficulties of surviving on meagre benefits. She was supported publicly by some figures from the left, just as she was condemned by those on the right. For a while, the Greens polling surged: the party polled as high as fifteen percent in the Colmar Brunton poll in late July.

Part of the surge came at Labour's expense. Andrew Little, who disapproved of Turei's stance, telling reporters, 'We can never condone breaking the rules',[5] was one of the first to hear news of his party's dismal ratings. It came on a Wednesday morning, 26 July – Jacinda Ardern's birthday. Ardern had just attended a Tawa Rotary Club campaign function in Wellington, where she was presented with a birthday cake – cheekily, with blue sponge hidden beneath the icing, blue of course being the colour of the National Party. The club members waited expectantly for her to 'eat the opponents', phones in hand to take a photo for a meme or social media sensation. They were to be disappointed. Ardern enjoyed the joke but dodged the gag, leaving the eating, more symbolically, to party workers and supporters.

From the Rotary function, Ardern went on to a meeting with Little at Weta Digital, the pre-eminent visual effects company, to discuss the controversial 'Hobbit law' – officially, the Employment Relations (Film Production Work) Amendment Act 2010. The law, which Weta's Sir Peter Jackson had championed prior to the filming of *The Hobbit*, nullified actors' rights to bargain collectively. While Ardern, as with the rest of Labour, had opposed it, she was among those in the party most interested in seeing *The Hobbit* made in New Zealand, which it was, in 2011.

Partway through the meeting, Little's phone vibrated in his suit pocket. He ignored it for a time. Curiosity got the better of him, though, as it invariably did. He plucked it out, opening the message for a quick sideways glance. It was the results from an internal Labour poll. Support for the party, the message revealed, had plummeted to twenty-three percent. It was a 'double-take moment',[6] Little later said. He was disconcerted, but seasoned party man that he is, he carried on with the meeting.

Later, in the car on the way to the office, the gravity of his situation descended on him. It was the depths of a Wellington winter, a wet and blustery one even for the Windy City, bleaker for Labour's woes. Eight weeks from the election, and despite his best efforts, Little knew he might lead his party to one of its worst defeats in history. Nothing he had said and done had reversed the party's fortunes. Even John Key's departure from politics hadn't helped, as Labour had anticipated. Key's anointed replacement, Prime Minister Bill English, was an experienced but dry politician, lacking Key's charisma and appeal. Labour had hoped to capitalise on his weaknesses, but he seemed to fare remarkably well on the campaign trail, leading Little as preferred prime minister by a wide margin.

Back in his office Little called Ardern for a meeting to discuss his thoughts. He was frank with her. 'I don't think I can do it,' he said. The polls were bad, he told her, and he asked her if she thought that his stepping down would make any difference. He then made a most unusual suggestion: 'I'm wondering whether you should do this job instead.'[7]

Ardern had seen the internal poll message earlier, and already sent him an encouraging though 'Pollyanna' kind of message, she later said, to 'hang in there'. As they sat together, she gave him advice that is very characteristic of her – advice she would have given herself under the circumstances: 'You must stick at it and carry on'; Little 'should stay the course, because stability matter[s]'.[8]

Unconvinced, Little said he would talk to his other cabinet colleagues, which he did.

More bad polling news came on Friday, with word of the TVNZ poll, to be released the following day. It told the same tale as the internal Labour poll: the party was down to twenty-four percent support, which meant that the internal poll was no aberration – save for an electoral miracle, Labour was headed for an ignominious defeat. Little and Ardern briefed all the caucus members personally on the poll, knowing the alarm it would cause that weekend.

Saturday and Sunday brought the matter to a head. Little honestly, but unwisely, perhaps, admitted in interviews with Radio New Zealand political reporters Corin Dann and Guy Espiner that he had raised with his senior colleagues the 'valid option' of resignation following the poll results. At a fundraising function held at Ardern and Clarke Gayford's Point Chevalier home on Saturday night, Little and Ardern managed to keep the mood upbeat for the event, but a senior party member gave him the tap on the shoulder he was expecting. There were no recriminations – he hadn't done anything wrong. Another simply said, 'We've got to do what's right for the party.' Little didn't argue.

22

The Worst Job in Politics

Leader of the opposition is the worst job in politics, pundits say – in the Westminster system, at least. The post entails a good deal of responsibility, but no real power, and as the New Zealand Labour leaders' short-lived careers between 2008 and 2014 demonstrate, a number of colleagues are always waiting in the wings, readying themselves to push their leader into the orchestra pit and claim centre stage when they falter – all for the good of the party, of course. The role is especially thankless when the party is riven with bickering and infighting, such as it was for much of the first half of the 2010s.

At any rate, nothing in the Labour Party's fortunes up to this point in 2017 was unusual for New Zealand politics. Underperforming leaders of the opposition are as much an element of the country's social landscape as are victorious captains of the national rugby team, with its seventy-seven percent winning record. Even Helen Clark had been in a similar position to Andrew Little. It was in May 1996. Then, Labour had shown a miserable sixteen percent support in a TV3–CM research poll, against New Zealand First's twenty-five percent and the ruling National Party's forty percent. Labour leader in opposition, Clark had failed to connect with voters, just as Little had twenty-one years later. With her rating for preferred prime minister at a pitiful three percent, she faced a revolt from senior MPs, little more than four months from the 1996 election.

Then, under more dire circumstances than those of 2017, Clark 'faced down' the challenge to her leadership. According to Annette King, one of a delegation of five shadow cabinet members who visited her office on 27 May 1996 to ask her to resign the leadership, 'Helen just looked at us, she stared at us, and it was obvious she was going nowhere'. The five backed down; the party was beaten in the election convincingly.

Pre-APEC meal, Seoul Universty, 11 August 1998. Closest to camera (*on right*) Christina McCombie and Jacinda Ardern.

Left to right: Elene Ly, Paul Lowe (recipient of the Prime Minister's Science Teacher Prize), Jacinda Ardern, Virginia Dawson and an APEC youth festival student, 16 August 1998.

The late Tania Lineham (1966–2018), the other lead teacher on the trip (recipient of the Prime Minister's Science Teacher Prize, 2015), with Jacinda and (*right*) Nicholas Moore.

Tania Lineham with other teachers in Seoul.

Labour MP Jacinda Ardern performs her DJ set in the Thunderdome during the Laneway Festival, Auckland, 27 January 2014.

Labour MP Louisa Wall (*centre*) is applauded by fellow Labour MPs – (*from left to right*) David Shearer, Trevor Mallard, Maryan Street and Jacinda Ardern – after the third reading and vote on the Marriage Equality Bill at Parliament House, Wellington, 17 April 2013.

MARTY MELVILLE/AFP/GETTY IMAGES

The new leader of the Labour Party speaks at her first press conference at Parliament in Wellington, 1 August 2017.

DAVE ROWLAND/GETTY IMAGES

The proud mentor: former Prime Minister Helen Clark is greeted by Jacinda Ardern, Leader of the Labour Party, at the party's general election campaign launch, Auckland, 20 August 2017.

PHIL WALTER/GETTY IMAGES

Jacinda chatting with children at the launch of 'Vector Lights on Harbour Bridge', which featured a ground-breaking renewable-energy technology-powered light show, 27 January 2018.

DON EMMERT/ AFP VIA GETTY IMAGES

Jacinda Ardern holds her daughter Neve, as partner Clarke Gayford looks on during the Nelson Mandela Peace Summit at the United Nations, 24 September 2018.

New Zealand Prime Minister Jacinda Ardern speaks during the General Debate of the 73rd session of the General Assembly at the United Nations, New York, 27 September 2018.

TIMOTHY A. CLARY/AFP VIA GETTY IMAGES

Jacinda Ardern comforts Naima Abdi at the Kilbirnie Mosque on 17 March 2019 in Wellington, following the Christchurch mosque shootings.

Whakatane Fire Station, 10 December 2019: Jacinda Ardern meets the first responders who helped the injured in the White Island volcano eruption the day before.

Prime Minister Jacinda Ardern gives one of her regular COVID-19 updates in 2020.

New Zealand chef Will Mordido, founder of Buko pop-up restaurant, with his mother, Fe Mordido, and Jacinda Ardern after the annual Labour Party Dinner, 25 November 2019.

OFFICE OF THE PRIME MINISTER OF NEW ZEALAND

Labour leader Jacinda Ardern delivers her victory speech at Auckland Town Hall, 17 October 2020.

LYNN GRIEVESON – NEWSROOM/GETTY IMAGES

Dressed casually in jeans and trainers, the re-elected prime minister talks to reporters at a café near her home in Auckland, the morning after her landslide victory, 18 October 2020.

Andrew Little was a very different person to Helen Clark, and a very different leader. The manner in which he dealt with his leadership woes was highly unusual – if not unprecedented – in New Zealand politics and, indeed, in politics elsewhere.

At first, he did what was only to be expected, consulting senior party figures after the poll shock of 26 July. One of those was King, his former deputy, for whom he had always had great respect. Her advice was measured, thoughtful. She didn't advise him to resign. She did, however, tell him the sentiment of the party, and laid out his two options: he could 'stare it down', and stay as leader, which was risky, she said. Equally risky was the other option, one that had been floated by numerous party figures. That was, he should stand aside and let Jacinda Ardern take the leadership because, she said, 'the indications are that Jacinda could pull it off'.[1]

Regardless of King's thoughts on the matter, Ardern stood by her party leader throughout, loyally. Many politicians would find her actions during this period baffling. Little was wounded politically – at least as leader. Most in Ardern's position would have publicly professed their allegiance to their stricken party leader, while canvassing support for a leadership challenge. The more Machiavellian might have waited, positioning for a challenge after the inevitable loss on election day. The latter course of action is essentially how Helen Clark was elected Labour leader in 1993, against her well-liked party leader, Mike Moore. Jacinda Ardern, in contrast, seemed to campaign against herself.

Her refusal to confront the issue did nothing to evade it. On each subsequent day after her 26 July discussion with Little, she was approached with increasingly urgent pleas from senior Labour figures to take over the reins of the party. Each time, she rebuffed them. Reportedly, seven times in all she was approached – a number that gives her demurring an air of biblical renunciation. To every appeal from her colleagues, she recalled, she said 'No, no, no'.

A major part of this was her ethics – loyalty to her leader. Another factor was her anxious feeling that she was not ready, that she could not live up to the expectations thrust upon her. Despite all the indications of her competence and popularity, it seems she felt she might not do as good a job as she should. Typically, she was worried that she might disappoint those who had vested so much hope in her. In fact, she had expressed just such feelings, in an interview with *Next* magazine, weeks earlier. She candidly spoke of her anxiety, her lack of desire to lead the party or become prime minister: 'I hate letting people down,' she said. 'I hate feeling like I'm not doing the job as well as I should.'[2]

Perhaps this was simply Ardern's overdeveloped sense of duty, which, coupled with her stringent self-assessments, made her a rare politician indeed. In politics, where evading responsibility, passing the buck, is *de rigueur* – even a defence mechanism for professional and personal survival – here was a woman who seemed prone to shouldering it, perhaps even beyond what would be reasonable.

Ironically, while her own sense of duty – and the anxiety it evoked – seemed to be holding her back from taking up what others saw as her duty to the party, it was ultimately duty to the party that brought Ardern into the limelight.

*

On Monday 31 July, the media smelled blood. The Labour caucus roiled with debate and discontent, some of which leaked to journalists. Reports emerged that senior members of the party were plotting to remove Little, just as others quoted Ardern as saying she was not thinking about a plan B, that she supported him. Political commentators' analyses were damning. Little's revelations of his offering to resign were as damaging as the party's lamentable polling itself, they said. There needed to be clarity for Labour.

Still, Andrew Little did his duty for the party, aware of his miserable situation. He attended a campaign launch for the electorate of East Coast Bays in northern Auckland, a conservative seat that Labour candidate Naisi Chen had no credible hope of winning. He made every effort to hide his downcast look, but none too successfully. His features, which have a naturally grave kind of set, bore a sad expression.

Afterwards, Little and his staff headed back to Auckland city centre, to the Stamford Plaza Hotel, where he met with his chief of staff, Neale Jones, chief press secretary, Mike Jaspers, and Willie

Jackson, a former Alliance politician and radio personality who was running for Labour for the first time. The group sat in the lobby bar and over a beer, discussed the party's downward spiral in the polls. They weighed Little's options.

Unlike so many leaders when circumstances and their party turn against them, Little was realistic, pragmatic. As he spoke with his three associates, he telephoned party whip Kris Faafoi and Annette King, among others. Their message was solemn: 'This is getting difficult, this is getting really difficult.'³

Ardern was more reserved. A few kilometres away, in Point Chevalier, she took Little's call while she and her friends enjoyed a late birthday celebration at her home. As they ate chicken and sipped tea, she made it clear to them she didn't want to be leader, but if she was asked to take the job, she would do it. And that is evidently the message she conveyed to Little.

A Labour insider reportedly gave an edgy, dramatic summation of Little's last days at Labour's helm: 'In the corner of the Labour caucus room is a locked box with a whole lot of sharpened knives. Little pretty much went and unlocked the box and said, "Pull out your weapons and stab me." '⁴ No one pulled a metaphorical weapon on Andrew Little, as events would transpire – there was no need. But if he had held more concern for his personal ambition than the party, he could very well have defended a leadership challenge. His massive union support, which had led him to prevail in the 2014 leadership contest with Grant Robertson, meant he could hardly be removed by coercion. In a strange turn of fate, the woman whom he and others had prevailed upon to abdicate for the sake of the party a few months earlier, Annette King, was now guiding him to do likewise.

Little finally made his mind up, in the hotel at half-past ten that night. He spoke with his wife Leigh on the telephone. Like Jacinda, Leigh told him he shouldn't quit, that he could 'get them over the line'. Andrew was firm, though, telling her simply, 'It's over.'⁵ He didn't yet tell his colleagues he was standing down, simply asking his team to cancel all his morning appointments.

The following day, 1 August, Andrew Little, Jacinda Ardern and their Labour colleagues flew together from Auckland to Wellington, a trip from the nation's commercial centre to its political capital. A common weekly ritual for politicians, the flight, at a little less than 500 kilometres due south, takes barely an hour. No sooner have you climbed to flying altitude, perhaps catching glimpses of Mt Taranaki's snow-capped peak through the long, white cloud cover, than you are headed back to terra firma.

Ardern would sometimes use her time in those lofty altitudes to relax, to sit back and flick through a magazine; indulge herself in a way that she simply wouldn't normally allow herself. In this flight, she could not comprehend the shifts in the land below, with her at their epicentre, changing her life forever.

At the gate in Wellington airport, Little was buttonholed by a sole journalist, who asked him if he was going to offer his resignation. 'Um, no, look, these issues are for a separate discussion,' he said. He fumbled with further questions, disengaging as smoothly as good grace would allow. In his government car, however, he broke the news to his colleagues. He was quitting.

From there, the Labour Party machinery went into overdrive. Neale Jones's first call was to Ardern, who, like Little, was on her way to Parliament from the airport, but in a taxi. It was a simple call, with a message made brief by the urgency of timing: she was going to be the leader of the party, Jones told her – that very morning.

Ardern sighed, as if a tremendous, unseen weight had been lowered onto her shoulders. She was hardly prepared; she had packed only her usual clothes for a week in Parliament. She had less than an hour to ready herself for the announcement.

As Ardern's new advisers – her former leader's old advisers – left her to plan her speech, Little was giving his final appearance as leader of the Labour Party. Flanked by party whips Kris Faafoi and Carmel Sepuloni, he made one of his best television appearances. He stood in the second-floor caucus room in Parliament, before a cluster of microphones and the media, his considered, husky intonation punctuated by the clicking and whirring of digital camera shutters.

It was a hastily planned press conference; reporters were unusually excited, blurting out their questions over one another even more than usual. In announcing his resignation, Little said, 'the party and the people who we are campaigning for would be better served by a new leader'. 'I have absolute confidence in Jacinda,' he declared, saying there would be a 'fresh face and a fresh voice . . . a fresh approach' from his party.[6]

If breathtaking speed is any indication of power, the force propelling Ardern to the party leadership was irresistible. Little's press conference to announce his resignation was scheduled for 10 a.m. He walked away from the reporters almost directly into the caucus meeting at 10.30. All the arrangements for Ardern's unanimous election had been made in advance, naturally; the ratification of her leadership at the caucus gathering that followed was swift. Afterwards, Little was joined by his wife Leigh at his now former office, to pack his belongings into cardboard boxes. By 2 P.M., he was gone and eating lunch with Leigh, the way made absolutely clear for Ardern.

As Little was clearing out his office, Jacinda Ardern herself fronted the media. Wearing her power colours, a red blazer over a black dress, she strode through Parliament's stately Edwardian Grand Hall to its wood-panelled Legislative Council Chamber, her team in a phalanx: the new deputy leader, Kelvin Davis, the first Māori in the position, beside her, Grant Robertson bringing up the rear. She entered first, standing in front of a red Labour Party backboard, decorated with silver fern party logos.

'Everyone knows that I have just accepted – with short notice – the worst job in politics,' she said. 'But I welcome this job.' She planned to 'take stock' for seventy-two hours to contemplate her campaign, which she promised would be characterised by 'relentless positivity'. She was, she said, 'privileged and honoured to be the leader of the Labour Party'.

The new Labour leader spoke with authority, appearing confident; almost relaxed, which is astounding given the suddenness of her appointment. But it was in her answers to questions that the gathering truly saw the kind of leadership they could expect from Jacinda Ardern. She smiled, sharing quips with journalists whom she addressed by their first name, charming and surprising some of the most cynical commentators of New Zealand politics.

She and Winston Peters shared a liking for single malt scotch, Ardern said, in reply to a query how she might get along with the crotchety New Zealand First leader. Only the day before, Labour's Stuart Nash had stated publicly that changing leader would be a 'disaster' for Labour, a reporter pointed out. Red-faced, Nash was about to step forward to address his *volte-face*, when Jacinda interjected: 'Stuart has already acknowledged that he was wrong,' she said. It would have been hard not to laugh. When a reporter questioned her ability to handle a fractious alliance with the Greens and New Zealand First, she said, 'I used to be the president of an international youth organisation that had members from Lebanon, Palestine and Israel. I think I can do this.'[7]

Witty politicians are not uncommon in New Zealand, and the country has had more than its share of eloquent leaders. David Lange, Labour prime minister (1984–9), was both. He famously silenced an interjection at an Oxford Union debate in March 1985 where he spoke against nuclear weapons, saying, 'If you hold your breath just for a moment . . . I can smell the uranium on it as you lean forward!' Ardern was different. She made no attempt at eloquence – she uttered the odd 'um' here and there. Her cleverness, though, was engaging, the kind that relaxed the press gallery: she disarmed rather than engaged in the usual parry and thrust with journalists. The mood of her delivery, its friendliness that makes the listener feel that somehow he or she is being spoken to directly, is rare. One has to look hard to find another politician with such a direct approach to communication.

Perhaps one must not only look far, but quite some distance into the past. The closest parallel with Ardern's press conferences might not be a woman, or even a New Zealander. Perhaps her charm over the media, the manner and ease with which she reaches out to reporters and even the public directly, are somehow reminiscent of one of the twentieth century's greatest names: US president John F. Kennedy. Kennedy was the first president to address the public directly on a regular basis. If he were in power today, he would probably use social media as effectively as Ardern.

Ardern's first appearance as Labour leader gave the nation a foretaste of her many press conferences and social media posts: their sincerity, sense of humour, simplicity, an unusual humanity that in other public figures might seem mawkish or feigned. She showed an utter lack of fear of revealing herself: 'Mum and Dad are going to get a surprise,' she said, telling reporters she had yet to inform her parents of her promotion. For a people known to trim and weed out tall poppies, this informality, this expression of being overawed by her elevation, was endearing.

Perhaps just as endearing was Clarke Gayford's post on social media, from Australia. Directly after Ardern's speech he tweeted a picture of himself on a boat with a colleague, both clad in scuba gear, the sea in the background: 'Have been underwater filming all day off Sunshine Coast, I miss anything?'[8]

23

Woman of Mettle

Open, patient with journalists (sometimes to the point of indulgence), authentic and approachable as Jacinda Ardern may be, there are limits to her charm. A reporter would find them less than one day after she became leader, over a key feminist principle – one that goes to the very heart of women's rights.

Perhaps best described as a practical feminist, Ardern might be a feminist in the same way as she was a Mormon: feminism is simply a part of her, unobtrusive as it is intrinsic. Strong, independent, accomplished women who might be classified as benevolent matriarchs are to be found in her family tree as in her career: Gwladys Ardern and Kate Wiltshire, Helen Clark and Annette King. Nevertheless, she has had to deal with the gamut of issues affecting women, plus the added strain and magnification of her life in the public eye.

Ardern is acutely aware of what her women predecessors, Clark and Jenny Shipley, understood. Shipley herself commented, 'If Helen Clark and I took the bait every time someone fusses about our hair or our glasses or our clothing, we'd spend a lot of time on it.' Add to that minor sexist infractions, which Ardern shrugs off as good-humouredly as she does personal jibes. And consider people's attention, which is a valuable commodity in politics, not to be wasted on trivialities.

When, on a television panel in August 2015, the former rugby league coach Graham Lowe described Ardern as 'a pretty little thing', there were howls of disgust. It was a comment straight out of a 1950s black-and-white television variety show. The presenter, Hilary Barry, tweeted, 'Rest assured he won't leave [the studio] without bruised shins.' Ardern simply replied, 'I thank you Hilary. I hope your shoes were pointy.' She let the matter rest there, later saying, when the furore over the comment had settled down, 'I didn't think it was a big deal. It just exploded around me. I thought the response [Lowe] got was disproportionate.'[1]

Even when she was offended, Ardern refused to rise to the bait. A couple of months before Lowe's gaffe, in June 2015, she found herself on the receiving end of a sexist remark – in Parliament, no less. When she asked Minister for Small Business Craig Foss a pointed question, to 'confirm . . . that there was nothing new in the Budget for small business other than . . . the survey he just announced', Foss replied with cringeworthy, patronising smarm. 'I welcome the member's megawatt smile and sparkling brown eyes,' he said.[2]

Along with Ardern's ire, Foss earned himself a well-deserved rebuke from the Speaker of the House for his unprofessional behaviour. Knowing the minister had intended to rile her and deflect attention from her questions, Ardern didn't bite back. She felt strongly enough about the incident, though, to mention it in an interview more than a year later.

Ardern usually brushed off offensive remarks and sexism with good humour. When during David Cunliffe's leadership she was portrayed in a Southland newspaper cartoon as a ring girl in stilettos – a depiction she found 'pretty demeaning and pretty awful' – she simply said, 'Surely the good people of Southland deserve better cartoons'. A few weeks after she ascended to the Labour leadership, Opportunities Party leader Gareth Morgan took a nasty swipe at her on social media, tweeting that Ardern 'should be required to show she's more than lipstick on a pig'. Ardern still didn't cry foul, though she might well have garnered sympathy if she had. She laughed it off, posing for a photograph with someone dressed as the Muppets figure Miss Piggy and tweeting it.

The key to her thinking and her sense of proportion was revealed in an interview in September 2015. Sexist comments were frustrating, she conceded, though 'I always take it in the context in which it's issued. For instance, you know, Graham Lowe, did he intend to offend me? No. I doubt very much he did. But some of the commentary that occurred afterwards, some of that I found very hard to read . . . I got into politics to make a difference, and I want people to scrutinise my ideas, the alternatives I put up, not whether or not my hair means I'm not credible enough to do the job.'

Other such minor issues entered public discourse. One was nicknames. Although her mother would occasionally call her Cindy, Jacinda disliked the name. Once when Jacinda was in high school, she and her friends visited the canteen. Laurell heard one of them call her Jac, as most school friends would. Laurell objected. 'You can call her Jacinda, or Cindy,' she told them, to Jacinda's chagrin. Jacinda spoke of her feelings on nicknames to a *New York Times* columnist in September 2018, 'Back in the early days of my political career, I was called Socialist Cindy. I just hate the nickname Cindy.'

One would think she might object, therefore, when some New Zealanders began referring to her affectionately as Aunty Cindy. One journalist even took up her cause with her article in September 2020, 'She's not a doll, so don't call the prime minister Cindy'. A Twitter user likewise complained, 'Aunty Cindy? Show a bit of respect.' Jacinda took the sting out of the argument, saying on the Edge's breakfast show, 'I don't mind at all. For me, if people feel familiar, then that's a good thing,' she said. 'There's some nicknames I'm no fan of, but that's a different story.' She was 'totally fine' with being called 'babe' by the show's (female) producer when they talked, too, she said. In another radio interview, in August 2020, she elaborated: 'Actually when I was a kid I didn't like being called Cindy, but I have to say when you chuck Aunty in the front of it, I actually don't mind that . . . I take the word "Aunty" as an affectionate term.'

Perhaps this was Ardern's expansiveness, generosity of spirit. While to some a nickname such as Aunty Cindy might have seemed a little demeaning, Ardern recognised that in context it was a term of endearment that could be appreciated. Anyhow, as an Edge breakfast show host observed, 'Aunty Cindy' was far preferable to 'Piggy Muldoon'.

Ardern might judiciously avoid being sidetracked, but she would quickly show that when faced with a substantive issue, she has no qualms about making a stand. As Labour leader, her first was on an issue that confronts almost every woman of working age.

It began innocently enough, mere hours – seven, in fact – after Ardern took on the mantle of leadership, during an interview with a panel including Jesse Mulligan on the current affairs programme *The Project*. This was Ardern's first primetime interview as Labour leader. Mulligan's questioning seemed sympathetic and on the face of it, innocuous. Did Ardern feel, as so many New Zealand women did, that they had to make a choice between having children and having a career, or had she already made such a choice?

Ardern had 'no problem' with the question, she said. Her case was the same as 'the woman who works three jobs, or who might be in a position where [she is] juggling lots of responsibilities. You've just got to take every day as it comes and . . . make the best of the lot you're given.'

While Ardern might have been untroubled by Mulligan's querying, many feminists promptly tweeted their objections. Typical was Hilary Barry's tweet: 'I see @jacindaardern has already been asked about babies vs career. Please can every nob who asks that ask the same of [Prime Minister] Bill English?'

The matter might have gone no further, had not a more confrontational media personality, the former international cricketer Mark Richardson, decided to pursue it more antagonistically the following morning on the *AM Show*. 'If you are an employer of a company you need to know that type of thing from the woman you are employing . . . the question is, is it OK for a PM to take maternity leave while in office?'

Ardern's answer was delivered with a kind of controlled anger, a powerful, righteous indignation that is so unusual for her. It took listeners and the panel aback. While confirming to host Duncan Garner that whether she might have a child was an appropriate question, 'because I open myself up to it', she pointed and wagged her finger at Richardson. 'But you,' she said, turning to him and glaring. 'It is totally unacceptable in 2017 to say that women should have to answer that question in the workplace.' Richardson's features betrayed his shock. 'That is unacceptable . . . It is the woman's decision about when they choose to have children. It should not predetermine whether or not they are given a job or have job opportunities,' Ardern said. Richardson clasped his hands, then folded his arms, looking away nervously. One of his country's all-time finest batsmen had been clean bowled on air by Ardern's first delivery, and he knew it.

Public figures immediately leapt to her defence. Equal Human Rights Commissioner Dr Jackie Blue was among the first to weigh in, writing, 'Quite frankly, whether a woman intends on having children or not, is none of their bloody business. Oh, and by the way, it's illegal to ask those questions.'[3] Ardern's stand was promptly affirmed by the Human Rights Commission's Facebook post, that it is unlawful for employers to ask about contraception, family planning or pregnancy. The post went viral, and the issue made its way around the globe – even going as far as the *Washington Post* and US radio.

Jacinda Ardern had waited to show her true feminist colours, and when she did, had hit hard and on a point that mattered to women, all over the world. For the many who had said or thought Ardern was 'too nice' to be prime minister, her effective silencing of the shock jock Richardson was a revelation. But there was to be further evidence of her toughness, measured though it was, in the following days.

On 3 August, two days into Jacinda's leadership, the political bomb sitting under Metiria Turei exploded. Sleuthing from *Newshub* reporters revealed that aside from her welfare transgressions, she had been enrolled to vote at the address of her former partner, an address that she had never occupied. She had, she said, enrolled to vote there because 'my best friend was standing for election in that seat, and I wanted to support her'.[4]

As co-leader of the Greens, Turei could expect a ministerial position in a Labour-led government. In the midst of a complex and quickly changing election campaign, though, she was not merely being investigated for welfare fraud, but potentially for an electoral offence as well. Turei – a lawyer, no less – could conceivably head a department where she would administer the very same laws she had broken.

The situation quickly deteriorated. The media bayed for her blood, while two of her party members, David Clendon and Kennedy Graham, resigned from the party over the issue. On one occasion, she was accosted by reporters, looking shamefaced and shaken as she left Work and Income, the welfare office, where she had been interviewed regarding her disclosures.

It's hard not to feel sympathy for Metiria Turei, though she was mostly responsible for her own plight. Her misdeeds from a quarter of a century earlier when she was a student in her early twenties, minor in the scheme of things, had come back to haunt her, and in spectacular fashion. Some columnists were quick to point out that male politicians – indeed, the most prominent – had committed legal and financial offences of a similar seriousness. Bill English, while deputy prime minister and finance minister, claimed accommodation allowances for his home in Wellington, which was owned by his family trust. He maintained his property in his electorate, in Dipton, Southland, was his 'primary residence', despite conceding he spent little time there. Under pressure from media and the opposition, 'Double-Dipper Bill English' repaid some $32,000 to the government, simply saying it was 'a bad look'.[5]

English's predecessor as prime minister, John Key, had his own scandal with a false registration of his address. He began his career in Parliament having enrolled to vote at a home he owned but where he never lived in the electorate of Helensville. The Electoral Act 1993's rules for determining one's place of residence include the phrase 'where that person chooses to make his or her home'. Key's explanation for his breaching the rules was that 'it was nothing to do with anything cute. People knew we were building in Parnell.'[6]

Nothing much came of either of these matters – not to the extent that it affected the two men's careers. There was, it seemed, one set of rules for wealthy men in politics who trod the verges of law and propriety for convenience or financial gain, and another for a Māori single mother who confessed to a historical fraud, done to help feed herself and her daughter.

Some people did show sympathy for Turei's plight, particularly in the working-class suburbs of Auckland, such as Manuwera. In a neighbourhood where reporters were told the number of beggars on the streets was much increased under the National Party, one woman even described her as a hero. But she didn't get much sympathy from Jacinda Ardern, though she might have hoped for some. Certainly, Ardern would have felt better inclined toward Turei had she at some earlier time made efforts to pay back the money she had wrongfully received. For the policeman's daughter from Murupara, Turei's deliberate breaking of the law, in two instances and without any apparent contrition, was unacceptable.

Ardern enunciated her thoughts on the issue simply yet clearly on the *AM Show*: 'When you're lawmakers, you can't condone lawbreaking . . . you have to be very clear about when what you've done in your past has been right or it's been wrong.'[7]

Not that Ardern hadn't broken the law herself before Turei's matter came to light. She admitted her infraction to a reporter – in fact, she even revealed her offence in an interview, which is how it came to light. In March 2017, in the days following her appointment as deputy leader, she made it into the news with her own, though unintentional, illegal act. 'Labour's new deputy Jacinda Ardern in the poo for installing her own loo,'[8] was the *New Zealand Herald*'s droll headline.

The furore began after Jacinda and Clarke had spruced up their Point Chevalier home the previous year. With their country backgrounds, both are handy, practical people. They had painted their walls and even did some plumbing, replacing their toilet pan themselves. Jacinda later described her DIY work as her 'proudest moment'. Her breach of the law only came to be known when a 'concerned member of the public' lodged a report with the Plumbers, Gasfitters, and Drainlayers Board after the interview.

In some parts of Auckland – but not any in Wellington – installing your own toilet pan is an offence under the Plumbers, Gasfitters, and Drainlayers Act 2006, apparently. In a strange twist, if Jacinda and Clarke had fitted the toilet pan at an address just one kilometre away from their home, they wouldn't have committed an offence.

Obviously Jacinda's breach of the law 'wasn't vindictive', she said, or culpable. 'I literally didn't know,' she told a reporter.[9] After an apology to the Plumbers, Gasfitters and Drainlayers Board, the matter went no further.

Naturally, Metiria Turei's breaches of the law were not to be so easily assuaged. As recriminations and speculation raged, Turei scheduled a press conference on 4 August, ruling herself out of a ministerial position in a Labour–Greens coalition. At a Labour press conference shortly afterwards, Ardern said Turei's was 'an incredibly sad set of circumstances, but I think Metiria has made the right decision'.[10]

The decision to walk the plank may have been Turei's, but it came with a push from Ardern, even if indirectly. Earlier, Ardern had reportedly assigned Grant Robertson and Neale Jones the duty of speaking with the Greens' other co-leader, James Shaw. Their message from Ardern was clear: Turei had to recuse herself in advance from a ministerial post, or Ardern would herself announce that Turei would not be assigned a cabinet or ministerial position in a Labour-led government. Ardern effectively gave Turei no option, but she took it, anyway.

New Zealand was used to the smiling, personable Jacinda Ardern, the 'softer face of Labour' as a journalist described her: the woman who loves children, charms an audience, doesn't easily take offence and smiles readily. Now, in her first three days as Labour leader, the public had its first glimpses of Ardern's will. As a *Stuff* opinion column headline noted, 'Jacinda Ardern shows her steel in week one'.[11] It would not be the last week in which New Zealand would witness, and appreciate, Jacinda Ardern's mettle.

24

Tied to the West Island

There would be other clues as to the kind of prime minister Jacinda Ardern would become. The next came in the form of a diplomatic spat, minor in the scheme of things for New Zealand, but a major affair in Australia.

The fracas began with Chris Hipkins, Ardern's loyal lieutenant, questioning Minister of Internal Affairs Peter Dunne in Parliament on 9 August 2017. Hipkins asked, 'Would a child born in Australia to a New Zealand father automatically have New Zealand citizenship?' Among the usual, meandering language of parliamentarians, Dunne replied in the affirmative: 'The child will be a New Zealand citizen by descent . . .'

The question sounded routine, but Dunne's answer sent a legal and political tidal wave across the Tasman Sea, almost swamping Australia's Liberal and National Party coalition government under Malcolm Turnbull. Australia's deputy prime minister, Barnaby Joyce, was very nearly swept away.

Joyce, a colourful National Party politician with a ruddy face and volatility to match, is notorious internationally for his long-standing public feud with Hollywood star Johnny Depp. Their mutual loathing began in May 2015, when it emerged Depp and his then partner Amber Heard had brought their two Yorkshire terriers, Pistol and Boo, along with them in their private jet to Australia, without a permit. Joyce, who was then agricultural minister, famously blustered that 'It's time that Pistol and Boo buggered off back to the United States', or be euthanised. Depp and Heard were forced to make an apology on video. Later, on the *Jimmy Kimmel Show Live!*, Depp described Joyce as looking 'some-how inbred with a tomato'.

Allegations of vegetable genes aside, Joyce is from the West Island, as Australia is sometimes jokingly referred to by Kiwis. He was born in Tamworth, in New England, a dry farming region in the north-west of New South Wales, known for its sheep, wheat, cattle and the annual Tamworth Country Music Festival. Dunne's answer to Hipkin's question, however, threw Joyce's legal nationality into question. His father was from Hampden in North Otago, New Zealand, and emigrated to Australia after the Second World War, which meant that Joyce was also a citizen of New Zealand by descent – a dual citizen, ergo ineligible for a seat in the Australian parliament under section 44(i) of the Australian constitution. Joyce, who said he was 'shocked' to discover he was a New Zealand citizen, was forced to resign his deputy prime ministership – and his seat, though he soon won it back in a by-election.

Joyce's humiliation provoked an uproar. For most Australians, Joyce, a man who roughhoused his way through public life, had got his comeuppance. The internet was abuzz with Australians' hackneyed New Zealand jokes, suggesting Joyce had an unnatural fondness for sheep (the New Zealander equivalents are jibes at Australia's convict roots). Back in The Land of the Long White Cloud, Joyce was laughingly nominated for New Zealander of the Year. A gleeful Bill Shorten, Jacinda Ardern's Australian counterpart, began an address to his caucus with the Māori greeting 'kia ora', while referring to the hapless Joyce as 'leader of the dual Nationals'.

Cartoonists had a field day. One drew a double-headed kiwi with a bird's head wearing a troubled expression at one end and Joyce's face as its posterior: 'the New England Kiwi'. Another had the Yorkshire terriers Pistol and Boo, tormenting a bereft Joyce, directing a video. One dog held a clapperboard, 'Foreign declaration apology video', while the other applied makeup. 'Just read out the script on the autocue, bro, and no one need get euthanised.'

The Australian government was not amused. Joyce's resignation, along with those of other members in a similar situation, meant its lower house majority was briefly lost. On 16 August 2017, Foreign Minister Julie Bishop declared she 'would find it very difficult to build trust with members of a political party that had been used by the Australian Labor Party to seek to undermine the Australian government'. Hipkins' question, urged by an Australian Labor Party staffer, had the whiff of collusion, a backroom settling of scores – bipartisan, it seemed – with Australia's government over its highly contentious deportation policy. Ardern would later make a stand for New Zealand over the issue, as we shall see. But at this time, she was dismayed by the distraction as the election campaign heated up. She moved swiftly to contain the issue, calling the Australian high commissioner and countering claims New Zealand Labour were involved in the mess. She tweeted, 'I value our relationship with the Australian Govt highly. I won't let disappointing and false claims stand in the way of that relationship.'[1]

Typically for Ardern, she healed the rift, meeting with Bishop in February the following year at Winston Peters' Auckland home. Bishop posted a picture of the pair together, smiling and standing close, enjoying a 'memorable evening'.

In the final analysis, the matter served Ardern well, oddly enough. Any doubts as to her ability to handle international relations calmly but without buckling were assuaged. The incident also underlined the close and sometimes complex relationship between the two countries.

Despite fierce rivalry on the sports field that often seems hostile to the rest of the world (the scandal of Australian Trevor Chappell's underarm bowling in February 1981 comes to mind here), Australia and New Zealand are tied to each other by friendship, sharing culture, kinship and geography. Their troops fought together at Gallipoli and on the Western Front during the First World War, and in numerous conflicts since.

In any event, there are many Australians with New Zealand connections and family, just as there are New Zealanders with Australian family and antecedents. Australians and New Zealanders are brothers and sisters.

Jacinda Ardern herself is a case in point. She is part Australian: her great-grandfather, Edwin Daniel McVicar, was born in Newcastle, New South Wales, a second-generation Australian of a free settler family. Edwin emigrated to New Zealand in his youth, volunteering for service in the First World War in 1916 as an Australian and New Zealand Army Corps (ANZAC) rifleman. The lithe farmhand late of Te Awamutu found himself in France with A Company in October 1916, at the tender age of eighteen. There, he endured the horrors of trench warfare, 'acquitt[ing] himself very creditably', according to official documents. A Lewis (machine gun) gunner, twice Edwin was wounded in action, both times by gunshot.

Perhaps it's appropriate that the future prime minister's ancestor took part in a historic event. It was during the Battle of Passchendaele, on 12 October 1917, known later as the darkest day of New Zealand's history. Some 845 New Zealand soldiers perished then in the machine-gun kill zone, fallen in mud and bloody shell craters for a vain thrust to take the small Belgian village of the same name.

Edwin was lucky, if one can call it luck, that he was wounded. His abdomen was grazed and his hip seriously injured with a perforating wound from an enemy round. It took him months to recover. Almost exactly a year later, he was taken from the Western Front to the general hospital in Camiers with a bullet wound to his left calf. This saw the end of the war for him: peace was declared before Edwin was discharged from hospital.

Remarkably, the experience of some of the bloodiest action in military history didn't dampen his enthusiasm for the military. In November 1940, well into his forties, Edwin reported for a medical examination lobbying successfully for enlistment as a medical orderly in the Second World War. Though he made concerted efforts to be posted overseas for active service, the closest he came to the enemy was with N Force, a small New Zealand Army unit of infantry and artillery that garrisoned Norfolk Island. He never saw action there.

Perhaps Jacinda has inherited her great-grandfather's tenacity, along with his links to the West Island. With her humour, sense of fairness, persistence and humility, it seems fitting that she has an Anzac digger (soldier) ancestor, one whose background traverses both nations of the corps. Jacinda still has many distant relatives in Australia, through the McVicar and Carter families in particular, and with a number of keen genealogists in her family, she is aware of her Australian connection. She knows, too, the increasing bond between the nations that, like that between siblings, strengthens as they mature. A Lowy Institute study a few years ago found that Australians regard New Zealanders as their best friends internationally.

Indeed, they might well have been people of the same nation, had events unfolded differently. New Zealand very nearly became part of Australia.

New Zealand's link to Australia began in earnest when Captain Arthur Phillip was appointed its governor by royal commission in 1788 as part of New South Wales (the Crown neglected to consult the Māori on their country's annexation by a new colony, some 1,200 miles away). At the Australasian Federation Conference held in Melbourne in February 1890, New Zealand's leaders were even invited to join the Australian Federation of States. While they remained non-committal on the issue, the framing of Australia's constitution moved ahead. Patriotic Kiwis might well be aghast to discover their sovereign nation is listed in Section 6 of the Commonwealth of Australia Constitution Act 1900, as a mere Australian state: the lost seventh state of the Commonwealth.

New Zealand has maintained its independence – fiercely, at times – but the country's love for the West Island and Australia's indulgence meant, as the former prime minister Geoffrey Palmer once said, New Zealand 'gained most of the advantages of being a state of Australia without becoming one'. Around 600,000 of New Zealand's people, somewhere in the order of twelve percent of the population, happily call Australia home.

The bigger nation will likely always be the elder sibling of the two countries. This hasn't prevented Jacinda Ardern making a firm stand for New Zealand, however, on an issue that she, along with most New Zealanders, feels is 'corrosive' to the countries' relationship. The issue stems from Australia's Migration Amendment (Character and General Visa Cancellation) Act 2014, which mandated the deportation of any non-citizen who had been sentenced to twelve months or more of imprisonment, or been found guilty of a child sex offence. More controversial were the sweeping powers it conferred on the minister to deport undesirable 'non-citizens': arbitrarily, without crucial rights afforded by natural justice.

The latter provision in particular bore down heavily on New Zealanders, who, used to the free flow of people across the Tasman for generations, were caught by surprise with its draconian measures. People who for all intents and purposes are Australian save for their paperwork – and who may never have even set foot in New Zealand – have been summarily sent there. In one famous case, the father of Australian Football League star Dustin Martin, Shane

Martin, a heavily tattooed former Rebels motorcycle club president, was deported in April 2016 to New Zealand, along with numerous other bikers.

With his son's fame – the younger Martin won a coveted Brownlow Medal, the highest individual award in Australian rules football – Shane Martin's case received considerable publicity. The most difficult cases for New Zealand, though, are those of anonymous criminals, often with mental health issues, many with few or no close family members in New Zealand. Most have been ostensibly Australian, Kiwis in the eyes of the law only.

Freshly released from Australian prisons, these '501s', so named for the section of the legislation they are deported under, are forcibly taken from custody to the airport. They make their 'walk of shame' through the concourse, handcuffed and trussed by body belts, chains from their torsos to their elbows tinkling as they go. Taken aboard a charter flight, they are flown, *Con Air* style, to Auckland or Wellington. There, these 'Aussie' criminals or 'non-citizens', unwanted by the country they have called their own, become New Zealand's problem. And a problem they usually are. Deracinated and traumatised, the 501s routinely end up on the wrong side of the law; there's talk of a forty percent recidivism rate for returning offenders. Gang membership has reportedly increased by a quarter in five years, their ranks adopting a more brazen style: contract killings, power struggles and ostentatious, gold-plated motorcycles; globalised crime, as it were.

The 501 deportee issue has rankled in New Zealand. Diplomatic pot shots were fired over the Tasman before Ardern's administration, and after she took over the Beehive. In July 2019, Acting Prime Minister Winston Peters told reporters that parts of Australia's legislation were 'ridiculous', and suggested Australian politicians 'tidy it up'. He was backed by Andrew Little – by this time, a highly regarded justice minister and a Labour Party hero – who described the 501 deportations as a 'serious point of tension'.

Australian politicians were unrepentant, much less apologetic. The architect of the Section 501 imbroglio, Australian immigration minister Peter Dutton, an impassive former Queensland policeman with a penchant for collecting portfolios, merely uttered the rhetoric of his government 'try[ing] to deport . . . paedophiles'.[2] Ardern's discussions on the matter with Australian prime minister Scott Morrison were to no avail.

Ardern had long been criticised in Labour backrooms for avoiding confrontation; she 'backed down' when challenged, it was rumoured. Perhaps she simply stayed with her strength, which was in negotiation, rallying people together. The woman who studied conflict and consensus in university seems to have no stomach for gratuitous verbal assaults. The peacemaker, in her family as elsewhere, would, however, emulate the Anzac spirit a number of times during her tenure as prime minister. One was her 'Big Norm moment', where she stood up to a larger, more powerful country on this point of principle. But rather than sending navy frigates as Norman Kirk did to protest against French nuclear tests, she sent herself – and she delivered her broadside personally.

Ardern's appearance in Sydney with Scott Morrison on 28 February 2020 was sensational, by anyone's reckoning. It will surely be marked in history as one of the most remarkable joint press conferences ever held between the nations. The pair presented themselves behind twin podiums adorned with the Australian coat of arms, out on the lawn at Kirribilli House, the prime minister's residence in Sydney. It's a delightful location at Kirribilli Point, one of dozens of pieces of land jutting out like jigsaw puzzle pieces into the harbour. Cameras trained on the pair captured the Sydney Opera House's iconic segmented arches and the grey coat-hanger sweep of the Harbour Bridge, out of focus across the water. The waves, a tinge of turquoise within their grey, danced behind the lighter shades of Ardern's blazer. Ardern might have been a guest at Sydney Harbour yet oddly, she seemed to belong there as much as Morrison.

She was present for the annual Australia–New Zealand Leaders' Meeting, for bilateral talks. Held at the prime minister's residence, it would seem to be a venue for trans-Tasman cooperation, as it was stated. Morrison had at least some forewarning of Ardern's intentions, which were shrewdly leaked to the New Zealand press corps at the last moment.

Ardern did indeed begin by talking of friendship. There were nervous chuckles between the pair early in her speech. A few minutes along, though, she spoke of New Zealanders as 'Australia's best migrants' whose 'rights are being eroded'. Then, she let loose the salvo the New Zealand press was waiting for. Raising the subject of deportations, she said that while New Zealand respected Australia's rights to deport foreign criminals, 'we have a simple request: send back Kiwis . . . genuine Kiwis. Do not deport your people, and your problems . . . we will own our own people. We ask that Australia stops exporting theirs.'[3]

She thanked Prime Minister Morrison for the opportunity to discuss these issues. As if he had any choice. Throughout, Morrison had stood with a pained half-smirk on his face as Ardern spoke. His lips pursed with tension, he looked every bit as uncomfortable as Mark Richardson had when he was hit by an Ardern precision strike. Morrison even mounted a defence, which descended into a polite but strained debate – one with a somewhat familial tenor – as Ardern took her right of reply. This was not simply done for publicity. She meant what she said, and it showed.

Ardern ended the appearance with a characteristic, light-hearted jibe. When a journalist tried to ask a question of Morrison after he finished, Morrison cut him off. 'He's one of yours,' Ardern said with a laugh as she and Morrison walked away from their podiums. Morrison couldn't help but snort a pained chuckle.

It was an extraordinary event, unprecedented in trans-Tasman relations. Not even the most confrontational New Zealand prime minister had openly chastised their Australian counterpart in a joint press conference – in front of Sydney Harbour, at the prime minister's own residence, no less. It was an utter humiliation for Morrison, worsened in the knowledge that Ardern might be more favoured as a prime minister – an Australian prime minister – than he was.

Just a few weeks after this event, an opinion poll showed Jacinda Ardern as Australians' most trusted political leader – far ahead of any local politician. Nine months earlier, an astonishing sixty-nine percent of Australians surveyed, agreed that she represented her country well and was an inspirational leader. A *Guardian* article of July 2019, 'Jacinda Ardern prime minister of Australasia? If only it was that simple',[4] spoke of a longing in Australia for someone like Ardern in the nation's top job. 'Can we swap? Can we have her?' Australians often asked.

Perhaps if Ardern had emigrated to Australia in her childhood, as had many of her contemporaries, she might well have ended up in

Kirribilli House herself. There's no great stretch here: she boasts early Australian heritage, and embodies so many characteristics cherished in both countries: humility, tenacity, frankness and a tendency to self-deprecation.

Had history played out differently, if New Zealand had actually become the seventh Australian state, rather than a hopeful entry in Australia's constitution, there would likely be an office of the prime minister of Australasia. In 2020, this could well have been held by one Jacinda Kate Laurell Ardern.

25

Stardust and Jacindamania

Before August 2017, Jacinda Ardern wouldn't have dreamed she would stand at Kirribilli House as her nation's prime minister a couple of years later, much less visit the Queen at Buckingham Palace. Indeed, a few days before Ardern was appointed Labour's leader on 1 August 2017, no one could have foreseen the turn of events from then to October, let alone the dramas and achievements beyond.

As August 2017 began, however, the public mood shifted, and dramatically. Ardern's act of throwing herself into the breach, so far behind in the polls and so close to the election, seemed to ignite a kind of passion in the media as in the electorate. Some part of it may have been New Zealand's egalitarian sentiment – everywhere, people love an underdog, and no more so than in Aotearoa, the Land of the Long White Cloud. The Kiwi battler is widely celebrated. And Jacinda Ardern was a battler. More than this, though, was that her humility, her charm and positivity, were refreshing to New Zealanders. She connected with them on a visceral level, representing the better parts of themselves, their aspirations.

Even hardened political journalists seemed swept up in the excitement. With headlines including 'Labour's A-bomb has the X-factor' and 'Labour's golden girl steps up', and the somewhat tongue-in-cheek comment column, 'A ray of sunshine penetrates the smog as Jacinda Ardern becomes Labour leader', it seemed the 'relentless positivity' Ardern promised was infectious, and journalists themselves had caught it.

Exasperated by the coverage, National Party minister Gerry Brownlee, gifted a set of cheerleader's pompoms to journalist Patrick Gower, who had said 'the mood for change is strong', and suggested Ardern could win the election.

Not many pundits fancied Ardern's chances against Bill English, however. The wily old man of New Zealand politics, Winston Peters, described Labour's change of leader as 'a very desperate move . . . A move . . . so filled with risk you have to wonder why they did it.' Others felt that the best Ardern could hope for was to salvage what she could for Labour; she might, like an Ernest Shackleton, lead her party heroically away from ruination.

The odds against Ardern taking office were grim. Bringing the party from less than twenty-five percent support to victory seemed improbable, if not impossible. The only consolation for Labour was that many voters were undecided. Still, Ardern's leadership galvanised many in the centre and left who had stood aloof from politics. In hours, donations began streaming into Labour's coffers, at one point at a rate of $700 per minute. Within a mere ten days, 3,500 people, mostly women, had volunteered to work for the party. The first week saw a 'poll quake' rise of nine points for Labour. The effect of Ardern taking the helm was breathtaking.

The frenetic pace of the campaign, which 'made a whirlwind seem like a gentle breeze',[1] Ardern would later say, had begun on the very day she took up the leadership. Annette King recalls the bedlam at the party offices that morning, where 'everyone was running around'. The pace didn't relent for more than two months. Ardern's earlier fears that she was 'not ready to do this' had evaporated. There was no time for such feelings. Ardern would later say she had 'PET, post-election trauma', and much of the campaign 'remain[s] a blur'.[2]

The first three days saw a flurry of activity in Labour's backrooms, with Ardern's self-imposed seventy-two-hour campaign revamp. The Labour campaign had more than a suggestion of Kiwi number-8 wire (a New Zealand expression for makeshift ingenuity, based on fencing wire). It became a can-do, make-it-happen-now, let's-pull-together affair.

Jacinda acknowledged Labour had to lift its game. The party television advertisements could not be edited – they would have to be discarded, and a new set filmed. Billboards were hastily pulled down and new ones soon erected, bearing Ardern's face against a white background. The former campaign slogan, the fairly insipid 'A Fresh Approach', would go too.

But what would replace it? Ardern 'angsted' over the new slogan – she knew campaigns can be won or lost on strength of slogans. Many a campaign slogan has become a political epitaph. Eventually, she had some help, intentional or otherwise. Her first Facebook post as leader, she ended with the words 'Let's do this'. Halfway through the seventy-two hours, Ardern received a text message from a journalist who asked if she intended this to be her campaign slogan.

It couldn't have come at a better time. 'Let's Do This' reminded her of her hero Big Norm Kirk's simple slogan for the November 1972 election, 'It's Time' (the slogan was so catchy, and successful, it was used by the Australian Labor Party for its triumphant campaign which followed). It also seemed reminiscent of Barack Obama's 'Yes we can', which was equally successful. The matter was settled.

The campaigning itself began well. Ardern made the astute decision to have Annette King accompany her on the hustings, which, she later said cheerily, was 'totally selfish'. As well as relying on King's wealth of political knowledge and campaigning acumen, she simply enjoyed her company: she could discuss the challenges facing Labour, and lean on the older woman's inner strength, her calm under fire, a quality that Ardern was developing.

King's presence alone was a boon. In so many photographs taken of Ardern during the campaign, Aunty Annette can be seen, hovering around her 'niece'. A woman who doesn't take herself too seriously, King was introduced in jest as 'the Queen Mother' at events.

Her advice to Ardern was as simple as it was invaluable: 'just be yourself'. It worked spectacularly. Crowds flocked to hear Ardern speak; people thronged to take a selfie with her. She was herself taken aback by the effect of her charisma, shocked by the sheer numbers and the enthusiasm of her supporters. The first Auckland event of the campaign, on transport, augured signs of the campaign ahead. Normally, a politician can expect a small turnout to such an event, but Jacinda found herself looking out on a whole square packed with people.

In days, the polls showed a dramatic upswing: the effects of the charismatic 'rock star' politician who had overturned the perception of Labour from that of a passionless, rather negative party to a cheery and hopeful one, in a matter of weeks. Aptly, her campaign volunteers looked like a fan club. At almost every appearance they surrounded Ardern, wearing their white shirts emblazoned with 'Let's Do This' in red.

Her appeal to people seemed inescapable. Ardern earned New Zealanders' respect for her hands-on, down-to-earth approach. She picked up tools and helped erect the first campaign billboard, putting to good use the skills she had learned on the farm during her childhood. She spoke of issues in a manner that resonated with people. She wore bright colours and vivid lipstick. She smiled her toothy smile incessantly – as she said later, 'I struggle not to smile. I look like I'm pouting [when I don't]'[3] – and her public loved it.

Ardern spoke, too, on issues that struck a chord with voters, issues that had for years been overlooked in favour of economic expediency. The gap between rich and poor, widening over the preceding decade, the need for decent jobs, homelessness, mental health. And the issue of climate change, which Ardern referred to in terms of a 'nuclear-free moment'.[4] Here, she invoked the spirit of Labour prime minister David Lange, who with the help of the courageous Marilyn Waring, brought the watershed issue to the electorate in 1984.

The official Labour campaign launch on 20 August saw Ardern speak with more conviction and confidence than ever, to a standing-room-only audience at Auckland Town Hall. The party faithful were so numerous, they spilled over into the Concert Chamber and the nearby Q Theatre, where the event was hastily screened live.

By then, pundits spoke of the 'Jacinda effect' and 'Jacindamania' that had Labour's polling surge steeply upward. Ardern was compared to Obama, Justin Trudeau, her old boss Tony Blair – and even, paradoxically, her party's former nemesis, John Key, for her charisma and hold over the nation's imagination. At least, she was mobbed, particularly by children – just as Key had been three years earlier – when she visited malls, and almost anywhere else. In her first mall walkabout on 22 August at the Plaza in Palmerston North, she meant to meet the local Labour team for lunch. She never got to the table, waylaid by well-wishers who flocked to her. One gushed to a reporter she was 'a breath of fresh air'. A man asked to hug her: 'Of course, you don't need to ask,' she replied, and obliged.

Ardern might have appealed more to women during the campaign, especially during its initial stages. For New Zealand men, though, who perhaps felt their leaders had misunderstood them – David Cunliffe's 'apology' is a case in point – Ardern's warmth was a delight. She represented a brand of feminism, and in her they saw the kind of woman they could embrace – literally. Women were taken with Jacindamania first, but the Jacindamania surge in the polls came from men as well as women.

The first material sign that the gap between Labour and the government was narrowing came on 18 August with a Roy Morgan poll, which showed that combined support for Labour and the Greens placed them neck and neck with the National Party. Gary Morgan from Roy Morgan spoke of the 'wildcard New Zealand First, on 11.5% support now appearing to hold all the aces'.[5] Morgan's card game and poker metaphor might have been muddled, but his judgement was accurate. Metiria Turei folded her hand, resigning on 9 August, which meant Winston Peters had won the round between the parties. New Zealand First appeared to gain from the Greens' lost gamble.

But the election campaign still had its rounds to play. Peters' fresh pile of electoral chips, amassed on the table in front of him, was too much for the Nationals, his former party. It seems someone in the party played an aggressive hand in a bid to take them.

On 27 August, Peters was forced to reveal publicly that he had been overpaid superannuation, which had come to his notice when the Ministry of Social Development contacted him the previous month. The amount was relatively small. Paid fortnightly over approximately seven years, it totalled some $18,000 including interest and penalties, it was reported. There was no suggestion of culpability: the overpayment was the result of an error, evidently; Peters had corrected the matter within twenty-four hours, he said.

How the matter came to the media's notice, though, took far longer to uncover – years, in fact. The leak of Peters' private information would prove infinitely more expensive for the National Party, too, than it would for New Zealand First. Its timing seemed too convenient to be a casual slip from Social Development Minister Anne Tolley's office, which was the official explanation. Perhaps somebody in the National Party backrooms thought Peters could be brought down as Turei had been. Looking at his career, they should have known better. The old-school Peters had been hit below the belt, and he was sore, his exasperation while discussing the matter on RNZ palpable. Anyone with a modicum of judgement could see this wily veteran would sneak in a head butt or throw an elbow to even the score.

All the while, Labour climbed in the polls. Before Jacinda and after Jacinda were different epochs of Labour's fortunes, the polling graph now showing their dizzying rise. At the end of August, after exactly one month of Ardern at the helm, Labour had edged above the National Party, for the first time in twelve years.

*

For the National Party, for Bill English in particular, Ardern's elevation to the Labour leadership was a misery. English, a solid performer with a good fiscal brain, had the decided edge in experience and perhaps endurance, but simply didn't possess any of the charisma, the emotional appeal of his new Labour opponent.

His change in fortunes was confounding for him. English entered the campaign 'confident but paranoid',[6] he says (the latter justifiably so, with hindsight). As the campaign began, he looked certain to prevail, and convincingly against a man whose conservative, somewhat bland style, stolidity and reticence to engage, matched him well. Indeed, the similarity between English and Andrew Little made for a boring contest.

With Ardern substituted for Little when the bell rang for the second round, English found himself utterly unprepared, flat-footed against a younger, more enthusiastic and energetic opponent who was as far removed from him in style and skills as could be imagined. Her obvious enjoyment of connecting with people contrasted with his formal, distant approach, as with almost everything else. The only commonalities between the pair, it seemed, was their candidacy for the prime ministership, their rural backgrounds and their love for literature. With Ardern turning the contest into her own match, scoring points at will, English struggled.

Well funded, cohesive, and properly organised, English and the

Nationals wouldn't give in so easily, however. Under pressure, party strategists plotted ways to take away Ardern's initiative, to turn the contest into one on English's terms.

Prime Minister Bill English had a decent reputation. His tenure of minister of finance and deputy prime minister for more than eight years between 2008 and 2016, then the prime ministership from December 2016, meant voters knew exactly what they were getting: more of the same. This was not bad for most voters, though vexing for those with a social conscience and concern for the environment.

A socially conservative politician with the demeanour of an accountant, English was known for being responsible, and tight with the purse strings. He celebrated budget surpluses with relish. In October 2016, he tweeted a picture of himself, shirt and tie at his desk, grinning widely, about to devour a steak and cheese pie. 'A good surplus warrants a good pie' was his caption. The surpluses, however, came along with growing poverty in Aotearoa.

Nevertheless, dependability, sound fiscal management, stability and experience were English's strong suits. His party also liked to use a heavier hand, so to speak, with law and order issues, favouring boot camps for offenders and crackdowns on gangs and methamphetamine traffickers. English's proven record, and law and order, would become the focus of his party's campaign.

As September began, and with the contest becoming 'nerve-rackingly close', according to one columnist, the National Party's strategy shifted from touting English's experience and achievements, to discrediting Ardern. Almost swamped by the Jacindamania surge in August, English jettisoned his usual decorum, and his party began taking a more aggressive approach to the campaign.

The opening gambit was to be Ardern's old sparring partner Paula Bennett. On 3 September, speaking on the National Party's proposal to empower the police to search without warrants, Bennett said of criminals, 'Some have fewer human rights than others.' She tweeted later, 'Scum gangs that peddle drugs don't deserve protection. They have zero regard for the harm they cause.'[7]

With Judith 'Crusher' Collins and Bennett in the National government's ministry, no one would accuse the party of being overly empathetic or soft-hearted. Indeed, Bennett seemed to be trying to distinguish herself from Ardern, playing on swing voters' concerns for law and order as she did. She had overstepped, however. With an outcry from prominent figures over her gaffes, from outgoing associate minister of health Peter Dunne to the human rights commissioner, English said hers was 'not an accurate reflection' of party policy. She 'misspoke', a journalist wryly paraphrased for him, conjuring that word so favoured by US politicians to cover a multitude of verbal sins.

At any rate, if Bennett planned to engage Ardern in the hope she might show herself to be soft on crime, she failed. She should have remembered Ardern's early contributions to parliamentary debate on justice and the penal system. The policeman's daughter had been involved in a review of policing in England and Wales in her twenties; her understanding of crime and punishment was deeper and more nuanced than most would expect of her. Ardern simply said she would like to 'see the detail' of the National Party's policy.

More effective was the National Party's undermining of Labour with explosive claims about its fiscal plan, and an outright assault on Jacindamania through targeted advertisements. These were calibrated so as not to be too negative in a way that might alienate Kiwis, who are less tolerant of attack advertisements than voters in some democracies. But enough to be an antidote to Ardern's 'relentless positivity' nonetheless.

The first was a statement on 4 September by the National Party's finance spokesperson, Steven Joyce, that there was a $11.7 billion 'black hole' in Labour's fiscal plan. He timed his bombshell cleverly, detonating it to the media in the hours before a leaders' televised debate.

Ardern was visiting a fibreglass insulation factory when she heard of it. Outside the factory before a scrum of reporters, she stuck first to her own schedule, telling them Labour intended to see that the country's 600,000 uninsulated homes were insulated, so they were 'warm and dry'. It is a worthy policy: a recent article reported that somewhere in the order of forty-five percent of New Zealand's houses are so cold in winter you can see the vapour of your breath. Ardern kept her focus on the 'four things that matter to people' that Big Norm Kirk had spoken of, which she quoted in her campaign launch speech: 'They have to have somewhere to live, they have to have food to eat, they have to have clothing to wear, and they have to have something to hope for.'[8]

When pressed on Joyce's claim, Ardern was unruffled. Grant Robertson, Labour's finance spokesperson, had already briefed her. 'I'm absolutely confident what we're saying in our budget is right,' he had said. 'We've done the sums, run the figures, had them independently judged.' Ardern told reporters, 'It's a campaign period. Of course Mr Joyce is going to level criticisms at [our budget]. That's what political parties do.'[9] She was emphatic. She stood by Labour's figures.

So did a veritable honour roll of economists. Robertson labelled Joyce's claim a 'desperate, cynical attempt to create a diversion'.[10] If this was the case, as it appears to have been, it was by no means the last. The National Party's 'Taxinda' slurs and 'Let's Tax This' advertisements likewise attempted to portray Labour, and Ardern in particular, as fiscally irresponsible, hell-bent on increasing taxes to fund the party's social and environmental programmes.

Evidently, the advertisements were effective. Under pressure from the party and voters, Ardern and Robertson announced on 14 September there would be no new taxes until after the 2020 election under a Labour government. It was an embarrassing *volte-face* from her earlier 'captain's call' not to rule out a capital gains tax (CGT). She had proposed forming a working group to consider the CGT as a means of venting some of the hot air away from Auckland's overheated housing market. With her party's campaign heading towards a reef in the form of the taxation issue, Ardern had little choice but to change tack.

By this stage, the campaign was in its final weeks, and beginning to take its toll. A general election campaign is gruelling for anyone in politics, but most of all for a party leader – especially one such as Ardern, who had never before campaigned nationally. Nevertheless, she found ways to manage as she always had.

One works with what one has; Jacinda Ardern doesn't seem to possess an iron constitution, an attribute so useful for a politician. She instead seems powered by stores of nervous energy, which may sometimes run low. With these, and mental focus, she wills herself onward nonetheless. Curiously, she often uses the word 'robust', though it hardly fits her. Perhaps she speaks the word to somehow invoke and so develop it as a characteristic within herself.

At any rate, 'resilient' would better describe Ardern. She simply never gives up – even when under extreme pressure; indeed, especially under pressure. Her resilience would be tested over the last weeks of the campaign. Surely, the 2017 election would have been challenge enough without the personal sorrow she endured as the election day drew near.

*

Ardern's decision to have Annette King with her on her campaign tour would prove not so much selfish as inspired. Most of the time, she travelled in a government car, accompanied by a press secretary and Diplomatic Protection Service officers, while King would follow in one of the support cars. From time to time, Ardern would ask King to sit with her in her car: sometimes just for the company; other times to talk, usually about mundane matters away from politics. When they did talk about leadership, King continually bolstered Ardern's confidence, 'reinforcing that I just needed to keep being myself', she recalls.[11]

King saw Ardern's confidence grow as the campaign progressed. 'She just got better and better every meeting,' she says.[12] The South Island leg of their tour was particularly successful. One stretch was memorable for the scenery, as much as for the glimpse of Ardern at her best.

It was a trip from Greymouth, a town on the narrow plain hugging the South Island's west coast, overlooked by the foothills of the majestic Southern Alps. From Greymouth, the motorcade headed inland on State Highway 73. It's a route best taken at leisure, across quintessential New Zealand terrain. The road meanders through valleys, beside lush riverside fields and between mountains. The countryside is exquisite here, rugged, verdant for the several metres of rain that falls each year. Across narrow one-lane bridges, the route takes you onto open, sweeping roads that carve their path along the valley floor, beside river plains with gravel and rocks strewn across their breadth.

Halfway through the journey, road works halted Ardern's

motorcade; a long line of cars, already parked, waited for their way to clear. The early spring sunshine warmed the chill from the air. Ardern stepped out of her car; King and the Diplomatic Protection Service officers followed.

The other motorists were delighted. Stepping out of their cars, they crowded around, chatting with Ardern as she and King munched on lollies. 'She was so engaging and this was so natural to her,'[13] King recalls. The effect of her presence on these people was captivating. Here was Ardern in her element: campaigning, but in a way that seemed to be simply relating, conversing with people. Perhaps it was. Meeting people on the campaign trail seemed as normal for her as chatting with friends.

What Ardern didn't show to the public then was her private worry for her family back in Morrinsville. Her 85-year-old grandfather, Eric Bottomley, had fallen ill and been admitted to the Waikato Hospital in Hamilton. He recovered, but on 12 September, the hospital tried to discharge him – at 11.30 P.M., and his home was nearly an hour's drive away. Thankfully, a family member intervened; Eric was allowed to leave the following morning. Jacinda did not blame the hospital, but spoke of the underfunded, overstretched health system that led to such mistreatment.

Worse was to come. As Jacinda, Annette and their entourage made their way down the west coast, Jacinda discovered that journalists were seeking her grandfather, to verify her comments. She felt, as she later recounted, 'absolutely gutted . . . I thought, did I make a mistake in mentioning that? How can I protect my family?'[14] In the midst of all these goings on, her grandmother, Margaret Bottomley, had a major stroke and was herself hospitalised.

All the while, the National Party harped on about Labour's tax policy. Ardern remembers being 'spliced between trying to deal with the tax issue and this personal grief I had. Do I need to be at home? How do I see my family?'[15] King, a woman who maintained a solid balance between her personal and professional lives, was the perfect person to have with her, she says, to help her through both her family issues and her political challenges. 'The role she played', Ardern says, 'was almost like a family member for me.'[16]

Her mind and heart might have been in Morrinsville with her

family, but Ardern kept to her tight schedule. After a campaign rally in Hamilton on 17 September, she went to see her grandmother at Te Aroha Community Hospital. Margaret Bottomley passed away the following night at the age of eighty-one.

She would be sorely missed. Margaret was the kind of woman who personifies the spirit of community in her country town. Her grandma, Jacinda later wrote in a Facebook post, was 'a kind woman who worked so hard her whole life but never hesitated to help someone else'.[17]

Fate can be cruel at times; people more so. Hours before Jacinda's grandmother died, hundreds of farmers gathered in Morrinsville around the Mega Cow to protest against Labour's proposed water tax. Though the gathering's mood was genial, the rhetoric was harsh, its placards contentious. Myrtle, the tractor Jacinda's distant cousin Shane Ardern had driven up the steps of Parliament fourteen years earlier, made an appearance, bearing poorly written signs: 'FART RED FOR LAbOUR' (*sic*) and 'THIEVING TAX HUNGRY SOCIALIST WANNA BE GOVERNMENT'. One man carried aloft a sign saying, 'SHE'S A PRETTY COMMUNIST'.

Helen Clarke and others took up her cause, but Ardern showed just how strong she had become, and none of the grief that she was experiencing. A reporter asked her for her comment on the sign. She simply laughed. 'I'm a pretty communist? Did they intend that to be a compliment or an insult? I'm not entirely sure,' she said.[18] She took the protest in remarkably good spirit, though its convening in her home town clearly targeted her: 'Having grown up in Morrinsville, I've always known that there are people who take a different view when it comes to politics than I do.'[19]

Jacinda had come a long way from being the girl her family felt was too thin-skinned for politics. She was no longer the highly strung young woman of her early years in the party. As the election campaign drew to a close, she had shown a remarkable endurance, and astonishing clarity of thought and purpose, for someone thrown into the leadership role so late in the campaign. She had been pitted against a seasoned, strong opponent in Bill English, too, and had more than held her own in public debate against him.

The debates showed New Zealanders just how good the young

Labour leader could be. The only criticisms Ardern heard from her performances there concerned her look. What she wore was bland; there was not enough colour. And her hairstyle: she received so much negative feedback about having her hair tied back in the first debate – mainly from women – that she changed it. She listened to these comments, well meant as they were, leaving her hair free and wearing blazers with shades of red for the following appearances.

Ardern also showed 'she could have some bite in there', as King commented approvingly.[20] She pursued English in the final minutes of their last debate. 'You've had nine years to trial your solutions, and they haven't worked very well,' she said. 'You discovered poverty last week . . . why are there kids sleeping in cars? Then why are kids going to school without food in their tummies? . . . We could never afford poverty, and you've been content to let it slide . . .'[21] English defended himself, but he was clearly on the back foot.

There was one exchange between the pair in their televised debates, in their third round, as it were, that illustrated the hope Ardern represented to New Zealanders. 'Now the stardust has settled, you're starting to see the policy,' English said. Ardern fired back, 'This stardust won't settle, because none of us should settle.'[22]

And it didn't.

26

Victory Day for Winston

The final days of a campaign are a frantic rush before the election silence, which in New Zealand as in most democracies means there is no campaigning on election day itself. Ardern had marked election day in her diary and looked at it with dread. There was little outward sign of anything other than good cheer on her, though, as the day approached.

The day before the polls, Ardern travelled some 140 kilometres to Te Aroha for her grandmother's funeral service, then returned to Auckland for an appearance at Manukau Shopping Centre. There, she mingled comfortably with voters, taking selfies, smiling broadly all the while. One would hardly believe she had just attended a funeral, let alone that of a beloved family member. All she would say about her loss was, 'My grandmother was a wonderful woman and I know she would have liked to have been here for tomorrow.'[1]

The following day, rather than taking a well-earned rest, Jacinda took to her fence with a paintbrush, perhaps to expend some of that Ardern nervous energy. Or simply to use the time judiciously – Jacinda is an 'active relaxer', she says[2] – and do as she was told. With characteristic directness, her mother had said the day she became leader, she should fix her fence. In the early evening, Jacinda gave a Facebook live feed as Clarke cooked bass fish bites and sausages ('the more processed, the better') with buttered white bread. Ross and Laurell Ardern and other family members watched with them as the poll results streamed live onto their television.

The early results gave them scant hope, and guaranteed uncertainty. After the runaway Jacindamania surge of August, the National Party had clawed back its advantage in September, and it showed.

There was to be no outcome that night, in any event. Save for an electoral landslide, nothing could come to much without post-election deals. No party since the MMP voting system was introduced in 1996 had won an outright majority of seats in a general election. Alliances with minor parties – the Greens, ACT and New Zealand First, but particularly the latter – would decide which party would govern.

The shape of the voting showed itself early; a record 1.24 million votes had been cast in advance. By 7.30 P.M., with ten percent of votes counted, it was becoming clear the National Party had prevailed as the leading party, 9.9% ahead of Labour. The Greens, already more or less married to Labour by their memorandum of understanding and a mutual enmity towards the National Party, had won some 5.9% of the party vote. New Zealand First, Winston Peters' party, which had remained aloof from the two larger parties, held 7.1%. There might be some small gains and losses around the edges as counting continued and special votes trickled in, but the essential proportions would remain.

Inside her Point Chevalier home, Jacinda stood in the kitchen, taking over cooking duties with the sausages while Clarke served them with white bread and sauce to the reporters waiting outside.

This was vintage Jacinda: caring about people most others cared to forget. A day earlier, she had telephoned a hapless journalist who had been assigned to cover her grandmother's funeral at St David's Church in Te Aroha. Clarke was in no mood to listen to his apology for intruding on the funeral outside the church, but the journalist was surprised to receive Jacinda's call later. To his astonishment, she reassured him. There were no hard feelings, she said. She knew he was simply doing his job.

While Jacinda ate a casual, homely dinner, some 230 kilometres north, at the Duke of Marlborough Hotel in Russell in the Bay of Islands, Winston Peters and his supporters were enjoying a more salubrious setting. The site of the nation's first white settlement, Russell is a picturesque location. The sky here is the bluest of blues, it is said, second only in the depth of its colour to Rio de Janeiro's. Now, the blue had faded, the day was over; what it held for Peters had been decided, for better or worse.

Sitting at a table with his brother Wayne and a New Zealand First supporter, Winston was photographed in the hotel at a dinner table. The men smiled as if sharing a joke; yachts and pleasure boats on the rippling waters, a pastel sunset, and the land on the far side of the bay made an exquisite backdrop. Perhaps they were having a chuckle at a coincidence that shows just how small Aotearoa really is. Former National Party prime minister Dame Jenny Shipley, who had sacked Peters acrimoniously in 1998, was sitting down for dinner just metres away in the same hotel. The suggestion Peters' old foe should stroll over to their function room to join the New Zealand First function would surely have made them chuckle.

Peters was putting on a brave face. The setting and the black-and-white-balloons that decorated the room belied a muted celebration. He was disappointed: both he and his party had come up short in the election. New Zealand First's vote share was diminished. Peters himself had lost his seat of Northland to the National Party's Matt King in a contentious campaign, leaving him, as one journalist remarked, 'a kingmaker without a kingdom'.[3]

The shrewd Peters knew better; the poker analogy that he would make was closer to the truth. With his number-one ranking on the party list and some seven percent of the party vote, he was still in the game, though with a smaller pile of chips. He stood at the podium shortly before 10 P.M.: an early announcement so his supporters could make their way home on the last ferry across the bay to Paihia.

It would have been a strange Winston Peters press conference indeed without a cutting remark for the press corps: 'We took a bus in the winter cold freezing months from Kaitaia to Invercargill and coast to coast, and we barely saw any [reporters] – anyways, better late than never.'[4] New Zealand First, Peters said, didn't hold 'all the cards but we do have the main cards – we're not going to squander that opportunity'. He spoke of the 'balance of legal responsibility', saying, 'We're not going to be hasty with that.'[5] There was to be no immediate decision on which party New Zealand First might form a government with, and reporters were to be patient, he stressed.

After making his statement to the media, then a few words to his colleagues, the old rugby player stepped away from the microphones, fighting his way out of the media scrum. There was to be no more said – this was his final word for the evening.

In Auckland, as Ardern made her way out of her home for the Labour Party function, reporters asked for her comment on the result. 'Obviously, we hoped for better,' she said, the trademark Ardern self-criticism coming to the fore. At the Aotea Centre, a performing arts theatre hired for their event, Labour supporters chanted, 'Jacinda, Jacinda.' But her speech was downbeat. 'I haven't done as well for [New Zealanders] as I would have liked,' she said.[6] Her staff, despondent with the margin by which Bill English's National Party led, held back their streamer cannon fire. Ardern had rallied her troops and led them in a valiant battle, but they knew they had lost, and convincingly.

English was buoyant, his mood celebratory, his speech almost a victory declaration. Speaking of the 'strong and stable' government New Zealand would have under a National Party and New Zealand First coalition, he claimed the 'moral authority' for the first attempt at forming a government.

Peters must have laughed at the irony of it. The very man who had helped jettison him from his party two-and-a-half decades earlier now clamoured to bring him into the fold, as if it were his right. The National Party leader's staking a moral claim to government was mere rhetoric. There was as much hope for Ardern as for English, and it rested with the man who had so often led parties to victory, one way or another. Perhaps the shrewdest politician New Zealand had seen, Winston Peters was not giving the slightest hint as to whom he might pledge his allegiance.

*

Women are inclined towards relationships; men are more interested in practical matters. Put another way, men prefer working with things and women prefer working with people. Or so the psychologists tell us. Of intelligence, there is nothing between the sexes (though looking at the relative success of countries led by women in combating COVID-19, one might be led to believe otherwise). Interests and inclinations are where the differences lie.

But this is a generalisation, of little use beyond discussion, for most of us live in the spaces between certainties and averages. Granted, Jacinda Ardern is a classic 'people person', whose life from an early age as much as her political career shows her focus on human welfare and relationships: in her family, her social circle, her society. Likewise, Bill English conforms to the masculine stereotype, which made the 2017 New Zealand general election rather interesting.

After years of both parties jostling to claim the centre, there was a refreshing ideological space between them. While Ardern spoke of protecting the environment, jobs with living wages, initiatives for mental health, and ensuring homes were liveable, English promoted an ambitious $10.5 billion plan to build ten 'Roads of National Significance'. They were opposites: male and female, left and right.

Winston Peters was far less easy to define. Indeed, journalists have long abandoned their attempts to figure out the man, remaining content to merely report his one-liners, his controversies, his insults, his idiosyncrasies. As one political scribe said, 'He's one hell of a puzzle.' They're all wary of him. And his tongue. He once called a *New Zealand Herald* columnist a 'smart alec, arrogant, quiche-eating, chardonnay-drinking, pinky finger-pointing snobbery, fart blossom'.[7] He could be punitive, too. 'Putting things in inverted commas will not save you from a defamation writ,' he once quipped, but he was serious.[8]

Undoubtedly, though, Peters is someone who values relationships highly, and maintains them well. Despite his bluntness domestically, he has many friends overseas, some of whom might not be expected to nurture a fondness for him. There's a famous shot of his greeting US secretary of state Condoleezza Rice in 2008 on the tarmac with open arms and a broad grin. Hers too are open, her features lit up with her own smile. The media might find him cranky, stubborn or wily, and David Seymour from ACT may say he's 'a terrible guy', but Winston Raymond Peters has his own brand of charm, humanity and honour.

Perhaps Ardern saw something in the irascible old uncle of New Zealand politics that some of her colleagues might have overlooked. Annette King was by her side, advising her. She never had any trouble with Peters, she said. He always did what he said he was going to do.

At any rate, while Bill English was keen to merely downplay his and the National Party's long and turbulent history with Peters, Ardern was quick to stress the importance of her relationship with the man. Perhaps it's simply women's common sense. Even Judith Collins would later write, 'Friends are gold under MMP.'

*

When the special votes were counted, Labour's position had improved, though only marginally. The National Party held fifty-six seats, Labour forty-six, New Zealand First nine, the Green Party eight and ACT one. The Māori Party had lost both its seats. ACT's David Seymour throwing in his lot with the National Party didn't amount to much for them, just as the Greens allying themselves with Labour wouldn't mean Ardern could govern.

None of this was a surprise to New Zealanders, least of all those in politics. They'd all heard the joke, that MMP is a system in which voters get to choose their favourite candidate and party, and then Winston Peters decides who wins. Peters held the cards. The two major parties would have to negotiate with him, and the canny leader of New Zealand First would decide on the basis of these talks – and other talks with his own party – where on the table he would lay his aces.

No one expected he would rush. Peters hadn't been kingmaker three times before in New Zealand without knowing how to extract concessions from the major parties – slowly, politely, with protracted discussion. The protocol for the talks themselves would be brokered, which itself took time.

Thus, for weeks after the election day, the nation remained in a political limbo. Technically, the National Party under Prime Minister Bill English was still in power, but the government machinery was in neutral, freewheeling while their leader and cabinet negotiated with Peters and his team.

The National Party's negotiations might have been a fine balancing act, but for Ardern, there was the juggling of not one but two potential coalition partners, without whose support there could be no Labour-led coalition. The Green Party and New Zealand First's mutual dislike, if not outright antipathy, made finding common ground all the more difficult. Still, Ardern undertook the talks with aplomb. She shuttled between meetings, with the Greens in the Leader's Lounge in the Opposition Wing and New Zealand First on the second floor. Annette King joined Ardern and the Labour leadership in the talks. The way Ardern balanced both parties' needs while staying true to herself and Labour's principles was 'remarkable', she says.[9]

The New Zealand First leader kept to his word – he was not going to be hasty as he worked through policies, one portfolio at a time, details with clarifications, back and forward. He and his party representatives were meticulous as they were inscrutable: Peters gave no indication of his thinking, at any juncture. These were blind negotiations in the sense that neither the National Party nor Labour had any clue as to what Peters was discussing with the other. They could only guess.

Neither party was sure of Peters' commitment to their negotiations, either. Could he have already decided which party he would join in government? Ardern and her team worried. Was he merely going through the motions of negotiating with them so he could bring pressure to bear on English; squeeze concessions from the National Party? In 1996, he was rumoured to have done just that to Helen Clark's Labour Party, over a marathon seven weeks of talks. Their doubts were justified.

King's advice to Ardern was invaluable, she says: 'She gave me the reassurance that I should follow my gut, and a lot of times in that negotiation I did.'[10]

Peters had his party's manifesto to guide the talks, but he often entrusted his capable lieutenant Tracey Martin to head the discussion for his party. For weeks, Ardern and her party's leaders met with New Zealand First's daily, sometimes twice daily. A staffer trundled in with ginger nut biscuits and tea from time to time.

King was quietly confident from the beginning of their chances of hammering out a deal with Peters. She had witnessed the way the National Party Speaker, David Carter, had treated him over the years, ejecting him from Parliament numerous times and addressing him in a disrespectful manner. The National Party had just conducted a bruising campaign against him in Northland, and Peters had lost his seat. Surely, the insults he bore from the National Party would weigh on his decision; the leak of his superannuation overpayment, likewise.

Another factor in Ardern's favour was that Peters might not feel he could trust the National Party as he could her and the Labour team. His relationship with Bill English himself was fraught. In 1992, English, a young MP at the time, seconded the motion that saw Peters expelled from the National Party caucus. Peters' sacking by the National Party prime minister Jenny Shipley in 1998 had demonstrated to him that carefully negotiated coalition agreements hold little value without trust. As with the rest of her colleagues, Ardern had a clean slate with the man. She was noted in Parliament, too, for keeping her word.

More important, perhaps, was Ardern's potential. A cooperative, progressive woman, voters and politicians alike saw she could bring transformation to New Zealand. English's National Party might make some adjustments, but would hardly change its direction after three terms in government. And change was what Peters spoke of: in leadership, and policy.

Indications as to his thinking were revealed in an interview conducted not long beforehand. His words were ominous for champions of the status quo. Peters had met with a journalist and camera crew, who made a pleasant document of his day during the campaign at his Northland office. Among more mundane discussion, he lamented the comparative decline in New Zealand's prosperity: 'If . . . you examined New Zealand – where it once was as a country in the Western world to where it is now . . . you'd have to admit we've done very, very badly,' he said.[11]

The formal talks with Peters concluded on 12 October. From there, the New Zealand First leader took his negotiations to his party board, after which further discussions ensued. As the days progressed, King noticed that Peters and his team had been spending more time with Labour, and less with the National Party – surely a promising sign.

On the last day of negotiations, 19 October, King and New Zealand First's Shane Jones – a colourful, controversial former Labour minister – liaised with their party leaders as the negotiations reached their conclusion. The final hours saw a simple misunderstanding that very nearly undid all of Ardern's careful work.

There was a troubling silence from New Zealand First, for the first time since negotiations began. Peters had made no contact; Ardern and her team began to worry. At mid-morning, the mood in the office darkened, the Labour team now convinced Peters had chosen the National Party. Someone drafted up a press release: Labour was withdrawing from the negotiations.

King's intuition told her there was still hope. She sent a text to Shane Jones: 'All ka pai [All good]?' Jones replied immediately with a telephone call. Peters, he told her, had not heard from Ardern – he was waiting for her call. Ardern promptly called Peters. The two spoke, ironing out a few small details that had arisen during their talks. It was a cordial discussion. Labour still had a chance.

It was now twenty-six days after the election. At 6.30 P.M., Peters walked into the Beehive Theatrette and took to the rostrum in front of twin New Zealand national flags. He wore a sober, dark grey suit, a white shirt and a black tie with white polka dots, matching the handkerchief in his breast pocket – black and white, New Zealand First's party colours. There had been no leaks, no indication as to what he might say. The only clue was a cryptic text message a prominent New Zealand First member had sent a Labour staffer that morning. 'Ka pai [well done],' was all it said. Was it meant to be a sign to reassure, or mislead them? Did it mean anything at all? No one could tell.

Ardern, Clarke Gayford, Grant Robertson, King and some Labour MPs stood in the Leader of the Opposition's lounge, watching Peters on a television monitor. Peters, an egalitarian Kiwi with a penchant for theatre, would afford the Labour leadership and their National Party counterparts the same treatment as the voters they represented. 'This decision is owed first to the New Zealand people,' Peters said. They would all hear his decision on who would govern the nation, on national television, at the same time – news time.

King sat on a couch, while Ardern, wearing her red blazer, stood nearby. She couldn't bear to sit; her anxiety wouldn't let her as she watched Peters speak.

And speak Peters did, in what could be one of the finest moments of his long career. He spoke eloquently, in measured tones for six-and-a-half minutes. He even quoted the Rolling Stones classic 'You Can't Always Get What You Want' in talking of the policies that 'survived the negotiations'. When he referred to economics, groans and sighs filled Ardern's office. Labour hadn't campaigned on economics. This was Bill English's hobby horse.

Peters continued his oration. Ardern watched the screen, hands clasped together, thumbs under her chin, forefingers over lips with nerves, her eyes unblinking. By her side, stood Robertson, one hand holding his elbow, his jaw supported by the other palm, eyes closed behind spectacles, lips tight as he listened. It seemed Peters was playing showman, bringing everyone's expectation to fever pitch for the sheer devilment of it.

Just as it seemed he would segue to another, considered monologue, Peters came to the point. 'Far too many New Zealanders have come to view today's capitalism not as their friend but as their foe, and they are not all wrong,' he said.[12]

The office erupted for a moment, then fell silent as Peters continued. Surely, they had won.

'We had a choice to make, for a modified status quo or for change. That's why in the end we chose a coalition government of New Zealand First with the New Zealand Labour Party.'

The office exploded with cheers. Ardern turned, tears in her eyes, throwing herself into a tight hug with Robertson, her political partner. Their faces beamed with joy. Gayford took a couple of shots of the moment for posterity.

From youngest deputy leader to the youngest leader in Labour's history, from the worst job in politics with a party languishing in the polls, Jacinda Ardern had swept her party into government – with hope, with empathy. To use a most appropriate cliché, the Labour Party had snatched victory from the jaws of defeat. Pizzas were ordered, and a bottle of single malt whisky was opened for their impromptu celebration. A few months earlier, no one could have predicted the turn of events, that Ardern would be Aotearoa's prime minister.

Nor could anyone have foreseen the challenges that would face her and the nation in her first term in power.

27

Paddles the Polydactyl Cat

Paddles' rise in fortunes was almost as spectacular as her owner's. She, like Jacinda, seemed born for greatness, finding fame young. From the SPCA, an animal rescue centre in Auckland, the ginger-and-white polydactyl cat – with opposable 'thumbs', like a human hand, as it were – rose to take pride of place in the most prominent household of the land. She became the 'first cat'.

Named after New Zealand's cricketing great Sir Richard Hadlee, who was nicknamed Paddles for his large feet, Paddles the cat seemed the perfect pet for Jacinda. She was special, yet remarkably normal. This extraordinary cat had a certain presence, and seemed quite at home in the public eye, as well.

She was a homebody, anyhow, sleeping comfortably on furniture and the plush carpet in the Ardern–Gayford home in Point Chevalier, as if she owned the place. Jacinda held a barbeque for Labour figures the day after the 2017 election; Paddles walked freely among the guests, as if it were her own party. Jacinda stood for the press outside her home holding Paddles, who looked as if she hadn't the slightest worry. An animal lover from her childhood, Jacinda carried Paddles with adoring care. Paddles sat on her lap while she worked from home.

Like her illustrious owner, Paddles was vocal. So much so, she very nearly sparked a diplomatic incident. When US president Donald Trump telephoned to congratulate Jacinda on her electoral victory, Paddles wasn't the slightest impressed, trotting into the room and sitting on the chair, mewing loudly beside her. Clarke had to hastily grab her and take her away so Jacinda could hear the president. Was Paddles showing her displeasure? Or was this just her Kiwi nature, showing neither fear of authority nor favour of rank?

Anyhow, within days of Jacinda's taking office, Paddles had become an internet celebrity. Like her 'mother', she was a dab hand at social media. A cartoonist gave a rendering of her, thumbs and all: 'Introducing Paddles, the new PM – Prime Moggie'. A Twitter account appeared: 'Hi, I'm Paddles and I am the First Cat of New Zealand. I have opposable thumbs, I'm purrty special.' A sleeping Paddles was pictured with a pair of spectacles hanging from her 'thumb'. Her biography there showed her full name as Paddles Ardern-Gayford. She was, it said, 'proud to serve as the First Cat of New Zealand. Have thumbs, will tweet.' She even connected with some famous felines overseas, who also seemed remarkably adept with the keyboard: Larry the cat and his sister Evie, at 10 Downing Street in London.

Alas, a star that shines so bright may not shine for long. So it was for Paddles Ardern-Gayford. On 7 November, the day of the new Parliament's opening, a neighbour, Chris, was hurrying back to work in his car after a lunch break. As he took a bend in the road, a cat streaked in front of him; he felt the bump as it ran under the wheel. Chris stopped, but the cat ran away and disappeared. He walked along the footpath, scanning the front lawns as he went, hoping to find it uninjured.

A woman emerged from her house. When Chris told her he had run over a ginger cat, she looked troubled. 'That's my neighbour's cat,' she said.

'Not that neighbour?' he asked, pointing at Jacinda and Clarke's home.

She nodded gravely. Chris's stomach churned.

The pair soon found Paddles' lifeless body next to a fence nearby. Chris was horrified. He had just killed the prime minister's beloved pet. What would he do?

Later, he knocked on Jacinda's door to apologise. Clarke answered. He was kind, understanding, but clearly upset. Chris wrote a condolence card to which his seven-year-old daughter contributed, asking Jacinda not to send her dad to jail.

Naturally, Jacinda was distraught over the loss of her beloved Paddles, made all the worse coming so soon after the death of her grandmother. She didn't show her grief publicly, though she posted on Facebook, 'To anyone who has ever lost a pet, you'll know how sad we feel.' She urged people, who so wished, to donate to the SPCA in Paddles' memory.

A month passed; Chris missed a telephone call. It went to voice-mail. Jacinda left a message: 'Sorry you had to go through that, thank you for stopping by and thanks for the card.'

Some time later, he saw Jacinda in a park by the beach, with her family. How would he handle the situation? Chris couldn't avoid her: his young son began playing rather boisterously with Jacinda's niece on the playground equipment, while Jacinda hovered over them. He worried. He'd killed Jacinda's cat and he couldn't face even the remot-est prospect that his son would hurt the little girl accidentally, so he stood nearby. Chris plucked up the courage to speak, identifying himself to Jacinda and apologising for running over Paddles.

Remarkably, she apologised to him: 'I said, "I'm so sorry," and then she said, "No, I'm sorry," and it kind of went round in circles,' Chris remembers.

The loss of Paddles was more than simply the loss of a pet for Jacinda, and Chris knew this. This personable cat represented the child she and Clarke could not have for themselves. The couple had sought a doctor's advice over Jacinda's failure to conceive; they would need medical intervention, they were told. It was a blow for the woman who so loved children, who had always aspired to be a mother. Stoic as she is, she soon came to terms with the fact that she and Clarke would need fertility treatment, perhaps even IVF, to achieve her dream.

Or so it appeared. Triumph tinged with sadness, the 'whirlwind' of her life since her thirty-seventh birthday held yet another surprise for Jacinda in the Land of the Long White Cloud.

28

Mother of the Nation

On 13 October, in the midst of negotiations with Winston Peters and New Zealand First, Jacinda and Clarke discovered Jacinda was pregnant. They were thrilled, and it was a blessed surprise to them. Somehow, in the turmoil and sadness of the campaign's final days, Jacinda had conceived. They kept their delight and their news a secret for as long as Jacinda could conceal it under her garments. She hid her morning sickness. Even though 'it was terrible' – for sixteen weeks of her pregnancy, she 'just wanted to throw up all of the time' – she gave no indication of it during those delicate negotiations to form a government. For the opening of Parliament on 7 November, her nausea was especially bad. She sat through the Governor General's speech, 'wondering what the fastest route to the bathroom was', but with no way to leave with grace, she just 'concentrated hard on the words being spoken . . . and hoped for the best.'[1] Thankfully for her and the occasion, this worked.

The news Jacinda was pregnant came to Clarke in the wake of an argument. He was in Whananaki, Northland, filming for his television show, *Fish of the Day*, while in Wellington Jacinda sweated over the tail end of Labour's negotiations with Winston Peters. 'I'd called [Clarke] and we'd had a little bit of an argument about whether or not he was going to be able to get to Wellington for [Peters'] announcement,' Jacinda says. 'When I got the result of my test, I thought, Oh my word, I'm going to have to call him back. I called him back, and he was kind of exasperated.' Until, of course, she told him their news. Clarke was overjoyed. Needless to say, he hurried back to Auckland to be with her.

A few months later, on 19 January 2018, with the bump beginning to show, Jacinda and Clarke announced they were expecting their first baby.

It began with an announcement to the Labour caucus in the morn-ing. Later in the day came a post on Facebook: a photograph of two large fishhooks, and a smaller one placed neatly within one of them. 'Clarke and I are really excited that in June our team will expand from two to three, and that we'll be joining the many parents out there who wear two hats. I'll be prime minister AND a mum, and Clarke will be "first man of fishing" and stay at home dad.'[2] The post would provoke a media blitz, a journalist predictably dubbed 'Jacindababymania', across the world.

Ardern was well aware that her baby would be quite a novelty, sought after by the press and the public. She was keen that the 'royal baby', as the expected child was quickly dubbed, would not suffer with the media's attention. She also knew, though, that inevitably, 'this will be a wee one a village will raise'. She seemed to understand that it was best to appeal to New Zealanders' good sense, to let them be part of her experience. Her message was clear: 'We are going to make this work, and New Zealand is going to help us raise our first child.'

She was correct. Most New Zealanders were happy for Ardern, excited at the prospect at their prime minister having a baby. They were supportive, and more than a little fascinated. She had been the youngest leader of New Zealand since 1856, the world's youngest female head of government, and now she would be only the second elected national leader to give birth while in office.

There were some, however, who expressed worry. How would she cope with raising her child while running the country? What would happen during the six weeks of maternity leave that she said she would take? What kind of an acting prime minister would Winston Peters (who had been appointed deputy prime minister as part of the coalition negotiations) make? Or, more to the point, what kind of mischief might he create?

Helen Clark's congratulatory tweet put the issue in perspective. She wished the couple 'all the best [for the pregnancy]: a super busy year coming up & much to look forward to. Every #woman should have the choice of combining family & career.'[3] She saw her protégée enjoying the kind of freedom she might have wanted decades earlier, and seemed to savour it vicariously.

Of the doubters, Ardern was dismissive, in several interviews. 'I'm just pregnant, not incapacitated,' she said. 'I am not the first woman to multitask.'⁴ 'I know these are special circumstances, but there will be many women who will have done this well before I have.'⁵

She was quite correct. On 25 January 1990, Prime Minister Benazir Bhutto of Pakistan gave birth to a daughter, Bakhtawar Bhutto-Zardari, though in vastly different circumstances. Under siege politically from the army, Bhutto kept her pregnancy under wraps, so to speak. Dressing in her hijab and flowing salwars and keeping a strict silence on the matter meant not even cabinet members knew of it, until she delivered Bakhtawar by caesarean section. She returned to work as soon as doctors allowed her – remarkably, as she later wrote, 'reading government papers and signing government files'⁶ the following day.

Ardern's experience of pregnancy, childbirth and motherhood in office was as different from Bhutto-Zardari's as could be imagined. Naturally, the whole affair was very public. As the day approached, many Kiwis suggested names for the baby. There were offers, also, for Jacinda to bury her placenta on the lands where the Waitangi Treaty was signed. This was a touching honour indeed.

The Māori and pākehā alike embracing Jacinda and Clarke's baby was welcome, as were the suggestions for names. The suggestions placed Jacinda and Clarke, though, in an invidious position: if they accepted one, they would undoubtedly offend another. They were delighted, at any rate, that their baby, whose sex they knew but were keeping to themselves, would become the Māori's mokopuna (grand-child, or grand-niece or nephew) and the pākehā's 'first baby'. All New Zealanders would share Jacinda and Clarke's joy, bringing the nation together.

In the months before her delivery, when the baby was awaited with as much anticipation by the public as by her family, Ardern didn't simply stick to her work schedule. She made bold state-ments for her nation's indigenous people that resonated across the world.

The first came with a historic event, one that in recent years has been the locus of vituperation, infighting and bitterness. Ardern was invited to speak at the upper marae (Māori meeting grounds) of the

Waitangi Treaty site on Waitangi Day, New Zealand's nation day, in February 2018. It was an honour for any prime minister, but especially for Ardern, as she would be the first woman prime minister to do so.

Previous appearances on the marae by a woman prime minister, however, had ended in tears – literally. Helen Clark attended the event in February 2004, but was jostled and jeered, leaving her shaken. She very nearly fell among the crush around her. Only sympathetic Māori, one of whom, with knives in his belt, threw himself into the fray, and plainclothes police with MPs, saved her.

A few years earlier, it was perhaps worse. In February 1998, Clark had been invited to speak at Waitangi, but in the midst of an internal Māori dispute was accosted and prevented from addressing the gathering. She sat quietly among her supporters instead, a borrowed maroon handkerchief in hand, her blue eyes glistening, wiping away tears of humiliation and shock. It was one of the rare occasions that New Zealanders witnessed raw emotion from the redoubtable Helen Clark.

It was hardly better at Waitangi for Clark's successor, John Key. Key was accosted by two brothers at Waitangi in 2009, who grabbed him and yelled, 'You're not going to the marae!' The prime minister nearly lost his suit jacket in the confrontation. The men were subdued by surrounding Māori, who comforted the unusually perturbed Key. In 2016, Key was represented at the event by Steven Joyce, his economic development minister. Joyce was hit by a flying dildo a protester hurled at him. Prime Minister Bill English declined an invitation to attend Waitangi Day at the marae in 2017.

One year later, and Ardern was determined to make Waitangi Day a departure from the anger, politicking and divisiveness that had marred the event for decades.

She had her own memories of Waitangi decades earlier, which had nothing to do with politics. Jacinda and Louise had visited the Waitangi Treaty grounds with their parents when Jacinda was seven. Ross and Laurell stood on the edge of the grounds; Ross gave Jacinda the family's camera and asked her to take a shot of him and Laurell. Just as the shutter was about to click, Ross swung Laurell into a tight embrace and kissed her on the lips. The girls were suitably embarrassed.

This year, the event was carefully planned so no one should be embarrassed, let alone manhandled. It was held on the upper marae for logistical and political reasons – it is more spacious, and neutral ground there. Ardern arrived with Gayford, accompanied by Winston Peters. Joyce, now the National Party's spokesperson for finance and infrastructure, attended alongside them, with a delegation from Parliament. It was to be the very opposite of a partisan event.

Women traditionally have not been allowed to speak at the marae. It was a great honour for her, Ardern said in her speech, which she delivered after she and her delegation had been treated to the pōwhiri (Māori ceremony of welcome, involving speeches, singing, dancing and finally the hongi). To the delight of the audience, she addressed the gathering first in te reo Māori, which she read from cue cards. 'We did not come simply for the beauty and the hospitality of the North,' she told the gathering. 'We came because there is work to do . . . [to] turn talk to action' on 'education, health, employment, roads, housing.' The clear message of her address was the government's willingness to work with the Māori, to deal constructively with the issues facing them.

It was all very well received. Some of her parliamentary colleagues had tears in their eyes at the pōwhiri. Even Winston Peters seemed touched by the event, which he told reporters was 'very harmonious. You'd have to go back forty years to see that.' There were, indeed, shades of Norman Kirk's appearance at the marae in 1973, where he walked hand-in-hand with a young Māori boy to the ceremony.

Ardern had her diplomatic protection officers, but she hardly needed them. As she walked around at Waitangi, looking charismatic in a black dress, with her hair down and her baby bump there for all to see, she was mobbed as much by children asking for selfies as she was by adults. They would sidle up to her with a shy, self-conscious shuffle that was becoming so familiar to her security detail and aides. The officers had to relax their protocols, because so many of her fans would want to touch her. Naturally, her admirers meant no harm – they simply wanted to connect with her. Ardern just smiled. A New Zealand Herald article, 'Everyone falls in love with Jacinda Ardern at Waitangi', nicely summed up her appearance. The following morning, Jacinda made perhaps her most lasting contribution to the Waitangi Day commemorations. 'She wanted to give something back to the people,' minister Kelvin Davis said, so rather than the 'fairly exclusive' breakfast prime ministers were treated to in earlier years, she and her ministers took to the grill. Wearing aprons and with tongs in hand, they cooked and served a free barbecue breakfast of eggs, bacon butties, bread and sausages to the public. The barbecue was enthusiastically received, such that Ardern needed to apologise to the crowd that they had run out of food. A powerful statement of national unity and service – leaders breaking bread with the people, as it were – the barbecue at Waitangi Day was repeated in 2019, 2020 and 2021. After Waitangi Day 2021, Jacinda wrote that she hoped the barbecue would become 'a tradition that continues'.

Another touching show of national unity came a few months later, in April, while Ardern was beginning to make her presence felt on an international stage. By this time, she was heavily pregnant. She visited France's President Emmanuel Macron within the majesty of the Élysée Palace on 16 April, ostensibly to win support for a free trade agreement between New Zealand and the European Union. While there, she had a brief one-on-one with Canadian prime minister Justin Trudeau, the other of the triumvirate of young, charismatic leaders from the West, all in Paris at the one time. From Paris, Ardern went to meet Angela Merkel in Berlin the following day, where she made strong statements against the use of chemical weapons in Syria: a 'blatant breach of international law' that 'cannot be left unchallenged',[7] Ardern told reporters.

The ultimate purpose of Ardern's overseas visit was to attend the Commonwealth Heads of Government meeting (CHOGM) in London, which may indeed be the last attended by Her Majesty Queen Elizabeth II. On this trip, the 'first man of fishing' Clarke Gayford would be seen as he so rarely had been before: in a suit and tie, then a tuxedo.

Ardern's attire was far more spectacular. She looked striking enough in Berlin, in all black – appropriate garb for a patriotic New Zealander. In London, she upped the ante, featuring perhaps the most graceful, regal attire ever worn by a New Zealand prime minister at an international event. For the CHOGM dinner at Buckingham Palace on 19

April, Ardern wore a dress of a deep yellow-mustard hue, cut perfectly for her bulge. Over her shoulders was the mantle of her nation, a kahu huruhuru, a Māori cloak made from fibre interwoven with native New Zealand bird feathers.

The effect was breathtaking. The kahu huruhuru is one of the most prestigious garments for the Māori. Denoting status, it is a symbol of mana (power) that Ardern wore easily: it looked as if it were made just for her. Even the Queen, who had been gifted a similar garment in her youth, wearing it at official events in New Zealand since, looked impressed as she spoke with Ardern. The garment was 'highly coveted among the princesses at the dinner . . . They made a beeline for her,' Gayford later commented.

Ardern spoke in even, clear tones as she raised a toast to the Commonwealth at the banquet. Earlier, she had been granted an audience with the Queen, one of only a few – no small feat for an avowed republican. She had made quite an impression on the gathering of leaders, as she had on her royal hosts.

New Zealanders were delighted, especially the Māori. Much as Ardern was a pākehā, she was their leader, who represented all citizens of Aotearoa. She had been respectful with the kahu huruhuru, which was offered with the Māori's blessing; Ngāti Rānana, London's Māori club, which loaned the garment, said it was 'an honour' that she wore it. Ardern, a leader who advocated that all children learn te reo Māori at school, sent an unequivocal message to the world at Buckingham Palace: Māori culture was New Zealand culture, cherished by New Zealanders of all racial backgrounds.

The New Zealand leader was making her presence felt globally, even at this early stage of her tenure – well before the dramatic events that characterised her first term in office. Immediately after her appearance at the CHOGM, Ardern was included in the *Time* 100 list of the most influential people in the world. 'She's not just leading a country. She's changing the game,' Sheryl Sandberg, the COO of Facebook, wrote. This could only benefit women and girls, throughout the world.

Sandberg, along with women from all walks of life, was intrigued to see how Ardern would juggle the duties of motherhood and the state – no mean feat, they knew well. They awaited the baby's arrival with keen interest.

*

It was if the baby wanted to heighten the expectation, or to be born on one of the most spiritually powerful days of the year, according to ancient tradition. Everyone was kept waiting with bated breath. Jacinda's due date was 17 June. *The Spinoff*, a Kiwi news website, launched a live blog on the day, but all it could report was 'No baby', showcasing such Kiwi wit as, 'Unfortunately there is no baby. However here is a picture of a baby,' above a Christmas-card rendering of the Nativity. Keeping a low profile, Jacinda was photographed working from home, looking over government papers.

Finally, on the morning of the winter solstice, Thursday 21 June, Clarke drove Jacinda to Auckland City Hospital, a five-kilometre trip across the suburbs. There were strict controls on the media, which was needed with the sheer number of reporters converging on the place. At 6.15 P.M., Jacinda posted on Instagram: 'Welcome to our village wee one. Feeling very lucky to have a healthy baby girl that arrived at 4.45 P.M. weighing 3.31kg (7.3lb). Thank you so much for your best wishes and your kindness. We're all doing really well thanks to the wonderful team at Auckland City Hospital.'

Beside these words was a touching photograph: Jacinda sitting up in the bed, beaming a satisfied smile, babe in arms. Her face showed a mix of joy and fatigue. Clarke knelt beside her and their baby, looking suitably proud. At last, Jacinda had the complete family she had so long wished for.

The joy of the event was reflected in the words of New Zealand's poet laureate, Selina Tusitala Marsh:

The baby's here, the baby's here!
Aotearoa, New Zealand, what a year!

Joy, but also hard work that only women can truly appreciate. It had not been an easy delivery, with Jacinda in labour for nearly twelve hours. Needless to say, this takes enormous effort. Jacinda's first meal after delivery was Marmite on toast and a cup of Milo (an Australian malted chocolate drink), the media reported. The next morning, she regained her strength with a plate of macaroni cheese, which her 'wonderful midwife Libby' had made her that morning, after hearing her say she had 'a wee craving yesterday'. Cheese is an Ardern passion.

Jacinda posed with Libby and baby for a photograph, still looking tired. The baby had been active the night before, keeping her awake. The little one had quite an appetite, according to a spokesperson from Jacinda's office. Jacinda decided to stay in the hospital another night to recuperate.

Laurell and Ross were thrilled at the arrival of their new grand-daughter. Jacinda posted on Facebook a touching photograph of Ross helping to zip her into her black ankle boot a few weeks earlier, when she could no longer reach her feet. It must have brought back memories more than three decades old. Laurell and Ross spoke to the media from Nelson, a town on Tasman Bay in the South Island, after the delivery. 'The baby was looking up at Jacinda and it looked like she was in awe of her and I couldn't get over how alert it was just after being born,' Laurell said. 'So, I'm dying to see it and hold her and just see what she's like.'[8]

Jacinda's baby was a special baby and being born on the Southern Hemisphere's winter solstice, in the midst of Matariki (Māori new year) festivals and celebrations, she deserved a special name. Coincidentally, she was born sixty-five years to the day after Benazir Bhutto, the first elected national leader to bear a child while in office. Deciding a name before the baby was born had gone 'terribly', Jacinda said before she had gone to hospital. It was a 'struggle' for months. After seeing their beautiful little girl for the first time, though, she and Clarke received inspiration, as parents often do.

On 24 June, Jacinda and Clarke stood in the hospital foyer before a bushel of microphones, cameras and press some way back, for a media appearance. Cradled in Jacinda's arms, their baby wore a light-green knitted hat Libby had gifted her, that looked like the infant's 'first fishing hat', the midwife said. They had decided, Jacinda announced, their child would be called Neve Te Aroha Ardern Gayford, or Neve Gayford. 'When we met her we thought she looked like she suited the name,' Jacinda said. Ardern Gayford wouldn't be a double-barrelled surname: honouring a tradition in Jacinda's family, as in many, her family name would be a middle name for her child.

Neve means 'bright and radiant and snow, which seemed like a good combination for Matariki and for solstice',⁹ Jacinda explained. Te Aroha, the name of the mountain whose silhouette filled the eastern skyline across the pastures from Jacinda's home in Morrinsville, means the place of love. It is also the name of the town beneath the mountain where the Ardern family settled. 'Te Aroha was our way of reflecting the amount of love this baby has been shown before she arrived and all of the names we were gifted along the way'¹⁰ by a number of iwi or tribes, Jacinda said. This was vintage, tactful Jacinda: she had avoided offending anyone, yet somehow taken pains to meet everyone's needs.

She might have offended someone, just a little. Neve's 'great-aunt' Annette King (now Dame Annette, her title awarded in the 2018 New Year's Honours list), was on a boat off the coast of France when she heard the news. She sent her warmest congratulations, saying she was 'absolutely delighted'. 'I am going to suggest', she commented, 'that Annie would be a good name – or Annette if you prefer the longer version.'

In any event, with Neve's name as with her appearance at Buckingham Palace, Jacinda managed to honour Aotearoa's mixed Māori and pākehā heritage.

Mixed heritage is perhaps an understatement – Neve is a typical Kiwi for her gloriously eclectic background. An episode of the TVNZ1 investigatory series *DNA Detectives* aired in November 2017 showed Jacinda had forebears from '[the] UK, Ireland, France, Germany, Scandinavia and western and eastern Europe'. In the episode, she met her fourth cousin Lana, in Greece. The resemblance between the two women is astonishing ('You have my teeth,' Jacinda exclaimed, the pair flashing near-identical toothy smiles at their meeting). On her father's side of the family, Neve has Māori ancestors along with the European, and appropriate to the growing Indian population in Aotearoa, her own link to India, with one ancestor on her father's side born in Byculla, a neighbourhood in Mumbai.

Congratulations came from all parts of the world for this truly international baby. From Canada, Jacinda's mentor, the former prime minister Helen Clark, said it was a very proud day for the couple. Messages came from all walks of life: Queen Elizabeth, pop stars such as Pink, prime ministers, National Party opponents and Bakhtawar Bhutto-Zardari, to name just a few. Neve was inundated with presents, too. Never one to waste anything, Jacinda said many of the baby clothes and the like would be recycled, passed onto other new parents.

For the next six weeks, Jacinda would be on maternity leave, beginning on the day she went to hospital. She could settle into motherhood – as much as a prime minister can, anyhow. Winston Peters would be acting prime minister. The old charmer told TVNZ1's *Breakfast*, 'We'll bother each other when we have to', which would be as little as necessary.

This would be the last time for years that Jacinda could enjoy any stretch of private time, being a mother for little Neve. Her maternal role would become public, broadening its scope and sense beyond all expectation, in her first term in office.

29

Changing the Game, Slowly

'It's really, really nice to be back amongst you all,' Jacinda Ardern told her cabinet colleagues on 2 August 2018 when she returned from maternity leave. 'Shall we get on with it?' The last six weeks at home with Neve, she said, had 'been wonderful'.

Ardern was applauded and cheered by her ministers, as was Winston Peters for his time as acting prime minister, though it was perhaps more for relief than praise. New Zealand's government had been more-or-less 'steady as she goes' while Ardern was on leave. As Peters himself said, 'The sky didn't fall in.'

It hadn't been all peace and happiness. The National Party president, Peter Goodfellow, had raised Peters' ire and risked a legal writ by describing him as 'whiskey-swilling, cigarette-smoking, double-breasted and irrational'.[1] The nation's nurses went on strike; Peters was engaged in suing the very government he had headed, for the breach of privacy over his superannuation overpayment. He had fired a couple of verbal shells across the Tasman Sea at the Australian government, as well, one in connection with a seventeen-year-old New Zealand boy in an adult detention centre. 'You're a signatory [to UN conventions],' he said. 'Live up to it.'[2] He also declared Australia should change its national flag, which is remarkably similar to New Zealand's, 'and honour the fact'[3] that the design originated in New Zealand (a questionable assertion). Stirring controversy, as he often does, he suggested Australia change its national anthem to 'Waltzing Matilda' (many Australians might well agree with him here).

All this was the least of Ardern's worries. Presenting the government as a cohesive whole, making it function was in itself a Herculean task. Soon after taking office, Ardern found herself playing the role of a patient matriarch in a dysfunctional family, riven with differences.

Naturally, Peters was the short-tempered great-uncle of the family. Then there were the fractious teenagers, including New Zealand First's leading light Shane Jones, described by the *Northland Age* as 'part jester, part genius'.[4] Jones could be relied on to court controversy, at times speaking his mind beyond decorum. The Greens were idealistic youngsters, utterly ignored and sidelined by their great-uncle, who scorned their 'woke pixie dust';[5] the Labour ministers the energetic young guns who felt frustrated by their strange domestic arrangement, exasperated by their adopted siblings and hampered progress.

Somehow, Ardern had to bring all these opposing forces together as a viable coalition. It's a mercy she studied conflict and consensus in university. Her knowledge of history served her well, too: she understood the fate of Prime Minister Jenny Shipley's government, which foundered not long after jettisoning Peters as deputy prime minister and treasurer in 1998.

Humility is a characteristic more innate than acquired. It is one Ardern exhibited comfortably and readily during her first term in government. By happy coincidence, her natural humility, her enormous reserves of patience, were a prerequisite if she was to make a success of her premiership. Indeed, they were key to her political survival.

Just over a month after she returned from maternity leave in September 2018, a *Newshub* article entitled 'Jacinda Ardern and the Winston Peters dilemma: Do nothing or take the nuclear option' discussed the stark choices the prime minister faced with her broadest of broad coalitions. The journalist's thesis was that Ardern had little choice but to indulge Peters or face the ruination of her government.[6]

The article came hard on the heels of a series of high-profile, embarrassing, abrupt changes of tack for the government. Justice Minister Andrew Little's plans to repeal the 'three strikes' criminal legislation were scuppered when Peters pulled his support for the bill at the eleventh hour. The Employment Relations Amendment Bill, one of Labour's flagship policies, and the government's new Crown–Māori Relations Agency met the same fate. Worse, their sponsors, such as Little and deputy Labour leader Kelvin Davis, learned of Peters' decisions the same way they had learned of his decision to join Labour in a coalition: via the media.

Just the day before the *Newshub* article was published, on 12 September 2018, the National Party's Gerry Brownlee targeted Peters in Parliament: 'Quite clearly . . . [Peters] still hasn't stopped acting as prime minister. He has the veto on everything this Government does.'[7] While this was obviously an exaggeration, theatrical in its rendering, New Zealand First was exercising a good deal of influence in the coalition government – certainly, it seemed, more than its share of the party vote would warrant.

The National Party was sure to make political capital from Labour's dilemma. Earlier, Simon Bridges had accused Ardern of being 'weak and indecisive'. It was a gratuitous attack, churlish to almost anyone with a thorough knowledge of New Zealand politics. Ardern pointed out that hers was the first 'pure' coalition government since the advent of MMP in 1996: neither of the two parties in coalition, Labour or New Zealand First (who governed with a confidence-and-supply agreement from the Greens) had won a plurality, unlike every other MMP government before. Without New Zealand First and the Greens, there would simply be no Labour-led government. The political journalist Tracy Watkins succinctly expressed the Labour leader's predicament: 'the way the numbers fell on election night means either minor party could hold Labour hostage to their programme should they wish'.[8]

Given the circumstances, Ardern's ability to keep her divergent alliance together says nothing of weakness, a good deal about her lack of egotism and much about her strength. Merely functioning with all the opposing elements within your own party – the Labour caucus, with its factions and competing personalities – is challenge enough for most politicians. To unite your own party, then bring together such wildly varying ideologies as Labour, New Zealand First (with its farrago of left and right, and socially conservative policies) and the Greens, takes almighty forbearance.

The job of prime minister is hard enough at the best of times. Watkins noted, 'The pressure is massive, the hours are punishing, the scrutiny is immense and you can't walk away and shut the door on everyone for a day.'[9] Add to that the strain, however joyful, of new motherhood.

Ardern herself brushed aside the National Party's criticism, telling a BBC reporter, 'It takes courage and strength to be empathetic. And I am very proudly an empathetic, compassionately driven politician . . . I am trying to chart a different path. That will attract critics.'[10]

One can only conclude Ardern had an expansive, philosophical view of her role in government. With her Christian upbringing and long-held fascination with Te Whiti's non-violent campaign in the late nineteenth century, and Gandhi's in the twentieth century, she knew well the strength of turning the other cheek. This way, Labour might suffer its humiliating reversals, but there would also be progress, even if it was not the swift transformation that Ardern's rise had promised. For every disappointment there was an achievement; for every backdown, Labour saw a triumph of implementation. In any event, where there could be agreement, Ardern lost no time in acting, the government setting to work with a 100-day plan.

Housing had been an issue of major concern to voters. By barring foreign speculators from buying existing homes in New Zealand, the Labour-led government managed to take some of the heat out of the property market. Single-use plastic bags, the curse of the waterways and a landfill nightmare, were banned. The sale of government homes was halted; although there was a slow start to KiwiBuild, a scheme to help New Zealanders buy their own homes, the building of state houses increased, exceeding targets. By mid-2019 there were somewhere in the order of nine times as many government homes being constructed as there were in 2016: 2,700, as opposed to 282.[11] Cold and damp rental homes, an issue that Ardern underscored on the election trail, had long called for action. The government passed the Healthy Homes Guarantee Act 2017 just months after she came to office. The act set minimum standards for rental accommodation, mandating insulation and heating.

Also within months of Ardern's government taking office, students had cause to celebrate, with their first-year fees waived for post-secondary-school education or training. Student allowances and living cost loans were also raised. Paid parental leave was extended to twenty-six weeks from 1 July 2020, a policy designed to give young ones the best start in life (in July 2012, Ardern had described in Parliament the first six months as 'the most crucial period of a child's development that we could possibly invest in'); a tax cut planned by the National Party government of some $1.5 billion per year was scrapped to pay for a families package, with the aim of lifting tens of thousands of children out of poverty.

In so many interviews, as in Supriya's, Ardern mentioned the profound effect of witnessing the poverty of children in her early childhood home town of Murupara. By the middle of the 2010s, with the absence of a government programme to tackle the issue, deprivation in schools had become almost endemic in some regions, especially in Northland, the areas surrounding Murupara. The need had become so pressing that while the National Party was in power, a biker gang, Tribal Huk, took its own initiative in distributing lunches to school children in Waikato. Ardern's government began a comprehensive programme to feed underprivileged children in 2019, introducing free, healthy daily lunches to students in schools with high levels of disadvantage.

Underprivileged children come from households gripped by poverty, often through no fault of the parents. Ardern had spoken numerous times in Parliament on the issue of the working poor. Early in her first term, the minimum hourly wage was raised to $16.50, and each year thereafter, taking it to $20 in 2021 – closer to the living wage of $22.10.[12]

Health too saw some positive change. Two budgets gave an enormous injection of capital, more than $2 billion, to build more hospital and healthcare facilities, with a particular focus on mental health. On 30 May 2019, Finance Minister Grant Robertson handed down a budget explicitly centred around its people's well-being. The Wellbeing Budget meant the nation would dedicate billions over the following four years to alleviating child poverty and domestic violence, and to improving mental health.

Interestingly, some of the inspiration for the budget seems to have come from the work of Marilyn Waring, Ardern's teenage heroine. As a pioneer in the field of feminist economics, Waring sought to broaden

the definition of economic prosperity beyond the dry economic defini-
tions of GDP, which had ascribed no value to women's care of families,
the environment and matters of general well-being. The Labour-led
coalition government headed by Ardern was the first in the Western
world to design its entire budget according to well-being factors, and to
instruct its ministers to pursue policies that enhance well-being.[13]

Naturally, none of this change was easy to effect within the coalition framework. But while New Zealand First might sometimes have
played the part of 'handbrake', as Peters described his party's role
during the 2020 election campaign, it also conceded on some key
issues. If it managed to water down the Climate Change Response
(Zero Carbon) Amendment Bill, it had to swallow a ban on all new
permits for oil and gas exploration, which many scientists supported
for reducing the nation's carbon emissions.

Indeed, all sides had to give ground in the coalition. But along
with the loss of cornerstone policies, Ardern's Labour Party had to
accept a leisurely rate of change. Ardern spoke of her feelings on this
openly, but not with the least rancour. 'Pace is something that always
does frustrate me,' she told the *Stuff* journalist Henry Cook in October
2019. 'You just face the reality of politics . . . that's something that I
was absolutely prepared for coming in with a three-party government,
which I think has actually delivered a huge amount, given that we are
three diverse parties.'[14]

Diverse personalities, too. Underpinning her first term in office
was the grace with which Ardern conducted her relationship with
Peters: her absolute, uncomplaining commitment to a consensus-
based regime. This put her in a league of her own in New Zealand
politics. Prime Minister Jim Bolger sacked Peters as minister of Māori
affairs in 1991 after he criticised the government. When as New
Zealand First leader Peters returned to cabinet as treasurer in 1996,
the pair made some effort to cooperate.

The nation's first woman prime minister, Jenny Shipley, handled
her differences with Peters in cabinet in a vastly different fashion –
authoritatively, that is: sacking him in August 1998 over his 'refusal to
accept Cabinet collective responsibility'.[15] Specifically, Peters had
publicly criticised the government's privatisation of Wellington
airport.

'Consensus' wasn't a word so often used by Shipley. She accused Peters of impugning her integrity, and charged that he had brought disrepute to the nation, while inviting New Zealand First's MPs to 'waka jump' (literally 'canoe jump', or jump ship) into the government. In the November 1999 general election, she was soundly beaten by Helen Clark.

Ardern's experience of New Zealand First and Winston Peters couldn't be further from Shipley's. Rather than merely suffer his foibles, she seemed to genuinely appreciate him. She spoke highly of the man: when asked to describe him in three words, she said, 'experienced, respectful and humorous'.[16] This was not simply flattery for convenience. Even after the 2020 election and months after Peters was ousted, she referred to their 'decent relationship'. In Parliament, the old-school, chivalrous Peters was Ardern's champion. Hers is the only government that he joined as a cabinet minister and survived a full term, without being sacked. 'I never questioned that we could make this work,' Ardern says. 'We just operate in a really respectful way. We talk often. There is no challenge that can't be worked through in my view.'[17]

There was not the least public expression of bitterness when consensus could not be reached between the parties, either. As the news reached the media that Labour's vaunted Auckland Light Rail project had been stymied by New Zealand First, Ardern and her transport minister, Phil Twyford, merely stated they were 'disappointed'. A glass-half-full kind of person, Ardern seemed much more inclined to celebrate the government's successes rather than dwell on lost opportunities. 'Look, ultimately, this is an MMP government,'[18] Jacinda told a journalist when prodded about the light rail project. That is, you win some; you lose some.

In November 2019, she took up a challenge from her team to list all her government's achievements in a two-minute video. It was an exuberant performance, going viral in the coming days throughout the world. Jacinda went overtime, however, taking two minutes fifty-six seconds, which she acknowledged at the end of the video with a cheeky, triumphant grin: 'But a great list.'

Winston Peters himself spoke positively of his term in coalition with Ardern's government. In one of the last sittings of Parliament before the 2020 election, he said, 'We've got over 190 bills passed. That suggests we have got by on agreeing on most . . . things. Or if we couldn't, we compromised, and got there in the end.'[19]

Ardern might have been slower in changing the game than she would ideally have liked. There were ways, however, in which she was doing so immediately.

30

Carving a Path

Helen Clark and Annette King's generation prepared the way for women such as her, Jacinda Ardern said. There was still much work to do, though, before a woman holding high office was treated as a 'normal' phenomenon throughout the world. Like Clark before her, Ardern felt the need to stress that her gender was not a substantive issue for her political career. 'I want to be a good leader, not a good lady leader,' she said. 'I don't want to be known simply as the woman who gave birth.'[1]

When she spoke those words, it was nearly a year into her first term. She could not have known the events ahead of her that would make any suggestion of her being remembered simply as the 'woman who gave birth' seem mildly ridiculous. Nevertheless, giving birth and holding the highest executive role in a Western democracy meant she would first become famous for this. Inevitably, she was an inspiration for women throughout the world, for successfully juggling the duties of prime ministership and motherhood.

For her stamina alone in this, Ardern deserved plaudits. Not that she herself was satisfied. True to her nature, she felt 'the guilt of whether or not I'm a good enough daughter, sister, partner, mother'.[2] Women know this guilt well, as Ardern noted: 'Show me a woman who doesn't.'[3] She was at pains to point out to a BBC interviewer, too, that she is 'a mother, not a superwoman'.[4]

Others might beg to differ. Ardern's schedule was punishing, particularly in the months after Neve's birth. Being a mother itself is a full-time job. Leading a coalition government at the same time as nursing an infant is almost unthinkable. Her spokesperson said, 'It's not unusual for a day to start as early as 6 A.M. and finish as late as 10.30 P.M. once travel is factored in, with considerable volumes of reading required outside those times.'[5] That is, Ardern would often read cabinet papers until midnight or later before feeding Neve, sleeping, then waking up early to head to the Beehive again. She enjoys reading briefing books – up to 1000 pages in a weekend, she says, often in the car, which would make her carsick. She is enthusiastic about her work, too. But all these intense hours required prodigious willpower. There was no time for cooking, reading recipe books or watching 'bad crime shows', which Jacinda says are her favourite ways to unwind. Just work and motherhood, for now. Little wonder she began drinking coffee, much to Clarke Gayford's chagrin, after quitting years earlier. Whatever it takes to get you through the day.

Adjustments were made so motherhood could take its place beside prime ministership. Neve would find her place in the Beehive on the ninth floor near her mother, her cot in a small room, a converted kitchenette. Ardern would attend parliamentary sessions and cabinet meetings, conduct interviews and hold press conferences, with her baby in the background and on her mind, stepping out on breaks to express milk or feed Neve herself. She would sometimes nurse her while she was doing radio interviews or on conference calls, even with cabinet ministers.

Thankfully, Ardern had Gayford to rely on as the full-time carer for their baby. As he told a journalist, 'It was a no-brainer to say, "Right, I'll take care of [Neve], you take care of the country." '[6] Still, he would find himself having to rush through the Beehive with Neve, knock on doors and interrupt meetings so the little one could see her mother and be fed.

Official engagements outside Auckland and Wellington were more of a challenge, especially those overseas. Perhaps the sacrifices Ardern and Gayford made in discomfort on their trips abroad was worthwhile, for everyone. Just by Jacinda, Clarke and Neve functioning normally as a family, New Zealand could show the world the way for women, as it had done with women's franchise, one-and-a-quarter centuries earlier.

To say one of Ardern's trips saw a watershed moment for women's empowerment is not an exaggeration. A historic event occurred simply in the course of her official visit to the United States in late September 2018. With Gayford and Neve in tow, she flew to New

York, not in one of the New Zealand Air Force Boeing 757-200s, but on a commercial flight. Travelling on commercial flights is not uncommon for New Zealand prime ministers. A prime minister with a sense of economy, Jacinda was at pains to keep waste and unnecessary travel expenses to a minimum. Ministers were encouraged to use vans and carpool, rather than travel separately to events in government cars.

Their salaries were also kept trim. A month earlier, Ardern had scotched a three percent pay rise for politicians that would have seen her paid an extra $12,000. Even then, she couldn't escape censure for alleged unnecessary expenditure. Just days before she was due to travel to New York, Ardern came under fire in the media for taking a government flight back from a Pacific Islands Forum meeting in Nauru on 5 September, so she could care for Neve. Media articles suggested the trip cost the New Zealand government some $80,000.

Never mind, as Winston Peters was quick to point out, that other, less senior government figures had previously made similar use of government transport, without question. Or that the purported costs of Ardern's travel were inflated because the cost of staff was constant: they were on duty and paid, whether they took the flight or not. And the plane would have needed to take another flight to the Marshall Islands anyhow so it didn't block the tarmac of Nauru International Airport's single runway. Or that Ardern had tried to 'hitch a ride' with the Australian contingent to the meeting to save costs. Peters quickly denounced the 'craven, cowardly trolls' who attempted to make an issue of the plane trip.

For Ardern, this was perhaps her worst, as she described it, 'damned if I do, damned if I don't'[7] experience of prime ministership and motherhood. The Pacific Islands Forum is of vital importance in the region. If she had not made the trip to Nauru, she would have been their first prime minister not to attend the meeting, outside an election cycle, since 1971. Neve could not accompany her to Nauru, as her immune system was not sufficiently developed, and she was too young for inoculations. If Ardern had not departed early, she would have left Neve without breast milk.

Other nation's people would hardly have cared for such an expense, given it was for work, not pleasure. In the US, President Trump cost his taxpayers in excess of US$102 million in taking several trips so he could play golf, according to a *HuffPost* article.[8] News media reported that President Barack Obama's 'date' and Broadway show with his wife Michelle in late May 2009 – at the height of the global recession, no less – cost his country in the order of US$250,000. Little came of either of these profligacies – Obama was even lauded by some Americans for being romantic. It's hard not to feel that Jacinda Ardern was being punished for being a woman, and having a baby while in office.

In any event, when she was accompanied by Clarke on their flight to New York on 22 September 2018, she had no paid nanny to help them care for their baby. They shared their parental duties; naturally, Clarke shouldering as much of the load as he could. Jacinda paid for Clarke and Neve's travel herself.

With typical thoughtfulness, she apologised in advance to the other passengers on their seventeen-hour flight for any disturbance her daughter might cause. Perhaps it was in response to the 'look that you get when you walk onto a plane with a little one, that stare from other passengers', she spoke of jokingly on the *Today* show in New York.[9] Surely, the other people on the flight understood. They might even have found some novelty in listening to the 'first baby's' cries and gurgling. In any event, Neve wasn't much disturbance. 'She is a good baby, I can't complain,' Jacinda said.[10]

Ardern's first event was a speech in the Big Apple at the Social Good Summit, in the 92nd Street Y in uptown Manhattan. The audience was so enthusiastic, it was almost as if she were speaking to a home crowd. She made a point that she had been making about women in politics for some time, though now with greater authority: 'We've had three female prime ministers,' she said, referring to the US not yet having a woman president. 'It's really not a big deal, guys.' The audience was taken with her utter lack of affectation that is so very New Zealand.

On Monday 24 September came a highlight of the visit. Ardern spoke at the Nelson Mandela Peace Summit, part of the annual United Nations General Assembly. Accompanying her were Gayford and Neve – the first infant to appear on the floor of the General Assembly. Neve even had her own United Nations ID tag, which

Gayford proudly showed on Twitter. 'I wish I could have captured the startled look[s] [from] a Japanese delegation . . . who walked into a meeting room in the middle of a nappy change,' he wrote. Photographers' images of the baby, Jacinda and Clarke, surrounded by beaming, well-wishing delegates, quickly circulated on the internet.

It was a historic moment for the United Nations, as for women. Ardern had instantly become, as one headline declared, 'a model for all working mothers'.[11]

The message was liberating. Women don't need to pretend they are men to occupy high office. They can have a supportive partner, one who helps them raise their children. They can be mothers without their maternal duties being seen as an impediment to their career; children can be part of their lives, not hidden away at home. If a prime minister, a respected world leader, can bring her infant daughter onto the floor of the United Nations General Assembly – with her nation's and the UN's blessing – employers everywhere must take notice.

Three days later, she addressed the UN General Assembly. With clarity and gravitas, she spoke of maintaining connectedness, the challenge of climate change, reforming the UN, and universal values. Her closing words were profound: 'Me Too must become We Too. We are all in this together . . . If I could distil it down into one concept that we are pursuing in New Zealand it is simple and it is this. Kindness,' she said. She concluded with her vow that 'New Zealand remains committed to . . . being pragmatic, empathetic, strong and kind. The next generation after all, deserves no less. Tena koutou, tena koutou, tena tatou katoa [Greetings, greetings, greetings to us all].' It was an extraordinary speech, with an inspiring ending.[12]

*

Jacinda Ardern's oration could hardly have contrasted more with President Donald Trump's jingoistic rhetoric at the Assembly two days earlier. President Trump declared, in his forthright, stony manner, 'America is governed by Americans. We reject the ideology of globalism, and we embrace the doctrine of patriotism.' Trump faced laughter from parts of the Assembly during his speech for his claim that '[his] administration accomplished more than almost any administration in the history of our country'.[13]

Ardern and Trump were often compared – or rather, contrasted – from the moment she took office. Astoundingly, she was once actually likened to the maverick US president. In September 2017, the *Wall Street Journal* tweeted, 'Meet New Zealand's Justin Trudeau – except she's more like Trump on immigration.' She said the tweet was 'offensive' and 'infuriated' her.[14] It was also substantively incorrect.

The pair first met at an Asia-Pacific Economic Cooperation (APEC) summit at the coastal resort city of Da Nang, Vietnam, in November 2017. Trump reportedly mistook Ardern for Sophie Grégoire Trudeau, spouse of Canada's prime minister, Justin Trudeau. When he realised his mistake, Trump said jokingly, 'This lady caused a lot of upset in her country' when she was elected. Quick with her riposte as usual, Ardern told Trump with a laugh, 'You know, no one marched when I was elected.'

Trump didn't appear the least offended with Ardern's reply. His response might have been different had she told him that she had joined the marchers herself when he took office. With some 1,000 women and men on the morning of 21 January 2017, Ardern had taken to the streets outside the US consulate-general in Auckland, demonstrating for women's rights. She was photographed that day with her friend Lizzie Marvelly. The pair held a placard together, smiling widely, Ardern with cool sunglasses on her head. She later addressed the crowd on the grassed slopes of Myers Park nearby. 'We know the power of the collective,' she told protesters. 'You shut down Queen Street without one police officer in sight.'[15]

Ardern's and Trump's differences would continue. In mid-July 2019, President Trump was accused of racism, after tweeting that certain Democratic congresswomen should 'go back' to the countries where they 'originally came from'. Ardern was fierce in her criticism of Trump's comment on RNZ. She said that while she didn't interfere in another nation's politics, 'I completely and utterly disagree with him. I'm quite proud that in New Zealand we take the opposite view.'[16]

Relentlessly positive as she is, though, Ardern identifies a favourable attribute in President Donald Trump, one few of her political leaning would acknowledge. He is 'consistent', she says. 'He is the same person that you see behind the scenes as he is in the public or through the media.'[17]

The pair met formally again in late September 2019 for what Ardern's office described as a bilateral meeting. It was held in New York's Intercontinental Hotel in the usual diplomatic setting: blue curtains behind pairs of the two nation's flags, leather chairs, and a table between the two leaders bearing an arrangement of hydrangeas. Despite all this formality, Trump's press schedule noted the meeting offhandedly as a 'pull-aside'. It's thuggish terminology, conjuring images of Trump collaring Ardern on the street, dragging the poor woman into a dingy New York alleyway to deliver her a stern warning. Simply, Trump's administration didn't ascribe the meeting as much importance as it did to bilateral meetings that the president conducted the same day with the leaders of Pakistan, Poland, Egypt and Singapore. As so often, New Zealand had been underestimated.

Not that there was the least hint of unfriendliness between Ardern and Trump. It seems that Jacinda charmed the notoriously fickle US president. Like her policeman father Ross, she is noted for being willing to deal with 'anyone', even someone diametrically opposed to her, politically, ideologically and stylistically. The pair had a 25-minute *tête-à-tête* that Ardern later described as 'excellent'. Trump tweeted it was 'A wonderful meeting!'; that the *New Zealand Herald*'s tweet, 'President Trump views New Zealand very warmly, views the relationship very warmly and holds New Zealand in very high regard', was 'True'.

The pair stood and posed in front of their nations' flags afterwards for a photograph. Ardern is wearing a red trouser suit with an ivory blouse, Trump a blue suit with red tie. The pair match colours pleasantly with their flags, but their body language contrasts appropriately: Ardern's hands are held together in front of her body; Trump is grinning, giving a thumbs-up sign.

Their meeting was in the normal, pre-pandemic times. Neither of the leaders could have guessed what lay ahead, just months later. In the midst of perhaps the worst worldwide health and economic crises in more than a century, the two would exchange words again, in a more public arena.

31

Acclaim and the Ides of March

New York loved Jacinda Ardern. At least much of the city, and indeed America, seemed taken with her during her first official visit there in September 2018. For America, as for much of the world, her appearance in New York was her formal debut, as it were, and she impressed mightily. Her looks and sartorial style, more akin to those of an actor than an executive head of state, were no doubt part of her allure: New York loves glamour. But it was her easy, straightforward manner, speaking frankly about the ordinary concerns of life – concerns that politicians so often seem awkward or artificial in discussing – that endeared her to Americans.

The New Zealand prime minister adapted remarkably well to the varied audiences she addressed in New York. These ranged from the formal at the UN, to semi-formal at the Social Good Summit (a UN-sponsored convocation 'which brings together global citizens from every walk of life to share their ideas and energy to create the world we all deserve'), to more casual but high-profile appearances on major television networks. When she told hosts on the *Today* show that 'the joy [of motherhood] . . . has far surpassed my expectations', she was utterly genuine, as she was when she said 'you can be strong and you can be kind', speaking of a 'compassionate government'.[1]

The Late Show with comedian Steven Colbert on 26 September 2018 was more entertaining. To the Trump-baiting Colbert, who suggested that the Assembly audience the previous day had laughed at the president, Jacinda tactfully described the incident as 'a little laugh, and [Trump] said, "I didn't expect that response," . . . then people laughed with him.'

'That was very diplomatically stated,' Colbert said. 'No war between the United States and New Zealand, then.'[2]

Ardern was as humorous as her host, easy with her banter. 'I do find it slightly offensive that everyone thinks that every New Zealander starred in either *Lord of the Rings* or *The Hobbit*,' she said, while admitting, to the audience's mirth, that she had auditioned unsuccessfully for *The Hobbit*. When Colbert spoke of being 'a little bit obsessed' with J. R. R. Tolkien, Ardern announced that he was invited to New Zealand. There, he would attend a ceremony for becoming a citizen of Hobbiton. He would receive a mug, and a citizenship certificate drawn up by the official calligrapher from *The Lord of the Rings* and *The Hobbit*, she said. 'Come to New Zealand and we'll make the ceremony official. There's a direct flight from Chicago, it's nice and easy.'

It was an unusually casual, friendly appearance for a government leader. Americans who watched Ardern were almost universally positive in their comments. One viewer tweeted, 'We need someone like her running this country!'

Behind the scenes, it was anything but easy and casual. Ardern had been juggling her schedule of meetings and appearances with three-month-old Neve, naturally. She had bought some wireless breast pumps in the US, so she could express milk in between engagements. Thankfully, there was more than just Clarke Gayford to help her with carer duties. Even her foreign policy adviser Paula Wilson would hold Neve, journalist Sophia Hollander from the *New Yorker* noted. It was 'all hands on deck . . . she has a lot of uncles and aunties,' Ardern explained.

She didn't mind revealing herself, or her fashion secrets, either. Hollander accompanied Ardern, baby and Gayford from their suite at the Plaza Hotel by car to the Ed Sullivan Theater for her *Late Show* appearance. With Neve in a car seat beside her, Ardern slipped on a second Spanx underskirt beneath her patterned silk dress. 'I'm normal . . . there are normal people in politics who consider whether they should wear one or two layers of Spanx', she said.[3]

Never mind the double layer of Spanx. Whatever it took, New Zealanders of all political persuasions couldn't have been happier with Ardern's New York trip. Her appearance on *The Late Show* may have been seen by 3.6 million viewers; the *Today* show interview might have reached as many as 4.2 million. The charming, smiling prime minister, who embodied her people's open friendliness better than any celebrity might, couldn't have been a better ambassador for Aotearoa. For the country whose tourism industry employs more than eight percent of the workforce and contributes around one-fifth of foreign exchange earnings, she was a star.

*

Jacinda Ardern would soon become an ambassador for aspirations more universal than tourism.

She was already an ambassador for women, and for racial reconciliation in Aotearoa, which she was serious enough to implement in her own home. Jacinda and Clarke didn't want their part-Māori daughter suffering as had so many Māori of previous generations, such as Winston Peters. Māori on his father's side, Peters grew up in the 1940s and 1950s, when speaking te reo Māori was actively discouraged by the government. His English is expressive and eloquent, but he is not fluent in the language of his Māori ancestors. Jacinda and Clarke vowed early on that Neve would be raised speaking te reo along with English.

With the same dedication as her own mother, who used flash cards to teach her two daughters, Jacinda would place te reo numbers on the family refrigerator for Neve so she could learn some of her ancestors', and her nation's, indigenous language. She would also play her Anika Moa songs in te reo, particularly 'Colours are Beautiful'.

Just as Ardern's international public appearances in the latter part of 2018 were gathering acclaim overseas, there were murmurs of dissatisfaction at home. The surge of Jacindamania had to recede at some point, at any rate – a politician's popularity ebbs and flows with time. In October 2018, a journalist from *The Guardian* questioned the government's delivery of transformation in an article headed 'Ardern's first year: New Zealand grapples with hangover from Jacindamania'. The piece suggested that 'more promise than action' had prompted calls for 'less hui [meetings] more do-ey'.[4]

Mid-term blues were nothing new in Aotearoa. They dogged Prime Minister John Key, as they do leaders in any democracy. In May 2012, Key showed his disenchantment on a visit to Holy Family

School in Porirua East, Wellington, when he asked a group of students if any of them had dreamed of becoming the nation's prime minister. Hands shot into the air. With an uncharacteristically subdued expression on his features, Key said, 'Frankly, the way it's going at the moment, you can have the job.' He was hardly jesting. Implosions in the National Party's coalition partners ACT and the Māori Party and the embarrassing leak of National Party Board minutes weighed heavily on the prime minister. The same day, his answer to a radio interviewer on coalition options was a sigh and the comment that it was going to be 'a long two-and-a-half years'.

The sixth Labour government was bound to suffer its own midterm blues. It had delivered on some of its promises; it was committed to change. But Ardern had been elected to office on her people's hope, far more than most politicians. Hope is usually followed by disenchantment in politics. The competing interests, the usual tug of war between the elected officials and the bureaucracy which impede progress at the best of times, were added now to Ardern's challenges in reaching agreement with her restive coalition. Delays and disappointment were inevitable.

Ardern could offer her country more than change, however. An incident in early 2019 showed New Zealanders an aspect of their leader that her friends and family knew well. She would be there in their hour of need; without hesitation, she would rush to the front line.

Perhaps climate change, which Ardern spoke of so often, played its part in the crisis of early February 2019. Most of New Zealand is a lush landscape. That summer, though, saw near-record warm conditions in the South Island and drought in the north of the island, which meant conditions remarkably similar to those in the closest (and the driest) habitable continent: Australia.

The city of Nelson and the surrounding area in the South Island basked in the sunniest weather of the season. On 5 February at Pigeon Valley near the town of Wakefield, an agricultural contractor ploughed a paddock. Behind his tractor, the plough's discs broke through the earth, hitting rocks. Sparks flew, igniting the tinder-dry grass above. The contractor tried to quell the flames but was pushed back by their heat. Soon, the whole paddock was ablaze. Fanned by strong, gusting winds, the fire spread rapidly to the plantation of young pines on a slope nearby.

The resulting blaze claimed 2,343 hectares of forest, destroying property and pastures. People were evacuated from their homes; the town of Wakefield itself was threatened, engulfed by smoke for days.

On 7 February as the bushfire raged, Ardern travelled to Nelson with minister Kris Faafoi and Damien O'Connor, the member for the electorate of West Coast-Tasman. There, she visited the Emergency Co-ordination Centre where Tasman District Council and Civil Defence were coordinating the firefighting effort. Backed by some 150 firefighters on the ground, a fleet of helicopters and planes fought the blaze, dropping fire retardant.

From the ground, she posted live on Facebook, the aircraft flying through the smoke far in the background as if in battle. She gave a practical and sensible, matter-of-fact report on the situation, during which she announced an immediate $20,000 grant for a mayoral fund. This, she said, was 'to pick up any gaps that might exist' in the funding of the relief effort for the disaster.

Just over a week later, on Valentine's Day, 14 February 2019, Ardern returned. 'What's the damage?' she promptly asked area representatives at the Emergency Response Office in Richmond. She announced a further $100,000 for the mayoral relief fund, plus another $50,000 for rural support. She praised the 'incredible work' of firefighters, then chatted with the children whose school had been temporarily relocated to Hope Community Church. There was some laughter when she was presented with a red gerbera for Valentine's Day. 'That's the most I'll get, because Clarke had food poisoning,' Ardern said.[5]

A few words she added about the disaster seem eerily correct in hindsight. 'We do have to make sure we're prepared for these kind of events,' she said. 'We need to always be ready, always be prepared.'[6]

*

Few could have foreseen, let alone prepared for, the incident a month and a day later. Events in the inner western suburbs of Christchurch on 15 March 2019 would change the course of Ardern's government, bringing the international spotlight to bear on New Zealand and questioning the values of the nation. As Ardern would declare, the day was to be among the darkest in New Zealand's history.

Brenton Harrison Tarrant had brooded over his appalling acts from the time he entered New Zealand in August 2017. Rage seethed behind his nondescript demeanour. The 28-year-old Australian white supremacist harboured a virulent, irrational hatred of immigrants – especially Muslims – and of Islam itself.

Disciplined and methodical, Tarrant planned carefully. He amassed weaponry, trained in marksmanship and lifted weights with dedication. He surveyed his targets with drones and recces. He even obtained plans of buildings. On Friday 15 March 2019, Tarrant drove from his home in Dunedin. At 1.26 p.m., he posted on his Facebook status a link to seven file sharing websites that contained a 74-page manifesto. Two minutes later, he posted a disturbing, jaunty message on the internet message board 8chan, which ended with, 'If I don't survive the attack, goodbye, godbless and I will see you all in Valhalla!' The message directed readers to Tarrant's Facebook page and to his manifesto.

At 1.31 and 1.32 p.m., he sent messages to his mother and sister, telling them of his plans and instructing them how to deal with the police when, inevitably, they would visit. He then emailed his manifesto to thirty-four addresses, mostly international media. The subject of the email was, 'On the attack in New Zealand today'. 'I was the partisan (*sic*) that committed the assault', its message began. Ardern's office was among the recipients, as were National Party leader Simon Bridges and New Zealand Parliament Speaker Trevor Mallard.

The manifesto attached to the email, entitled 'The Great Replacement', begins with Dylan Thomas's poem 'Do not go gentle into that good night', before descending into a rambling, bitter monologue. Unedited, the document seems hastily written, with a tone perhaps of an angrier, abridged *Mein Kampf*. Its intent is clear, however, as is Tarrant's hatred. Tarrant rails against an imagined 'white genocide', claiming that 'radicalisation is the rational response to degeneration'. The heinous crimes he would commit, he declares, are for the purpose of 'destabilising and polarising Western society'.

At 1.33, he started live-streaming footage from his GoPro head-cam, on Facebook and a white extremist chat site. Wearing a

military-style outfit – a ballistic and tactical vest bristling with ammunition and a scabbard holding a bayonet-style knife, adorned with
neo-Nazi symbols – Tarrant drove in his silver Subaru Outback hatch-
back. From an industrial estate on Leslie Hills Drive in Riccarton, an
inner western suburb of Christchurch, Tarrant headed south onto
Mandeville Street and Blenheim Road, before turning north up
Deans Avenue.

His vehicle carried an arsenal of weaponry, with six high-powered
firearms, including three semi-automatic carbines, a lever-action fire-
arm and two shotguns. Incredibly, Tarrant had obtained his weapons
legally. Every one of them had white supremacist graffiti scrawled over
its surfaces and on its magazines. Three were arrayed neatly on the
passenger seat beside him, while his main weapon, a semi-automatic
rifle, lay alongside his right leg as he drove, its mounted tactical strobe
flashing. The other two were in the rear compartment of the vehicle,
along with four red plastic petrol cans – crude incendiary devices.

An audio speaker attached to Tarrant's vest played his macabre
soundtrack as he followed Google Maps: a Serbian nationalist polka
praising Radovan Karadžić, the convicted Bosnian Serb war criminal.
It was followed by the march 'The British Grenadiers'; later, the
bizarre 'Fire' by the Crazy World of Arthur Brown ('I am the god of
hellfire' is the opening line), and a remix version of a German para-
trooper song, 'Grün ist unser Fallschirm'.

The killer's behaviour was chillingly matter of fact. A brief glimpse
of his face as he took off his GoPro camera shows hard features, a piti-
less expression. At 1.39 p.m., he parked his car in the laneway beside
the Al Noor Mosque, alighted with his automatic rifle, opened the
rear hatch and took out a shotgun. From there, he walked briskly
with the weapons along a footpath and through the mosque car park,
'The British Grenadiers' playing on his vest's audio speaker. Tarrant
lowered his shotgun and began his cowardly attack on the worshippers inside – men, women and children – who were preparing for
their *namaz*, Friday prayers.

His first victim was 71-year-old Haji-Daoud Nabi, a decent,
friendly man whose final act of hospitality was greeting the approaching killer from the mosque's doorway. 'Hello brother,' Nabi said,
before he was gunned down.

Tarrant's assault at the Al Noor Mosque claimed another forty-three lives, with thirty-five more injured.

Six minutes after he arrived, Tarrant drove away from the mosque, shooting rounds randomly at passers-by through his windscreen and side window in frustration. He swore. 'It did not go as planned,' he explained to his online audience. 'I should have stayed longer. There was time for the fuel.' Tarrant was disappointed: he had lost his nerve; abandoned his plan to burn the mosque to the ground.

The killer drove erratically at speeds of up to 130 kilometres per hour, north along Deans Avenue, which skirts Hagley Park, along Harper Avenue then onto Bealey Avenue. As he rambled, almost incoherently, music from his vest's audio speaker can be heard: Manuel's 'Gas Gas Gas', a song featured heavily in computer games and the *Initial D* manga series, and coopted for memes and automotive nihilism. Tarrant seemed utterly enthralled with his perverse fantasy, a warped belief that he was undertaking a military operation. He referred to his massacre of the unarmed, peaceful worshippers as a 'firefight'.

In a few minutes, the killer reached the Linwood Islamic Centre, some six kilometres from the Al Noor Mosque. There, at 1.52 P.M., he launched a similar attack. Seven more worshippers were mortally wounded before the slaughter was curtailed; five were injured.

Many more lives would have been taken, had it not been for the quick thinking of the imam and a worshipper. When he heard shots being fired outside, Imam Alabi Lateef Zikrullah ran through his congregation towards the door. 'Go down! Down! Down! Down!' he yelled. He reached the door before Tarrant could enter, locking it. It didn't stop the killer, but it slowed him down. Frustrated, Tarrant fired through the windows.

Abdul Aziz Wahabzada, a member of the congregation, picked up the only weapon he could lay his hands on, a credit card reader, and charging at Tarrant, threw it at him. Tarrant ducked, picked up his automatic rifle and fired as Wahabzada took cover behind some cars. Wahabzada screamed at him, 'Come over here, I'm here!', hoping to draw the killer away as he returned to the mosque. Tarrant shot more worshippers before retreating to his car. Wahabzada picked up Tarrant's discarded, empty shotgun and hurled it like a spear at Tarrant, breaking the car's rear side window.

Tarrant swore at him then drove away, running a red light to avoid Wahabzada, who, incredibly, pursued him on foot. Driving at speeds approaching 120 kilometres per hour, Tarrant headed towards his third target: another mosque some ninety-four kilometres away, in Ashburton.

Mercifully, he never got there. A couple of minutes later, at 1.57, two armed police officers in a patrol car spotted Tarrant's Subaru driving west towards them on Brougham Street in Sydenham. Making a quick U-turn, they began their high-speed pursuit; within a minute, they had intercepted Tarrant. Lights flashing, their patrol car rammed the Subaru hard against the kerb, lifting its wheels off the ground with the force, the front right one spinning in the air. The officers leapt from their vehicle and surrounded Tarrant's, weapons trained on the killer. Tarrant surrendered without resisting. Dragged from his car by one officer while the other held him at gunpoint, he was laid out, handcuffed on the pavement in seconds.

It was 1.59 P.M., 15 March 2019. Tarrant's short, diabolical reign of terror was over. But the suffering he had inflicted continued, radiating outwards from the sites of the atrocities to the whole of New Zealand, and rapidly across the globe.

Fifty-one people – peaceful worshippers – had been mortally wounded; another forty were injured, many seriously. The Christchurch mosque shootings, as the events came to be known, were the worst mass murder by a lone gunman in the nation's history, and by far, New Zealand's most heinous terrorist attack. Tarrant admitted later in a police interview that he was 'going into both mosques to kill as many people as [he] could'. The manner in which he did so made his crimes ineffably depraved.

With Tarrant's attack steeped in grandiosity, it's difficult to ascertain which of his actions were planned and symbolic, and which were simply dramatic flourishes of a mentally disturbed extremist, seeking attention for his cause. The white supremacist graffiti on his weaponry spoke of self-righteousness and self-justification as much as malevolence. Names of European military leaders who resisted the Ottoman invasions were scribbled alongside a reference to Ebba Akerlund, an eleven-year-old girl who was killed in an Islamic extremist attack in Stockholm in April 2017. 'Kebab remover' was written on his assault rifle, along with 'welcome to hell'.

Then there were Tarrant's symbols: historical dates, the Odin's Cross, the Black Sun. Even the date of the attack might have been chosen for its symbolism by the killer, who exhibited a keen, though perverse, interest in history. Was it a coincidence that this day was the Ides of March, an ancient Roman day of religious sacrifice, the ominous day upon which Julius Caesar was brutally assassinated in 44 BC and which would change the course of ancient history, fore-shadowing two centuries of tyranny? Had Tarrant planned for his attack to fall on this date, as coolly as he had prepared himself for his killing? As carefully as he had choreographed his attack with music?

What goes without question is Tarrant's clear intent to destroy racial and religious tolerance in New Zealand, to make immigrants fear for their safety – to damage the nation's international reputation. His use of technology, of social media, meant his crime's effect would be like a natural disaster, swift and devastating.

As news of the attack flooded the airways and internet, the nation's people reeled in shock. In the West, there was disbelief; in the Muslim world, anguish. How on earth could this happen in New Zealand, one of the most peaceful countries in the world?

32

They Are Us

Jacinda Ardern had a full morning on 15 March 2019, as usual. From 7.30 A.M., she conducted a handful of early radio interviews by telephone, as is common for her. At 9.00, she he held an hour-long meeting with health care cooperative representatives in a medical centre in Mangere, a suburb in Auckland's south, before heading to the airport nearby and boarding a plane. She and her team flew to New Plymouth, a brief flight of around fifty minutes.

At midday, she surprised and delighted a group of a few hundred students, arriving unannounced at Puke Ariki, a park complex by the New Plymouth foreshore. Because New Zealand Standard Time is 12 hours ahead of GMT (Greenwich Mean Time), the teenagers were among the first to begin the worldwide climate change lunchtime 'strike'. Ardern joined them, speaking in support of their strike, which had been approved by local school principals. She thanked the students 'for raising the awareness, not just here in New Zealand but from around the world'. Climate change, Jacinda said, 'is the biggest challenge we will tackle globally in my lifetime and in your lifetime'.[1]

From Puke Ariki, Ardern and her entourage headed to the Novotel New Plymouth Hobson, where, matching words from her previous speech with a plan, she launched the H_2 (Hydrogen) Taranaki Roadmap. Hydrogen, an ecologically sound fuel, was already being produced at Taranaki. The Roadmap laid out ways that could make the region a global leader in hydrogen production.

The H_2 Taranaki Roadmap launch over, Ardern set off in a minivan – carpooling, as usual – with Justice Minister Andrew Little and her staff, to visit the site of a new school. Afterwards, it was to have been an evening of joy, of celebration: Ardern had been invited to open the WOMAD music festival at the TSB Bowl of Brooklands, a picturesque venue with a broad lawn surrounded by trees, its stage overlooking a lake. She was scheduled to stay and enjoy the music with the rest of the audience; she loved music festivals. Tonight, she could mix business with pleasure, as it were. Or so it was planned.

At around 1.50 P.M., the minivan had just picked up the local mayor, when Ardern's new press secretary, Kelly Spring, received an urgent call. The chief press secretary, Andrew Campbell, had some disturbing news. There was an 'evolving incident' in Christchurch, Campbell said. Spring handed the phone to Ardern. A shooting had occurred at a mosque in Christchurch, he told her. Details were sketchy – police had only just arrived at the scene, and radio reports indicated the perpetrator or perpetrators were still at large – but it was clear there were numerous casualties.

Ardern stopped the van. She directed the driver to head to New Plymouth police station, without delay. Inside this concrete vault of a building with its steel-slatted front, Jacinda sat with Kelly Spring in an upper room for several hours, receiving updates from over the police radio.

At first, with the scale of the killing and the two targets, it was thought the attacks might involve a number of assailants. The incendiary devices in the rear of Brenton Tarrant's Subaru indicated a danger of explosives being detonated elsewhere. Schools, malls and workplaces in the area were immediately locked down.

When the state of affairs in Christchurch had been ascertained, and police were confident the threat had been contained, Ardern and her team headed to the Devon Hotel in New Plymouth for a press conference. There, Ardern delivered an extraordinary address, all the more so for the scant time she had to prepare. While waiting in the police station, she jotted notes of the back of an A4-size sheet of paper, the front of which was printed with the running order of a function the previous evening. As she did, she had an 'overwhelming sense,' she later said, 'of, here are people who've made New Zealand their home. Regardless of whether someone had been in New Zealand for a generation or whether . . . they moved here a year ago . . . they should have been safe and they should have been able to worship here.' Among the words she scribbled in hurried letters, Ardern high-lighted three lines in fluorescent orange:

> One person custody may be other offndr.
> Act of exraordnry violence. It has no place in NZ.
> They are us.

Ardern called Grant Robertson, a former diplomat, to focus her thoughts for what would be one of the most important speeches of her tenure. At 4.20 p.m., she entered a large event room at the hotel, empty save for a table with a black tablecloth, a cluster of microphones on it; two television cameras in front, a backdrop of sombre curtains behind. She took her place at the table. In the national broadcast that followed, Ardern's words were delivered with an emphatic tone, though she almost choked with emotion when she spoke of the victims:

> Whilst I cannot give any confirmation at this stage around fatalities and casualties, what I can say is that it is clear that this is one of New Zealand's darkest days. Clearly, what has happened here is an extraordinary and unprecedented act of violence.
>   Many of those who will have been directly affected by this shooting may be migrants to New Zealand, they may even be refugees here. They have chosen to make New Zealand their home, and it is their home. They are us.
>   The person who has perpetuated this violence against us is not . . . I would describe it as . . . an act that has absolutely no place in New Zealand. This is not who we are . . . The people who were the subject of this attack today, New Zealand is their home. They should be safe here.
>   The person who has perpetuated this violent act against them, they have no place in New Zealand society.[2]

There was no time or opportunity for questions. 'If you'll excuse me, I'm very happy to update you again once I've met with agencies upon my landing. Thank you,' Ardern said.

At 5.52 P.M., Ardern posted a tweet, reiterating her message to the media, before boarding a Defence Force plane and flying to

Wellington. On the way, she typed more notes into her phone for a more detailed press conference. At the Beehive, which unusually was guarded by a formidable contingent of armed police, she met with ministers, senior police and intelligence officials to convene a one-hour gathering, later termed the Christchurch attack response meeting. This group would convene numerous times in the coming days.

The firearms the gunman had used in the shootings, Ardern was told, were registered and legally in his possession as a licensed gun holder: Tarrant held an A-category gun licence. Police still deliberated over whether there were other attackers. Three other known extremists were arrested, but later released. Tarrant was, it transpires, what has become known as a lone-wolf attacker.

At 7.30 P.M., Ardern addressed the media again, with a more comprehensive statement. The first part of her address dealt with the formal details of the incident, discussing the government's response to the attack, before her words took on an unusual tone for a national leader. She spoke of the victims and their families with sensitivity:

> Christchurch was the home of these victims . . . where they were parts of communities that they loved and who loved them in return. It was a place that many came to for its safety. A place where they were free to practise their culture and their religion . . . We [in New Zealand] were not chosen for this act of violence because we condone racism, because we are an enclave for extremism. We were chosen . . . because we represent diversity, kindness, compassion. A home for those who share our values. Refuge for those who need it. And those values will not and cannot be shaken by this attack.

Significantly, Ardern made no resort to the language of retribution, anger or even justice. The most she directed at the attacker was 'the strongest possible condemnation of [his] ideology . . . You may have chosen us – but we utterly reject and condemn you.'[3]

In the hours after the press conference, calls came from New Zealand's most significant allies, in their order of importance. Ardern spoke first with the Australian prime minister, Scott Morrison, then the following morning, with US president Donald Trump. Trump asked what assistance and support he might provide. 'My message was,' Ardern told reporters later that morning, ' "Sympathy and love for all Muslim communities." '[4]

Earlier, on that weekend morning, when most New Zealanders slept, Winston Peters had been called by his chief of staff. Ardern had a special request for her deputy prime minister. It was for his backing on changes to gun laws. Previously, Peters had rejected calls for the ban of various firearms. Now, without hesitation, he pledged his support for Ardern's call for the restriction of certain types of semi-automatic firearms and high-capacity magazines. With Peters' support, she announced her intention at her address later that morning: 'I can tell you one thing right now,' she declared. 'Our gun laws will change.' Significantly, without the kind of equivocation other Western leaders had shown after white supremacist attacks, Ardern termed the shootings a 'terrorist act'.[5]

Far more remarkable than her stand on gun control, however, was the way in which she immediately reached out to the victims of the shootings, and their families. At 11 A.M. on 16 March, she boarded one of the New Zealand Air Force Boeing 757-200s, along with Peters, National Party leader Simon Bridges and Green Party leader James Shaw. Together, they travelled to Christchurch. Around noon, the multi-party delegation arrived at a meeting organised with Muslim community representatives affiliated with the Canterbury Refugee Resettlement and Resources Centre. For security reasons, the media had not been informed of the address; instead they had to follow the prime ministerial delegation in convoy.

Significantly, Ardern wore a scarf covering her head: a black hijab to match her black outfit. She met and spoke with local Muslim leaders. She addressed them in a small, crowded room. 'I have many roles in my role as prime minister but at the moment I have three incredibly important jobs. One is to bring with me the message of love and support and grief of the people of New Zealand,' she said, gesturing to her parliamentary colleagues. 'New Zealand is united in grief. This is not New Zealand. The only part of the incident we have seen over the past 24 to 36 hours that is New Zealand, is the support that you are seeing now.'[6] She had tears in her eyes as she spoke.

What Ardern said was absolutely correct, too. New Zealanders of all walks of life indeed offered their support, leaving bouquets of

flowers and messages of sympathy on Deans Avenue the morning
after the shootings, as close to the mosque as police would allow.
Messages appeared on the footpath; cards propped up next to flowers:
'We love you / We grieve with you / This is not New Zealand / Al
salam Alaikum'; 'Home grown love for all'.

For a week, thousands of flowers and teddy bears and messages
lined Deans Avenue; traffic cones set in place to direct traffic were
used to hold flower arrangements. Locals made tea and coffee and
brought home-made biscuits to the police guarding the mosque. A
local biker gang, the Mongrel Mob, offered to provide security for any
mosque that required it. Other biker gangs followed suit, throughout
New Zealand. This was surely the spontaneous reaction of Aotearoa's
people, but Jacinda Ardern had facilitated it by her words.

Practical concerns were also addressed with Muslim community
leaders. Ardern assured them that Accident Compensation Corporation
payments for funeral expenses would be made to the bereaved.

She met families and friends of the victims in a tightly packed
room on the city side of Hagley Park. The press was not allowed
inside, though some of those present recorded Ardern's address on
their mobile phones. Several used Facetime to relay her appearance
live to overseas loved ones. '*Al-salam alaikum*,' Ardern said, a microphone in one hand, the other placed over her heart in the Islamic
traditional manner. 'Peace be upon you, peace be upon all of us.'

Her sensitivity and diplomacy were needed. She had been briefed
before she had arrived about the fraught communication between the
police and victims' families, who clamoured for their loved ones'
remains. Islamic custom requires that a deceased's corpse be washed
with warm water and interred as soon as possible after death; burial
within 24 hours is all but mandatory. The police crime scene investigation, victim identification procedure and collection of forensic
evidence, though, meant there were delays in handing over the
victims' bodies to relatives. 'I remember just asking people if they
could sit,' Ardern later said. 'And we had silence for a moment, and
then I just tried to talk it through.' She told those gathered she understood their need to have their family members' remains as soon as
possible. Many bodies still remained in the mosque, as police could
not be confident it was safe to remove them, she explained. She

assured them the police would work as quickly as possible; updates would be imminent.

Her voice trembled as she spoke, almost breaking, as she said, 'You have our love and our support. You have it now, you have it for the coming days, you have it for the coming weeks. You have it because this is your home. *Al-salam alaikum*.'[7]

In between two media conferences and a briefing from the Canterbury District police commander on the situation in Christchurch, Ardern met with first responders to the tragedy: police and ambulance officers. She could well understand, knowing her father's job, the kind of stress they had endured. She then made her way to Christchurch Hospital. Two kilometres from the Al Noor Mosque, the hospital had been overrun, with some fifty patients suffering from gunshot wounds admitted the previous afternoon. Nurses' leave was cancelled, extra doctors and surgeons were brought in; seven operating theatres were opened, where only three were usually in use. Without media, Ardern alone visited victims and their loved ones, embracing those less seriously injured, holding hands of others, comforting those in grief with her words. She was at the hospital for an hour.

Afterwards, at Christchurch airport, she gave interviews before taking a flight back to Wellington, where another Christchurch attack response meeting was convened at the Beehive.

The following day, after midday, Ardern attended Kilbirnie Mosque with Grant Robertson and Clark Gayford beside her, meeting with members of Wellington's Muslim community. She comforted the crying, traumatised members of the mosque's congregation, embracing the women who came to her. One was a mother with her infant son; another, Naima Abdi, a thirty-year-old woman who was born in Somalia. Abdi greeted people outside the mosque. As Ardern walked by her, they spoke. Abdi tightly hugged Ardern, a box of tissues still in her hand. 'We'll get through this together,' Ardern told Abdi as she held her.

The photographer Hagen Hopkins had walked to the mosque from his home, just two minutes away. He took shots sparingly, and one of them was of Ardern and Abdi. This would become an iconic image of Ardern's, and New Zealand's, compassionate response to the

15 March attack. Hopkins captured a beautiful moment perfectly. Ardern's eyes are gently closed, her mouth soft with empathy. There is no formality, no distance: Abdi is held utterly within Ardern's embrace, as close as one would hold a dear family member in bereavement. After its projection onto the Burj Khalifa in Dubai, it became a mural to grace the side of a 25-metre-tall silo in Melbourne's inner suburb of Brunswick.

Another photograph that stood apart from the thousands taken in the aftermath of the mosque shootings had been taken the previous day, when Ardern was meeting Muslim community leaders in Christchurch. Photographer Kirk Hargreaves was late to the event; the room was already packed with members of the Muslim community when he arrived. He tried to peer in from outside, but with the sun's rays reflected on the windowpane, he couldn't see inside the building. Hargreaves took out his camera anyhow.

Focusing through the window, he caught sight of Ardern. 'Her face was like a wee bubble out of darkness,' he says.[8] He could hardly believe it was her – she was wearing a hijab – though her concern was clearly visible. A reflection of colourful flowers from the garden below show on the pane like the light in stained glass, giving the image a dreamy translucence and somewhat religious mood.

The following Friday, 22 March, thousands gathered in Hagley Park, opposite the Al Noor Mosque, for a call to prayer, which was broadcast live on radio and national television. The event was to mark a national day of reflection for the attack.

Taking Ardern's lead, women from all communities and religions arrived at the event wearing scarves as hijabs. Many in attendance, along with mourners, performed a haka, one of numerous throughout the country to honour the victims of the attack. The imam of the Al Noor Mosque, Gamal Fouda, addressed the gathering. While the gunman 'broke the hearts of millions around the world', he said, 'today, from the same place, I look out and I see the love and compassion.'[9] Afterwards, a national two-minute silence was observed.

Ardern spoke before the call to prayer: 'New Zealand mourns with you, we are one,' she said. 'According to the Prophet Muhammad . . . the believers in their mutual kindness, compassion and sympathy are just like one body. When any part of the body suffers, the whole body feels pain.'[10]

It was a sizeable gathering, but nowhere near the magnitude of the memorial service, Ko Tātou, Tātou – We Are One, on the morning of Friday 29 March, two weeks after the attack. Somewhere in the region of 20,000 New Zealanders packed the broad grassy expanse of Hagley Park for the service, which was broadcast live. Along with leaders from across the Pacific, Australian prime minister Scott Morrison attended. The audience enjoyed performances by Yusuf Islam (formerly Cat Stevens), Marlon Williams, Maisey Rika, Hollie Smith and Teeks.

Ardern was given a standing ovation when she took to the stage. She wore a kahu huruhuru over a black dress: a serious yet charismatic outfit. Her words were once again inspired: 'The world has been stuck in a vicious cycle of extremism breeding extremism and it must end,' she declared. 'We cannot confront these issues alone, none of us can . . . The answer lies in our humanity. But for now we will remember the tears of our nation and the new resolve we have formed.'[11]

One sentence she said reflects much that she stands for: 'We each hold the power – in our words, in our actions, in our daily acts of kindness – let that be the legacy of the fifteenth of March.'[12] These were humane words from an unusually humane leader, whose response to terrorism departed from those of many leaders before her. Indeed, much can be learned from Prime Minister Jacinda Ardern's handling of the Christchurch mosque shootings. She mourned with those who mourned, which was the right moral and human response to their tragedy. Her fellow New Zealanders did likewise.

Some leaders might also have done so in similar circumstances. Few, though, could have committed themselves to such a gesture as she did, that in exquisite form crystallised her words 'they are us' – that is, by wearing a garment, a symbol of a faith not her own.

Before she left Wellington, Ardern had sought a scarf in Premier House, the prime minister's official residence, but there was none to be found. So she called a friend to borrow her black scarf, one with a neat, embroidered hem. It was the closest to a hijab she could muster, and it suited the ex-Mormon, agnostic prime minister remarkably well.

Unquestionably, wearing a hijab in the company of Muslims – a sincere and 'intuitive' gesture – said more even than Ardern's thoughtful, compassionate words. The image of a Western leader dressed as a Muslim, mourning with Muslims, comforting them in grief, was profound. It reassured the Islamic world, powerfully. Accustomed in recent years to Western defensiveness or aggression, Muslims everywhere were touched by Ardern's open-hearted embraces of Muslim women in Christchurch and in Wellington. For Muslims, the images of Jacinda Ardern in a hijab that flashed across the globe could not have been more heartening.

With empathy, competent administration, sincerity and healing words, Ardern had guided her nation through a tragedy, one that could easily have jarred its harmony and spoiled its international reputation. Her actions and words touched hearts and soothed hurts across the globe.

Perhaps from the bloodshed emerged a kind of moral victory. Ardern's largely instinctive response to the carnage of 15 March 2019 – compassion, thoughtfulness, articulate moral leadership – showed the best of Aotearoa and her people, the very opposite of what the attacker had desired, and demonstrated to the world another way to deal with the worst of humanity.

33

Engagement

Even Judith Collins, Jacinda Ardern's inveterate opponent, publicly applauded her handling of the Christchurch mosque shootings. It was 'outstanding', a visibly touched Collins told Parliament on 20 March. Collins also supported Ardern's wearing a hijab, or 'scarf', as she described the garment.

The day before, four days after the Christchurch mosque shootings, the House saw a rare show of unity, both politically and spiritually. A multi-faith delegation, with representatives of the Islamic, Jewish, Buddhist, Sikh, Hindu and Rātana (a Māori Christian movement) faiths, together with those of the Catholic, Anglican and Presbyterian denominations in their robes and vestments, joined Speaker Trevor Mallard, who was in his, for the Speaker's procession into the debating chamber. The group stood together for prayer in solidarity with their Muslim brothers and sisters, for their grief, in honour of those who had died. 'I've asked a group of religious leaders to come into Parliament with me as a sign of unity and togetherness so our prayer period today will be slightly extended,'[1] the Speaker said. Imam Nizam ul-Haq Thanvi delivered the prayer in Arabic, which was translated by his colleague into English. The prayer blessed Ardern and those who had responded: police, ambulance and medical personnel. It also blessed those who had lost their lives.

Mallard opened with the traditional Muslim greeting of '*Al-salam alaikum*', as did others who spoke. Parliament heard Ardern's most resolute, forceful oration yet. She was dressed in black, accentuating her pallor and rings of fatigue under her eyes. Her face was stony, with angles wrought by the emotion of the preceding days, but her voice was as powerful as her words: 'The families of the fallen will have justice. He sought many things from his act of terror, but one was notoriety. And that is why you will never hear me mention his name. He is a terrorist; he is a criminal; he is an extremist. But he will, when I speak, be nameless . . . I implore you, speak the names of those who are lost . . . we in New Zealand will give him nothing, not even his name.'

The government, and the country, took Ardern's lead. On 23 March New Zealand's chief censor deemed the killer's manifesto and the video of his attack objectionable under the Films, Videos, and Publications Classification Act 1993, making it 'illegal to have a copy of the video or document, or to share these with others'. On 1 May, New Zealand's media organisations RNZ, Stuff, Mediaworks, TVNZ and New Zealand Media and Entertainment (NZME) announced voluntarily agreed protocols to suppress white supremacist or terrorist content, messages or symbols in their coverage of Brenton Tarrant's trial. On video, white supremacist hand signals and the like would appear pixelated; white supremacist tirades would be given scant coverage. The killer would not be allowed to exploit court proceedings and his appearances to promote his ideology.

Ardern's speech in Parliament also signalled her determination to rein in the excesses that had facilitated Tarrant's atrocity. 'We will also look at the role social media played and what steps we can take, including on the international stage and in unison with our partners,' she said. '[Social media platforms] are the publisher, not just the postman. There cannot be a case of all profit, no responsibility.'[2]

This signalled her initiative, the Christchurch Call to Action Summit. On 29 April, Ardern told journalists a 'core group of leaders' had been invited for a conference in Paris the following month to discuss ways of curbing extremist, violent content on social media. The summit would be held on 15 May with the G7 digital ministers' 'Tech for Humanity' meeting and France's 'Tech for Good' conference. With trademark diplomacy, Ardern had found an ally in French president Emmanuel Macron, who would co-chair the summit with her. She had won the support of German chancellor Angela Merkel, too.

Also invited to the Paris summit were representatives of tech companies, whom Ardern said they were 'calling on . . . to join with us and help achieve our goal of eliminating violent extremism online'.³ The killer's 16-minute, 55-second Facebook live streaming of his attack showed the yawning gaps in the social media giant's systems. In the twenty-nine minutes before Tarrant's online atrocity was reported, it had been viewed by hundreds and shared thousands of times by Facebook users. The video stayed on Facebook for hours, allowing it to go viral; it appeared on the extremist 8Chan message board and was re-uploaded to Facebook. The social media platform removed it some 1.5 million times in the twenty-four hours following the shootings: an astonishing indictment of online behaviour, speaking of ghoulish curiosity and indifference to human suffering.

While the tech giants quickly made overtures to Ardern in the days after the shootings, Ardern had left them on tenterhooks while she shored up support for the Christchurch Call. After a few weeks, she spoke directly with Microsoft president Brad Smith, Facebook's Mark Zuckerberg, Susan Wojcicki, the CEO of YouTube and Twitter's Jack Dorsey. Under pressure, Facebook capitulated a day before the Paris meeting convened. While live streaming would remain on the platform, it would see tighter rules and a 'one-strike policy' banning those who violated them. Facebook assured the media that had the new rules been in place in March, they would have stopped the Christchurch killer from live streaming his crimes from his account.

On 15 May in the sumptuous, gilt-ornamented Élysée Palace in Paris, Ardern and President Macron sat with world leaders to launch the Christchurch Call. Most of the hard work had been done beforehand. After a day of discussions, which from all accounts had a fairly genial air, the Christchurch Call to Action document was ratified. Signatories to the agreement were the European Commission, the Council of Europe, UNESCO and the governments of forty-seven countries, along with Amazon, Dailymotion, Facebook, Google, Microsoft, Qwant, Twitter and YouTube.

Though it was a non-binding agreement, there was a sting in the tail of the Christchurch Call, which was led by New Zealand business figures. The NZ Superannuation Fund had joined forces with twenty-three overseas institutional investors with assets of more than $800 billion, to lobby Facebook, Google and Twitter on the issue of objectionable content, 'such as the shootings that took place in

Christchurch'. Ardern led with diplomacy, smiles and persuasive arguments at the Paris summit, but Kiwis backed her to the hilt.

Diplomacy of a more traditional kind had been needed – and urgently so – in the days following the shootings. The firebrand nationalist president of Turkey, Recep Tayyip Erdoğan, screened Tarrant's footage at his election campaign rallies, edited with music for dramatic effect, arousing anti-Western sentiment among voters. There was worse. Erdoğan openly threatened Australian and New Zealand tourists who he imagined might harbour anti-Turkish senti-ments. 'Your grandparents came here and returned in coffins,' he blustered, referring to the Gallipoli campaign. 'Have no doubt: we will send you back like your grandfathers.'[4]

This might have been mere rhetoric, Erdoğan ranting on the hustings to whip up support. But it didn't bode well for New Zealanders and Australians taking part in the annual Anzac Day pilgrimage to Gallipoli on 25 April, just weeks later. The Australian prime minister, Scott Morrison, summoned the Turkish ambassador in Canberra, demanding Erdoğan withdraw his 'highly offensive' and 'highly reckless' statements.

Ardern went a step further. It would fall to deputy prime minis-ter and foreign minister Winston Peters to 'confront' the comments and 'set the record straight, face to face' in Turkey, she told report-ers.[5] Actually, a personal visit to Turkey was Peters' idea, reportedly. He had to go and deal with the situation himself, he told Ardern, and never one to reject a good idea just because it isn't hers, she agreed.

Peters travelled to Istanbul on 22 March. He attracted some criti-cism in the media for 'backpedalling', taking a conciliatory approach in Istanbul – and for allegedly snoozing, translator's headphones on his head, through part of President Erdoğan's speech at the emergency Organisation of Islamic Co-operation (OIC) meeting.

Peters claimed to be in 'deep contemplation'; the kinder journalists noted he was jetlagged. Nevertheless, his legendary charm (overseas, at least) seemed to have its effect, with Erdoğan's tone softening in the following days. He spoke warmly of Peters' presence at the OIC, saying Ardern's 'reaction to the terror attack, empathy and solidarity with all Muslims should be a model for all the [world's] leaders'.[6]

Some of the more lavish compliments come from those least expected to proffer them.

Prime Minister Jacinda Ardern was now an unlikely Western star in the Muslim political sphere. Leaders in the Muslim world, men whose ideas, ideologies and lifestyles were far removed in most respects from Ardern's, appreciated her efforts, and deeply so.

Behind the scenes, Ardern had engaged with them. In the hectic week following the shootings, she found time to speak over the telephone with the crown prince of Dubai, the crown prince of Abu Dhabi, the emir of Qatar, the crown prince of Jordan and the prime minister of Pakistan. Little wonder Dubai's Sheikh Mohammed bin Rashid al-Maktoum honoured Ardern on the evening of 22 March, with the projection of her portrait onto the Burj Khalifa. Perhaps he felt it was the least he could do to acknowledge her compassion.

*

The day before Hagen Hopkins' picture of Ardern graced the Burj Khalifa, Clarke Gayford posted a touching photograph on Twitter. It was of Neve's tiny, soft hand grasping his finger. 'For her 9-month birthday today we received the gift of crawling. While her mum got her the gift of having a safer country to grow up in.' This was in response to Ardern's announcement of sweeping changes to firearms legislation, which was passed as an order by the Executive Council of ministers: the Arms (Military Style Semi-automatic Firearms) Order 2019, came into effect at 3 P.M. on 21 March 2019.

Assault rifles and military-style semi-automatic weapons were banned, Ardern told reporters, along with high-capacity magazines and components that could be used to allow guns to fire at the rate of automatic or semi-automatic weapons. A gun buyback scheme would be set in place to pay owners for weapons surrendered pursuant to the legislation.

The rationale behind Ardern's changes to gun laws was sound and practical, as she made clear in Supriya's interview. New Zealand is 'quite a rural nation. And so we use guns for legitimate purposes, pest control in particular,' she said, 'to protect our native flora and fauna, for animal welfare issues . . . what it's been about us for us is trying to remove the use of weapons . . . for the purposes of harming others.'

Ardern's rationale was simple enough, and an overwhelming majority of New Zealanders agreed. On 10 April, the Arms (Prohibited Firearms, Magazines, and Parts) Amendment Act 2019 passed its third reading with almost unanimous support – 119:1 votes for the bill, the only dissent from ACT's David Seymour. The bipartisan support for the reforms was impressive. As Minister of Police Stuart Nash told the House, 'Every single MP except one acknowledged that things needed to change, and this is incredible.' The Act became law on 11 April.

Ardern didn't take much personal credit. When in an interview in May CNN journalist Christiane Amanpour lauded her achievement, saying, 'Even President Obama couldn't do that in the United States,' she gently brushed aside the compliment. The legislation was for measures that 'New Zealanders by and large absolutely agreed with,' she said. 'Australia experienced a massacre and changed their laws, New Zealand had its experience and changed its laws. To be honest with you, I do not understand the United States.'[7]

Ardern might have had difficulty in understanding the US in some ways, but at least once the US media summed her up precisely, and only months after she was elected. *Vogue* magazine's lead feature in February 2018 was titled 'New Zealand's prime minister, Jacinda Ardern, is young, forward-looking, and unabashedly liberal – call her the Anti-Trump'.

*

Occasionally, though, the media could seem to misread Ardern and, occasionally, the quick-thinking prime minister would be caught flat-footed. While in London in January 2019 for a meeting with her UK counterpart over post-Brexit trade, Ardern found herself in one such moment with BBC2 presenter Victoria Derbyshire. As the interview drew to its conclusion, Derbyshire asked, 'Can you imagine asking . . . Clarke Gayford to marry you, or will you wait for him to ask you?'

Ardern threw her head back in laughter. 'No, I would not ask, no, no,' she replied emphatically.

'You're a feminist?' Derbyshire queried, pushing the point.

Ardern looked flummoxed. Was this really a matter of feminism? It was rare, if ever, that her feminist credentials were questioned. 'Oh absolutely, absolutely I am a feminist,' she said. 'But no, I want to put him through the pain and torture of having to agonise about that question himself, that's letting him off the hook, absolutely not.'

'OK, fair enough,' Derbyshire said. 'We await that day.'[8]

That day wasn't far away. Indeed, reporters had speculated – incorrectly, as it happened – it had already come and gone. In December 2017 and then in October 2018, reporters spied a ring on Ardern's finger that they guessed was an engagement ring. Ardern quickly dispelled any notion it was for her engagement, telling them she had simply moved the exquisite silver ring with its inset onyx onto her left hand to ease her eczema.

Journalists are not so easily deterred. Actually, it was not a journalist but an intern, a journalism student whose sharp eyes helped break one of the biggest stories of the year for New Zealand's social pages. On Friday 3 May 2019, the student noticed something significant, when along with Andrew Little and other dignitaries Ardern visited the Pike River coal mine to celebrate the scheduled re-entry to the drift (horizontal passage) there. The mine had remained closed since the Pike River Mine disaster on 19 November 2010, which claimed twenty-nine lives.

Though Ardern met with bereaved relatives of the lost miners, the day was something of a disappointment, as the re-entry had to be postponed for technical reasons. But there was some intrigue. The journalism student saw Ardern was wearing a fine diamond ring that she hadn't worn just a few days earlier.

The student did what all journalists worth their salt would do: follow up with an enquiry, in this instance to the prime minister's office. Is this ring for Jacinda's engagement?

Indeed it is, Ardern's spokesman confirmed.

The media buzzed with excitement. Reporters had to wait until the following Monday and Ardern's regular weekly post-cabinet press conference at the Beehive Theatrette to question her. As soon as the opportunity presented itself, they quizzed Jacinda on her engagement. From the lectern, she said she was 'surprised by [Clarke's] question', and as with many other couples, they hadn't made 'any plans at all' for their nuptials. When a journalist asked her to tell more about the proposal, saying 'the public are hungry [for more information] . . . trust me', Jacinda smiled as broadly as ever, but bashfully. 'Are they, are they really?' Unusually, she stumbled over her words for a moment. 'Look . . . ah . . . There are some things I wouldn't mind keeping for us,' she said. Then, obliging as she is, she proceeded to give a brief outline of Clarke's proposal.

It happened over the preceding Easter weekend, she said, while they were sitting at the lookout on Mokotahi Hill, a delightful spot overlooking Hawkes Bay on the east coast of the North Island. The vista there takes in rugged grassy hills and bleached cliffs at the water's edge above seas that glisten aquamarine under the sun. This is a special place for Clarke. His family owns a bach (pronounced 'batch', a Kiwi term for a small holiday home) in nearby Mahia; Hawkes Bay was where he had enjoyed many blissful summer days, surfing and fishing.

A prime minister can rarely find privacy, and never so in public. For this joyous occasion, there was a Diplomatic Protection Service officer present and some Mahia locals, who apparently had no clue as to the significance of the event they witnessed. An opportunistic dog saw something special was happening and wanted to join Jacinda and Clarke's celebration. A little too keenly: it tried to steal the chocolate cake Clarke had brought.

There was no getting down on one knee to pop the question; Jacinda didn't make Clarke agonise as she had suggested she would a few months earlier on the BBC. Rather than put him through 'pain and torture', she let her fisherman off the hook easily, by the sound of things. Perhaps it was simply that he caught her unawares: she was wearing trackpants for this momentous occasion.

Naturally, Clarke had planned his proposal carefully. He had asked both Laurell and Ross for their permission before he popped the question. In his pocket, he kept the family heirloom that would seal their engagement: his grandmother's elegant art deco ring, with two bead-set diamonds. He quietly proposed; she accepted, and he slipped the ring on her finger. But it was too big for her ring finger, she later explained, so she wore it on her middle finger instead.

News of Ardern's engagement set off the kind of speculation that one might see for the expected nuptials of royals or film stars. The *New Zealand Herald* indulged itself with the article 'Wedding of the Year: Ideas for Jacinda Ardern and Clark Gayford's nuptials'. Kiwi designers, who have always been favoured by the prime minister, were named and compared. Several event planners gave somewhat contrasting ideas on the kind of wedding Jacinda and Clarke might like. A cheese stack cake, for a ceremony at a Hawkes Bay vineyard. Or barefoot on the beach. Perhaps in a garden in the Bay of Islands. Or something more traditional?

It seems everyone was getting ahead of themselves. With New Zealand's year of crises – there is hardly space in a prime minister's schedule for personal business at the best of times – Jacinda and Clarke had given little, if any, serious thought to wedding plans.

*

One serious attempt to bring the couple to the altar, so to speak, came out of the blue. It came from a man whose whole career has been one of apparent light-heartedness, silliness and satire.

Perhaps it was for Ardern's utter lack of pretence in a world of make-believe. Or perhaps it was for her refreshing contrast to many of her foreign counterparts, her innate modesty. In any event, in her two appearances on *The Late Show with Stephen Colbert*, Ardern had made a sincere impression on the host. So much so, Colbert even described himself on air as her 'admirer' and 'personal friend'.

During both appearances, Jacinda invited him to New Zealand, assuring him she would personally meet him at the airport.

In October 2019, Colbert took Ardern up on her offer, arriving comically with his suitcase, a travel pillow around his neck, at Auckland airport. As she had promised, Ardern was there to pick him up – unsurprisingly of the ecologically aware prime minister, in her electric car, a white Hyundai Ioniq. Ardern drove Colbert from the airport through traffic in an astonishing media appearance for a world leader.

Colbert said, 'I just hope I'm not cutting into executive time.'

'I'm a woman, I multi-task, so do not worry,' Ardern replied. The pair launched into a spoof of James Corden's *Carpool Karaoke*, singing their own *a cappella* version of the chorus from Queen's 'Bohemian Rhapsody'. At her home in Sandringham, Ardern sat for an interview with Colbert. After some banter, he congratulated her on her engagement. 'When is the wedding?' he asked.

'We don't know,' Ardern replied.

'Do you need an officiant? Because I can legally marry people, I've married people before,' he said. Colbert's face became solemn, devoid of his usual sardonic expression. He meant it.

Colbert might have joked about his accreditation as a minister, which he said was 'the most prestigious ministry certification you can get online while also being on the toilet', but it seemed he truly enjoys helping couples tie the knot. He was the celebrant for an on-air wedding in October 2013; the couple had been forced to postpone their wedding due to a government shutdown.

Ardern took Colbert's offer in the spirit in which he delivered it. 'Can you? That would be really something if you came back and . . .'

'I'd be thrilled to,' Colbert said.

'Clarke!' Ardern called out to her partner, who was in the other room. 'What do you think of that?'

'Uh, I mean, sure, let's . . . let's talk,' Gayford called back, none too convincingly.

' "Let's talk"? He hates the idea!' Colbert said.

That put the matter to rest. The interview finished. Ardern and Gayford treated Colbert and the singer Lorde to a 'state dinner': a barbecue spread of sausages and buttered white bread in the garden. After he aired the footage of his visit and interview as part of a week-long series, 'The Newest Zealander', Colbert simply said, 'Thank you, Prime Minister Ardern. And thank you, Lorde.'[9]

'Thank you, Stephen Colbert' was New Zealand's grateful response. Colbert's trip was a publicity bonanza for the tourist industry. 'The Newest Zealander' aired as a regular feature on *The Late Show* for several days, exhibiting the delights of the country: shearing sheep, singing the national anthem (badly) in a bar, playing rugby, taking a helicopter ride over the majestic Southern Alps, landing on a glacier – 'It's more than beautiful . . . it's absolutely spiritual,' a visibly touched Colbert said – and toasting the experience with a shot of hip-flask whisky on the rocks (glacier ice). Colbert wrapped up the series with an amazing tribute. 'It's the most beautiful country in the world, with the nicest people,' he declared as he lay in an inflatable raft, elated after a bungee jump.

The only regret for New Zealanders, perhaps, was that Clarke Gayford didn't take up Colbert's offer for a wedding.

34

Whakaari

For a tourist looking out across the Bay of Plenty, White Island seems benign enough. From the town of Whakatane, it's little more than a bulge on the horizon through the haze of a summer afternoon. If one didn't know otherwise, the steam that hovers above its contours might be mistaken for smoke from fires. One cannot see its barrenness, the imposing geology; it doesn't possess a classic cone shape to reveal its true nature. Little shows that this is Aotearoa's most active volcano.

The Māori view the island as a living ancestor, and surely it is alive, in a geological sense. They call it Te Puia Whakaari, a far more fitting title than the beguilingly bland English name for the place. Whakaari means 'dramatic'; te puia whakaari, 'the dramatic volcano'.

Drama – or the notion of it, at least – is what attracted more than 10,000 visitors each year from around the world to Whakaari. Despite the dangers – or because of them – people flock to experience the stark, brutal majesty, the menace of an active volcano.

There was no easier place to do so than White Island. Whakaari's flank on the southern side had collapsed into the sea in some past eruption, creating a unique, amphitheatre-shaped caldera, just a few metres above sea level. There was no need to scale any mountainous flank. Small children and the elderly could happily join young, fit adults on a tour: unquestionably, it was the easiest, the least threatening walk into the throat of an active volcano.

Otherwise, Whakaari is fairly typical of its kind. The air in its crater is acerbic, sulphur-dioxide laden, like a match that has just been struck. Sucking on lollies and occasionally donning masks to soothe their throats, visitors trod over the powdery, light-grey ash, marvelling at this almost alien landscape.

Parts of Whakaari's crater were tinged a light yellow with sulphur; hot streams, streaking the landscape ochre, ran past the walking trails. Mud puddles boiled like a dish from some subterranean kitchen; the caldera's flanks towered some 300 metres high over the drama with awesome majesty. For the tour's highlight, visitors would stand above Whakaari's green acid lake, scalding hot in the centre of the crater, marvelling at the clouds of steam rising from its acrid, bubbling surface, before ambling back to the concrete jetty or helipad.

Compared to New Zealand's more hair-raising adventure tourism activities – jetboating's terrifying high-speed turns and splashes in cool rivers, skydiving over snowy peaks, bungee jumping and mountaineering – a boat trip or helicopter ride to White Island must have seemed like a peaceful day out.

*

Monday 9 December 2019 seemed like any other day during the warmer months, the peak tourist season: the skies clear blue, seas calm while three boats plied their forty-kilometre route from Whakatane to the island. In the early afternoon, just after 2 P.M., two remained in the waters off Whakaari in Crater Bay. One, the *Phoenix*, had just weighed anchor for the return to Whakatane. The other, *Te Puia Whakaari*, was moored some 100 metres from the shore, waiting for two tour groups. A helicopter and its pilot waited. Some visitors from *Te Puia Whakaari* stood on the jetty; others were trekking back from the crater.

A few moments after 2.10 P.M., passengers from the *Phoenix* looked out at the island in horror. A gargantuan steam and ash cloud, white, light-grey and leaden, was silently billowing from the crater, balling and rising over the island. In moments, this superheated pyroclastic flow had swallowed everything in the caldera, spilling out towards the boats at around 100 kilometres per hour from the gap in the caldera's flank. Some passengers panicked. The *Phoenix*'s crew ordered them into the cabin, the captain opening the throttle wide and motoring away as the cloud bore down on them.

It was not a moment too soon. Crater Bay, and the rest of the island, was in seconds shrouded in ash and steam.

In a minute or two the eruption was over, the cloud reaching 3,000 metres into the atmosphere. The *Phoenix* followed a wide arc, speeding back into Crater Bay.

Everything on Whakaari was now monochrome pale grey, shrouded in volcanic ash – including the passengers on the jetty and *Te Puia Whakaari*. The force of the blast had blown the Volcanic Air Safaris helicopter from its landing. Grey and stricken, it sat among the ash, blades hopelessly bent to the ground. Tourists stood and sat on the jetty as before. But while they looked unhurt from a distance, they had suffered horrific burns. The *Phoenix* crew, led by Paul Kingi, launched a dinghy, rushing them aboard in several trips. The passengers and crew on board helped with first aid, pouring bottled water on the burned survivors and comforting them as the launch sped back to Whakatane. On the way, St John ambulance paramedics boarded from a rescue vessel to assist.

A couple of people on the island had escaped almost unscathed. From *Te Puia Whakaari,* skipper David Plews had radioed a desperate warning as he saw the eruption. 'Evacuate, evacuate, evacuate!' On the island, helicopter pilot Brian Depauw screamed at his clients, 'Jump into the water!' Two plunged into the sea with him, the blackness above enveloping everything as they submerged.

Those closest to the crater stood little chance. Astonishingly, an Australian teenager, Jesse Langford, staggered from the ash to the beach, his entire body burned horribly. Kingi ferried him to *Te Puia Whakaari*, which rushed him to Whakatane. With the risk of further eruptions, it was a brave decision for Kingi to remain on the island to search for survivors.

The ash cloud high above the island meant news of the blast spread quickly. What happened next demonstrates the spirit of Whakatane's people, so typical of New Zealanders from all walks of life. Within minutes of the disaster, the helicopter tour operators and a local flying instructor had coordinated by mobile phone and radio. They knew what had to be done – they must launch their own rescue mission.

Just after 2.50, Jason Hill and Tom Storey in one chopper, and then Mark Law in another, lifted off from Kahu NZ's hangar in Whakatane. A short while later, Volcanic Air's Tim Barrow and Graeme Hopcroft took off from Rotorua. With the veteran airman John Funnel circling the island in his light plane to provide radio coverage, these brave men would put their own lives in danger to aid the seriously injured victims stranded in Whakaari's crater.

It was just as well. With the danger of the volcano erupting again, the national air desk had diverted rescue flights to Whakatane. It was too dangerous to fly emergency services helicopters to White Island, the authorities decided. The helicopter tour operators were on their own. They would be the ones to ferry the stricken tourists from Whakaari's crater to Whakatane, without medical support.

Upon landing, the men donned respirators to save them from the gases in the crater. Braving hot ash in some places thirty centimetres deep, they defied the risk of another eruption as they scoured the caldera for survivors.

Footprints in fresh ash told of the guides' last, valiant efforts for their group. Their medical kit lay open – they had attempted to administer first aid to the victims. One guide, the expert Hayden Inman-Marshall, had led some of his group towards the jetty then doubled back inland in the darkness to guide others, before succumbing to his injuries. His young colleague Tipene Maangi had collapsed with an asthma inhaler in his hand, apparently reaching out to hand it to someone in his group. The pair had placed masks on stricken, unconscious tourists after the eruption.

The pilots loaded survivors aboard the helicopters, rushing the victims across the water to a fleet of waiting ambulances and medical helicopters, twenty minutes' flight away in Whakatane. 'I wish I could have sped that flight up 100 times and had those guys back at Whakatane in a millisecond,' Tim Barrow later said.

The pilots' heroism saved two lives. For most, though, they could do little. Of the twenty-one tourists in the caldera when Whakaari erupted, only three would live.

The human loss from the disaster was heartrending. An entire family, the Hollanders from Sydney, perished – father, mother and two teenage sons. Other families, such as Jesse Langford's, were devastated, with only a sole survivor of the calamity. Finally, the volcano's eruption would claim twenty-two souls. Most were Australian tourists from the cruise liner *Ovation of the Seas*. Many others, including guides, had suffered terrible burns, some of the worst seen by medical experts. And Whakatane had lost two of its loved sons.

*

Most prime ministers face disasters, national calamities at least once in their tenure. But for the third time in 2019, not even nine months after the Christchurch mosque shootings, Jacinda Ardern found herself leading the nation through a crisis.

Two crises, actually, simultaneously. Before news of the eruption reached the Beehive, Ardern was chairing her regular Monday afternoon cabinet meeting. The major order of business was to coordinate relief for a disaster – one that seemed to speak to her urgency for climate change action – that had affected around a thousand foreign tourists. Over the weekend, extreme weather had lashed the South Island. Severe thunderstorms, hail and driving rain, with some 300,000 lightning strikes recorded on Sunday alone, had led to flooding then landslides. Major roads, including parts of State Highway 1, the premier road which runs the length of the country, remained closed, submerged by floodwaters. The Rangitata River, whose valley was the setting for the city of Edoras in *Lord of the Rings*, had burst its banks, effectively isolating the southern half of the South Island. Numerous towns including Fox Glacier and Franz Josef had been cut off, leaving hundreds of foreign tourists stranded. Many had been forced to sleep in their cars, hungry and exhausted.

Ardern's cabinet meeting was cut short as updates from Whakaari's disaster trickled in. Radio messages relayed by John Funnel over the volcano and emergency services updates from Whakatane indicated the gravity of the situation, but no clear information as to the exact number of casualties.

In front of the customary dark curtains and New Zealand flags, Ardern stood at the lectern in the Parliament Buildings at 4 P.M. She apologised to reporters for the delay in the press conference, which she said was on account of her 'wanting to [have] the most up-to-date information . . . to share' regarding the Whakaari disaster. She gave a brief outline of the information available, saying that police had asked the public to avoid the Whakatane Heads and Muriwai Drive area so it would be clear for the emergency services. She informed journalists there would be a joint press conference at 5.30 P.M. with the National Emergency Management Agency and the police, with updates on the 'evolving situation' at Whakatane. As if one disaster were not enough to manage, Ardern then outlined the relief effort for the stricken South Island with Minister of Transport Phil Twyford, which included immediate grants of $100,000 to mayoral relief funds.

Ardern moved quickly. After a further briefing at the Beehive and a media appearance, she took a flight to Whakatane airport, where she held a late-night briefing with Minister of Civil Defence Peeni Henare, local parliamentarian Tamati Coffey, Whakatane's mayor, Māori representatives and officials. Early the next morning, she convened another meeting at Whakatane District Council before a 7 A.M. press conference, followed by four television and radio interviews.

Dressed in sober black, Ardern took her place before the cameras on the lawn outside Whakatane District Council Buildings, for an interview with TVNZ Breakfast reporter John Campbell. She spoke in a considered tone, acknowledging the eruption was 'devastating'. Victims had been taken to hospitals throughout the country, she said, 'utilising the best expertise in care'. She spoke of the importance for police of 'making sure that we [know] precisely who those potential victims are'.

Campbell's question 'Were [the tourists] at greater risk . . . than they should have been?' was perhaps poorly timed given the loss and grief of the disaster, but it was inescapable. Weeks earlier, with increasing geothermal activity and swelling in the crater, New Zealand's GeoNet raised the level of alert for the island to level 2, the highest before an eruption. On 3 December, the warning took on a darker tone: 'The volcano may be entering a period where eruptive activity is more likely than normal.' Geysers of mud and debris shooting up to thirty metres into the air from its crater were ominous, surely a sign to keep people far from the island.

Ardern's reply was typically level-headed, common-sense: 'Today, the focus is on providing that critical care for those who've been injured . . . We do and will ensure that the appropriate authorities answer those questions.'

Her priority was indeed the survivors. At 9.30 A.M., Ardern went to Whakatane Hospital, where she met with staff and patients. Thirty-one burns victims from Whakaari, many of them in critical condition, were spread over hospitals throughout New Zealand's main centres. The country's burns units were at capacity.

An hour later, at Whakatane Fire Station, Ardern met with the first responders: the police, ambulance and rescue personnel. Greeting them with warm hugs and handshakes, she chatted with them and gave a brief address. While the atmosphere was subdued, her message was positive, appreciative. 'What a community that exists here,' she said. 'Firefighters, police, St John [ambulance] all on the ground and assisting. They have done an incredible job in difficult circumstances.'[1] She described the pilots who had landed on the island after the eruption as 'incredibly brave'. The expression on her face as she spoke to them was of acknowledgement, of admiration: as the daughter of an emergency services officer, she understood implicitly the magnitude of their actions.

In Parliament later that day, she again paid tribute to the courageous pilots, whose 'own personal safety was the last thing on their minds' when they undertook their rescue mission. Referring to the efforts of police, rescue, ambulance and volunteers, she declared, 'There is no limit to New Zealand's capacity to mobilise, to respond, to care and embrace those impacted by tragedy. We are a nation full of ordinary people who do extraordinary things.'[2]

Ardern spoke to the world as much as her people, with language that was especially moving for such a formal arena:

> To those who have lost or are missing family and friends, we share in your grief and sorrow, and we are devastated. To our international partners and friends, we will do everything we can to support you as you have supported us in times past. In particular, our family in Australia has been heavily impacted . . . I say to those who have lost and grieve: you are forever linked to our nation and we will hold you close.

The prime minister would pursue matters in the following days with the kind of rigorous engagement that was becoming familiar.

On 12 December, she visited patients at the burns unit in Christchurch Hospital; a week later, she did so at Middlemore Hospital in Otahuhu.

The nation's hospitals were the unsung heroes of the White Island disaster. Immediately following the eruption, the medical professionals had swung into action. Their prompt action saved numerous victims of Whakaari, and meant that survivors of the disaster could heal and lead functional lives. Specialist surgeons from Australia and Canada came to help with the huge workload of skin graft operations; a massive global order of 120 square metres of skin for grafts was quickly filled. It would not be until April 2020 that the last patients in New Zealand were discharged.

On the afternoon of 13 December, Ardern met with personnel on HMNZS *Wellington*. The navy patrol vessel was engaged in a search – for remains rather than survivors – which had been hampered by bad weather and the threat of a second eruption. Ardern spoke of the 'enormous duty of care' to recover the victims' bodies. Six were recovered from the island by military personnel from the Explosive Ordinance Disposal Squadron, who were equipped with closed-circuit breathing apparatus and protective suits. Tragically, the remaining two – those of Hayden Marshall-Inman and Winona Langford, Jesse Langford's sister – had been washed by rains into the sea. Despite searches by divers of the toxic waters around the island and local police and community efforts for weeks afterwards, they were never recovered.

In a press conference later that afternoon held at Whakatane District Council, Ardern called on New Zealanders to observe a minute's silence at 2.11 P.M. on the following Monday, in memory of the victims of the Whakaari eruption: 'Wherever you are in New Zealand or around the world, this is a moment we can stand alongside those who have lost loved ones in this extraordinary tragedy,' she said. 'Together we can express our sorrow for those who have died and been hurt and our support for their grieving families and friends.'[3]

Precisely a week after the eruption, Ardern stood with her ministers at the cabinet round table in the Beehive, silent in commemoration of those who had perished. Hagen Hopkins captured the moment with another touching image of Ardern to add to his portfolio. With her long black blazer, the ministers' heads bowed and hands clasped in front of them, it gives the impression of a priest leading her congregation in prayer.

Along with Ardern and her cabinet, New Zealanders widely observed the minute's silence. Social media reports told of drivers pulling their cars to the side of the road. School children stood in silent contemplation; embassies of citizens who had perished in the eruption paid their minute's tribute before flags flown at half-mast.

Ardern's human and humane actions had once again embodied her nation's spirit, her people's wishes; she had more than lived up to Aotearoa's aspirations. Certainly, she had personified the Kiwi concern for others that had characterised New Zealand's, and especially Whakatane's, response to the disaster.

The people in the Bay of Plenty did everything that could be expected of them, and more. Along with their courageous emergency effort, locals had arranged memorial services and left floral tributes at the waterfront. A Māori blessing welcomed grieving relatives on a White Island Tours trip to the island. There was a makeshift shrine and a tearful send-off for the *Ovation of the Seas* at the Port of Tauranga, with dozens of people on the wharf. Amazingly, numerous Kiwis throughout New Zealand even offered to donate some of their own skin to help the burns victims. New Zealanders and their prime minister showed they cared for their visitors.

The world noticed. Overseas, the Kiwi effort and Ardern's leadership after the Whakaari eruption was widely praised, particularly in Australia, which had lost seventeen of its citizens in the calamity. Ardern was described online as 'classy' for her 'measured' and 'calm' response.

An obvious empathy underpinned Jacinda Ardern's actions. But her eminently sensible, practical leadership in the hours and days following Whakaari's eruption was more than a touching display of humanity. In her public briefings, Ardern was concise and direct, deferring to the experts: the police, the National Emergency Management Agency, the military and health professionals. She empowered them, providing them with moral leadership along with the authority of her office, fostering an approach that saw the arms of government gracefully cooperate.

Prime Minister Ardern had long been recognised as a compassionate leader. Now, in a year that had seen a bushfire, a terrorist attack, floods and a volcanic eruption, there was no question as to her effectiveness, which she had demonstrated could happily coexist with her empathy. One could indeed argue that her empathy made Ardern a more effective leader for her people. Clearly, she could be relied upon when a leader is most needed: in times of crisis.

The defining crisis of Jacinda Ardern's first term was just months away.

35

Cometh the Hour, Cometh the Woman

Gregor Fountain recalls a charming incident in the mid-2000s, when he accompanied a high-school group on a London trip. He was the head of history at Wellington College at the time, he told Supriya. By then more Jacinda Ardern's friend than former teacher, he took the opportunity to meet up with her – this was during her OE, when she was working in the Cabinet Office.

Ardern saw Fountain in Whitehall, where she gave him a guided tour. She took him into the bowels of the buildings, the underground bunkers where the British government functioned during the Blitz, pointing out the small room where she had been told Prime Minister Winston Churchill watched films during the Second World War. 'It was this lovely moment of student-turned-teacher,' Fountain recalls.

Ardern's interest in Churchill is intriguing, not least because he seems to represent – politically, at least – so much that she stands against. A staunch imperialist and hard-boiled conservative, Churchill declared he wouldn't be 'henpecked' into supporting women's suffrage. He had no time for decolonisation, let alone the kind of indigenous rights that Ardern viewed as just and fair. Old-fashioned even for his own time, Churchill snarled with contempt for her hero Mahatma Gandhi, who was, he declared in 1931, 'an Inner Temple lawyer, now become a seditious fakir . . . striding half-naked up the steps of the Viceregal Palace'.[1]

Suffice it to say, there are few ideological similarities between Ardern and the cigar-smoking, top-hat-wearing, acid-tongued Churchill. Yet Ardern's masterful leadership in yet another crisis, the COVID-19 pandemic in New Zealand, showed aspects of the great British leader. With Churchill's odious views on race and his conservative politics, Ardern may be reticent to acknowledge him, but the British Bulldog seems to be a major inspiration for her. Perhaps even as powerful as Big Norm Kirk and that other celebrated crisis leader, Ernest Shackleton.

The parallels are there as evidence.

*

On 23 April 2020, UN secretary-general António Guterres recorded a video message for UN staff. His words were sobering: 'We are together facing,' he declared, 'the biggest global crisis since the Second World War.'[2]

Jacinda Ardern could hardly have found a better role model for leading New Zealand through the COVID-19 crisis than the man who led Britain through its Darkest Hour. The Western world as we know it would probably not exist without Winston Churchill, widely recognised as the greatest crisis leader in history.

Churchill came to power in spectacular fashion, early in the war. Upon the outbreak of Nazi aggression in September 1939, his warnings of the threat Nazi Germany posed to world peace, unfashionable in a political climate of appeasement little more than a year earlier, quickly became confirmed truth. When Prime Minister Neville Chamberlain resigned on 10 May, Churchill was just the man to take his place.

The British had great trust in Churchill. He was viewed as a man willing to speak the truth, even at the expense of his career. This trust would prove crucial to his success.

His communication was equally important. Churchill was not a natural orator: he had a raspy voice and a lisp, his speech was often punctuated with a stammer. But he honed his skills assiduously. On 4 June 1940, under the threat of invasion, Churchill gave perhaps the most famous of all inspirational speeches.

Honest and emboldening, it set a pattern for his oratory during the war. While he spoke frankly of the dire situation Britain faced, with an invasion by Nazi German forces imminent, he exhorted his people with stirring rhetoric: 'We shall fight on the beaches, we shall fight on the landing grounds, we shall fight in the fields

and in the streets, we shall fight in the hills; we shall never surren-
der'. His speech roused his people like none of that era, and
perhaps none since. Churchill's friend and Labour MP Josiah
Wedgwood declared it 'worth 1,000 guns and the speeches of
1,000 years'.[3]

While Churchill knew the power in words, he also understood the
power of well-timed symbolic acts, of making a statement for his
people. On 24 August, when German bombs hit civilian targets in
London, he immediately ordered a retaliatory bombing attack on
Berlin. When air raid sirens sounded during the Blitz, Churchill often
took to the nearest rooftop, fearlessly surveying the action with his
aides and staff, and sometimes even guests. At first, anti-aircraft guns
stayed fairly quiet during night raids, because gunners could not readily see their targets, and were loath to waste precious ammunition.
Hearing of Londoners' dismay that the Nazi planes ruled the skies
uncontested, Churchill ordered the gunners to fire at will during
raids. Morale soared.

Churchill also made use of personal symbols, several of which
became emblematic of him. In the media of the day, newspapers and
cinema newsreels, a scowling Churchill would be seen, bowler hat on
his bald head, cigar between his teeth and holding his fingers in a
trademark V-sign for victory for the cameras. His confidence was
infectious. When he was amid a crowd, he would place his bowler hat
on the point of his walking stick and twirl it playfully above his head
to show his presence to those farthest away. With the prime minister
so utterly self-possessed and indomitable, so fearless, Britons couldn't
help but take courage.

Like any great leader, Churchill made sure he was there for his
people, personally. Hours after the first raid of the Blitz on 7 September
1940, the British Bulldog toured London's devastated docklands in
the East End. Through streets strewn with rubble, past wrecked buildings he walked with his entourage. His aides were apprehensive that
he might be blamed for the catastrophe. They need not have worried.
Locals flocked to Churchill, heartened by their leader coming to their
side in their time of suffering. Churchill's public appearances continued throughout the war. His walking through charred ruins in defiance of the Nazi bombing raids gave us some of the defining images

of this great man. Their effect in bolstering his people's spirits can hardly be overstated.

Churchill vexed his generals with questioning and debates on strategy. He sought and heeded specialist advice, though, only interfering where he felt it would prove constructive. His reduced, five-man War Cabinet was streamlined to bypass the usual bureaucratic hurdles between experts and decision makers, proving agile in the shifting fortunes of war.

The cabinet itself spoke of the man's genius. Comprising some of Churchill's former opponents – including Clement Attlee, the man who would ultimately succeed him – it was the heart of his National Government. Churchill understood that to defeat the Nazis, political and ideological foes must for the war effort combine their energies that would otherwise be wasted in party politicking. With representatives of all parties, his government steered the nation to victory, only dissolving once Nazi Germany surrendered in May 1945.

In the decades since Prime Minister Winston Churchill left office, many historians, scholars and management experts have studied this great leader – his strengths, his methods, his effectiveness. So, too, it seems, did a young New Zealand woman on her OE, just a decade before she would lead her country.

*

A war with an invisible enemy, the COVID-19 pandemic has seen more tactical blunders and shoddy administration than inspirational leadership. Prosperity has scarcely played a part in the matter. Developed nations along with those poorer have lurched from procrastination to crisis management, shattering lives and economies as quickly as their politicians shifted blame.

Some success stories have emerged, however, and these share an indisputable pattern. Three of the countries that have fared best in containing COVID-19 and limiting its casualties have been led by women.[4] These stellar women's performances could hardly contrast more starkly with those of some of their male counterparts.

Scientist that she is, German chancellor Angela Merkel took a rational approach, calmly telling her people that the virus could infect as much as seventy percent of the population. 'It's serious', and they had to be 'taking it seriously', she said. Germans heeded her words – at least for the first months of the pandemic. Taiwan's President Tsai Ing-wen promptly introduced 124 measures that arrested the transmission of COVID-19 in her country. In Iceland, Prime Minister Katrín Jakobsdóttir instituted free coronavirus testing and a tracing regime that has become world best practice.

The effectiveness of women leaders in tackling COVID-19 – at least in comparison to their male counterparts – is measureable, and dramatic. On average, countries led by women have suffered little more than half the number of coronavirus deaths of countries run by men.

A 2020 British study, 'Leading the Fight against the Pandemic: Does Gender "Really" Matter?', conducted by Supriya Garikipati and Uma Kambhampati, investigates the phenomenon. The paper suggests women leaders' concern for their citizens' welfare, which led them to act quickly and decisively with lockdowns and other measures – along with men's risk aversion to financial loss (that is, the effects of a lockdown on the economy) – explains the astounding difference in casualties.

Qualitative analysis of the evidence varies, naturally. Some journalists have praised women leaders' governance, while others flay the abysmal performance of male leaders who have dithered and blustered through the crisis, particularly in the US, the UK and Brazil (significantly, all three of those leaders have contracted the virus). Women are performing as leaders should, they say. The men, the strongmen particularly, have let us down.

Of the women leaders, Jacinda Ardern is among those most praised for her conduct in the campaign against COVID-19. Unarguably, New Zealand's geographic isolation and her nation's unitary government (New Zealand has no states) have afforded Ardern an advantage in fighting the disease, as has its later onset. But while her counterparts across the Tasman Sea have struggled with outbreaks of the virus and recriminations, Kiwis have cooperated with the government's measures, harsh as they have been, largely without complaint.

Ardern possessed a huge advantage over most leaders as the COVID-19 crisis hit. Like Churchill when he assumed office in 1940, she enjoyed New Zealanders' trust. Tested in two major crises, Ardern was widely acknowledged for her honesty and ability, even by those who would never vote Labour. A Colmar Brunton poll taken in April 2020, during the country's rigorous lockdown, indicated eighty-eight percent of New Zealanders trusted the government's decisions in controlling COVID-19. As Helen Clark said, Kiwis 'may even think, "Well, I don't understand why [the government] did that, but I know she's got our back." '[5] Eighty-four percent approved of the government's approach.

Possessing advantages alone amounts to little; taking the best course of action requires judgement and a plan. Ardern's strategy of 'going hard early' meant the virus couldn't get a foothold in New Zealand as it had in other countries. On 2 February, Jacinda announced a ban on foreign travellers from mainland China entering the country. Her reaction was swift, coming just a couple of days after the World Health Organization's declaration on 30 January of a 'public health emergency of international concern'.

Speed was of the essence; the usual consultative departmental processes were bypassed, government analyst Clinton Watson told a reporter: 'We had to make some blunt decisions . . . in order to avoid total calamity.'[6] Agile decision making was as important in combating COVID-19 as it would have been in battling any invader.

After the virus inevitably made its way to New Zealand, via a traveller from Iran, Ardern's government closed the borders on 19 March. Only residents and citizens could return, but they would have to self-isolate for fourteen days after they arrived ('managed isolation' was introduced on 10 April). On 21 March, Ardern announced the centrepiece of New Zealand's response to tackling the virus, the four-level Alert System: Prepare; Reduce; Restrict; Lockdown.

Reportedly, Ardern herself initiated the system. It's not hard to discern her influence in the alerts and their language: the care, the caution and the thoughtfulness.

Her televised announcement for the Alert System was familiar in style. She began her address, 'I'm speaking directly to all New Zealanders today, to give you as much certainty and clarity as we can as we fight COVID-19.'[7] Her speech was sensible, direct, reassuring, while acknowledging the 'anxiety and uncertainty' of the pandemic and the government's response.

In explaining the impending Alert Level 2, Ardern assured New Zealanders of access to essential services, supermarkets and pharmacies, which probably lessened the severity of panic buying. She concluded her speech with a hallmark exhortation: 'Be strong, be kind, and unite against COVID-19.'

By explaining the reasons for the government's actions and its objectives, along with the Alert System, Ardern brought her people into her confidence; she made it clear what was expected of them, while establishing the basis for a united national effort. She also acknowledged the sacrifice New Zealanders would have to make. She seems to have absorbed the lessons of Churchill's example in the Second World War – instinctively, or otherwise. This wasn't a leader ordering people about. This was an enlightened leader urging her people to willingly join the fight against an unseen foe.

The New Zealand campaign against COVID-19 began with sound intelligence. Throughout the early days of the coronavirus, New Zealand's experts took advantage of learning from other countries' mistakes. They could see from the pandemonium in Italy and Spain – overwhelmed hospitals, bodies piled into army trucks, coffins lined up in churches – that firm measures were needed. Behind the scenes, Ardern secured support from business leaders for a ratcheting up of the regime to Alert Level 4: Lockdown.

At 1.30 P.M. on 23 March, Ardern held her regular Monday post-cabinet-meeting press conference in the Parliament Buildings. Beside her was her political partner and minister, Grant Robertson. She spoke with conviction. 'We currently have 102 cases, but so did Italy once,' she said. 'Like the rest of the world, we are facing the potential for devastating impacts from this virus. But through decisive action and working together, we do have a small window to get ahead of it.'[8] She did not mince her words. If firm measures were not adopted, 'our health system will be inundated, and tens of thousands of New Zealanders will die,' she said.

Ardern proceeded to outline what Alert Level 4 entailed. There were to be no mixed messages in Aotearoa as there were across the Ditch. There, in the wake of a muddling press conference, the cricketing great Shane Warne thundered on Twitter, 'Listening to the [Australian prime minister Scott Morrison] . . . what I understood was, "It's essential, unless it's not. Then it's essentially not essential. I can't be clearer." Plus people can buy a new shirt at a shopping centre? WTF?'

New Zealand's lockdown would be the most stringent in the world at the time, but the objectives and the details were clearly stated. Schools would close, along with all non-essential businesses; non-essential travel was to cease; people would have to stay at home.

Elimination, and not flattening the curve of infection, was the objective. It was either this, or the kind of calamity seen in Spain and Italy in the preceding weeks. 'I remember my chief science adviser [Professor Juliet Gerrard] bringing me a graph that showed me what flattening the curve would look like for New Zealand,' Ardern later said. 'And where our hospital and health capacity was. And the curve wasn't sitting under that line. So we knew that flattening the curve wasn't sufficient for us.' It was an ambitious goal, but aiming for elimination would save lives, even if it were not achieved.

It wasn't just science that informed the decision to try to eliminate COVID-19. Jacinda's daily walks between Premier House to the Beehive, about one kilometre, had given her some insight into New Zealanders' fear of the disease. She saw people loading bags of flour into their cars; she heard conversations on the street. Hence, she knew 'we had to lift our communication . . . so we could just take people with us.' Clarity was key to its success, as was Ardern's open acknowledgement of the toll the lockdown would exact on Kiwis. 'I do not underestimate what I'm asking New Zealanders to do, I know it's huge,' she said at her 23 March press conference.[9]

Here, she exhibited her enlightened leadership. Direction giving, the stuff of governments throughout the world, formed part of the speech – there was no question that the lockdown was mandatory, as lockdowns are, everywhere. Her speech was far more nuanced, though, than speeches given around the same time by her counterparts, such as that of the British prime minister Boris Johnson, an alumnus of Eton and Oxford.

When Ardern spoke logically of the danger of the virus, she was informing her people of the threat they collectively faced, which explained the reasons for the measures that she had directed. She then acknowledged the sacrifice that Kiwis collectively would have to make

– a message of empathy that reached out to them on a human level – which in effect asked for their cooperation. Ardern's speech hence took on the nature of a nation-building exercise, beyond its purpose as a public health and administrative message.

Her next communication on 25 March assumed a more familial character when she hosted a coronavirus live stream session from her home. Wearing minimal makeup and dressed in a sage-green sweat-shirt that had seen better days, Ardern apologised for the 'casual attire', which was for 'the messy business' of putting Neve to bed, she explained. This was as endearing to Jacinda's admirers overseas as to Kiwis, who don't like too much pomp and ceremony.

She spoke of the lag in COVID-19 infection, saying, 'We won't see positive benefits of all of the effort that you're about to put in . . . for a few days yet . . . so don't be disheartened.' Smiling, optimistic, Ardern was just as reassuring in her manner as her words. She asked people to 'check in on your neighbours, especially . . . [the] elderly, give them a call, see what their needs are . . . if you can help them, go out and grab their essentials and pop them on the front door for them.'[10]

Here, Ardern was going much further than almost any leader in her COVID-19 briefing, save for one of the spiritual kind. She wasn't asking New Zealanders to do something she wouldn't do herself. The woman who 'got into politics to make a difference' was, in the midst of a crisis, doing just that, suggesting ways Kiwis could be kinder, become more active in their community. Ardern somehow found a way to make her country better from adversity.

Ardern's COVID-19 daily press conferences and her more infor-mal live streams, a mainstay of her war on the virus, will likely become case studies for management and leadership in the years to come. They were of the highest order; government at its best. The press conferences saw not the slightest sugarcoating: no attempt to withhold information or manipulate data or facts was to be heard. There was no finessing of figures. It was clear to all and sundry, too, that the government was acting under expert advice – she often appeared with Dr Ashley Bloomfield, the director-general of health, whom she described later as a 'studious, evidence-based and optimis-tic leader'.[11] She deferred to Bloomfield, a telegenic man who quickly earned New Zealanders' respect for his clear, concise and informative briefings.

Ardern's language itself revealed much, and conveyed a good deal. 'We', 'our' and 'us' were the regular pronouns in her presentations. Not in the least condescending, she didn't preach to her people. Human and humane, she spoke of living in a lockdown 'bubble'; her Facebook question-and-answer live stream sessions opened with a friendly 'Kia ora' and her usual smile, a casual chat about the weather and what was on her agenda for the day. Often at lunchtime, her dressed-down, homely chats managed to make communicating government restrictions and pandemic information palatable. She would pick questions from those sent to her, answering them in a frank and engaging manner, with an optimistic mood.

Ardern's formal presentations were equally cordial. Press conferences can be fraught affairs, especially in difficult times, but she wasn't crotchety with journalists. Quite the contrary. When at a COVID-19 press conference on 16 April she called for a question from the *New Zealand Herald*'s Jason Walls, the reporter went blank. 'Sorry, it doesn't matter,' he said. Ardern's surprising response quickly made waves across the internet. 'We'll come back to you, no problem,' she said. 'I do worry about your sleep at the moment though, Jason.'[12]

Many Americans were delighted at Ardern's show of human concern, and her sense of humour, after the exasperating confrontations typical of President Trump's press conferences. John (@johnsbig73) tweeted, 'Time to move to New Zealand!' Joyce Karam, the Washington correspondent for the United Arab Emirates newspaper *The National*, wrote, 'At a time when journalists are under attack by US President, expelled by China, Egypt and censored by many authoritarian states, it's heartening to see civility in leadership.'[13]

At another press conference with Ardern and Bloomfield a few days later, an Australian Sky News journalist also forgot his question. Befuddled, or perhaps a little starstruck by the prime minister, he directed it to Ardern while speaking to Bloomfield. Ardern, smiling that broad smile of hers, pointed towards the good doctor beside her, the Beehive Theatrette filled with reporters' chuckling.

While the media bonhomie might have been inspired by Ardern's charm and charisma, it came about in an environment of trust.

Journalists weren't the least antagonistic because there was simply no reason to be so. From Bloomfield, Ardern or Grant Robertson, the media could expect transparency: straightforward, factual, informative briefings; honest replies to questions; and sound governmental strategy.

The press could see, too, by the figures and their own reckoning, the war on COVID-19 was being won. On 20 April, Ardern announced, 'We have done what very few countries have been able to do. We have stopped a wave of devastation.'[14] With a transmission rate of 0.48, as against the world average of 2.5, the lockdown could ease to Alert Level 3 restrictions after a week.

Three weeks later, with COVID-19 cases dwindling, Ardern announced the further easing of restrictions to Alert Level 2. Workers could return to their offices; schools would reopen; retail stores and restaurants would be free to resume trade. Ardern thanked her 'team of five million' – a memorable, inspired way of referring to her people – for the efforts and sacrifice of perhaps the harshest lockdown in a democracy. 'Kiwis from all walks of life were resolute and determined – determined that this was a war we could eventually win, but only if we acted together,' she said. She was careful to note, though, that 'we may have won a few battles but we have not won the war'.[15]

New Zealand's happiest day since the COVID-19 pandemic struck came with Ardern's announcement on 8 June that there were no active COVID-19 cases. 'I did a little dance,' she said, in response to a journalist's question about her own reaction to the news. Neve 'joined in, having absolutely no idea why I was dancing around the lounge, but enjoying it nonetheless'.

Coronavirus had been beaten, but not eradicated. Naturally cautious, Ardern warned the following day of inevitable further cases. She might have been disappointed and cut her celebratory dance short, had she known the new cases of the disease could easily have been avoided.

*

Even wars of the victorious are beset with failure and loss. The New Zealand campaign against COVID-19 has been largely successful, though various blunders very nearly saw the sacrifices of the lock-down and Alert System restrictions undone.

The first was an indiscretion, more of a public confidence issue than anything else. Still, it threatened to undermine Jacinda Ardern's brilliant leadership during the lockdown. On 2 April, Minister of Health David Clark was photographed by a vigilant member of the public driving his van, his image emblazoned on its side, to a park two kilometres away from his Dunedin home, where he took a ride on his mountain bike.

In normal circumstances, this would be perfectly routine behav-iour. But in the lockdown it was baffling and embarrassing for Ardern and the government. The minister principally responsible for the COVID-19 lockdown was clearly flouting the Alert Level 4 advice of his government, administered by his own department. That is, New Zealanders were to avoid high-risk exercise and to confine exercise to their local areas.

Ardern promptly issued a statement: 'I spoke to the health minis-ter last night, who apologised to me.' Her right-hand man, Grant Robertson, weighed in, saying, 'He needs to lead by example, and he didn't do that in this case.' Clark didn't heed Robertson's words. A few days later, it emerged he had driven with his family twenty kilometres to the beach for a walk. Jacinda acted quickly and decisively. The minister would ordinarily have been sacked, she said, but in the midst of the campaign against the COVID-19 pandemic, he was needed. He would instead be demoted, losing his portfolio of associate finance minister. 'I expect better, and so does New Zealand,' Ardern wrote in her media statement.[16] Clark's hold on his portfolio seemed tenuous, and he resigned at the beginning of July.

As the lockdown looked to ease to Alert Level 3 in late April, Ardern saw some dissent over government strategy. It came from one of her old friends. Disagreeing with the government's decision to reopen schools, her former school principal John Inger wrote in a school newsletter that it was a 'potential disaster'; that parents might simply want this because their young ones were a 'pain in the neck'.[17]

Reporters gleefully raised it with Ardern at her press conference. 'Mr Inger,' she said, with mock irritation. Making light of Inger's statement, she suggested he might have had her in mind, with her two parents being essential workers. She made it quite clear, however, that she disagreed with his comment.

After the easing of the lockdown, there was no disaster. New Zealand saw a further easing on 9 June to Alert Level 1. This return to essentially normal life, however, was brief. The virus soon found its way through chinks in the nation's defence.

During the first months of the pandemic, some 70,000 Kiwis made their way back to Aotearoa from their OEs and overseas jaunts. As the nation began to return to normal living, two women who had recently arrived from the UK, quarantined in an Auckland hotel, were allowed leave on compassionate grounds to visit a dying relative in Wellington. The pair had not been tested for coronavirus. They drove in a borrowed car, becoming lost as they went. So they visited a friend for directions, whom they gave a 'kiss and a cuddle', it was later revealed. One of the women became ill on their journey. Both later tested positive for COVID-19. They had had contact, it emerged, with hundreds of people.

The protocols were clear: the women should have been tested before they left isolation. It was a blunder in implementation, though, rather than policy. Ardern nevertheless faced the issue squarely, saying, 'It is totally unacceptable that procedures we were advised were in place were not.' Dr Ashley Bloomfield did likewise: 'I am taking responsibility,' he declared, 'for ensuring this does not happen again.'[18]

This was not mere public relations spin. There was no attempt to shift blame, or indeed to blame anyone. As quickly and decisively as she had acted against the virus, Ardern took measures to correct the deficiencies in the quarantine system. Looking to the military in this most unusual war, she appointed Air Commodore Darryn (Digby) Webb, the second in charge of New Zealand's armed forces, to supervise the quarantine. Housing Minister Megan Woods, an energetic woman noted for her competence and ability to juggle punishing work demands, was charged with working alongside Webb to oversee a review of managed isolation.

The review was prompt and frank in its findings. On 29 June, Ardern spoke of the review, which found the quarantine system to be under 'extreme stress'. She said, however, that New Zealanders should feel assured of the government's response, because her team had 'adjusted our settings every step of the way based on what we've learnt, based on what we know is working and based on what needs to be done . . . we have been very agile.' As for the deficiencies in the system, 'we have all been taking responsibility for this. There is not one person to blame . . . we just have to fix it.'[19]

In these few sentences, Ardern articulated some key reasons for New Zealand's success in containing the pandemic: observing, learning, constantly adjusting the government's approach. This, and rolling up your sleeves and dealing with challenges as they presented themselves. New Zealand's government didn't waste time and energy on manoeuvring, obfuscating and passing the buck, which has blighted the coronavirus response in the US.

President Donald Trump's leadership, his response to the pandemic, could barely be further from Jacinda Ardern's. The *Washington Post* wrote of 'Trumpian mismanagement' of the COVID-19 crisis, the president's name a self-explanatory adjective.

In February, the early days of the pandemic, Trump claimed the virus was 'very much under control in the USA'.[20] In March, he continued to downplay the coronavirus's threat, comparing it to seasonal flu. As the pandemic took hold later in the month, he turned on the media, calling a journalist who asked a 'nasty question' a 'terrible reporter'.[21]

The following month, he urged his supporters to 'liberate' Michigan, Minnesota and Virginia – that is, breach those states' lockdowns. On 30 April, Trump's administration allowed the federal 'stay at home' guidelines to expire, leaving the states to their own devices. As the number of deaths soared in May, Trump began to deny blame for the catastrophe, while pushing for non-essential businesses to be allowed to reopen. In a bizarre statement on 11 May, he claimed, 'We have met the moment and we have prevailed.'

Trump's tweet was almost as fatuous as his public musing in April: 'And then I see the disinfectant, where it knocks it out in a minute. One minute. And is there a way we can do something like that, by injection inside or almost a cleaning . . .'

Vacillating, denying responsibility, playing party politics and flouting expert advice were just some of President Trump's failures during the COVID-19 crisis. With such leadership, little wonder that the

US has perhaps the worst rate of COVID-19 infection in the world, and one of the highest numbers of COVID-related deaths.

Incredibly, Trump spoke derisively of New Zealand's COVID-19 situation. When news of a cluster of cases in Auckland hit the news in August, he and Ardern shared a terse public exchange. On 17 August, President Trump spoke before supporters at a Minnesota airport. 'You see what's going on in New Zealand? They beat [the virus] . . . it was like front-page [news] . . . because they wanted to show me some-thing,' Trump said. 'Big surge in New Zealand. So you know, it's terrible, we don't want that . . .'[22]

It's hard not to laugh at the gall of the man. The *Washington Post* article headline, 'Trump warns of a "big surge" of coronavirus in New Zealand, which had just recorded nine new cases', brought some perspective to the matter. That, and the horrendous figures from the US. On the very day Trump spoke, 33,326 new cases of coronavirus were reported across the country. *The Guardian* noted that Trump's 'comments fail to reflect that 22 people have died from coronavirus in New Zealand, versus 170,000 in the US'.[23]

Journalists buttonholed Ardern over Trump's comments the following day at Parliament House. She was on her 'Tile Run', a Kiwi institution where politicians run the gauntlet of reporters as they cross the chequered tiles of the corridors. The Tile Run is an opportu-nity for journalists to put hard questions to their leaders, freed from the constraints of a press conference. A long-time master of the Tile Run, Winston Peters took lessons from his old party leader, Robert Muldoon, delighting in 'counterpunching' hapless journalists with insults and quips.

Naturally, Ardern was less confrontational. But she was firm when confronted with Trump's egregious misrepresentation. 'Obviously I don't think there's any comparison between New Zealand's current cluster and the tens of thousands of cases that are being seen daily in the United States.' Trump's assertion was 'patently wrong,' she said.[24] Nevertheless, she later said the August Auckland COVID-19 outbreak was 'a real psychological blow for people' that she herself felt.

President Donald Trump and Prime Minister Jacinda Ardern share a fascination for Winston Churchill, but little else. Astonishingly, given Trump's botched crisis management and divisiveness, the White

House compared him to the wartime leader, even as coronavirus ravaged his nation. 'Trump is no Churchill,' the US newspaper headlines blared in disgust.[25]

If there is a Winston Churchill of the war against COVID-19, for her success in rallying her country to fight the virus, there's a good argument to say it's Prime Minister Jacinda Ardern.

36

The COVID Election

Much was outstanding and historic about the 2020 New Zealand general election. For only the second time in the nation's history, two women leaders vied for their nation's prime ministership. The polls were postponed from 19 September to check a minor cluster of COVID-19, an unprecedented but widely supported decision. Polling day, 17 October, gave Aotearoa a unitary government for the first time under the MMP system; a thumping Labour victory, the biggest since Norman Kirk stormed into office in 1972. More significantly, forty-eight percent of the new parliament would be women, who accounted for fifty-five percent of Labour's sixty-four seats – numbers Helen Clark and Annette King could only have dreamed of when they began their parliamentary careers in the 1980s.

The campaign, though, seemed dull by the measure of New Zealand elections. Months of lockdowns and Alert Levels, and the looming shadow of the coronavirus had left Kiwis ambivalent about run-of-the-mill political issues. It was, as veteran political commentator Jack Vowles would later say, a 'COVID election'. In the war against the virus, security and stability mattered most; with even dyed-in-the-wool National Party voters at ease having Aunty Jacinda in the Beehive, the election's result was a fait accompli. Labour's campaign slogan, 'Let's keep moving', might as well have been 'Don't change horses midstream'. Kiwis seemed to want the election over with, to regroup and rebuild, to get on with their lives.

The year started with some doubts, however. Discontent from the left over the slow progress in housing, welfare and alleviating poverty – due mostly to the restraints of the coalition – gave cause for worry in Labour. But while COVID-19 forced the nation onto a war footing and Ardern's able leadership tilted the contest firmly towards Labour, woes in the opposition also helped the government.

Leadership coups diminished the National Party in the months before the election. Though intelligent and well presented, National Party leader Simon Bridges, Ardern's old television and parliamentary sparring partner, never quite connected with the public. Party backrooms hummed with intrigue as Bridges' approval ratings slumped in the first months of 2020. He soon had enough of it, bringing matters to a head in a leadership ballot on 22 May. He was narrowly defeated, reportedly by a single vote. Bridges and his deputy, Paula Bennett, were replaced by Todd Muller and Ardern's former opponent Nikki Kaye.

This was just the beginning of a bloodletting in the National Party's ranks, and women fared worst – senior, talented women, at that. Bennett resigned, along with Anne Tolley, a veteran who had also held several portfolios.

In any event, Muller never seemed comfortable in his new role. With his leadership marred by trouble reining in a restive caucus, he abandoned the leadership on 14 July. It later emerged Muller had suffered from severe anxiety soon after taking up the post. He served just fifty-three days in post, a record short term as party leader.

Kaye's unexpected announcement on 16 July that she would leave politics only worsened matters for the party. She was followed that very day by Amy Adams, another National Party stalwart. Kaye was a formidable campaigner, one of the party's young leadership hopes, a former minister with a promising future. Suffering from breast cancer, which caused her to take sick leave in September 2016, gave her a different perspective, she says: 'There's always been a calculation of the greatest amount of contribution I can make versus being able to live and have a life.'[1] She chose a life over the bruising world of politics.

Her resignation was a blow her party could ill afford. The National Party had lost four respected women parliamentarians in a couple of months. And in a curious mirroring of Ardern's situation heading into the 2017 general election, Judith Collins had risen to the leadership, her party well behind in the polls, just two months before the election.

Pitting Collins against Ardern would have made for an interesting match under normal circumstances. Tempting though it might be to cast this as a contest between absolute opposites – young versus old, left versus right, a tough slugger taking on the popular champion – the truth about Judith Collins is far more intriguing.

There's no doubt she has cultivated the 'iron woman' persona of 'Crusher' Collins throughout her career. Nicky Hager's 2014 book *Dirty Politics* showed how Collins revelled in the Machiavellian cut-and-thrust of political life. One of her leaked emails read, 'If you can't be loved, then best to be feared', a clear nod to the Renaissance thinker. Her instruction to the right-wing blogger Cameron Slater, 'always reward with Double [*sic*]' – that is, retaliate with twice the force – sounds more like advice from a feudal lord than a government minister.

One can guess that Collins's 'Crusher' behaviour is a means of coping in the rough-and-tumble of New Zealand politics. She seems to have made Crusher a career persona – like a professional wrestling 'villain' alter-ego, if you will. She was known for having shooting-range terrorist targets peppered with bullet holes hung in her office, just to make a point. She didn't shoot them herself: she wasn't into violence, she said.

Collins didn't deny cultivating the Crusher persona. Curiously, the topic was raised by Jacinda Ardern at an arranged lunch interview with the pair, in December 2015. The lunch date was just the second time the two women had spoken personally. The first was some time earlier, on a plane, when they chatted about films and books. This time, they shared some interesting exchanges and opinions as they dined with journalist Simon Wilson. The women discovered they grew up in nearby Waikato country towns – Collins in Walton, just twenty kilometres from Morrinsville – though nearly a generation apart. Wilson noted the pair liked each other, that they seemed to agree with each other while debating points vigorously. They even identified each other's strong suits.

Ardern praised Collins for her resilience.

'You've got to be resilient,' Collins replied. '[Politics is] a tough environment.'

'Did you build that persona to survive?'

'Yeah, I have. I think when we're in the heat of battle, and it's all so exciting – it's after the kill, basically, when the blood is in the air – it is really easy to forget that the other side is actually human.'

Ardern noted then that she herself was 'seen as too nice, too soft, too sensitive, almost . . . the very opposite of Judith'.[2]

Nearly five years later, Kiwis had seen different aspects of both women. Jacinda Ardern, they discovered, might be nice, engaging and sensitive, but she could be strong – tough, even – when the situation demanded. In the wake of the Christchurch mosque shootings, Judith Collins had shown a softer side of her nature. On 20 March 2019, she addressed Parliament, thanking Ardern for her 'outstanding' response to the terrorist attack, and speaking in support of her wearing a headscarf. Collins's face was downcast, her voice quavered with emotion; she choked on tears as she spoke, enunciating each word to compose herself. The tragedy brought the humane Judith Collins to the fore.

When the women faced off on the hustings, it was clear to New Zealanders that Collins was the underdog. There was to be no mirroring of Ardern's miraculous coming-from-behind victory in 2017, however. Still, Collins wouldn't have survived nearly two decades in politics if she had been a quitter. She campaigned against Ardern about as well as anyone could have, under the circumstances.

Perhaps Collins felt constrained. Invoking Crusher, as she might have liked, would have been a risky tactic against the much-loved Aunty Cindy. Ardern's 'go hard early' COVID strategy had been vindicated; Kiwis looked at their own situation with relief, aghast at the mayhem of recurring COVID-19 outbreaks, rising death tolls and lockdowns in the US and UK. To criticise the government over its handling of COVID would have been counterproductive.

The National Party had learned its lesson already. Simon Bridges had suffered a backlash from his Facebook post in April flaying the government over its coronavirus policy. Harsh though the lockdowns were, National Party voters as much as Labour ones approved of the government's actions. Even Todd Muller had been forced to acknowledge the government's 'impressive' performance in containing COVID-19. So for the most part, Collins's campaigning was subdued. Ardern was herself low-key; months of COVID-19 seemed to have weighed on her, and she still faced the long haul of rebuilding the damaged economy if she won the election, which it indeed seemed she would.

Always in search of a conflict, political journalists bemoaned the pair's 'unmemorable', bland performance in their first of three televised debates. The second and third debates saw a little more energy. Perhaps the greatest interest came from a question relating to the referendum to legalise cannabis. The media was agog with Ardern's admission she had used the drug, 'a long time ago'.

There was some controversy during the campaign. In late August, Collins had to field questions from the media over her husband, David Wong-Tung, posting off-colour caricatures of Ardern on Facebook: one depicted her as a green 'Incredible Sulk', another as a milkmaid, captioned 'Cindy is milking the WuFlu for all it's worth now'.

Wong-Tung's actions were obviously unacceptable, but Collins sidestepped the issue with a glib explanation that women might anyhow relate to. She wouldn't have done it herself, she said. But '[my husband and I have] been together for forty-one years. I have never been able to get him to do anything I tell him to do . . . he's an adult, he makes his own decisions.' Was her husband sexist? reporters asked. 'He's married to me. How could he be sexist?' Collins replied. The gathered media personnel chuckled.[3]

There were other controversies, some of which came, not surprisingly, from Winston Peters. In early September, with New Zealand First languishing well below the five percent threshold in polling, he took aim at Labour over the government's COVID-19 response. 'We let our guard down,' Peters said. 'Too many things fell through the traps . . . The fact of the matter is that the Labour ministers are the only ones in charge of all that.'[4]

Perhaps it seems a little odd that a government minister – the deputy prime minister, no less – should attack his own government. But this was Winston Peters: the usual political rules haven't applied to the man throughout his four-decade career. His election strategy could be summed up in his claim that New Zealand First were 'a handbrake for silly ideas and a serious accelerator for good ideas'. The 'handbrake' would be applied against 'woke pixie dust' in Labour and the Greens, apparently. 'Every farmer should be really very worried if we don't get back,' he declared.[5]

While one centre-right party seemed headed for a polling shipwreck and another listed badly, the smallest had the wind behind it.

Founded in 1994 by Roger Douglas and Derek Quigley, ACT New Zealand had been a classical liberal, conservative and right-libertarian force in New Zealand politics until the 2011 general election. That year, it lost all but one seat in Parliament. With that one seat, it held tenuously to the National Party-led coalition until the 2017 election, when it went into opposition. The National Party's infighting – and voter disaffection with New Zealand First, whose alliance with Labour and cooperation with its policies had left many of their conservative constituents feeling disenfranchised – was a godsend to ACT leader David Seymour.

With his penchant for speaking his mind, and bluntly, one could be excused for describing the 37-year-old, part-Māori Seymour as a younger Winston Peters. Significantly, his was the sole dissenting vote against gun control legislation after the Christchurch mosque shootings. Seymour's contrarian streak anyhow seemed to resonate with some voters in a way that Peters' had, more than a generation earlier.

2020 would be Seymour's year, almost as much as it was Ardern's. He was about the same age as she was when her star rose. In twelve months, he had taken his party from one percent support to eight percent, leading into the election. Many of his new supporters had jumped ship from New Zealand First and the National Party.

As the signs for the National Party became ominous in the weeks before polling day, it made one last desperate push against Ardern and Labour. Knowing the effectiveness of attack advertising over taxation in the 2017 election, Collins's team ran a series of 'STOP THE WEALTH TAX' advertisements on Facebook, the banner surrounded by red and green. The advertisements spoke squarely to older voters: 'A wealth tax would be disastrous for retirees in New Zealand . . . you could be pinged $140 PER WEEK. Only a Party Vote for National will protect your retirement.'[6] In a Newstalk ZB interview on 12 October, Ardern countered the advertisements: 'We've said all along that is not our policy,' she said tersely. 'And nor . . . would that be part of the negotiations' with the Green Party after the election.

Last-minute jockeying amounted to less than ever, in any event, with close to half the votes already cast. A total of 1,976,996 New

Zealanders voted in advance. The question, anyhow, for political observers was not whether Jacinda Ardern would win. It was whether her Labour Party would achieve an outright majority.

Perhaps the only surprise of the election campaign was that there were still doubts of an emphatic Labour victory. An Australian news. com.au article on the election day, 'New Zealand Election 2020: Jacinda Ardern could lose election, even if Labour comes first', suggested that the 'shy Tory' factor might have skewed the polls; the nation's 'Byzantine' MMP system and 'lazy Labour voters' who were so certain of a victory, they wouldn't bother to vote, meant 'there is reason for Ms Ardern to be worried'. Maybe this was simply the writer's own trans-Tasman joke.

Hours later, the figures spoke emphatically of Kiwis' confidence in their leader. With a massive swing to the party, Labour claimed sixty-five seats of the 120-seat Parliament, nineteen more than in the 2017 election, and 50.01% of the party vote. Many former conservative electorates, such as National Party deputy leader Gerry Brownlee's seat of Ilam in Christchurch, had fallen in the Labour onslaught. The result meant Labour could govern without a coalition partner.

For the Nationals, it was a disaster, a rout. The party had lost twenty-three seats, garnering a mere 25.58% of the party vote. The minor parties saw as much of a change in fortunes. Deputy Prime Minister Winston Peters lost his list seat; polling just 2.6% of the party vote, New Zealand First was out of Parliament. The Greens and ACT were almost neck and neck at 7.86% and 7.58% of the party vote respectively. Both won ten seats, though for ACT, this represented a massive swing in the party's favour from the one seat in the previous parliament.

Of the two referendums that accompanied the election – on whether to legalise euthanasia and cannabis use – voters supported only the End of Life Choice Act 2019, which Ardern also backed. After refusing to divulge her position on the cannabis referendum, she confirmed after the election that she had voted in favour of the legislation, because she didn't want to see people jailed for using cannabis. She stressed that this was only her personal vote: 'On this occasion, I wanted New Zealanders to decide.'[7]

Ardern was gracious in victory. In her address to party members in

Auckland, she acknowledged her supporters and reached out to all Kiwis: 'Thank you to the many people who gave us their vote, who trusted us to continue with leading New Zealand's recovery . . . And to those amongst you who may not have supported Labour before . . . thank you. We will not take your support for granted. And I can promise you, we will be a party that governs for every New Zealander.'[8]

She aired her enlightened perspective of politics: 'We are living in an increasingly polarised world, a place where more and more people have lost the ability to see one another's point of view. I hope that [in] this election, New Zealand has shown that . . . as a nation, we can listen and we can debate. . . . Elections aren't always great at bringing people together, but they also don't need to tear one another apart.'[9]

Later, while addressing journalists, Ardern showed her awareness of the task ahead. While she said she was 'very pleased with the results tonight', she continued, 'I imagine I'll take a little moment later this evening and then first thing tomorrow we crack on with work.'[10]

Perhaps this best sums up the COVID election. For all the glory of the greatest Labour victory in half a century, the message it carried was clear as it was simple: Kiwis trusted Jacinda Ardern implicitly to lead Aotearoa through its worst crisis in seventy years. Her Labour Party had been granted a thumping mandate, an authority to govern that no other party had had in decades (though it would form a loose coalition with the Greens: 'Friends are gold under MMP,' as Judith Collins said). But there was no time for celebration or indulgence, little scope for grand visions. The challenges facing the nation were far too great.

37

Kindness and the Ardern Effect

During the 2020 election campaign, a heartbreaking story found its way into New Zealand's newspapers. In early August, a British family of four, Harry Jarman, Barbara Genda and their children, fourteen-year-old Eddie and thirteen-year-old Amelie, had been sailing their yacht, their only home, in Tahiti's waters, when tragedy struck. Eddie was snorkelling near the yacht to check its anchor when a rented motorboat sped past, striking him as he swam just below the surface. Amid the screaming and crying of his family, a woman boater dragged Eddie's limp body from the water. Despite emergency services' best efforts, the boy could not be revived.

The family had lost an engaging, talented young man, a son with 'an amazing zest for life', his parents said. Heartbroken, they abandoned their yachting voyage. They would need to sail their boat to New Zealand to sell it so they could resume their life in the UK. The New Zealand maritime border, though, was closed to foreign yachts due to COVID-19, except those in 'compelling' need of repair and refit, to the value of not less than $50,000. The Jarmans requested permission to enter New Zealand on humanitarian grounds, but were promptly rejected. Stranded in French Polynesia on their yacht with the cyclone season approaching, they appealed directly to Jacinda Ardern.

The Jarmans' case arose during an interview on 12 October on Newstalk ZB, among a bevy of issues leading up to the election. 'I did see a case recently which I thought . . . on humanitarian grounds . . . a reasonable case had been made,' Ardern said. 'I'm going to go back and look at that one . . . the case of a family who had a death on their yacht.'

Within a day, the Ministry of Health confirmed to the *New Zealand Herald* that the Jarmans' case was being reviewed 'as a matter of urgency'. By 2 November, in time so they could avoid the cyclone season, the Jarmans had been granted an exemption by the director-general of health to sail to New Zealand.

In the three years of her first term as prime minister, Ardern said she had 'learned how to use the levers [of government] to move more quickly'. The Jarmans' case demonstrates her willingness to operate these levers for decency and compassion. This wasn't a whim; rather, it is simply the manner in which Jacinda Ardern chooses to live. In early April 2019, a woman posted on Facebook her account of an incident where she was at the checkout of her supermarket with her two children, only to discover she had left her purse at home. She was preparing to leave her groceries behind when Ardern stepped in and paid for them. The woman was astonished as much as delighted. When reporters asked Ardern why she paid for the groceries, she simply replied, 'Because she was a mum.'[1]

The suggestion this might have been a political stunt could have found favour with Ardern's detractors, had others not made mention of incidents in her teenage years. Her generosity is an old habit, it seems. When she worked at the checkout in a Morrinsville supermarket, she was known to take money from her own pocket when customers were a few dollars short.

More instances of Ardern's thoughtfulness, her empathy emerged after the Facebook post. During Easter of 2014, she was stranded at Wellington airport after flights were cancelled due to stormy weather – a not-so-uncommon occurrence in the Windy City. She was one of the lucky few who could secure a rental car to make her trip by road. Instead of driving away by herself, however, she returned to the terminal in the car and offered lifts to the 'upset-looking group' from her flight who were not so fortunate. One traveller was due at a wedding; another a twenty-first birthday party, while the third just wanted to see her family. Ardern worked out a route with her new companions. Together, the four of them set out across the North Island, Ardern making sure they all reached their destinations in time for their engagements.

Other stories of Ardern's kindness filtered through to the media. She had sent a couple a hand-written, sixtieth wedding anniversary card. She donated readily to worthy causes. Cases came to light of people who had met her casually discovering to their delight, when they crossed paths a couple of years later, Jacinda remembered their meeting, and even their last conversation.

Such expressions of her well-rounded humanity have doubtless endeared Ardern to New Zealanders, just as they have found her fans around the world. The belief in her decency has at any rate demonstrated its currency when the prime minister asked for Kiwis' cooperation and sacrifice. New Zealanders were no more enthusiastic about lockdowns than Americans or Europeans during the COVID-19 crisis, but their confidence in Aunty Jacinda saw them largely willing to comply with government restrictions.

Doubtless, charm is part of Jacinda Ardern's leadership, with its undeniably feminine style. A self-described feminist who embodies feminism's values and lives according to its tenets, she is unabashed about her womanhood, natural glamour and maternal instincts. Kissing babies is a political trope; most leaders look for photo opportunities with children whether they genuinely like them or only, as in W. C. Fields' humorous quip, 'if they're properly cooked'. Ardern's interactions with children, though, reveal a true love of young ones, and a sometimes unusual humour from a leader of state.

Such was her dealing with an eleven-year-old girl in 2019 called Victoria, who sent the prime minister a letter, along with a $5 'bribe' to conduct research into dragons. Victoria wanted to be given telekinetic powers so she could become a dragon trainer, she wrote.

On prime ministerial letterhead, Jacinda replied, 'We were very interested to hear your suggestions about psychics and dragons, but unfortunately we are not currently doing any work in either of these areas. I am therefore returning your bribe money, and I wish you all the very best in your quest for telekinesis, telepathy and dragons.' She added a hand-written postscript, in rounded, printed letters: 'I'll still keep any eye out for those dragons. Do they wear suits?'

The picture that one must paint of Jacinda Ardern is of a genuine, thoughtful woman. Her detractors rarely cast credible doubt on her sincerity. 'What you see is what you get' is a comment one often hears from her friends and colleagues in describing her; she is indeed, bar her glamour, a mature version of the girl her teachers described.

Perhaps she is not so unusual. Everyone encounters thoughtful and generous souls who love children and possess an innate integrity. There are few, though, to be found in high office – fewer still who lead countries. Certainly, Ardern's kindness and humanity seem utterly incongruous with the world of politics. The characters most often seen walking the halls of government have a good dose of the 'dark triad': narcissism, Machiavellianism and psychopathy. *Vogue* magazine didn't dub Ardern the 'anti-Trump' without good reason. Perhaps it's an indictment of our systems of governance that some measure of the dark triad appears to be almost a prerequisite for high office.

The dark triad should be considered negative ego. Ego, which for the purposes of discussion may be defined as a sense of self-esteem and self-confidence, combined with a feeling of self-importance, is a necessary attribute for a political leader. Without self-confidence, a person would not feel able to appear in public and speak in the manner required of a public representative. Without self-esteem and a feeling of self-importance, a person wouldn't even contemplate running for office, much less seek to inspire a nation.

For all her humility, it would be naive to suggest that Jacinda Ardern doesn't possess a robust ego. It is the expression of her ego that distinguishes her. Ardern's determination to 'make a difference', to improve the living conditions for her people; to acknowledge her tendency for anxiety and sublimate this for perseverance, an absolute commitment to her duty, contrasts her with lesser leaders.

Through Ardern, New Zealand has shown a kind of moral leadership that it once did in granting women suffrage. The nation has demonstrated that an empathetic woman with a sense of humour and a good dose of humility – someone who speaks of being kind without mawkishness – can be a most effective leader. More effective, perhaps, than narcissistic leaders who preach *realpolitik* and make harsh decisions without qualms. A good dose of humanity – along with genuine, honest and persuasive rhetoric, for want of a better word – seems to have found its place in Aotearoa.

Internationally, Ardern's popularity could see the beginning of a profound shift. The Kiwi actor Sam Neill says, 'Wherever I go, people say . . . "Could we just borrow her for a while?" '[2] People throughout the world understand, to their delight, that Ardern's leadership functions well. Just as a new technology is embraced, voters will probably seek her kind of governance, across the globe. With her example in mind, they will begin to expect more from their own elected leaders.

*

Be that as it may, Ardern and her government face great challenges in the coming years. While her success in handling disasters of the natural and man-made variety in her first term is indisputable, it remains to be seen how she and her government will handle more entrenched problems. There are issues that cannot be solved with empathy and decent leadership alone. Some have their roots going back generations.

New Zealand's economy was already slowing when Ardern took office in 2017. COVID-19 has simply worsened the situation, and greatly so. The price and availability of housing is an issue that has been decades in the making; inexcusable levels of childhood poverty have blighted Aotearoa since Jacinda was a small child. Farmers have resisted environmental legislation stoutly for years.

Transformation, changing the status quo, is a difficult and more importantly an expensive business. New Zealand's economy contracted by an unprecedented 12.2% in the June quarter of 2020, largely as a result of lockdowns. Tourism, which accounts for some ten percent of New Zealand's GDP, was decimated by the COVID-19 travel restrictions and lockdowns. A struggling economy means sagging government revenues. No one could question Jacinda Ardern's mandate, her moral and legal authority to govern; nor could anyone say she lacks the will to improve the lives of underprivileged New Zealanders. With a paucity of funds, however, the transformation that Ardern promised when she first came to power appears elusive.

Regardless of her achievements in her second term in office, Ardern's legacy has in some respects already been set in place. Prime Minister Jacinda Ardern may well be remembered in much the same way as her hero, the great Ernest Shackleton from the Heroic Age of Antarctic exploration. The Antarctic explorer and geologist Sir Raymond Priestly commented, 'For scientific discovery give me Scott; for speed and efficiency of travel give me Amundsen; but when disaster strikes and all hope is gone, get down on your knees and pray for Shackleton.'[3] In time, when natural disasters occur and in moments of national emergency, New Zealanders will likely recall Prime Minister Jacinda Ardern with much of the same fondness.

Surely, this smiling, personable woman has guided New Zealand through some of the worst crises it has endured. But like Shackleton, Ardern might fall short of her goal of transformation, due simply to circumstance. If her first term is any indication, she will probably make whatever changes are feasible. She might personally have advocated free university study when she worked for Helen Clark's campaign in 2005, but it was her policy of interest-free student loans that prevailed, enduring nearly a decade of National Party government. Similarly, with a series of factors militating against radical transformation – the post COVID-19 economic adjustment, a mandate from a broad range of New Zealand voters and her favouring of consensus – Ardern is likely to pursue more modest, incremental change, policies that will long outlast her government. As she has said, she has always been the 'pragmatic idealist'.

In any event, Prime Minister Jacinda Ardern has shown the world a different face of power, that one might hope will become a more familiar expression of government as the century progresses. Having women such as Ardern hold high office may be rare now, as women's suffrage was a century ago. In future decades it should become as common, as expected and as unremarkable as it is in these times for women to cast their vote.

Acknowledgements

First and foremost we would like to thank Jacinda Ardern, prime minister of New Zealand, for taking the time to talk with Supriya Vani about her life and motivation. We would also like to thank officials in the Prime Minister's Office for their correspondence with Supriya over the last three years, which gave invaluable additional insights into the New Zealand prime minister's values and her unique approach to politics. The seed of this book was sown in 2017 when Supriya met Joanna Kempkers, New Zealand's high commissioner to India.

Writing a book is a challenge at the best of times. Needless to say, 2020 has been far from the best of times. We had planned on conducting numerous viva voce interviews in New Zealand, but of course COVID-19 put paid to this. Happily, messaging and Voice over IP (VoIP) and email, along with digital and print sources saved the day.

We would like to thank Kiwi journalists and their publications, TV and radio stations, and websites: the *New Zealand Herald*, the *New Zealand Listener*, *Newshub*, *Newsroom*, *Next*, *Noted*, *Now to Love*, *Otago Connection*, the *Otago Daily Times,* the *Otago Post,* Radio New Zealand (RNZ), the *Rotorua Daily Post*, *Scoop*, *Stuff,* the *Taranaki Daily News*, Television New Zealand (TVNZ), *Spinoff,* the *Standard,* and the *Waikato Times.*

We would also like to acknowledge the following international sources: *The Age*, the BBC, *The Conversation*, *Diplomacy and Beyond*, *Euronews*, the *Evening Standard* (London), *The Interpreter*, *The Guardian, Marie Claire*, Movehub, *the New Yorker* and *Time.*

We are grateful to the authors of the following books: Madeleine Chapman, *Jacinda Ardern: A New Kind of Leader*; Michelle Duff, *Jacinda Ardern: The Story Behind an Extraordinary Leader*; Claudia Pond Eyley and Dan Salmon, *Helen Clark: Inside Stories*; Nicky Hager, *Dirty Politics:*

How Attack Politics is Poisoning New Zealand's Political Environment; and John Harvey and Brent Edwards, *Annette King: The Authorised Biography.*

Of the many people we have been in touch with about this book and who have shared their experiences and knowledge, we are particularly grateful to Gregor Fountain, John Inger, Dame Annette King, Professor Stephen Levine, Paul Lowe and Colin Mathura-Jeffree.

For sourcing research material, M. Marie Issack's assistance has been invaluable, and we thank him wholeheartedly. We also thank Amanda Bentley for her help with genealogical research and her expertise in First World War history and documents, which gave us insights into Jacinda Ardern's family history.

We are grateful to our agent, Kathrin Scheel of This Book Travels, for helping us to get our book out in the world, where we have been fortunate to work with Bill Swainson at Oneworld, who has shepherded the book throughout. Authors have their blind spots: Bill's editorial clarity and our copy editor Jonathan Wadman's meticulous attention to detail – along with their absolute commitment to the book during the trying UK lockdown – have helped focus our narrative and refine the text. We are also grateful to Emily Hart at Hardie Grant for taking on the book in Australia and New Zealand, and for her comments on the final draft, and to Prema Govindan at HarperCollins India for taking on the book for the Indian subcontinent.

*

Personal acknowledgements:

Supriya Vani: Thanks to my parents Madhur Bhashini and Tarsem Lal, my brother Jai and sister Ishanu for being my support system. Thanks also to Sharon L. Shields, Katherine T. Osten, Obse Ababiya, Christian Marc and Mohinder Singh Miglani.

Carl A. Harte: Thanks to my partner Rajeshni Reddy for her support, and to my sons Zachary Harte and Hamish Harte for their interest in and comments on the text.

Finally, we acknowledge New Zealand, this exquisite land so far from the rest of the world, rich with scenery and characters that we hope come alive in our narrative. Without Kiwis' down-to-earth friendliness this book would not have been written. Aotearoa has shown the way to the rest of the world in the past, as it does now.

Supriya Vani, New York,
Carl A. Harte, Pondicherry,
1 March 2021

Notes

All website references were accessed 14–15 December 2020.

1 Volcanos and Seismic Shifts

1 Ann Pomeroy, 'Resilient Communities Murupara', Centre for Sustainability: Agriculture, Food, Energy and Environment University of Otago, Dunedin, June 2016.

2 Ewan McDonald, 'Laurell Ardern on motherhood and raising the future prime minister', *Mindfood*, 4 May 2020. https://www.mindfood.com/article/laurell-ardern-on-motherhood-and-raising-the-future-prime-minister/

3 'Woman's Day: Jacinda Ardern on her role model mum', *Now to Love*, 20 October 2017, https://www.nowtolove.co.nz/parenting/family/jacinda-ardern-on-her-role-model-mum-34346.

4 Ibid.

5 Wayne McClintock, 'Resource Community Formation & Change: A Case Study of Murupara', Working Paper 7, Taylor Baines & Associates, June 1998, ISSN 1176-3515.

6 Zizi Sparks, 'Jacinda Ardern organised, engaged and focused from age 5, says long-serving teacher', *Rotorua Daily Post*, 22 June 2018, https://www.nzherald.co.nz/rotorua-daily-post/news/jacinda-ardern-organised-engaged-and-focused-from-age-5-says-long-serving-teacher/2MTBRUEQGCNLNSGIL35VJFSKYI/

7 Praveen Menon, 'New Zealand's Ardern stays cool as earthquake strikes during live interview', Reuters, 24 May 2020, https://uk.reuters.com/article/uk-newzealand-quake/new-zealands-ardern-stays-cool-as-earthquake-strikes-during-live-interview-idUKKBN2300RT

2 A Peaceful Valley

1 Supriya Vani, interview with Jacinda Ardern, 30 April 2019.

2 Supriya Vani, interview with Jacinda Ardern, 30 April 2019.

3 Jacinda Ardern (2008), Maiden Statements, *New Zealand Parliamentary Debates*, vol. 651, p. 753, https://www.parliament.nz/en/pb/hansard-debates/

rhr/document/49HansS_20081216_00001012/ardern-jacinda-maiden
-statements

3 *The Activist Awakes*

1 Bruce Munro, 'Teachers who made a difference', *Otago Daily Times*, 21 January
   2019, https://www.odt.co.nz/lifestyle/magazine/teachers-who-made-difference
2 'An extraordinary job', *PPTA News*, 1 April 2019, https://www.ppta.org.nz/
   news-and-media/an-extraordinary-job
3 Paul Lowe, Whatsapp message to Supriya, 22 September 2020.
4 Jacinda Ardern, interview with Paul Lowe, 'Jacinda Crest Benefits', Morrinsville,
   11 February 2011. Morrinsville.
5 Jacinda Ardern, interview with Paul Lowe, 'Jacinda Crest Benefits', Morrinsville,
   11 February 2011.
6 'An extraordinary job', *PPTA News*, 1 April 2019, https://www.ppta.org.nz/
   news-and-media/an-extraordinary-job.
7 Madeleine Chapman, *Jacinda Ardern: A New Kind of Leader* (Cheltenham:
   History Press, 2020), p. 16.
8 Jacinda Ardern, Vehicle Confiscation and Seizure Bill – First Reading (2009),
   New Zealand Parliamentary Debates, vol. 654, p. 4123, https://www.parlia-
   ment.nz/mi/pb/hansard-debates/rhr/document/49HansS_20090602_
   00001174/ardern-jacinda-vehicle-confiscation-and-seizure-bill/
9 Kim Knight, 'The politics of life: the truth about Jacinda Ardern', *New Zealand
   Herald*, 29 January 2017, https://www.nzherald.co.nz/lifestyle/the-politics-of-
   life-the-truth-about-jacinda-ardern/4WEA6GJ4UZCLE23QCG23WTHR7I/
10 John Inger, Letter to Supriya, 'Re Jacinda Ardern', 7 September 2020.
11 Liam Fitzpatrick and Casey Quackenbush, 'Jacinda Ardern, New Zealand's 37
   -year-old leader, rolls up her sleeves', *Time*, 20 November 2017, https://time.
   com/5028891/jacinda-ardern-worlds-youngest-female-leader-new-zealand/
12 See for example Belinda Feek, 'Ardern's former teacher "emotional" at request to
   attend ceremony', *New Zealand Herald*, 24 October 2017, https://www.nzher-
   ald.co.nz/nz/arderns-former-teacher-emotional-at-request-to-attend-ceremony
   /WJMG2VX5FXUF6B643M3FAGLC6E/
13 Nikki Macdonald, 'Marilyn Waring: a woman's view of parliament from 1975
   to 1984', *Stuff*, 18 May 2019, https://www.stuff.co.nz/national/politics/
   112579830/marilyn-waring-a-womans-view-of-parliament-from-1975-to
   -1984
14 Amanda Hooton, '48 hours with Jacinda: warm, earnest, accessible – is our PM
   too good to be true?', *Stuff*, 31 Mar 2018, https://www.stuff.co.nz/life-style/
   well-good/inspire-me/102696690/48-hours-with-jacinda-warm-earnest-acces-
   sible-is-our-pm-too-good-to-be-true
15 Dan Satherley, Mitch McCann, 'Jacinda Ardern's parents knew 20 years ago
   she'd be Prime Minister', *Newshub*, https://www.newshub.co.nz/home/election/

2017/10/jacinda-ardern-s-parents-knew-20-years-ago-she-d-be-prime-minis-ter.html

16 Ibid.

4 Nature and Nurture

1 Supriya Vani, interview with Jacinda Ardern, 30 April 2019.
2 Mark Sainsbury, 'Jacinda Ardern: running on instinct', *Noted*, 17 September 2017.
3 Ibid.
4 'Appointment of high commissioner to Niue a great honour', press release, New Zealand Police, 16 October 2013, available at https://www.scoop.co.nz/stories/PO1310/S00175/appointment-of-high-commissioner-to-niue-a-great-honour.htm?from-mobile=bottom-link-01
5 'Removing fuel from grounded fishing trawler in Niue a difficult challenge – Niue police chief', Radio New Zealand, 12 March 2007, https://www.rnz.co.nz/international/pacific-news/168406/removing-fuel-from-grounded-fishing-trawler-in-niue-a-difficult-challenge-niue-police-chief
6 Jeff Neems, 'Damage right at top: cop', *Waikato Times*, 2 October 2009, www.stuff.co.nz/waikato-times/news/2924790/Damage-right-at-top-cop
7 'Home violence "swept under Pacific mat"', *Stuff*, 31 January 2009, http://www.stuff.co.nz/national/24745/Home-violence-swept-under-Pacific-mat

5 The Mighty Totara

1 *Inside New Zealand: Robert Muldoon – The Grim Face of Power* (1994), a four-part television documentary, dir. Neil Roberts and Louise Callan.
2 Ibid.
3 Ibid.
4 *Inquiry – The Late Mr Norman Kirk*', NZBC Television, 1974
5 Robert Muldoon, valedictory speech to the New Zealand parliament, *New Zealand Parliamentary Debates*, 17 December 1991, vol. 521.

6 Family and Politics

1 'End of the Road for Peters', *New Zealand Herald*, 8 November 2008, https://www.nzherald.co.nz/nz/end-of-the-road-for-winston-peters/VTF76W7K7UBNOT7PJ7JGC4WFRU/
2 Rt Hon. Winston Peters, *New Zealand Parliamentary Debates*, 12 February 2019, vol. 736, p. 9167.
3 Rt Hon. Winston Peters, 'Replacing Political Tyranny with Direct Democracy', speech, New Zealand First Party, 12 November 2003, available at https://www.

scoop.co.nz/stories/PA0311/S00254/replacing-political-tyranny-with-direct-democracy.htm

4 Guyon Espiner, 'Jenny Shipley: Winston could have been Prime Minister but for want of himself', *New Zealand Herald*, 28 April 2017, https://www.nzherald.co.nz/nz/jenny-shipley-winston-could-have-been-prime-minister-but-for-want-of-himself/3ZHGB5NT57OYN2Z4EOWPOSGEQU/

5 John Roughan, 'Peters deal would carry a price', *New Zealand Herald*, 24 January 2014, https://www.nzherald.co.nz/nz/john-roughan-peters-deal-would-carry-a-price/ZZPCIPZVK2YHGKQPTDABHCGLW4/

6 'Winston Peters' memorable quotes', *The Age*, 18 October 2005, https://www.theage.com.au/world/winston-peters-memorable-quotes-20051018-ge12mh.html

7 Claudia Pond Eyley and Dan Salmon, *Helen Clark: Inside Stories* (Auckland: Auckland University Press, 2015), p. 246.

8 Guyon Espiner, 'Jacinda Ardern: One to Watch', *Noted*, 21 July 2012. https://www.noted.co.nz/archive/listener-nz-2012/jacinda-ardern-one-to-watch/ (inactive)

9 Ibid.

10 Helen Harvey, 'Jacinda Ardern's aunty gets emotional as her niece is sworn in as Prime Minister', *Stuff*, 27 October 2017, https://www.stuff.co.nz/taranaki-daily-news/news/98307540/jacinda-arderns-aunty-gets-emotional-as-her-niece-is-sworn-in-as-prime-minister

7 Suffrage and Suffering

1 *Auckland Star*, 7 September 1933.

2 'Lyttelton by-election', *Manawatu Herald*, 14 September 1933, p. 3.

3 'Voice of women: seat in Parliament', *King Country Chronicle*, 9 September 1933, p. 4.

4 Ibid.

5 Hon. Ruth Dyson (2019), Women Winning the Right to Stand for Parliament – Centenary, *New Zealand Parliamentary Debates*, vol. 742, p. 14506.

6 Elizabeth McCombs, 'Woman's Way Is the Right Way', Speaking While Female, https://speakingwhilefemale.co/global-affairs-mccombs/

7 Ibid.

8 Ibid.

8 Emerging

1 Jo Moir, 'Ardern climbs Labour ladder', *Stuff*, 8 October 2012, http://www.stuff.co.nz/taranaki-daily-news/features/7778209/Ardern-climbs-Labour-ladder

2 Kim Knight, 'The politics of life: the truth about Jacinda Ardern', *New Zealand Herald*, 29 January 2017, https://www.nzherald.co.nz/lifestyle/the-politics-of-life-the-truth-about-jacinda-ardern/4WEA6GJ4UZCLE23QCG23WTHR7I/

3 Janet Quigley, Jacinda Ardern, Public Service Association (PSA) Biennial Congress, Wellington, 17 November, 2020. See also, Zane Small, 'Jacinda Ardern reflects on "awakening" teen work experience that entrenched her support for "vulnerable workers"' *Newshub*, 18 November 2020.

4 Liam Fitzpatrick and Casey Quackenbush, 'Jacinda Ardern, New Zealand's 37-year-old leader, rolls up her sleeves', *Time*, 20 November 2017, https://time.com/5028891/jacinda-ardern-worlds-youngest-female-leader-new-zealand/

5 Ibid.

6 ' "Be confident" urges Prime Minister at Convocation', *Otago Connection*, 20 February 2018, https://www.otago.ac.nz/otago-connection/otago676955.html

7 Ibid.

8 Mike Rann, 'The Ardern ascendancy', *The Interpreter*, 20 October 2017, https://www.lowyinstitute.org/the-interpreter/ardern-ascendancy

9 *When the Student Is Ready*

1 Claudia Pond Eyley and Dan Salmon, *Helen Clark: Inside Stories* (Auckland: Auckland University Press, 2015), p. 188.

2 Emma Clifton, 'Helen Clark on women in politics and why optimism is always the best policy', *Now to Love*, 1 November 2018, https://www.nowtolove.co.nz/lifestyle/career/helen-clark-new-book-women-equality-power-women-in-politics-39464

3 Eyley and Salmon, *Helen Clark*, p. 188.

4 Ibid.

5 Ibid.

6 Ibid.

7 *Ngati Apa v Attorney-General* [2003] 3 NZLR 643.

8 Catherine Woulfe, 'Jacinda Ardern: simply red', *Sunday News*, 16 March 2010, www.stuff.co.nz/sunday-news/entertainment/3409523/Jacinda-Ardern-Simply-red

9 Eyley and Salmon, *Helen Clark*, p. 235.

10 Adam Dudding, 'Jacinda Ardern: I didn't want to work for Tony Blair', *Stuff*, 27 August 2017, https://www.stuff.co.nz/national/politics/96123508/jacinda-ardern-i-didnt-want-to-work-for-tony-blair

11 Ibid.

12 Eyley and Salmon, *Helen Clark*, p. 235.

13 Mark Sainsbury, 'Jacinda Ardern: running on instinct', *Noted*, 17 September 2017.

10 *Mentor and Role Model*

1 Emma Clifton, 'Helen Clark on women in politics and why optimism is always the best policy', *Now to Love*, 1 November 2018, https://www.nowtolove.co.nz

/lifestyle/career/helen-clark-new-book-women-equality-power-women-in-poli-tics-39464

2 Jacinda Ardern, Maiden Statement, *New Zealand Parliamentary Debates*, vol. 651, p. 753, 16 December 2008, https://www.parliament.nz/en/pb/hansard-debates/rhr/document/49HansS_20081216_00001012/ardern-jacinda-maiden-statements.

3 Amanda Hooton, '48 hours with Jacinda: warm, earnest, accessible – is our PM too good to be true?', *Stuff*, 31 March 2018, https://www.stuff.co.nz/life-style/well-good/inspire-me/102696690/48-hours-with-jacinda-warm-earnest-acces-sible–is-our-pm-too-good-to-be-true

4 Carroll du Chateau, 'The transforming of Helen', *New Zealand Herald*, 16 November 2001, https://www.nzherald.co.nz/nz/the-transforming-of-helen/HUE5JFZXVQLGEKLH5IYDYRY5B4/

5 '"It's going to be a very interesting campaign" – Helen Clark believes Jacinda Ardern has what it takes', 1 News, TVNZ, 20 August 2020, https://www.tvnz.co.nz/one-news/new-zealand/its-going-very-interesting-campaign-helen-clark-believes-jacinda-ardern-has-takes

6 Claudia Pond Eyley and Dan Salmon, *Helen Clark: Inside Stories* (Auckland: Auckland University Press, 2015), p. 250.

7 Nicholas Jones, 'Helen Clark, Jenny Shipley recall the "nasty stuff"', *New Zealand Herald*, 5 May 2017, https://www.nzherald.co.nz/nz/helen-clark-jenny-shipley-recall-the-nasty-stuff/SIWAMCUXQMD4VYY3FVFHPPU5CE/

8 Eyley and Salmon, *Helen Clark*, p. 235.

11 Resolution

1 'MPs asked whether they have ever smoked cannabis', *New Zealand Herald*, 7 May 2019, https://www.nzherald.co.nz/nz/mps-asked-whether-they-have-ever-smoked-cannabis/XEFEIOOGSULLCXWM5Y4EPCEI2E/

2 R. Scott Lloyd, 'Elder Ian S. Ardern: "Go and do"', *Church News*, 23 April 2011, https://www.thechurchnews.com/leaders-and-ministry/2011-04-23/elder-ian-s-ardern-general-authority-seventy-2011-58526

3 'Michele Hewitson Interview: Jacinda Ardern', *New Zealand Herald*, 23 April 2014, https://www.nzherald.co.nz/nz/michele-hewitson-interview-jacinda-ardern/7RGYTF7JGSNTT6BYV2OTUGMA6I/

4 Joe Morgan, 'New Zealand's new Prime Minister left the Mormon church because she believes in gay rights', *Gay Star News*, 19 October 2017, https://www.gaystarnews.com/article/new-zealands-new-prime-minister-left-the-mormon-church-because-she-believes-in-gay-rights/#gs.s_fsgcc

5 Bruce R. McConkie, *Mormon Doctrine*, 2nd ed. (Salt Lake City: Bookcraft, 1966).

6 Liam Fitzpatrick and Casey Quackenbush, 'Jacinda Ardern, New Zealand's 37-year-old leader, rolls up her sleeves', *Time*, 20 November 2017, https://

time.com/5028891/jacinda-ardern-worlds-youngest-female-leader-new-
zealand/

7 Peter Hartcher, 'The leader's not for #turning: is Jacinda Ardern really the future
of liberal democracy?', *Sydney Morning Herald*, 9 October 2020, https://www.
smh.com.au/world/oceania/the-leader-s-not-for-turning-is-jacinda-ardern-
really-the-future-of-liberal-democracy-20200907-p55t86.html

8 Mark Sainsbury, 'Jacinda Ardern: running on instinct', *Noted*, 17 September
2017.

9 Spunky, 'How the church influenced the future prime minister', *Exponent II*, 31
March 2018, https://www.the-exponent.com/how-the-church-influenced-the-
future-prime-minister/

12 Overseas Experience

1 Adam Duddings, 'Jacinda Ardern: I didn't want to work for Tony Blair', *Stuff*,
27 August 2017, https://www.stuff.co.nz/national/politics/96123508/jacinda-
ardern-i-didnt-want-to-work-for-tony-blair

2 Ibid.

3 Ibid.

4 See for example ALL_YOUR_BASE, 'Jacinda Ardern to lead IUSY', *The
Standard*, 31 January 2008, https://thestandard.org.nz/ardern-to-lead-iusy/

5 Catherine Woulfe, 'Jacinda Ardern: simply red', *Sunday News*, 16 March 2010,
www.stuff.co.nz/sunday-news/entertainment/3409523/Jacinda-Ardern-Simply
-red

13 Baby of the House

1 Madeleine Chapman, *Jacinda Ardern: A New Kind of Leader* (Cheltenham:
History Press, 2020).

2 Eyley and Dan Salmon, *Helen Clark: Inside Stories* (Auckland: Auckland
University Press, 2015), p. 265.

3 'Young hot shot versus old head', *Waikato Times*, 31 January 2009, https://
www.stuff.co.nz/waikato-times/archived-sections/vote-08/694520/Young-hot-
shot-versus-old-head

4 Claudia Pond Eyley and Dan Salmon, *Helen Clark: Inside Stories* (Auckland:
Auckland University Press, 2015), p. 265.

5 This, and the subsequent quotes from Ardern's maiden speech to the New
Zealand Parliament, are from *New Zealand Parliamentary Debates*, vol. 651,
p.   753,   https://www.parliament.nz/en/pb/hansard-debates/rhr/document/
49HansS_20081216_00001012/ardern-jacinda-maiden-statements

14 Battle of the Babes

1 *New Zealand Listener*, 2011, quoted in Julia Gillard and Ngozi Okonjo-Iweala, *Women and Leadership: Real Lives, Real Lessons* (London: Transworld Digital, 2020).

2 Jonathan Milne, 'Nicola Kaye vs Jacinda Ardern', *Noted*, 24 September 2011, https://www.noted.co.nz/archive/listener-nz-2011/nicola-kaye-vs-jacinda-ardern/ (inactive)

3 Claire Trevett, 'MP vows no political spin in DJ stint', *New Zealand Herald*, 22 January 2014, https://www.nzherald.co.nz/entertainment/mp-vows-no-political-spin-in-dj-stint/MPDUZSXHKUSERR4E34O5UTOUYE/

15 Catch of a Lifetime

1 Guyon Espiner, 'Jacinda Ardern: One to Watch', *Noted*, 21 July 2012, https://www.noted.co.nz/archive/listener-nz-2012/jacinda-ardern-one-to-watch/ (inactive)

2 Isabelle Truman, 'Jacinda Ardern opens up about her pregnancy, finding love and running a country at 37', *Marie Claire Australia*, April 2018, https://www.marieclaire.com.au/jacinda-ardern-interview-pregnancy

3 Ibid.

4 Authors' email interview with Colin Mathura-Jeffree, 14 April 2020.

5 Kim Knight, 'Clarke Gayford: Jacinda Ardern is the best thing that's ever happened to me', *New Zealand Herald*, 17 July 2016, https://www.nzherald.co.nz/entertainment/clarke-gayford-jacinda-ardern-is-the-best-thing-thats-ever-happened-to-me/ZVB56DVTGKSZURO3M3A3B52LXA/

6 Ibid.

7 Kerry McIvor, 'Clarke Gayford talks fishing, fatherhood and hypnobirths', *New Zealand Woman's Weekly*, 6 March 2018, https://www.nowtolove.co.nz/parenting/family/clarke-gayford-talks-fishing-fatherhood-and-hypnobirths-36731

8 'Prior to dating the PM Clarke Gayford thought Danger was a "rad" middle name for a child', *New Zealand Herald*, 25 June 2018, https://www.nzherald.co.nz/nz/prior-to-dating-the-pm-clarke-gayford-thought-danger-was-a-rad-middle-name-for-a-child/WI4EJC7R2YHNJZKRFBDW6IQ2VM/

9 'Clarke Gayford reveals his first date with Prime Minister Jacinda Ardern', *New Zealand Woman's Weekly*, 25 February 2018, https://www.nowtolove.co.nz/celebrity/celeb-news/clarke-gayford-reveals-his-first-date-with-prime-minister-jacinda-ardern-36666

10 'Is romance blossoming for MP?', *New Zealand Herald*, 4 September 2014, https://www.nzherald.co.nz/entertainment/is-romance-blossoming-for-mp/OWVI6GIVWBJQM2CU5MYPVBGJYM/

11 Truman, 'Jacinda Ardern opens up about her pregnancy'.

12 'Clarke Gayford: I want to let you in on a secret', *New Zealand Herald*, 24 September 2017, https://www.nzherald.co.nz/nz/clarke-gayford-i-want-to-let-you-in-on-a-secret/6CHOMW5JT53V24G3UK2TZFACRY/

13 Emma Clifton, 'Labour's Jacinda Ardern reveals why she doesn't want to be Prime Minister', *Next*, 15 June 2017, https://www.nowtolove.co.nz/news/current-affairs/jacinda-ardern-labour-deputy-leader-personal-story-in-next-32958

14 Knight, 'Clarke Gayford: Jacinda Ardern is the best thing that's ever happened to me'.

16 Ambition or Ambivalence?

1 Lloyd Burr, 'Jacinda Ardern opens up on anxieties and having a family', *Newshub*, 15 June 2017, https://www.newshub.co.nz/home/politics/2017/06/poll-jacinda-ardern-s-popularity-plummets.html

2 'Things we learned about Jacinda Ardern', *Newshub*, 6 June 2014.

3 Jessica Kegu, 'New Zealand' prime minister says she and Trump had a "policy discussion" about gun control', *CBS News*, 25 September 2019.

4 Ibid.

5 Pauline Rose Clance and Suzanne Ament Imes, 'The Imposter Phenomenon in High Achieving Women: Dynamics and Therapeutic Intervention', *Psychotherapy: Theory, Research & Practice*, 15(3), 1978, 241–7.

6 Michelle Duff, *Jacinda Ardern: The Story Behind an Extraordinary Leader* (Auckland: Allen & Unwin, 2019), p. 55.

7 'No doubt in my mind, says Ardern', *New Zealand Herald*, 27 September 2017, https://www.nzherald.co.nz/nz/no-doubt-in-my-mind-says-ardern/FYMTWPBY7VONQVNA7O6XP6EZ2A/

17 Turmoil and Teflon John

1 Patrice Dougan and Cherie Howie, 'Election 2014: Cunliffe defends decision to stay on', *New Zealand Herald*, 20 September 2014, https://www.nzherald.co.nz/nz/election-2014-cunliffe-defends-decision-to-stay-on/WN5SBOEGCRV2VTA4GQ6VTWIYNQ/

2 Toby Manhire, 'New Zealand election: John Key's National party on course for victory, *The Guardian*, 20 September 2014, https://www.theguardian.com/world/2014/sep/20/new-zealand-election-john-keys-national-party-on-course-for-victory

3 Kelly Bertrand, 'Jacinda Ardern's country childhood', *New Zealand Woman's Weekly*, 30 June 2014, https://www.nowtolove.co.nz/celebrity/celeb-news/jacinda-arderns-country-childhood-2894

4 Sophie Ryan, 'Labour leadership race: Ardern joins Robertson', *New Zealand Herald*, 19 October 2014, https://www.nzherald.co.nz/nz/labour-leadership-race-ardern-joins-robertson/43RPFVAXQIZRJWWYVU7LFCBRZ4/

5 Dr Jarrod Gilbert, 'Life, kids and being Jacinda', *New Zealand Herald*, 18 January 2018, https://www.nzherald.co.nz/nz/life-kids-and-being-jacinda/ 4K7RICULEMUYCWEPIOPCDIIEQI/

6 'John Key likes . . . Johnny English?', *Stuff*, 25 November 2011, http://www. stuff.co.nz/the-press/6020881/John-Key-likes-Johnny-English

7 'John Key: Drug abuse major contributor to child poverty', *New Zealand Herald*, 15 December 2015, https://www.nzherald.co.nz/nz/john-key-drug-abuse-major-contributor-to-child-poverty/7GQ4GPMM5 WOQ46AIPCUDTN3SKY/

8 Claire Trevett, 'Food parcel families made poor choices, says Key', *New Zealand Herald*, 16 February 2011, https://www.nzherald.co.nz/nz/food-parcel-families -made-poor-choices-says-key/KDI3II47PEO6BANHQID5QWI2TA/

9 Stacey Kirk, Hamish Rutherford and Aimee Gulliver, 'Prime Minister John Key pulled waitress' ponytail', *Stuff*, 22 April 2015. https://www.stuff.co.nz/ national/politics/67949918/prime-minister-john-key-pulled-waitress -ponytail

10 'John Key's "Thank You for Your Honesty" made it onto Last Week Tonight', Radio Hauraki, 19 October 2015, https://www.hauraki.co.nz/the-feed/john-keys-thank-you-for-your-honesty-made-it-onto-last-week-tonight/

11 James Meikle, 'New Zealand's prime minister apologises for cannibalism joke', *The Guardian*, 13 May 2010. https://www.theguardian.com/world/2010/may/ 13/john-key-apologises-cannibalism-joke

12 'John Key steps down as Prime Minister of New Zealand – "I've got nothing left in the tank"', *New Zealand Herald*, 5 December 2016, https://www. nzherald.co.nz/nz/john-key-steps-down-as-prime-minister-of-new-zealand-ive-got-nothing-left-in-the-tank/ZAV2VV73IVKUBPDGABHNCPB4RM/

18 *Star on the Rise*

1 'National won't contest Mt Albert by-election', Radio New Zealand, 19 December 2016, https://www.rnz.co.nz/news/political/320794/national-won%27t-contest-mt-albert-by-election

2 'Jacinda Ardern wants to stand for Mt Albert', Radio New Zealand, 14 December 2016, https://www.rnz.co.nz/news/political/320379/jacinda-ardern -wants-to-stand-for-mt-albert

3 Kim Knight, 'The politics of life: the truth about Jacinda Ardern', *New Zealand Herald*, 29 January 2017 https://www.nzherald.co.nz/lifestyle/the-politics-of-life-the-truth-about-jacinda-ardern/4WEA6GJ4UZCLE23QCG23WTHR7I/

4 'Mt Albert by-election: Geoff Simmons will prove to be a thorn between the two roses of Ardern and Genter', 1 News, TVNZ, 1 February 2017, https:// www.tvnz.co.nz/one-news/new-zealand/mt-albert-election-geoff-simmons-prove-thorn-between-two-roses-arden-and-genter

5 Bryce Edwards, 'Political roundup: a boring but important Mt Albert by

-election', *New Zealand Herald*, 24 February 2017, https://www.nzherald.co.nz
/nz/political-roundup-a-boring-but-important-mt-albert-by-election/
YC3B7LHNHK6DU24RJ7JK7S2G2I/

6 Isaac Davison, 'Candidates brace for the polls . . . wait, what? There's a byelection?', *New Zealand Herald*, 17 February 2017, https://www.nzherald.co.nz/nz
/candidates-brace-for-the-polls-wait-what-theres-a-byelection/
7D27XPHUWUDLBT6QP7GVHHW4ZM/

7 Edwards, 'Political roundup'.

8 'WATCH: The Great Spinoff Mt Albert By-election Candidates' Debate', *The
Spinoff*, 16 February 2017, https://thespinoff.co.nz/politics/16-02-2017/watch
-the-great-spinoff-mt-albert-by-election-candidates-debate/

9 Sarah Robson, 'Labour's Jacinda Ardern wins Mt Albert by-election', RNZ, 25
February 2017, https://www.rnz.co.nz/news/political/325308/labour%27s-
jacinda-ardern-wins-mt-albert-by-election

10 'Mt Albert byelection: Andrew Little joins Jacinda Ardern for final day of
campaigning', *New Zealand Herald*, 24 February 2017, https://www.nzherald.
co.nz/nz/mt-albert-byelection-andrew-little-joins-jacinda-ardern-for-final-day-
of-campaigning/V6XTAIKGLWK6BOHSU45PHFTEBU/

11 'Andrew Little jokes Jacinda Ardern's Mt Albert by-election win was "a knife
edge result", 1 News, TVNZ, 25 February 2017, https://www.tvnz.co.nz/one-
news/new-zealand/watch-andrew-little-jokes-jacinda-arderns-mt-albert-elec-
tion-win-knife-edge-result

12 Jacinda Ardern, speech at Point Chevalier Bowling Club, 25 February 2017,
available at https://www.youtu.be/9TxKFp-tvnI

13 Ibid.

19 For the Party

1 Claire Trevett, 'Annette King lashes out at "ageist" idea of stepping to one side',
New Zealand Herald, 26 February 2017, https://www.nzherald.co.nz/nz/
annette-king-lashes-out-at-ageist-idea-of-stepping-to-one-side/
FXQ7M2ADJJTG55QXMPRNZ47XM4/

2 *New Zealand Parliamentary Debates*, 10 October 1984, vol. 458, p. 970.

3 John Harvey and Brent Edwards, *Annette King: The Authorised Biography*
(Auckland: Upstart Press, 2019), p.239.

4 Ibid.

5 'Things we learned about Jacinda Ardern', Newshub, 6 June 2014. https://www.
newshub.co.nz/politics/things-we-learned-about-jacinda-ardern-2014060616

6 John Harvey and Brent Edwards, *Annette King: The Authorised Biography*
(Auckland: Upstart Press, 2019), p. 279.

7 Ibid, p.270.

8 Ibid, p. 271.

9 Ibid, p. 274.

10 Audrey Young, 'Elevating Ardern now gives Little best shot', *New Zealand*

Herald, 27 January 2017, https://www.nzherald.co.nz/nz/audrey-young-elevat-ing - ardern - now - gives - little - best - shot / D6EWNLCTFSMDGZLF53XKOALBBY/

11 John Harvey and Brent Edwards, *Annette King: The Authorised Biography* (Auckland: Upstart Press, 2019), p. 222.

12 Ibid, p. 224.

13 'Andrew Little and Jacinda Ardern speak to John Campbell about her sudden deputy nomination', RNZ/YouTube, 28 February 2017, https://www.youtu.be /qnNOG7gyQDg

20 *Pull Up the Ladder, or the Woman?*

1 'Top quote for 2012: "Zip it sweetie"', *New Zealand Herald*, 20 December 2012,   https://www.nzherald.co.nz/nz/top-quote-for-2012-zip-it-sweetie/ 54O34DOWF6IMJ2BJQXW3YJKF5I/

2 Anthony Burns, 'All show and no substance', *The Standard*, 20 March 2017, https://thestandard.org.nz/all-show-and-no-substance/

3 Vernon Small, 'National's attack on Labour's deputy suggests concerns more than skin deep', Stuff, 16 March 2017.

4 Michele Hewitson, 'Interview: Jacinda Ardern', New Zealand Herald, 23 April 2014.

5 New Zealand Labour Party, 'Bennett bouncing all over the place on jobs', press release, 14 November 2012, available at https://www.scoop.co.nz/stories/ PA1211/S00242/bennett-bouncing-all-over-the-place-on-jobs.htm

6 New Zealand Labour Party, 'Bennett bouncing all over the place on jobs', press release, 14 November 2012, available at https://www.scoop.co.nz/stories/ PA1211/S00242/bennett-bouncing-all-over-the-place-on-jobs.htm

7 Gin Wigmore and Jacinda Ardern in Conversation, Sitting Room Only x Girl Gang, directed by Hannah Marshall, May 2018. https://www.youtube.com/ watch?v=enKLU31kpWg

8 'Jacinda Ardern on her groundbreaking first few months as PM', *Australian Woman's Weekly*, 1 February 2018. https://www.nowtolove.co.nz/lifestyle/ career/jacinda-ardern-on-her-groundbreaking-first-few-months-as-pm -36272

9 Gin Wigmore and Jacinda Ardern in Conversation, Sitting Room Only x Girl Gang, directed by Hannah Marshall, May 2018. https://www.youtube.com/ watch?v=enKLU31kpWg

10 Judith Collins, *Pull No Punches: Memoir of a Political Survivor*, Allen & Unwin, 2020.

21 *Turning Point*

1 Steve Braunias: 'On the campaign trail with Jacinda Ardern', *New Zealand Herald*, 9 September 2017. https://www.nzherald.co.nz/nz/steve-braunias-on-the-campaign-trail-with-jacinda-ardern/ZLE7IDNES5V4HB2Z BXTXWVOIQA/

2 Claire Trevett, 'Green Party's Metiria Turei "racist" call riles NZ First's Winston Peters', *New Zealand Herald*, 9 July 2017, https://www.nzherald.co.nz/nz/green -partys-metiria-turei-racist-call-riles-nz-firsts-winston-peters/ J5YNFJ6LFRKXVU7ERBSLCDEDGU/

3 Ibid.

4 Isaac Davison, 'Green Party co-leader Metiria Turei admits she lied to WINZ, as party announces radical welfare reforms', *New Zealand Herald*, 16 July 2017, https://www.nzherald.co.nz/nz/green-party-co-leader-metiria-turei-admits-she -lied-to-winz-as-party-announces-radical-welfare-reforms/ S7J4O2G32Q7ENBO26TA4QFF75Y/

5 ' "We can never condone breaking the rules" – Andrew Little won't support Metiria Turei's stance of not condemning benefit fraudsters', 1 News, TVNZ, 26 July 2017, https://www.tvnz.co.nz/one-news/new-zealand/we-can-never-condone-breaking-rules-andrew-little-wont-support-metiria-tureis-stance-not-condemning-benefit-fraudsters

6 Eugene Bingham and Paula Penfold, 'The Demise and Rise of Andrew Little', *Stuff*, https://interactives.stuff.co.nz/2017/12/the-demise-and-rise-of-andrew-little/

7 'Jacinda Ardern rejected Labour leadership "seven times" ', *New Zealand Herald*, 27 September 2017, https://www.nzherald.co.nz/nz/jacinda-ardern-rejected-labour-leadership-seven-times/T64CW2XOA2NS3QH657GI3WISEU/

8 Bingham and Penfold, 'The Demise and Rise of Andrew Little'; Mark Sainsbury, 'Jacinda Ardern: Running on instinct', *Noted*, 17 September 2017.

22 *The Worst Job in Politics*

1 John Harvey and Brent Edwards, *Annette King: The Authorised Biography* (Auckland: Upstart Press, 2019), p. 225.

2 'Jacinda Ardern reveals real reason she doesn't want to be PM', *Scoop* (quoting *Next* press release), 15 June 2017, https://www.scoop.co.nz/stories/BU1706/ S00451/jacinda-ardern-reveals-real-reason-she-doesnt-want-to-be-pm.htm

3 .Eugene Bingham, Paula Penfold, 'The Demise and Rise of Andrew Little', *Stuff*, December 2017. https://interactives.stuff.co.nz/2017/12/the-demise-and -rise-of-andrew-little/

4 Mark Sainsbury, 'Jacinda Ardern: Running on instinct', *Noted*, 17 September 2017.

5 Eugene Bingham and Paula Penfold, 'The Demise and Rise of Andrew Little',

Stuff, December 2017. https://interactives.stuff.co.nz/2017/12/the-demise-and
-rise-of-andrew-little/

6 'Little walks the plank', RNZ, 1 August 2017, https://www.rnz.co.nz/news/top
/336219/little-walks-the-plank

7 Stacey Kirk, 'Jacinda Ardern says she can handle it and her path to the top
would suggest she's right', *Stuff*, 1 August 2017, https://www.stuff.co.nz/
national/politics/95327574/jacinda-ardern-says-shes-can-handle-it-and-her-
path-to-the-top-would-suggest-shes-right

8 Clarke Gayford (@NZClarke), 'Have been underwater filming all day off
Sunshine Coast, I miss anything?', Twitter, 1 August 2017, https://twitter.com
/NZClarke/status/892274576121511941

23 *Woman of Mettle*

1 Dr Jarrod Gilbert, 'Life, kids and being Jacinda', *New Zealand Herald*, 18
January 2018, https://www.nzherald.co.nz/nz/life-kids-and-being-jacinda/
4K7RICULEMUYCWEPIOPCDIIEQI/

2 *New Zealand Parliamentary Debates*, vol. 706, p. 4706, https://www.parlia-
ment.nz/en/pb/hansard-debates/rhr/document/51HansS_20150624_
00000747/dean-jacqui-oral-questions-questions-to-ministers

3 Eleanor Ainge Roy, ' "Unacceptable": New Zealand's Labour leader asked about
baby plans seven hours into job', *The Guardian*, 2 August 2017, https://www.
theguardian.com/world/2017/aug/02/unacceptable-new-zealands-labour-
leader-asked-about-baby-plans-six-hours-into-job

4 'Turei admits enrolling to vote at different address in 1990s', RNZ, 4 August
2017. https://www.rnz.co.nz/news/political/336436/turei-admits-enrolling-to-
vote-at-different-address-in-1990s

5 Vernon Small, 'Bill English buckles over housing allowance', *Stuff*, 29 September
2009, https://www.stuff.co.nz/national/politics/2910957/Bill-English-buckles-
over-housing-allowance

6 'National MP's home away from home', *New Zealand Herald*, 26 January 2005.
https://www.nzherald.co.nz/nz/national-mps-home-away-from-home/
BFDKONJC3R5IKRYTTLEPGVAUVY/

7 ' "You can't condone lawbreaking" – Jacinda Ardern to Metiria Turei', *AM
Show*, 28 July 2017, reported on www.newshub.co.nz

8 Natalie Akoorie, 'Labour's new deputy Jacinda Ardern in the poo for installing
her own loo', *New Zealand Herald*, 10 March 2017, https://www.nzherald.
co.nz/nz/labours-new-deputy-jacinda-ardern-in-the-poo-for-installing-her-
own-loo/HEMDEBYRW35FRT4PKBHIO2PPXM/

9 Ibid.

10 Isaac Davison, 'Greens co-leader Metiria Turei's decision to rule out Cabinet
role follows warning from Jacinda Ardern', *New Zealand Herald*, 4 August
2017, https://www.nzherald.co.nz/nz/greens-co-leader-metiria-tureis-decision

-to-rule-out-cabinet-role-follows-warning-from-jacinda-ardern/
W4T756E5C4RW54C4OWRUIO6VPI/

11 Tracy Watkins, 'Jacinda Ardern shows her steel in week one', *Stuff*, 5 August
2017,   https://www.stuff.co.nz/national/politics/opinion/95467650/jacinda-
ardern-shows-her-steel-in-week-one

24 *Tied to the West Island*

1 Jacinda Ardern (@jacindaardern), 'I value our relationship with the Australian
Govt highly. I won't let disappointing & false claims stand in the way of that
relationship', Twitter, 15 August 2017, https://twitter.com/jacindaardern/status
/897289688519540736?lang=en

2 Patrick Keyzer and Dave Martin, 'No, Peter Dutton. Most deported Kiwis
aren't paedophiles and you're hurting our relationship with NZ', *The
Conversation*, 24 July 2019, https://theconversation.com/no-peter-dutton-most
-deported-kiwis-arent-paedophiles-and-youre-hurting-our-relationship-with-
nz-120655

3 Giovanni Torre, 'Stop deporting your people and problems, New Zealand PM
Jacinda Ardern tells Australia', *Daily Telegraph*, 28 February 2020, https://www.
telegraph.co.uk/news/2020/02/28/stop-deporting-people-problems-new-
zealand-prime-minister-tells/

4 Nicholas Reece, 'Jacinda Ardern prime minister of Australasia? If only it was
that simple', *The Guardian*, 19 July 2019, https://www.theguardian.com/world
/commentisfree/2019/jul/19/jacinda-ardern-prime-minister-of-australasia-if-
only-it-was-that-simple

25 *Stardust and Jacindamania*

1 'Stardust and substance: New book reveals how Jacinda Ardern led Labour into
government', *New Zealand Herald*, 12 September 2018. https://www.nzherald.
co.nz/nz/stardust-and-substance-new-book-reveals-how-jacinda-ardern-led-
labour-into-government/TFUB3GCBMCPKN4YXIHIEMLKNQA/

2 'Jacinda Ardern interrupts speech to warmly welcome delighted school kids
into room', 1 News, TVNZ, 5 December 2017, https://www.tvnz.co.nz/one-
news/new-zealand/watch-jacinda-ardern-interrupts-speech-warmly-welcome-
delighted-school-kids-into-room

3 Toby Manhire, 'Jacinda Ardern: "Very little of what I have done has been
deliberate. It's intuitive"', *The Guardian*, 6 April 2019, https://www.
theguardian.com/world/2019/apr/06/jacinda-ardern-intuitive-courage-new
-zealand

4 Claire Trevett, 'Jacinda Ardern's rallying cry: Climate change the nuclear-free
moment of her generation', *New Zealand Herald*, 20 August 2017, https://
www.nzherald.co.nz/nz/jacinda-arderns-rallying-cry-climate-change-the

-nuclear-free-moment-of-her-generation/
6LEDCNATMAFX2PWA3GHNLK7NUU/

5 'Jacinda Ardern's ascension to leadership revitalises Labour, up 2% to 32.5%; Turei scandal costs Greens support, down 4.5% to 9%', Roy Morgan, 18 August 2017, https://www.roymorgan.com/findings/7309-roy-morgan-new-zealand-voting-intention-august-2017-201708181513

6 '"Confident but paranoid": Bill English reflects on election 2017', *The Spinoff*, 14 September 2018, https://thespinoff.co.nz/politics/14-09-2018/confident-but-paranoid-bill-english-reflects-on-election-2017/

7 Demelza Leslie, 'Serious criminals "have fewer human rights" – National', RNZ, 3 September 2017. https://www.rnz.co.nz/news/election-2017/338588/serious-criminals-have-fewer-human-rights-national https://twitter.com/paula-lbennett/status/904189927813824512

8 George Andrews, 'The famous words that Norman Kirk did not say', the *Spinoff*, 1 August 2020. https://thespinoff.co.nz/politics/01-08-2020/the-famous-words-that-norman-kirk-did-not-say/

9 '$11.7b hole in Labour's books: Joyce', *Otago Daily Times*, 4 September 2017, https://www.odt.co.nz/news/election-2017/117b-hole-labours-books-joyce

10 '"I regard this as a desperate, cynical attempt by Steven Joyce to create a diversion" – Grant Robertson', 1 News, TVNZ, 4 September 2017, https://www.tvnz.co.nz/one-news/new-zealand/-regard-desperate-cynical-attempt-steven-joyce-create-diversion-grant-robertson

11 John Harvey and Brent Edwards, *Annette King: The Authorised Biography* (Auckland: Upstart Press, 2019), p. 277.

12 Ibid.

13 Ibid.

14 Madeleine Chapman, *Jacinda Ardern: A New Kind of Leader* (Cheltenham: History Press, 2020), p. 110.

15 John Harvey and Brent Edwards, *Annette King: The Authorised Biography* (Auckland: Upstart Press, 2019), p. 278.

16 Ibid., p. 275.

17 Jacinda Ardern, 'Came home to find my mum had left this for me – a picture of my Grandma standing by the car she lent me for the 2008 election . . .', Facebook, 27 September 2017, https://www.facebook.com/jacindaardern/photos/came-home-to-find-my-mum-had-left-this-for-me-a-picture-of-my-grandma-standing-b/10154729031982441/

18 'Jacinda Ardern laughs off "pretty communist" protest sign', *Newshub*, 18 September 2017, https://www.newshub.co.nz/home/election/2017/09/jacinda-ardern-laughs-off-pretty-communist-protest-sign.html

19 Ibid.

20 Harvey and Edwards, *Annette King*, p. 280.

21 'The debate's top five moments', RNZ, 20 September 2017, https://www.rnz.co.nz/news/election-2017/339856/the-debate-s-top-five-moments

22 Anna Jones, 'Jacinda Ardern: "Stardust" ousts experience in New Zealand',

BBC News, 19 October 2017, https://www.bbc.co.uk/news/world-asia
-41226232

26 Victory Day for Winston

1   Bernard Hickey, 'Election live: "You better bloody win, young lady"', *Newsroom*,
    22 September 2017, https://www.newsroom.co.nz/election-live-you-better-
    bloody-win-young-lady
2   'Open Minded', Episode 5, hosted by Sir John Kirwan, Mentemania, December
    2020.
3   Bernard Hickey and others, 'Election Live: Winston in the Kingmaker posi-
    tion', *Newsroom*, 24 September 2017, https://www.newsroom.co.nz/2017/09/
    23/49642/election-live-winston-in-kingmaker-position
4   Ibid.
5   Jo Moir, 'Next government in Winston Peters' hands, as Northland rejects the
    party leader', *Stuff*, 24 September 2017, https://www.stuff.co.nz/national/poli-
    tics/97175899/next-government-in-winston-peters-hands-as-northland-rejects
    -the-party-leader
6   Amy Wiggins, 'Jacinda Ardern: "I haven't done as well as I would have liked"',
    New Zealand Herald, 23 September 2017, https://www.nzherald.co.nz/nz/
    jacinda-ardern-i-havent-done-as-well-as-i-would-have-liked/
    BCGASI5NYDCHI3RFNBGEIRIMSE/
7   'Campaign diary: Winston's wacky wordplay', *New Zealand Herald*, 25 July
    2002, https://www.nzherald.co.nz/nz/icampaign-diaryi-winstons-wacky-word-
    play/GWQ7HLFZHZITRYK66KHLFBMM4Q/
8   Cliff Taylor, 'When Condoleezza met Winston', *New Zealand Herald*, 26 July
    2008,   https://www.nzherald.co.nz/nz/when-condoleezza-met-winston/
    NKBBQVSLKSKSMQDTIOUXTJUKQI/
9   John Harvey and Brent Edwards, *Annette King: The Authorised Biography*
    (Auckland: Upstart Press, 2019), p.282.
10 Ibid., p. 283.
11 Jo Moir, 'Winston Peters has made his choice – now he has three years to deliver the
    goods', *Stuff*, 19 October 2017, https://www.stuff.co.nz/national/politics/98047525
    /winston-peters-has-made-his-choice–now-he-has-three-years-to-deliver-the-goods
12 Michael Daly, 'Winston Peters wants "today's capitalism" to regain its "human
    face"', *Stuff*, 20 October 2017, https://www.stuff.co.nz/national/politics/
    98084598/winston-peters-wants-todays-capitalism-to-regain-its-human-face

28 Mother of the Nation

1   Jacinda Ardern, Facebook post, 29 November 2020, https://m.facebook.com/
    jacindaardern/photos/a.10151312135452441/10157500435832441/
    ?type=3&source=48

2 Jacinda Ardern, 'And we thought 2017 was a big year!', Facebook, 18 January 2018, https://www.facebook.com/jacindaardern/photos/a.1015131213545244 1.1073741827.45300632440/10154987366582441

3 Helen Clark (@HelenClarkNZ), 'Wishing @jacindaardern & @NZClarke all the best as they expect their 1st child in June . . .', Twitter, 18 January 2018, https://twitter.com/helenclarknz/status/954117595430404096?lang=en

4 Eleanor Ainge Roy, ' "I'm pregnant, not incapacitated": PM Jacinda Ardern on baby mania', *The Guardian*, 26 January 2018, https://www.theguardian.com/world/2018/jan/26/jacinda-ardern-pregnant-new-zealand-baby-mania

5 Charlotte Greenfield, 'New Zealand Prime Minister Jacinda Ardern pregnant with first child', Reuters, 18 January 2018, https://uk.reuters.com/article/uk-newzealand-politcs-ardern/new-zealand-prime-minister-jacinda-ardern-pregnant-with-first-child-idUKKBN1F736J

6 M. Ilyas Khan, 'Ardern and Bhutto: Two different pregnancies in power', BBC News, 21 June 2018, https://www.bbc.co.uk/news/world-asia-44568537

7 Stacey Kirk, 'Jacinda Ardern arrives for discussions with German Chancellor Angela Merkel', *Stuff*, 18 April 2018, https://www.stuff.co.nz/national/politics/103192807/prime-minister-jacinda-ardern-arrives-for-discussions-with-angela-merkel

8 'After giving birth, New Zealand PM craves mac-n-cheese', *Sydney Morning Herald*, 22 June 2018, https://www.smh.com.au/world/oceania/after-giving-birth-new-zealand-pm-craves-mac-n-cheese-20180622-p4zn6r.html

9 Bernard Lagan, 'Jacinda Ardern introduces baby daughter Neve Te Aroha to the world', *Sunday Times*, 24 June 2018, https://www.thetimes.co.uk/article/jacinda-ardern-introduces-baby-daughter-neve-te-aroha-to-the-world-9fb7c6q96

10 Naaman Zhou and Charles Anderson, 'Neve Te Aroha: New Zealand PM Jacinda Ardern reveals name of baby daughter', *The Guardian*, 24 June 2018. https://www.theguardian.com/world/2018/jun/24/neve-te-aroha-new-zealand-pm-jacinda-ardern-reveals-name-of-baby-daughter

29 *Changing the Game, Slowly*

1 Claire Trevett, 'National Party President Peter Goodfellow: National dodged a "whisky-swilling" bullet in Winston Peters', *New Zealand Herald*, 28 July 2018, https://www.nzherald.co.nz/nz/national-party-president-peter-goodfellow-national-dodged-a-whisky-swilling-bullet-in-winston-peters/7LAA4NFDYWBVSDBMSNY6ZENNDY/

2 'Winston Peters says Australia is ignoring UN obligations on children', RNZ, 3 July 2018, https://www.rnz.co.nz/news/political/360972/winston-peters-says-australia-is-ignoring-un-obligations-on-children

3 Elaine Ainge Roy, 'Stop copying New Zealand's flag, Winston Peters tells Australia', *The Guardian*, 25 July 2018, https://www.theguardian.com/world/2018/jul/25/new-zealand-flag-winston-peters-australia-copy

4 Peter Jackson, 'Shane Jones – jester or genius', *Northland Age*, 1 May 2018, https://www.nzherald.co.nz/northland-age/news/editorial-shane-jones-jester-or-genius/DS65BNQC7FFH3ZO52I33K6MIDU/

5 Jason Walls, ' "Woke pixie dust": NZ First leader Winston Peters takes aim at political allies in conference speech', *New Zealand Herald*, 20 July 2020, https://www.nzherald.co.nz/nz/woke-pixie-dust-nz-first-leader-winston-peters-takes-aim-at-political-allies-in-conference-speech/LDBEY54BPUVEJ2GVXWMWYUERLU/

6 Danyl McLauchlan, 'Jacinda Ardern and the Winston Peters dilemma: Do nothing or take the nuclear option', *Newshub*, 13 September 2018. https://www.newshub.co.nz/home/politics/2018/09/jacinda-ardern-and-the-winston-peters-dilemma-do-nothing-or-take-the-nuclear-option.html

7 *New Zealand Parliamentary Debates*, 12 September 2018, vol. 732, p. 6523, https://www.parliament.nz/en/pb/hansard-debates/rhr/combined/HansD_20180912_20180912

8 Tracy Watkins, 'Why National insists on calling Jacinda Ardern "weak"', *Stuff*, 13 September 2018, https://www.stuff.co.nz/national/politics/opinion/107025942/why-national-insists-on-calling-jacinda-ardern-weak

9 Ibid.

10 'Jacinda Ardern: "It takes strength to be an empathetic leader"', BBC News, 14 November 2018, https://www.bbc.co.uk/news/av/world-asia-46207254

11 Henry Cooke, 'While KiwiBuild falters, state house build rockets ahead with ninefold increase', *Stuff*, 11 June 2019, https://www.stuff.co.nz/national/politics/113402379/while-kiwibuild-falters-state-house-build-rockets-ahead-with-ninefold-increase-over-three-years

12 'Current minimum wage rates', Employment New Zealand, https://www.employment.govt.nz/hours-and-wages/pay/minimum-wage/minimum-wage-rates/; 'Previous minimum wage rates', Employment New Zealand, https://www.employment.govt.nz/hours-and-wages/pay/minimum-wage/previous-rates/; Living Wage Aotearoa New Zealand, https://www.livingwage.org.nz/about

13 Eleanor Ainge Roy, 'New Zealand's world-first "wellbeing" budget to focus on poverty and mental health', *The Guardian*, 14 May 2019, https://www.theguardian.com/world/2019/may/14/new-zealands-world-first-wellbeing-budget-to-focus-on-poverty-and-mental-health

14 'Two years in: How is PM Jacinda Ardern's Government doing?', *Stuff*, 26 October 2019, https://www.stuff.co.nz/national/politics/116855014/two-years-in-how-is-pm-jacinda-arderns-government-doing

15 'Dismissal of Rt Hon Winston Peters', New Zealand Government press release, 14 August 1998, https://www.beehive.govt.nz/release/dismissal-rt-hon-winston-peters

16 Tracy Watkins, 'Jacinda Ardern and Winston Peters on making their relationship work', *Stuff*, 25 October 2018. https://www.stuff.co.nz/national/politics/

108114509/jacinda-ardern-and-winston-peters-on-making-their-relationship-work

17 Ibid.

18 ' "This is MMP": PM responds to claim that Govt " tearing itself apart" ', *Otago Daily Times*, 24 June 2020, https://www.odt.co.nz/star-news/star-national/mmp-pm-responds-claims-govt-tearing-itself-apart

19 Henry Cooke, 'The last day of the coalition: Parliament wraps up with brutal jokes and moments of gratitude', *Stuff*, 6 August 2020, https://www.stuff.co.nz/national/politics/300076180/the-last-day-of-the-coalition-parliament-wraps-up-with-brutal-jokes-and-moments-of-gratitude

30 *Carving a Path*

1 Maureen Dowd, 'Lady of the Rings: Jacinda rules', *New York Times*, 8 September 2018, https://www.nytimes.com/2018/09/08/opinion/sunday/jacinda-ardern-new-zealand-prime-minister.html

2 'New Zealand's PM: How I Juggle Politics with Motherhood', *Victoria Derbyshire*, BBC2, 21 January 2019, https://www.bbc.co.uk/programmes/p06yp5j3

3 'New Zealand's PM: How I Juggle Politics with Motherhood', *Victoria Derbyshire*, BBC2, 21 January 2019, https://www.bbc.co.uk/programmes/p06yp5j3

4 Ibid.

5 Hao, 'Jacinda Ardern: Daily Routine', *Balance the Grind*, 7 July 2020. https://www.balancethegrind.com.au/daily-routines/jacinda-ardern-daily-routine/

6 Sophia Hollander, 'Jacinda Ardern's juggling act', *New Yorker*, 8 October 2018, https://www.newyorker.com/magazine/2018/10/08/jacinda-arderns-juggling-act

7 Siobhán O'Grady, ' "Damned if I did and damned if I didn't": New Zealand PM defends spending thousands on extra flight so she could breastfeed', *National Post*, 5 September 2018, https://nationalpost.com/news/world/damned-if-i-did-and-damned-if-i-didnt-new-zealand-pm-defends-spending-thousands-on-extra-flights-so-she-could-breastfeed

8 S. V. Date, 'Trump's golf costs: $102 million and counting, with taxpayers picking up the tab', *HuffPost*, 22 May 2019, https://www.huffingtonpost.co.uk/entry/trump-golf-102-million-taxpayers_n_5ce46727e4b09b23e65a01bb?ri18n=true

9 'New Zealand's prime minister Jacinda Ardern talks about being a new mom and world leader', *Today*/YouTube, 24 September 2018, https://youtu.be/rVEV7MpQU_M

10 Ibid.

11 Shelina Janmohamed, 'Jacinda Ardern is a model for all working mothers', *The National*, 27 September 2018, https://www.thenationalnews.com/opinion/comment/jacinda-ardern-is-a-model-for-all-working-mothers-1.774576

12 'Prime Minister Jacinda Ardern's statement to the United Nations General Assembly', *Stuff*, 28 September 2018, https://www.stuff.co.nz/national/politics /107445802/prime-minister-jacinda-arderns-statement-to-the-united-nations-general-assembly

13 'Remarks by President Trump to the 73rd Session of the United Nations General Assembly, New York, NY', 25 September 2018, https://www.white-house.gov/briefings-statements/remarks-president-trump-73rd-session-united-nations-general-assembly-new-york-ny/

14 Eleanor Ainge Roy, 'Jacinda Ardern "infuriated" by comparisons to Donald Trump', *The Guardian*, 18 April 2018, https://www.theguardian.com/world/2018/apr/18/jacinda-ardern-infuriated-with-comparisons-to-donald-trump

15 'New Zealanders march for women's rights in wake of Donald Trump's inauguration', *New Zealand Herald*, 20 January 2017, https://www.nzherald.co.nz/nz/new-zealanders-march-for-womens-rights-in-wake-of-donald-trumps-inauguration/T2NFMWZ6ZDBL2NMA3TPJUHAVNM/

16 Stewart Sowman-Lund, 'A brief history of Donald Trump v Jacinda Ardern', *New Zealand Herald*, 20 August 2020, https://www.nzherald.co.nz/nz/a-brief-history-of-donald-trump-v-jacinda-ardern/7TGK4RGBQ25YELU5AV6N67PU6I/

17 Audrey Young, 'Q & A with Jacinda Ardern: We have a role in taking a lead', *New Zealand Herald*, 15 November 2017, https://www.nzherald.co.nz/nz/q-a-with-jacinda-ardern-we-have-a-role-in-taking-a-lead/5VMRZKY4KXZOC2KXVHO4LM33HM/

31 Acclaim and the Ides of March

1 *Today* (@TODAYshow), 'The joy, though, has far surpassed my expectations', Twitter, 24 September 2018, https://twitter.com/todayshow/status/1044201298567008256?lang=en

2 'Prime Minister Jacinda Ardern explains why the UN laughed at Trump', *The Late Show with Stephen Colbert*/YouTube, 27 September 2018, https://www.youtu.be/aYsZv9JXmio

3 Sophia Hollander, 'Jacinda Ardern's juggling act', *New Yorker*, 8 October 2018, https://www.newyorker.com/magazine/2018/10/08/jacinda-arderns-juggling-act

4 Eleanor Ainge Roy, 'Ardern's first year: New Zealand grapples with hangover from Jacindamania', *The Guardian*, 21 October 2018. https://www.theguardian.com/world/2018/oct/21/jacinda-ardern-first-year-new-zealand-grapples-with-jacindamania-hangover

5 Joel MacManus, 'Nelson bush fire: PM Jacinda Ardern says NZ needs to prepare for more serious events', *Stuff*, 14 Feb 2019, https://www.stuff.co.nz/national/110602393/nelson-bush-fire-pm-jacinda-ardern-says-nz-needs-to-prepare-for-more-serious-events

6 Ibid.

32 *They Are Us*

1 Jane Matthews, 'Striking students in New Plymouth surprised by Prime Minister', *Stuff*, 15 March 2019, https://www.stuff.co.nz/environment/111310820/striking-students-in-new-plymouth-surprised-by-prime-minister

2 'Jacinda Ardern on the Christchurch shooting: "One of New Zealand's darkest days"', *The Guardian*, 15 March 2019, https://www.theguardian.com/world/2019/mar/15/one-of-new-zealands-darkest-days-jacinda-ardern-responds-to-christchurch-shooting

3 Anna Whyte, '"We utterly reject and condemn you" – PM denounces those responsible for Christchurch terror attacks that left 40 dead', 1 News, TVNZ, 15 March 2019, https://www.tvnz.co.nz/one-news/new-zealand/we-utterly-reject-and-condemn-you-pm-denounces-those-responsible-christchurch-terror-attacks-left-40-dead

4 Henry Cooke, 'PM Jacinda Ardern told Donald Trump: Send love to Muslims after mosque shooting', *Stuff*, 16 March 2019, https://www.stuff.co.nz/national/politics/111331484/pm-jacinda-ardern-told-donald-trump-send-love-to-muslims-after-mosque-shooting

5 Jon Swaine, 'New Zealand PM vows to toughen gun control laws after Christchurch attack', *The Guardian*, 15 March 2019, https://www.theguardian.com/world/2019/mar/15/new-zealand-prime-minister-gun-control-jacinda-ardern

6 Matthew Theunissen, 'Christchurch terror attack: the PM's role – bringing the "message of love and support and grief"', RNZ, 17 March 2019, https://www.rnz.co.nz/news/national/384877/christchurch-terror-attack-the-pm-s-role-bringing-the-message-of-love-and-support-and-grief

7 Madeleine Chapman, *Jacinda Ardern: A New Kind of Leader* (Cheltenham: History Press, 2020), p. 202.

8 '"I was struck by her humanity" – photographer who took incredible portrait of PM', 1 News, TVNZ, 19 March 2019, https://www.tvnz.co.nz/one-news/new-zealand/struck-her-humanity-photographer-took-incredible-portrait-pm

9 '"Broken-hearted but not broken": Al Noor imam's Christchurch speech in full', *The Guardian*, 22 March 2019, https://www.theguardian.com/world/2019/mar/22/broken-hearted-but-not-broken-al-noor-imams-christchurch-speech-in-full

10 Tom Westbrook, '"We are one" says PM Ardern as New Zealand mourns with prayers, silence', Reuters, 21 March 2019, https://uk.reuters.com/article/uk-newzealand-shootout/we-are-one-says-pm-ardern-as-new-zealand-mourns-with-prayers-silence-idUKKCN1R22FM

11 'New Zealand PM honoured at Christchurch memorial', *Diplomacy & Beyond*, 29 March 2019, https://diplomacybeyond.com/new-zealand-pm-honoured-at-christchurch-memorial/

12 Ibid.

33 Engagement

1 Phil Smith and Daniela Maoate-Cox, 'Praying with "strangers" in Parliament', RNZ, 19 March 2019, https://www.rnz.co.nz/national/programmes/the-house /audio/2018687276/praying-with-strangers-in-parliament

2 'Ministerial Statements – Mosque Terror Attacks – Christchurch', *New Zealand Parliamentary Debates*, 19 March 2019, vol. 737, p. 10072, https://www.parliament.nz/en/pb/hansard-debates/rhr/document/HansS_20190319_050700000 /ardern-jacinda

3 'France, New Zealand launch bid to end online extremism', France 24, 24 April 2019, https://www.france24.com/en/20190424-france-new-zealand-launch-bid-end-online-extremism-terrorism-social-media

4 'Erdogan says attackers targeting Turkey will go home "in caskets"', Reuters, 18 March 2019, https://uk.reuters.com/article/us-newzealand-shootout-erdogan/ erdogan-says-attackers-targeting-turkey-will-go-home-in-caskets -idUSKCN1QZ1QF

5 'NZ foreign minister headed to Turkey to "confront" Erdogan's mosque shooting comments', Reuters, 20 March 2019, https://uk.reuters.com/article/us-newzealand-shootout-erdogan/nz-foreign-minister-headed-to-turkey-to-confront-erdogans-mosque-shooting-comments-idUSKCN1R10B6

6 Patrick Wintour and Bethan McKernan, 'Erdoğan praises New Zealand PM after row over mosque attacks', *The Guardian*, 22 March 2019, https://www.theguardian.com/world/2019/mar/22/erdogan-praises-new-zealand-pm-row-mosque-attack-remarks

7 Eleanor Ainge Roy, '"I don't understand": Jacinda Ardern mystified by lack of US gun control, *The Guardian*, 15 May 2019, https://www.theguardian.com/world/2019/may/15/i-dont-understand-jacinda-ardern-mystified-by-lack-of-us-gun-control

8 'Jacinda Ardern asked by BBC if she'll propose to partner Clarke Gayford', *Stuff*, 23 January 2019, https://www.stuff.co.nz/national/politics/110097524/ jacinda-ardern-asked-by-bbc-if-shell-propose-to-partner-clarke-gayford

9 'Stephen Colbert: The Newest Zealander visits PM Jacinda Ardern', *The Late Show with Stephen Colbert*/YouTube, 19 November 2019, https://www.youtu. be/DUP0620uU84

34 Whakaari

1 'Jacinda Ardern thanks first responders from Whakaari/White Island eruption', *Stuff*, 10 December 2019, https://www.stuff.co.nz/national/118083649 /jacinda-ardern-thanks-first-responders-from-whakaariwhite-island -eruption

2 *New Zealand Parliamentary Debates*, 'Ministerial Statements – Whakaari/White Island – Eruption', 10 December 2019, vol. 743, p. 15671, https://www.

parliament.nz/en/pb/hansard-debates/rhr/document/HansS_20191210_050550000/ardern-jacinda

3 'A minute's silence for Whakaari White Island victims', New Zealand Government press release, 14 December 2019, https://www.beehive.govt.nz/release/minute's-silence-whakaari-white-island-victims

35 Cometh the Hour, Cometh the Woman

1 Quoted in 'India. The Beginning of the Road to Self-Rule', International Churchill Society, https://winstonchurchill.org/the-life-of-churchill/wilderness-years/india-3/

2 'The Secretary General: Video Message to Staff', 23 April 2020, transcript available at https://www.un.org/sites/un2.un.org/files/staffvideo-april2020.pdf; 'Transcript of UN secretary-general's virtual press encounter to launch the Report on the Socio-Economic Impacts of COVID-19', United Nations Secretary-General, 31 March 2020, https://www.un.org/sg/en/content/sg/press-encounter/2020-03-31/transcript-of-un-secretary-general's-virtual-press-encounter-launch-the-report-the-socio-economic-impacts-of-covid-19

3 Quoted in 'Churchill: Leader and Statesman', International Churchill Society, https://winstonchurchill.org/the-life-of-churchill/life/churchill-leader-and-statesman/

4 Beth Howell, 'The countries who've handled coronavirus the best – and worst', MoveHub, 4 December 2020, https://www.movehub.com/blog/best-and-worst-covid-responses/

5 Andrei Alexander Lux, 'Open, honest and effective: what makes Jacinda Ardern an authentic leader', The Conversation, 26 May 2020, https://theconversation.com/open-honest-and-effective-what-makes-jacinda-ardern-an-authentic-leader-132513

6 'Captaining a Team of 5 Million: New Zealand Beats Back Covid-19, March–June 2020' (Princeton study), https://successfulsocieties.princeton.edu/sites/successfulsocieties/files/NewZealand_COVID_Final.txt

7 'Nation steps up to COVID-19 Alert Level 2', Department of Internal Affairs, 21 March 2020, https://www.dia.govt.nz/press.nsf/d77da9b523f12931c-c256ac5000d19b6/f1ebaeee43690e66cc258532001329bd!OpenDocument

8 Ben McKay, '"We have 102 cases, so did Italy once": NZ enters coronavirus lockdown', Sydney Morning Herald, 23 March 2020, https://www.smh.com.au/world/oceania/we-have-102-cases-so-did-italy-once-nz-enters-coronavirus-lockdown-20200323-p54d07.html

9 'All of New Zealand must prepare to go in self-isolation now – Prime Minister', RNZ, 23 March 2020, https://www.rnz.co.nz/news/political/412403/all-of-new-zealand-must-prepare-to-go-in-self-isolation-now-prime-minister

10 'Jacinda Ardern hosts coronavirus Q&A from home after putting child to bed – video', The Guardian, 26 March 2020, https://www.theguardian.com/world/

video/2020/mar/26/jacinda-ardern-hosts-coronavirus-qa-from-home-after-putting-child-to-bed-video

11   'Covid 19 coronavirus: Traces of virus "survives on some surfaces for 28 days"', *New Zealand Herald*, 11 October 2020, https://www.nzherald.co.nz/world/covid-19-coronavirus-traces-of-virus-survives-on-some-surfaces-for-28-days/WI4TPH4UZDH5HNAJESRJSM5LG4/

12   'Covid 19 coronavirus: Americans lose it over Jacinda Ardern's light-hearted media moment', *New Zealand Herald*, 16 April 2020, https://www.nzherald.co.nz/nz/covid-19-coronavirus-americans-lose-it-over-jacinda-arderns-light-hearted-media-moment/M3VBAGKUIP4IEBEZQAWIWTLJ4Q/

13   Joyce Karam (@Joyce_Karam), 'At a time when journalists are under attack by US President, expelled by China, Egypt and censored by many authoritarian states, it's heartening to see civility in leadership', Twitter, 14 April 2020, https://twitter.com/joyce_karam/status/1250106828521865216

14   'Prime Minister's remarks on COVID-19 alert level decision – April 20', New Zealand Government, 20 April 2020, https://www.beehive.govt.nz/speech/prime-minister's-remarks-covid-19-alert-level-decision---april-20

15   'Level 2 announcement', New Zealand Government, 11 May 2020, https://www.beehive.govt.nz/speech/level-2-announcement

16   'PM on Clark – "I expect better and so does NZ"', RNZ, 7 April 2020, https://www.rnz.co.nz/news/political/413674/pm-on-clark-i-expect-better-and-so-does-nz

17   Derek Cheng, 'Covid 19 coronavirus: Jacinda Ardern's former school Morrinsville College warns parents to keep kids at home', *New Zealand Herald*, 22 April 2020, https://www.nzherald.co.nz/nz/covid-19-coronavirus-jacinda-arderns-former-school-morrinsville-college-warns-parents-to-keep-kids-at-home/YWKRZ5VJX62F7N6WRAMM3ER6OE/

18   Katarina Williams, 'Coronavirus: border bungle an "unacceptable failure" – Prime Minister Jacinda Ardern', *Stuff*, 17 June 2020, https://www.stuff.co.nz/national/health/coronavirus/121855818/coronavirus-border-bungle-an-unacceptable-failure--prime-minister-jacinda-ardern

19   'Prime Minister Jacinda Ardern looks to reassure public in wake of managed isolation review', RNZ, 29 June 2020, https://www.rnz.co.nz/news/political/420064/prime-minister-jacinda-ardern-looks-to-reassure-public-in-wake-of-managed-isolation-review

20   Tom McCarthy, '"It will disappear": the disinformation Trump spread about the coronavirus – timeline', *The Guardian*, 14 April 2020, https://www.theguardian.com/us-news/2020/apr/14/trump-coronavirus-alerts-disinformation-timeline

21   David Smith, 'Trump throws tantrum over coronavirus question: "You're a terrible reporter"', *The Guardian*, 21 March 2020, https://www.theguardian.com/us-news/2020/mar/20/trump-coronavirus-question-attack-reporter-over-fears

22   Praveen Menon, 'New Zealand's Ardern hits back at Trump over coronavirus "surge"', Reuters, 18 August 2020, https://uk.reuters.com/article/uk-health

-coronavirus-newzealand-cases/new-zealands-ardern-hits-back-at-trump-over-coronavirus-surge-idUKKCN25E04W

23 Eleanor Ainge Roy, 'Trump calls out New Zealand's "terrible" Covid surge, on day it records nine new cases', *The Guardian*, 22 August 2020, https://www.theguardian.com/world/2020/aug/18/trump-calls-out-new-zealands-big-surge-on-day-it-records-nine-covid-cases

24 Menon, 'New Zealand's Ardern hits back at Trump over coronavirus "surge"'.

25 See for example *Los Angeles Times*, 6 October 2020; *National Journal*, 18 October 2020.

36 *The COVID Election*

1 '"My time is up" – Teary Nikki Kaye reflects on retirement decision', 1 News, TVNZ, 16 July 2020, https://www.tvnz.co.nz/one-news/new-zealand/my-time-up-teary-nikki-kaye-reflects-retirement-decision

2 'Simon Wilson's Auckland election diary: Lunch with Judith and Jacinda', *New Zealand Herald*, 16 July 2020, https://www.nzherald.co.nz/nz/simon-wilsons-auckland-election-diary-lunch-with-judith-and-jacinda/Q6VIXL74ZDC23U74UXAR3EMW6Q/

3 'Collins' husband criticised for sharing anti-Ardern memes', *Otago Daily Times*, 31 August 2020, https://www.odt.co.nz/news/decision-2020/collins-husband-criticised-sharing-anti-ardern-memes

4 Henry Cooke, 'Election 2020: Winston Peters attacks government's coronavirus response as he relaunches election campaign', *Stuff*, 2 September 2020, https://www.stuff.co.nz/national/politics/300097515/election-2020-winston-peters-attacks-governments-coronavirus-response-as-he-relaunches-election-campaign

5 Jason Walls, '"A handbrake for silly ideas:" Peters to discuss coalition disagreements in conference speech', *New Zealand Herald*, 17 July 2020, https://www.nzherald.co.nz/nz/a-handbrake-for-silly-ideas-peters-to-discuss-coalition-disagreements-in-conference-speech/RTYAJP4FQIW46QJBIDVOEJVONA/

6 Farah Hancock, 'Wealth tax ads from National in final push', *Newsroom*, 15 October 2020, https://www.newsroom.co.nz/election-2020-wealth-tax-ads-from-national

7 'Ardern explains why she voted for cannabis reform', *Otago Daily Times*, 31 October 2020, https://www.odt.co.nz/star-news/star-national/ardern-explains-why-she-voted-cannabis-reform

8 Hannah Kronast, 'NZ Election 2020: Jacinda Ardern vows to govern for every New Zealander in victory speech', *Newshub*, 17 October 2020. https://www.newshub.co.nz/home/politics/2020/10/nz-election-2020-jacinda-ardern-vows-to-govern-for-every-new-zealander-in-victory-speech.html

9 Eleanor Ainge Roy and Charlotte Graham-McLay, 'Jacinda Ardern to govern New Zealand for second term after historic victory', *The Guardian*, 17 October

2020, https://www.theguardian.com/world/2020/oct/17/jacinda-arderns-labour-party-set-for-victory-in-new-zealand-election

10 'Jacinda Ardern's Labour Party secures victory in New Zealand election', *Euronews*, 17 October 2020, https://www.euronews.com/2020/10/17/jacinda-ardern-secures-second-term-in-new-zealand-election-after-rival-concedes

37 Kindness and the Ardern Effect

1 Ella Wills, 'New Zealand PM Jacinda Ardern pays for woman's groceries at supermarket after the mum leaves her purse at home', *Evening Standard* (London), 4 April 2019, https://www.standard.co.uk/news/world/new-zealand-pm-jacinda-ardern-pays-for-woman-s-supermarket-shopping-after-the-mum-leaves-her-purse-at-home-a4109191.html

2 Belinda Luscombe, 'A year after Christchurch, Jacinda Ardern has the world's attention. How will she use it?', *Time*, 20 February 2020, https://time.com/5787443/jacinda-ardern-christchurch-new-zealand-anniversary/

3 'Ernest Shackleton', Royal Society – Science in the Making, https://makingscience.royalsociety.org/s/rs/people/fst00000549

Bibliography

Madeleine Chapman, *Jacinda Ardern: A New Kind of Leader* (Cheltenham: History Press, 2020).

Pauline Rose Clance and Suzanne Ament Imes, 'The Imposter Phenomenon in High Achieving Women: Dynamics and Therapeutic Intervention', *Psychotherapy: Theory, Research & Practice*, 15(3), 1978, 241–7.

Michelle Duff, *Jacinda Ardern: The Story Behind an Extraordinary Leader* (Auckland: Allen & Unwin, 2019).

Claudia Pond Eyley and Dan Salmon, *Helen Clark: Inside Stories* (Auckland: Auckland University Press, 2015).

Julia Gillard and Ngozi Okonjo-Iweala, *Women and Leadership: Real Lives, Real Lessons* (London: Transworld Digital, 2020).

Nicky Hager, *Dirty Politics: How Attack Politics is Poisoning New Zealand's Political Environment* (Nelson, NZ: Craig Potton, 2014).

John Harvey and Brent Edwards, *Annette King: The Authorised Biography* (Auckland: Upstart Press, 2019).

Wayne McClintock, 'Resource Community Formation & Change: A Case Study of Murupara', Working Paper 7, Taylor Baines & Associates, June 1998, ISSN 1176-3515.

Bruce R. McConkie, *Mormon Doctrine*, 2nd ed. (Salt Lake City: Bookcraft, 1966).

Ann Pomeroy, 'Resilient Communities Murupara', Centre for Sustainability: Agriculture, Food, Energy and Environment University of Otago, Dunedin, June 2016.

Royal Commission of Inquiry into the terrorist attack on Christchurch masjidain on 15 March 2019, Report, 26 November 2020.

Index

A Note About the Authors

SUPRIYA VANI is a peace activist and author. As a human rights advocate, she actively participates at international peace organisations and forums, including the Permanent Secretariat of the World Summit of Nobel Peace Laureates, the Nobel Women's initiative, and Laureates and Leaders, World Academy of Arts and Science, and United Nations. As a journalist she has interviewed a number of women political figures, including prime minister of Iceland Katrín Jakobsdóttir, former president of Liberia Ellen Johnson Sirleaf, former prime minister of Australia Julia Gillard and Jacinda Ardern about female leadership. She is a recipient of an honorary James Patterson Fellowship from Vanderbilt University in Nashville, Tennessee. Her first book, *Battling Injustice: 16 Women Nobel Peace Laureates*, based on her interviews with all the women Nobel Peace Laureates, won praise from a number of prominent international figures including Nobel Peace Laureates Malala Yousafzai, His Holiness the Dalai Lama, Mikhail Gorbachev, and Former Secretary General of United Nations Ban Ki-Moon.

CARL A. HARTE is an Australian writer and book editor. The recipient of an eLit Gold Award for his book, *Building Your Own Home: Tips, Techniques and Thoughts for the Owner Builder*, he has also worked with a wide range of authors including the late former President of India, Dr A.P.J. Abdul Kalam, Om Swami, Lieutenant Governor Kiran Bedi, Arun Tiwari, Farahnaz Ispahani, Swami Agnivesh, Kishalay Bhattacharjee and Maxwell Pereira.